T0136984

Progress in IS

"PROGRESS in IS" encompasses the various areas of Information Systems in theory and practice, presenting cutting-edge advances in the field. It is aimed especially at researchers, doctoral students, and advanced practitioners. The series features both research monographs that make substantial contributions to our state of knowledge and handbooks and other edited volumes, in which a team of experts is organized by one or more leading authorities to write individual chapters on various aspects of the topic. "PROGRESS in IS" is edited by a global team of leading IS experts. The editorial board expressly welcomes new members to this group. Individual volumes in this series are supported by a minimum of two members of the editorial board, and a code of conduct mandatory for all members of the board ensures the quality and cutting-edge nature of the titles published under this series.

More information about this series at http://www.springer.com/series/10440

Jan vom Brocke · Alan Hevner ·
Alexander Maedche
Editors

Design Science Research.
Cases

 Springer

Editors
Jan vom Brocke
Department of Information Systems
University of Liechtenstein
Vaduz, Liechtenstein

Alan Hevner
Muma College of Business
University of South Florida
Tampa, FL, USA

Alexander Maedche
Institute of Information Systems
and Marketing (IISM)
Karlsruhe Institute of Technology (KIT)
Karlsruhe, Germany

ISSN 2196-8705   ISSN 2196-8713   (electronic)
Progress in IS
ISBN 978-3-030-46783-8   ISBN 978-3-030-46781-4   (eBook)
https://doi.org/10.1007/978-3-030-46781-4

This Springer imprint is published by the registered company Springer Nature Switzerland AG
The registered company address is: Gewerbestrasse 11, 6330 Cham, Switzerland

DSR Cases Book: Preface

The Design Science Research (DSR) paradigm has become central to Information Systems (IS) studies in the past 20 years. Simply stated, the goal of DSR is to generate knowledge on how to build innovative solutions to important problems in the form of models, methods, constructs, and instantiations. DSR aims to provide knowledge of how things can and should be constructed or arranged (i.e., designed). In this sense, design knowledge describes means-end relationships between problem and solution spaces.

DSR is ideally positioned to make both research and practical contributions. From a research point of view, it contributes to the technology body of knowledge in the form of innovative design artifacts. Furthermore, it also delivers design theories that extend and generalize the knowledge contribution from a scientific perspective. DSR also contributes practically by delivering actionable innovative solutions that solve real-world problems with prescriptive knowledge.

Despite the huge potentials and increasing impacts of DSR, there is currently no comprehensive collection of successful DSR cases available. This is regrettable because practitioners and scientists, who want to apply DSR are confronted with numerous questions regarding planning and implementation of comparable projects. Exemplary DSR cases offer opportunities to learn from documented experiences of others, and, as such, they complement existing sources.

This book provides a collection and documentation of DSR cases provided by experienced researchers in the field. It gives access to real-world DSR studies together with the reflection of the authors on their research process. These cases support researchers who want to engage in DSR with a valuable addition to existing introductions to DSR methods and processes. Readers will learn from the valuable experiences of a wide range of established colleagues who have extensively conducted DSR in many application contexts.

Moreover, the book also aims to increase the exchange of knowledge in the DSR field, as well as to invite colleagues to engage in this promising form of research. Specifically for IS researchers who would like become familiar with DSR, this book provides many examples illustrating how to plan and conduct DSR. These examples provide both inspiration and a source of reference. The book also showcases the range of DSR projects and gives an overview of colleagues highly active in the field.

Each chapter follows a unified presentation structure that makes the relevant case knowledge easily accessible and transferrable to other contexts:

- **Introduction**: A brief narrative of the entire story to grasp interest in the case is provided.
- **Context**: This section describes the business or the societal context, so that readers can relate the findings to their own context.
- **Journey**: DSR projects typically do not follow not a linear process, but rather a journey of continuous refinement of both problem and solution understanding. In this section of the case this journey is described. Here the DSR process is overviewed with an emphasis on the different types of activities conducted during the DSR project. Specifically, iterations of problem and solution understanding during the design process are presented.
- **Results**: The key results of the journey are documented, covering both scientific and practical contributions.
- **Key Learnings**: Finally, reflections and learnings made during the reported DSR project are documented. Notable successes and key limitations of the research are addressed. Future directions can be provided.

With the unified structure of each case, we hope to support readers effectively accessing the most relevant parts to build on in their own DSR work. The material presented in this book is complemented by online material for teaching, training, and consulting. The website http://www.dsr-cases.com makes available slides and additional content that can be helpful for using the cases both in teaching DSR and in preparing for DSR projects in practice.

We thank the following people and institutions for their continuous support toward the compilation of this book. First, we thank our research teams, specifically Charlotte Wehking and Michael Gau from the University of Liechtenstein and .... from Karlsruhe Institute of Technology.

We hope you will enjoy reading the book and learning from these DSR cases. We look forward to your feedback on how best to share knowledge and learning from DSR projects.

Vaduz, Liechtenstein   Jan vom Brocke
Tampa, USA   Alan Hevner
Karlsruhe, Germany   Alexander Maedche

Contents

Introduction to Design Science Research

Jan vom Brocke, Alan Hevner, and Alexander Maedche

Abstract Design Science Research (DSR) is a problem-solving paradigm that seeks to enhance human knowledge via the creation of innovative artifacts. Simply stated, DSR seeks to enhance technology and science knowledge bases via the creation of innovative artifacts that solve problems and improve the environment in which they are instantiated. The results of DSR include both the newly designed artifacts and design knowledge (DK) that provides a fuller understanding via design theories of why the artifacts enhance (or, disrupt) the relevant application contexts. The goal of this introduction chapter is to provide a brief survey of DSR concepts for better understanding of the following chapters that present DSR case studies.

1 Introduction to Design Science Research

The Design Science Research (DSR) paradigm has its roots in engineering and the sciences of the artificial (Simon, 1996). It is fundamentally a problem-solving paradigm. DSR seeks to enhance human knowledge with the creation of innovative artifacts and the generation of design knowledge (DK) via innovative solutions to real-world problems (Hevner, March, Park, & Ram, 2004). As such, this research paradigm has generated a surge of interest in the past twenty years, specifically due to its potential to contribute to fostering the innovation capabilities of organizations as well as contributing to the much needed sustainability transformation of society (Watson, Boudreau, & Chen, 2010; vom Brocke, Watson, Dwyer, Elliot, & Melville, 2013; vom Brocke, Winter, Hevner, & Maedche 2020).

J. vom Brocke (✉)
Department of Information Systems, University of Liechtenstein, Vaduz, Liechtenstein
e-mail: jan.vom.brocke@uni.li

A. Hevner
Muma College of Business, University of South Florida, Tampa, FL, USA

A. Maedche
Department of Information Systems, IISM - Information Systems and Marketing, Karlsruhe Institute of Technology, Karlsruhe, Germany

© Springer Nature Switzerland AG 2020
J. vom Brocke et al. (eds.), *Design Science Research. Cases*, Progress in IS,
https://doi.org/10.1007/978-3-030-46781-4_1

1

The goal of a DSR research project is to extend the boundaries of human and organizational capabilities by designing new and innovative artifacts represented by constructs, models, methods, and instantiations (Hevner et al., 2004; Gregor & Hevner, 2013). DSR aims to generate knowledge of how things can and should be constructed or arranged (i.e., designed), usually by human agency, to achieve a desired set of goals; referred to as design knowledge (DK). For example, DK in the Information Systems (IS) discipline includes knowledge of how to structure and construct a database system, how to model business processes, how to align IS with organizational strategy, how to deliver data analytics for effective decision making (e.g. Becker et al., 2015), as well as how to use information technology to support sustainable practices (Seidel et al., 2013; vom Brocke & Seidel, 2012a, b). DSR results in IS have been shown to create significant economic and societal impact (Gregor & Hevner, 2013; vom Brocke et al., 2013). Beyond the IS field, DSR is a central research paradigm in many other domains including engineering, architecture, business, economics, and other information technology-related disciplines for the creation of novel solutions to relevant design problems.

In the following, we introduce some essential frameworks and conceptualizations that we deem important in order to provide foundations on how to conduct DSR to scholarly standards. The cases presented in this book use such fundamentals in order to structure and document their DSR projects.

2   The DSR Framework

Figure 1 presents a conceptual framework for understanding, executing, and evaluating design science research (Hevner et al. 2004). The environment defines the problem space in which the phenomena of interest reside. It is composed of people, organizations, and existing or planned technologies. In it are the goals, tasks, problems, and opportunities that define needs as they are perceived by stakeholders within the organization. Needs are assessed and evaluated within the context of organizational strategies, structure, culture, and existing work processes. They are positioned relative to existing technology infrastructure, applications, communication architectures, and development capabilities. Together these define the "research problem" as perceived by the researcher. Framing research activities to address real stakeholder needs assures research relevance. The knowledge base provides the raw materials from and through which DSR is accomplished. The knowledge base is composed of Foundations and Methodologies. Prior research and results from reference disciplines provide foundational theories, frameworks, instruments, constructs, models, methods, and instantiations used in the build phase of a research study. Methodologies provide guidelines used in the evaluate phase. Rigor is achieved by appropriately applying existing foundations and methodologies.

DSR studies relevant problems in the real-world environment with various application domains. Research links to a "need" for solutions to be empirically investigated with people in organizations using specific technology. Often, the analysis

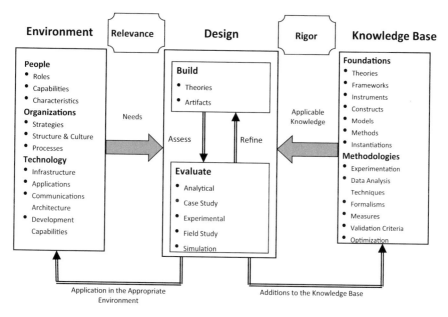

Fig. 1 Design science research framework (Adapted from (Hevner et al., 2004))

of the business environment and the derivation of specific needs to be solved build the starting point of a DSR project. However, also situations exist in which needs have already been studied and can be taken from extant research. DSR analyses the (academic) knowledge base in that it studies to which extent design knowledge is already available to solve a problem of interest. Such knowledge can take the form of theories, frameworks, instruments or design artifacts, such as constructs, models, methods or instantiations. In case knowledge is already available to solve a problem identified, this knowledge can be applied following "routine design", which does not constitute DSR. Else, DSR sets out to create an innovative solution to the problem, which, in most cases, builds on existing parts of a solution and combines, revises, and extends extant design knowledge. The design activities comprise of "build" and "evaluate" activities, typically following multiple iterations. In course of a DSR study, diverse research methods are applied, including those well established in social science research, such as interviews, surveys, literature reviews, or focus groups.

3   DSR Process

The performance of DSR projects has been based on several process models, such as Nunamaker, Chen and Purdin (1991), Walls, Widmeyer and El Sawy (1992), Hevner (2007), Kuchler and Vaishnavi (2008). The mostly widely referenced model is one proposed by Peffers et al. (2007). The design science research methodology (DSRM) process model is shown in Fig. 2. This DSR process includes six steps: problem identification and motivation, definition of the objectives for a solution, design and development, demonstration, evaluation, and communication; and four possible entry points: problem-centered initiation, objective-centered solution, design and development-centered initiation, and client/context initiation. A brief description of each DSR activity follows.

Activity 1. Problem identification and motivation. This activity defines the specific research problem and justifies the value of a solution. Justifying the value of a solution accomplishes two things: it motivates the researcher and the audience of the research to pursue the solution and it helps the audience to appreciate the researcher's understanding of the problem. Resources required for this activity include knowledge of the state of the problem and the importance of its solution.

Activity 2. Define the objectives for a solution. The objectives of a solution can be inferred from the problem definition and knowledge of what is possible and feasible. The objectives can be quantitative, e.g., terms in which a desirable solution would be better than current ones, or qualitative, e.g., a description of how a new artifact is expected to support solutions to problems not hitherto addressed. The objectives should be inferred rationally from the problem specification.

Activity 3. Design and development. An artifact is created. Conceptually, a DSR artifact can be any designed object in which a research contribution is embedded in the design. This activity includes determining the artifact's desired functionality and its architecture and then creating the actual artifact.

Activity 4. Demonstration. This activity demonstrates the use of the artifact to solve one or more instances of the problem. This could involve its use in experimentation, simulation, case study, proof, or other appropriate activity.

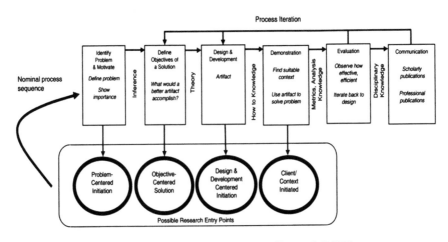

Fig. 2 DSR methodology process model (Adapted from Peffers et al. (2007))

Activity 5. Evaluation. The evaluation measures how well the artifact supports a solution to the problem. This activity involves comparing the objectives of a solution to actual observed results from use of the artifact in context. Depending on the nature of the problem venue and the artifact, evaluation could take many forms. At the end of this activity the researchers can decide whether to iterate back to step three to try to improve the effectiveness of the artifact or to continue on to communication and leave further improvement to subsequent projects.

Activity 6. Communication. Here all aspects of the problem and the designed artifact are communicated to the relevant stakeholders. Appropriate forms of communication are employed depending upon the research goals and the audience, such as practicing professionals.

4 DSR Evaluation

The process of conducting DSR has been further developed in many ways, specifically paying attention to the evaluation activities and allowing for a more concurrent and fine-grained evaluation of intermediate steps in the design process. While it is well-understood that also the Peffers et al. (2007) process should and would be conducted iteratively, evaluation only takes place after design, development and demonstration activities; missing out on the opportunity to inform the design in an early stage of the research process.

Sonnenberg and vom Brocke (2012) conceptualize concurrent evaluation according to different aspects of design as shown in Fig. 3. They build on prior work describing DSR activities within the overall DSR process, arguing that each of these activities progresses toward the intended artefacts differently and thus offer potential for concurrent (or formative) evaluation. Such evaluation can mitigate risk (Venable, vom Brocke, & Winter, 2019), as early feedback on the minute steps leading to the eventual artefact can be incorporated into the design process. The authors also assert that this type of evaluation can be more specific and better directed if the evaluation focuses on the different aspects of design when relevant decisions are being made during the design process.

To demonstrate, Sonnenberg and vom Brocke (2012) identify four evaluation types (Eval 1 to Eval 4) derived from typical DSR activities. Figure 3 shows a cyclic high-level DSR process that includes the activities of problem identification, design, construction, and use. In addition, Fig. 3 suggests that each DSR activity is followed by an evaluation activity, as follows:

- Eval 1: Evaluating the problem identification; criteria include importance, novelty, and feasibility
- Eval 2: Evaluating the solution design; criteria include simplicity, clarity, and consistency
- Eval 3: Evaluating the solution instantiation; criteria include ease of use, fidelity with real-world phenomena, and robustness

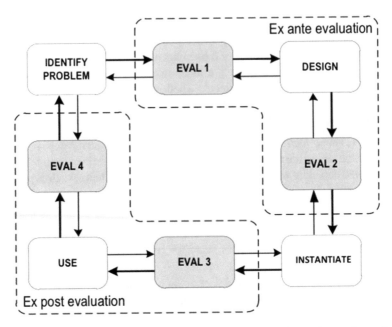

Fig. 3 Evaluation activities within the DSR process (Adapted from Sonnenberg and vom Brocke (2012))

- Eval 4: Evaluating the solution in use; criteria include effectiveness, efficiency, and external consistency.

Depending on when an evaluation occurs, *ex ante* and *ex post* evaluations are distinguished. *Ex ante* evaluations are conducted before the instantiation of any arte-facts, while *ex post* evaluations occur after the instantiation of any artefact (Venable, Pries-Heje, & Baskerville, 2016). The DSR process in Fig. 3 indicates that there are feedback loops from each evaluation activity to the preceding design activity. Overall, these feedback loops together form a feedback cycle that runs in the opposite direction to the DSR cycle.

5 Design Knowledge Framework

The design knowledge (DK) produced in a DSR project can be richly multifaceted. DK will include information about the important problem, the designed solution, and the evaluation evidence. Specifically it includes measures of timely progress on how well the problem solution satisfies the key stakeholders of a problem.

We consider these three components to constitute DK: the problem space, the solution space, and the evaluation. While we understand that both problem space knowledge and solution space knowledge exists independently, it is only through putting them in relation to one another that we refer to the respective knowledge as DK. Figure 4 provides a simple model conceptualizing important components of DK.

Information systems research consumes and produces two basic types of knowledge: (1) behavioral science-oriented research activities primarily grow propositional knowledge or Ω-knowledge (comprising descriptive and explanatory knowledge), and, (2) DSR-oriented research activities primarily grow applicable (or prescriptive) knowledge or λ-knowledge (Gregor & Hevner, 2013). Contributions to the λ knowledge base typically comprise knowledge about technological (i.e. digital) innovations that directly affect individuals, organizations, or society while also enabling the development of future innovations (Winter & Albani, 2013). Contributions to the Ω knowledge base enhance our understanding of the world and the phenomena our technologies harness (or cause). Research projects may combine both paradigms of inquiry and contribute to both knowledge bases.

The relationships of design knowledge produced and consumed in DSR projects and the (design) knowledge bases are shown in Fig. 1. This figure is adapted and simplified from (Drechsler & Hevner, 2018) and clearly illustrates paired modes of consuming and producing knowledge between the DSR project and the Ω and λ knowledge bases. The λ-knowledge is further divided into two sub-categories. The *Solution Design Entities* collect the prescriptive knowledge as represented in the tangible artifacts, systems, and processes designed and applied in the problem solution space. The growth of design theories around these solutions is captured in the *Solution Design Theories* knowledge base (Gregor & Hevner, 2013). Knowledge can be projected from the specific application solutions into nascent theories around

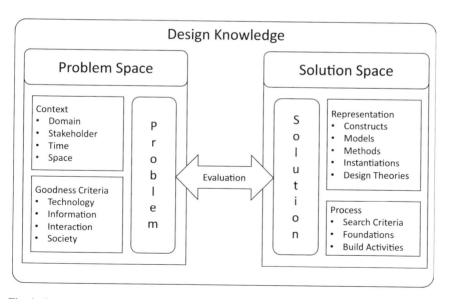

Fig. 4 Components of design knowledge for a specific DSR project

solution technologies, actions, systems, and design processes based on the new and interesting knowledge produced in a DSR project. Thus, we can describe the interactions of a specific DSR project with the extant knowledge bases in the following consuming and producing modes (Fig. 5):

- Descriptive (Ω) Knowledge: Ω-knowledge (or kernel knowledge) informs the understanding of a problem, its context, and the underlying design of a solution entity (Arrow 1). As results of the research project, the design and real-world application of solution entities or design knowledge enhances our descriptive understanding of how the world works via the testing and building of new Ω-knowledge (Arrow 2).
- Prescriptive (λ) Solution Design Entities: Existing solution entities, design processes, or design systems are re-used to inform novel designs of new entities, processes, or systems (Arrow 5) (vom Brocke & Buddendick, 2006). Within a DSR project, effective solution entities, design processes, or design systems are produced and contributed to new λ-knowledge (Arrow 6).
- Prescriptive (λ) Solution Design Theories: Solution design knowledge, in the form of growing design theories, informs the design of a solution entity, a design process or a design system (Arrow 3). Within a DSR project, effective principles, features, actions, or effects of a solution entity or a design process or system are generalized and codified in solution design knowledge (e.g. design theories or technological rules) (Arrow 4).

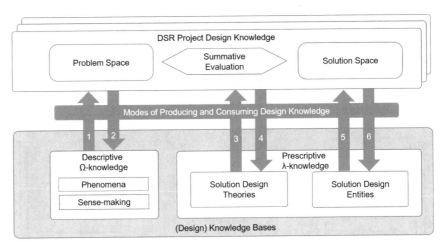

Fig. 5 DSR projects and modes of producing and consuming design knowledge (Adapted from Drechsler and Hevner (2018))

6 Three Types of Design Science Projects

In simple terms, a DSR project can make two types of contributions—it can contribute to design entities or to design theory—and conducting design processes in search of solutions to prob-lems and theorizing about such processes are what lead to these contributions (vom Brocke & Maedche, 2019). The two type of contributions and related activities are illustrated in Fig. 6.

Early contributions to DSR focused on contributions to design entities (e.g., Hevner et al. 2004; Peffers et al. 2007). Gregor and Jones (2007) introduce the idea of DSR projects' producing design theory and conceptualize the anatomy of a design theory by means of six core components: purpose and scope, constructs, principle of form and function, artifact mutability, testable propositions, and justificatory knowledge. Gregor and Hevner (2013) outline how both types of contributions relate to each another and how a DSR project can go beyond the design of design entities to contribute to design theory by theorizing about the design science process and the evaluation result achieved.

More recently, Chandra-Kruse, Seidel and vom Brocke (2019) suggest a third type of DSR project that builds on design processes that are not conducted as part of the DSR project itself but at another place and time. Such research opens DSR projects up to theorize about design that is not motivated by research but by something that happened in, for example, industry or society. Drawing from archeology research, researchers have described methods for investigating design processes and artifacts empirically to generate DK. In short, three types of DSR projects can be differentiated regarding the contribution they intend to make to DK: (1) projects that contribute to design entities, (2) projects that contribute to both design entities and design theory, and (3) projects that contribute to design theory without developing a design entity as part of the same project.

Given the complexity of DSR projects and the various ways a DSR project might contribute to DK, how comprehensively and effectively a DSR project is planned and communicated can affect its likelihood of success. Such planning and communication enables researchers to reflect on and receive feedback about their DSR project in its early stages and to question and update their scope as they progress in the project.

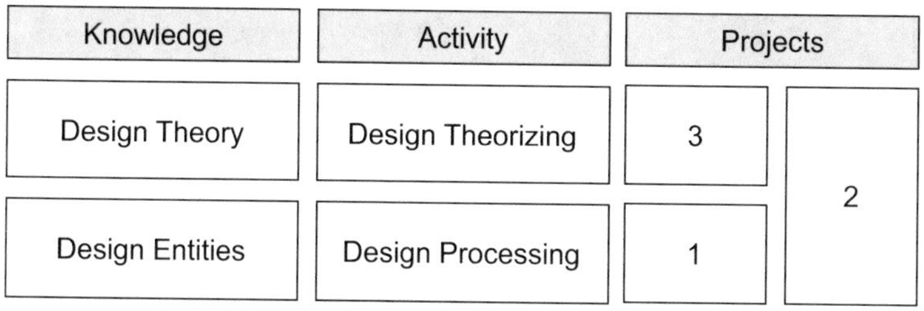

Knowledge	Activity	Projects	
Design Theory	Design Theorizing	3	2
Design Entities	Design Processing	1	

Fig. 6 DSR Projects' contributions to design knowledge

7   The Design Science Research Grid

The DSR Grid (vom Brocke & Maedche, 2019) enables researchers to effectively plan, coordinate and communicate their DSR projects. The DSR grid intends to put an entire DSR project on one page, highlighting its essential components in order to reflect and communicate its scope. Such representation of a DSR project helps to better plan and communicate a DSR project as well as to receive feedback from different stakeholders in an early stage and to question and update the scope as the project progresses. As shown in Fig. 7, the DSR Grid consists of the six most important dimensions of a DSR project.

Problem Description: What is the problem for which a DSR project must identify possible solution? Problems should be formulated by means of problem statements and characterized by positioning the problem in a problem space. Research has identified the context, described by the domain, the stakeholder, time and place, and goodness criteria, the last of which tells when a problem should be considered solved, as necessary to capture the problem appropriately (vom Brocke et al. 2020).

Input Knowledge: What prior knowledge will be used in the DSR project? As introduced above one can distinguish Ω-knowledge and λ-knowledge, the first being descriptive, explanatory, or predictive, and the second being prescriptive (Gregor & Hevner, 2013). Three types input—kernel theories, design theories, and design entities—can be differentiated for high-level communication about DSR projects.

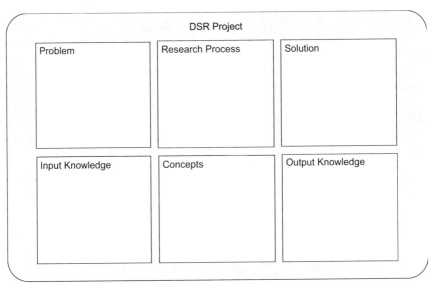

Fig. 7 DSR grid comprised of the six core dimensions of a DSR project

Research Process: What are the essential activities planned (or conducted) to make the intended contribution? When the intended contribution is design entities, the process includes build and evaluate activities (Hevner et al., 2004). In particular, these activities also include grounding the design (vom Brocke et al., 2020) by, for example, conducting literature reviews (Webster & Watson, 2002, vom Brocke et al. 2015), and meta-analysis (Denyer, Tranfield & Van Aken, 2008). In order to support concurrent design and evaluation, it is suggested to plan and document the build and evaluation activities in one. DSR tools have been developed (vom Brocke et al., 2017; Morana et al., 2018) to keep logs of the research process; such logs can complement a high-level list of research activities used to scope the DSR project in the process dimension. The process documented here may also include activities for theorizing about the design. While activities for processing the design can draw from DSR process models like the Peffers et al. (2007) model, activities for theorizing can draw from various research methods and strategies of inquiry, such as qualitative and quantitative empirical research.

Key concepts: What are the most important concepts used in the research performed in the DSR project? The words used to describe the research, such as the problem and solution space that the DSR project focuses on, as well as the concepts used to describe the process and input and output knowledge must be defined clearly. A clear definition of the key concepts is particularly important to ensure a rigorous execution of the evaluation activities.

Solution Description: What is the solution to the problem being investigated by a DSR project? The solution description clearly states the essential mechanisms of the solution (vom Brocke et al. 2020) and how the solution is positioned in solution space by characterizing its representation as a construct, a model, a method, an instantiation, or a design theory.

Output Knowledge: What knowledge is produced in the DSR project? Naturally, DSR projects produce DK, classified as λ-knowledge (Gregor & Hevner, 2013), but in contrast to the solution description, the DK generated through the project puts the problem and solution spaces in relation to each other (vom Brocke et al. 2020). If a DSR project does not intend to generate design theory but to generate design entities, the description of such entities does not constitute DK, as it is only the results of the design entity's evaluation in context that constitute DK. These results are then documented as output knowledge when the project is described.

Factors like the phase of the project (e.g., early planning or documenting completed research) and the stakeholder group (e.g., industry partners or editors) determine the perspectives from which and the detail with which the six dimensions may be described. Multiple versions of the dimensions will usually be created in iterations as a project progresses, but referring to the dimensions helps researchers to consider the core aspects of a DSR project from the outset and to discuss these aspects with stakeholder groups to shape the project's profile further as it goes along.

8 Conclusion

In this chapter, some important DSR concepts and models have been presented to provide a foundation for the planning, performing, and disseminating DK from specific DSR projects. In the following chapters, cases of DSR projects are presented as conducted by experienced researchers in the field. These cases serve as examples from which to learn in order to inform one's DSR projects. These case studies provide invaluable experiential knowledge of how fellow researchers have conducted DSR over the past decades. This case collection is intended to "live" in that we are always very happy to include new cases of diverse application environments. The richer the collection, the more useful for the community. Apart from enjoying to read the cases in the book, authors are cordially invited to get in touch and discuss how to add their own case to this collection.

References

Becker, J., vom Brocke, J., Heddier, M., & Seidel, S. (2015). In search of information systems (Grand) challenges: a community of inquirers perspective. *Business & Information Systems Engineering (BISE), 6*(1), 39–43.

Chandra-Kruse, L., Seidel, S., & vom Brocke, J. (2019). Design archaeology: Generating design knowledge from real-world artifact design. Paper presented at the 14th International Conference on Design Science Research in Information Systems and Technology, Worcester, MA.

Denyer, D., Tranfield, D., & van Aken, J. E. (2008). Developing design propositions through research synthesis. *Organization Studies, 29*(3), 393–413.

Drechsler, A., & Hevner, A. R. (2018). Utilizing, producing, and contributing design knowledge in DSR projects. In S. Chatterjee, K. Dutta, & R. Sundarraj (Eds.), *Lecture Notes in Computer Science* (Vol. 10844, pp. 82–97)., Designing for a Digital and Globalized World Cham, Switzerland: Springer.

Gregor, S., & Jones, D. (2007). The anatomy of a design theory. *Journal of the Association For Information Systems, 8*(5), 312–335.

Gregor, S., & Hevner, A. R. (2013). Positioning and presenting design science research for maximum impact. *MIS Quarterly, 37*(2), 337–355.

Hevner, A. R. (2007). A three cycle view of design science research. *Scandinavian Journal of Information Systems, 19*(2), 87–92.

Hevner, A. R., March, S. T., Park, J., & Ram, S. (2004). Design science in information systems. *MIS Quarterly, 28*(1), 75–105.

Morana, S., Scheid, M., Gau, M., Benke, I., vom Brocke, J., Fettke, P., & Maedche, A. (2018). Research Prototype: The Design Canvas in MyDesignProcess.com, in: DESRIST 2018 Conference Proceedings.

Nunamaker, J. F., Chen, M., & Purdin, T. D. (1991). Systems development in information systems research. *Journal of Management Information Systems, 7*(3), 89–106.

Peffers, K., Tuunanen, T., Rothenberger, M. A., & Chatterjee, S. (2007). A design science research methodology for information systems research. *Journal of Management Information Systems, 24*(3), 45–77.

Seidel, S., Recker, J., & vom Brocke, J. (2013). Sensemaking and sustainable practicing: functional affordances of information systems in green transformations. *Management Information Systems Quarterly (MISQ), 37*(4), 1275–1299.

Simon, H. A. (1996). *The sciences of the artificial.* Cambridge, MA: MIT Press.

Sonnenberg, C., & vom Brocke, J. (2012). Evaluations in the Science of the Artificial: Reconsidering the Build-evaluate Pattern in Design Science Research. In K. Peffers, M. Rothenberger, & B. Kuechler (Eds.), *Design science research in information systems and technology 2012, advances in theory and practice (Lecture Notes in Computer Science)* (pp. 381–397). NV, USA, Springer, Berlin, Heidelberg: Las Vegas.

Venable, J. R., Pries-Heje, J., & Baskerville, R. L. (2016). FEDS: A framework for evaluation in design science research. *European Journal Information Systems, 25*(1), 77–89.

Venable, J., vom Brocke, J., & Winter, R. (2019), Designing TRiDS: Treatments for risks in design science. *Australasian Journal of Information Systems (AJIS)*, June 2019.

vom Brocke J., Seidel S. (2012a) Environmental sustainability in design science research: direct and indirect effects of design artifacts. In: K. Peffers, M. Rothenberger, B. Kuechler (eds) Design Science Research in Information Systems. Advances in Theory and Practice. DESRIST 2012. Lecture Notes in Computer Science, vol 7286. Springer, Berlin, Heidelberg.

vom Brocke, J., & Seidel, S. (2012b). Environmental Sustainability in Design Science Research: Direct and Indirect Effects of Design Artifacts. Paper presented at the 7th international conference on Design Science Research in Information Systems, Las Vegas, USA.

vom Brocke, J., Fettke, P., Gau, M., Houy, C., Maedche, A., Morana, S., & Seidel, S. (2017). Tool-Support for Design Science Research: Design Principles and Instantiation (May 23, 2017). Available at SSRN: https://ssrn.com/abstract=2972803 or https://doi.org/10.2139/ssrn.2972803.

vom Brocke, J., & Maedche, A. (2019). The DSR grid: Six core dimensions for effectively planning and communicating design science research projects. *Electronic Markets, 29*(3), 379–385.

vom Brocke, J., Simons, A., Riemer, K., Niehaves, B., Plattfaut, R., & Cleven, A. (2015). Standing on the shoulders of giants: challenges and recommendations of literature search in information systems research. communications of the association for information systems. *Article, 37*(1), 205–224. Article 9.

vom Brocke, J., Watson, R., Dwyer, C., Elliot, S., & Melville, N. (2013). Green information systems: Directives for the IS discipline. *Communications of the Association for Information Systems (CAIS), 33*(30), 509–520.

vom Brocke, J., Winter, R., Hevner, A., & Maedche, A. (2020). Accumulation and evolution of design knowledge in design science research—a journey through time and space. *Journal of the Association for Information Systems (JAIS), forthcoming.*

Walls, J. G., Widmeyer, G. R., & El Sawy, O. A. (1992). Building an information system design theory for vigilant EIS. *Information Systems Research, 3*(1), 36–59.

Watson, R. T., Boudreau, M.-C., & Chen, A. J. W. (2010). Information systems and environ-mentally sustainable development: Energy Informatics and new directions for the IS com-munity. *MIS Quarterly, 34*(1), 23–38.

Webster J. and Watson R.T. (2002). Analyzing the past to prepare for the future: Writing a literature review. *MIS Quarterly, 26*(2), xiii–xxiii.

Winter, R., & Albani, A. (2013). Restructuring the design science research knowledge base: A onecycle view of design science research and its consequences for understanding organizational design problems. In R. Winter & A. Albani (Eds.), *Lecture Notes in Information Systems and Organisation* (Vol. 1, pp. 381–397)., Designing Organizational Systems: An Interdisciplinary Discourse Heidelberg, Germany: Springer.

DSR in Information Management

A Novel Approach to Collectively Determine Cybersecurity Performance Benchmark Data

Aiding Organizational Cybersecurity Assessment

Richard Baskerville and Vijay Vaishnavi

Abstract How do we determine cybersecurity performance benchmark data across organizations without the organizations revealing data points involving their frequency of information compromises? Disclosures of underlying data points are fundamentally inhibited by the need for privacy. It is a responsible organizational action to prevent the risk of expected or unexpected damages through data disclosure. Obtaining the data, especially valid and reliable data, necessary to calculate benchmarks, was thus an unsolvable wicked problem. The problem was therefore redefined as: How do we enable a distributed power-base of cybersecurity managers across organizations to *collectively* determine their benchmark data *without actually disclosing their own data points*? The core of the solution is a simple creative idea of having a protocol for a network of organizations to calculate benchmarks by distributing such calculations starting with some obfuscating data instead of centrally collecting the constituent data points of each organization. In this way, the confidential data of the organization would never be released beyond organizational systems. The fuller development of the protocol faced the issues of establishing trust in the network and preventing statistical compromises that were addressed through creative use of available technology, leading to the final solution, a distributed peer-to-peer architecture called Trusted Query Network (TQN). Distributed processing can induce trust and privacy into computer networks. In addition: (1) A research group representing multiple strengths and different but complementary backgrounds can be a very powerful asset in solving difficult problems. (2) Use of creativity is central to design science research but is particularly needed in solving apparently intractable problems. A group format can encourage free flow of ideas and brainstorming that are useful in spurring creativity. (3) It is very useful to be visionary in finding and solving challenging problems. Research groups provide the psychological strength to confront existing design challenges and to visualize their out-of-the-box solutions.

R. Baskerville (✉) · V. Vaishnavi
Georgia State University, Atlanta, Georgia
e-mail: baskerville@acm.org

V. Vaishnavi
e-mail: vvaishna@gsu.edu

© Springer Nature Switzerland AG 2020
J. vom Brocke et al. (eds.), *Design Science Research. Cases*, Progress in IS,
https://doi.org/10.1007/978-3-030-46781-4_2

1 Introduction

How well are today's organizations protecting their confidential information? As important as the answer to this question is, we don't really know the answer. It has been historically impossible to answer such a question because the underlying data is impossible to collect. Such a collection is impossible because the individual data points involve revealing the frequency of information compromises in organizations. Organizations are understandably reticent when it comes to admitting their information security compromises. As a result, we can only guess about the general status of our cybersecurity efforts. For example, the Privacy Rights Clearinghouse reports details of more than 10 billion compromised records since 2005.[1] This data comes from government reports or verifiable media sources. In an age of big data, is our average exposure of 800 million records annually a record that is spectacularly bad or spectacularly good? The data reveals that 14 publicly known breaches at Bank of America have exposed 1,894,326 records. By comparison, nine publicly known breaches at Citigroup have exposed 4,769,338 records. Does this mean that Citi (with annual revenue of around US$70b) is more careless than BoA (with annual revenue of around US$90b)? Instead, does it simply mean that Citi has been forced to disclose publicly more of its exposures than BoA? What if both of these records are much better than the average of actual exposures at all banks?

We cannot answer these questions because we lack benchmarks for cybersecurity performance. We lack such benchmarks because companies are understandably reluctant to admit their actual cybersecurity performance. What makes this problem worse is that these companies cannot know themselves whether their performance is comparably better than, or worse than, the cybersecurity performance benchmarks for their industry. Disclosures of underlying data points are fundamentally inhibited by the need for privacy. Disclosure inhibition is an inner impediment to the free expression of information. It is a responsible organizational action to prevent the risk of expected or unexpected damages through data disclosure. Thus the fundamental problem is *The Law of Private Data Disclosure* (Vaishnavi, Vandenberg, Baskerville, & Zheng, 2006):

$$\text{Private Data Disclosure} \Rightarrow \text{Risk}$$

That is, any information disclosure implies a risk to the discloser. The risk may vary in scale from trivial to fatal, but any disclosure involves risk. As a result few organizations share information about their cybersecurity breaches because such information is so sensitive (Vance, Lowry, & Wilson, 2016).

Under today's management theory, the capability to manage high quality processes depends on the availability of good metrics to guide decision making. It is a completely simple notion, like a speedometer for helping a driver manage the speed of the vehicle. The meter indicates speed, and the driver makes informed decisions

---

[1] Data reviewed on 29 December 2017 at https://www.privacyrights.org/data-breaches.

whether to go faster or slower. Of course, a poor manager may make poor decisions in terms of the metrics, just as a poor driver may precipitate a collision or get arrested.

Dedicated cybersecurity managers, such as a CISO (Chief Information Security Officer) need more information than just the organizational cybersecurity performance. They need cybersecurity performance benchmarks that provide reference points for their performance. Is the organization's number of cybersecurity incidents better or worse than similar organizations? Is the CISO and the security department doing a good job or a poor job relative to their peers? It is similar for driving. Drivers need some indication about how fast is too fast and how slow is too slow. The most obvious speed benchmark for drivers is a speed limit or speed recommendation. For drivers, these speed benchmarks are based on laws or road designs.

Of course, benchmarks for the metrics for cybersecurity managers are more complex. These are rarely set by laws or environmental designs, and more often based on comparative performance of similar organizations. For example, a measure like the rate of return on investment (ROI) may be regarded "good" or "bad" depending on comparative benchmarks. If an investment manager achieves an ROI of 6%, and the average ROI for other comparative investment managers is 8%, then it suggests the manager is making poor decisions and has room for improvement. On the other hand, if the average ROI for other comparative investment managers is 4%, then the 6% investment manager is making good decisions that could lead others to improve.

It is the value of the benchmarks as well as the performance metrics that most help managers to know if their decision making has been good or bad, better or worse, in comparison with other managers facing similar decisions. A focus purely on organizational metrics only solves part of the guidance issues for management decisions. It is the benchmarks that help determine the goals for the metrics values. The calculation of benchmarks across comparative organizations is often further complicated by the confidentiality of the underlying measures. For example, cybersecurity managers may want to use a metric such as the number of server compromises per month. Suppose the metric measure for December is 21. Is this good or bad? The cybersecurity manager can compare to November or January, but this is not as useful as accurately knowing what would be typical for this measure in other organizations. Is this number spectacularly high; or is it a tiny fraction of that normally found in other organizations? It is the benchmark that helps the cybersecurity manager decide if the server compromises are being overmanaged or undermanaged.

2 The Context

The problem with confidentiality of the measures most desirable for benchmarks is the extreme sensitivity of the metrics values for each organization. There has been some operational success with industry-based Information Sharing and Analysis Centers (ISACs)[2] that exchange threat and mitigation information. There has also

---

[2]https://www.nationalisacs.org/ (last accessed on 8 March 2018).

been similar success with a law-enforcement-based (i.e., FBI) operational information exchange intended to protect critical infrastructures (Infragard[3]). However, none
of these organizations track organizational cybersecurity performance information.
Attempts to create central databases for such confidential data have not only run
afoul of trust, but also risks of legal discovery, and freedom-of-information laws.
Examples include Purdue University Cerias Incident Response Data Base (CIRDB)[4]
project[5] and the CIFAC project (Rezmierski, Rothschild, Kazanis, & Rivas, 2005).
The purpose of these systems is to manage this sensitive point data centrally, rather
than sharing benchmark data at a collective level.

The specific setting for this problem was a U.S. state university system that
confronted the need to assess the cybersecurity performance across its 30 constituent
universities and colleges. Even when the cybersecurity breach reporting was made
mandatory, little data was collected, partly because the cybersecurity managers in
the various institutions did not know whether they were confessing to incompe-
tence or bragging about their competence. Members of the university system originally formed a team to investigate the creation of a national ISAC-like system for
collecting and reporting cybersecurity performance in higher education. Eventually
this effort gave way to a recognition that obtaining the data, especially valid and
reliable data, necessary to calculate benchmarks was a wicked problem. It involved
multiple, conflicting criteria at different levels of the data collection and disclosure
process. No one would willingly divulge their own data points until they had the
opportunity to compare their own data points to the collective benchmark. Based on
this observation, the problem was redefined as:

> How do we enable a distributed power-base of cybersecurity managers to collectively
> determine their benchmark data without actually disclosing their own data points?

The redefined problem operated under a fundamental assumption that cybersecurity managers, who are distributed across the population, would be motivated
to improve their cybersecurity performance as soon as they learned that they are
underperforming in relation to the benchmarks. As a natural outcome of the steadily
improving quality of the underperforming sector in the population, the benchmarks
will rise. As a natural outcome of the behavior above, the overall performance
of the population will rise. In other words, the way to improve the cybersecurity
performance of any sector is to develop and share benchmarks of performance.

3 The Journey

We will describe the design science research journey of this project in terms of Vaishnavi and Kuechler's general process model for design science research (Vaishnavi & Kuechler, 2015). This model describes an iterative process of problem awareness,

---

[3]https://www.infragard.org/ (last accessed on 8 March 2018).

[4]https://www.cerias.purdue.edu/site/news/view/cirdb_cassandra/ (last accessed on 8 March 2018).

[5]https://www.cerias.purdue.edu/site/about (last accessed on 12 March 2018).

solution suggestion, artifact development, evaluation, conclusion and knowledge flow circumscription. This model is depicted in Fig. 1.

Awareness of Problem. There can be multiple sources from which an awareness may arise of an interesting practical and research problem. The problem should be interesting because it is proving intractable. Intractable problems are those for which the solutions at hand are unsatisfying. Intractable problems are interesting when we discover that these problems are essentially not of the nature previously assumed. In the example above, we assume that the essence of the problem has to do with overcoming the unwillingness of cybersecurity managers to reveal unpleasant data. The problem becomes interesting when we assume the cybersecurity managers are behaving properly in withholding the data. It is a problem of helping them obtain the information they need to properly manage their cybersecurity operations.

Intractable problems are often interesting research problems because researchers may have been basing their knowledge on the wrong range of theories. Such a misalignment occurs because the practical problem has been misdiagnosed.

The output of the Awareness phase is a proposal, formal or informal, for a new design science research effort.

Suggestion. This phase follows from the proposal. Indeed, it is closely connected with awareness as indicated by the dotted line around proposal and tentative design. Both the Awareness and the Suggestion phases are likely to involve an *abductive reasoning process*. It is a reasoning process in which the designer observes the problem and then creates elements of the most likely solution (tentative design). This tentative design is the output of the Suggestion phase.

Development. In this phase, the tentative design is further developed and implemented. The implementation itself is sometimes very pedestrian. That is, it may not necessarily involve novelty or originality beyond the current state-of-the-art. The novel contribution is usually present in the artifact's design rather than in its

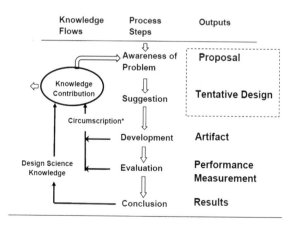

Fig. 1 Vaishnavi & Kuechler's design science research process model (2015, p. 13)

construction. Both the Development and the Conclusion phases (next) involve *deductive reasoning* in deducing the artifact's material characteristics from the tentative design.

Evaluation. In the Evaluation phase, the results of the artifact development are compared with the expectations that are either implicit or explicit in the Awareness and the Suggestion phases. When results embody essential deviations from expectations, we need tentative explanations to determine which further steps to follow next. These results and explanations often provide information that often helps refine our understanding of the problem, the utility of the suggestion, and the feasibility of the originally imagined artifact.

Conclusion. In terms of reasoning, this phase involves *reflection and abstraction*. We give consideration to the meaning of the more important and general outcomes of the previous phases. It is not necessary that the outcomes are optimal, only that they satisfice. But in producing these outcomes, we learn about the nature of the problem, the character of the solution, and the effect of the artifact. In other words, we not only seek to solve the problem, but also to learn about the environment that produces the problem and envelopes the solution-artifact.

Circumscription represents the major feedback loops that drive iteration in the design science research process. It is a rich notion about the common-sense value of knowledge and conjecture. McCarthy defined circumscription as "a rule of conjecture that can be used by a person or program for 'jumping to certain conclusions', namely … the objects they can determine to have certain properties or relations are the only objects that do" (McCarthy, 1980, p. 27). This aspect of the process informs us of the limits or boundaries of the knowledge discovered in each design science research cycle in two ways. First, we discover constraint knowledge about the theories underlying our design. This knowledge involves detecting and analyzing contradictions arising when things do not work according to theory. Second, a problem situation determines our awareness and suggestion, which in turn drive our conclusion to design and develop an artifact. In so doing, we create a new situation and we must again decide what to do. We create and use both knowledge about the specific situation and more general types of knowledge (like common sense). Accordingly, there are two types of arrows in the Fig. 1 representation of this process. Broad white arrows represent knowledge use, and narrow black arrows represent the generation of knowledge.

3.1 Lap 1—"Paper-Based Prototype"

Awareness of Problem. The problem and its origin, as it appeared to the design group, are described above in the introduction and the context sections. The important aspect of this awareness was the realization that it would not be possible to compel organizations to share such sensitive data. This aspect embodied our pre-theory as we approached the suggestion phase (Baskerville & Vaishnavi, 2016). An alternative was needed in which the benchmarks could be developed without any organizational disclosures.

Suggestion. At the design group's first meeting, the suggestion arose that it might be possible for a collective of organizations to calculate benchmarks by distributing such calculations instead of centrally collecting the constituent data points of each organization. In this way, the confidential data of the organization would never be released beyond organizational systems or organizational protection. Our solution to the underlying problem (The Law of Private Data Disclosure) was defined as:

(Disclose no private data) ^ (Disclose only aggregate data)

The design group devised a paper-based experiment in which slips of paper would be passed around the group members and each person would individually calculate their data's impact on the benchmark.

Development. Because this initial experiment was a simple paper-based prototype it materialized something like a design walk-through. Our first experiment was calculating the average age of the group members without any one person revealing his/her age.

The first person imagined three people of different ages. He then totaled these three people's ages (obfuscating data) with his own. He wrote the number of people ($n = 4$) and their total age on a slip of paper and passed this slip to another (randomly chosen) member of the design team.

The second person added his age to the total and incremented n. He wrote the new total and the new value of n on a new slip of paper. He passed this slip to another (randomly chosen) member of the design team.

The third person similarly added her age and incremented n. She passed along a new slip of paper with her results to the next person, and so on, until all members of the design group had a pass at the calculation.

The paper was returned to the first person (the initiator) who subtracted the total age of the three imaginary people and reduced n accordingly by three. He then divided the remaining total by the remaining n, producing the average age of the design group without anyone actually revealing his/her own age.

This exercise was repeated several times, with ongoing discussions about how to compromise the protocol and how to calculate more complex values.

Evaluation. While this early paper-based experiment seemed very promising, it was easy to imagine very simple compromises. For example, the group could collude against any one of its number to detect that member's confidential data. Any member of the group could bias the results by misadjusting the values of partial results and n. Everyone in the *network* had to *trust* its members to be accurate and not collude. It was clear that control over the network membership and the initiation of a calculation round (a *query*) would still require one member of the network to act as a controller to insure members were not misrepresenting themselves or their data, and that the progress of the query calculation was random. The design group also recognized that existing statistical theories about statistical data compromise would have to be considered in developing the protocols for various calculations.

Circumscription. Based on the experience and the evaluation, the design group decided to proceed to the design and development of a computer-based prototype that would emulate the paper-based prototype. This emulator would need to account for the various compromise paths and the need for a controller in the network. The proposed approach to distributed benchmark calculations would be named a *trusted query network* (TQN) because of the prominence of trust among the network of query calculators.

Conclusion. This lap of a rather simple looking 'paper-based prototype' provided a very powerful foundation for solving the research problem. It not only provided a deeper understanding of the problem but also contributed an elegant creative idea that needed further refinement and development.

3.2   Lap 2—"Simulation Prototype"

Awareness of Problem. In Lap 1, the basic problem at first seemed impossible at the outset. The initial suggestion, distribution of benchmark processing at first seemed to offer a simple and elegant solution. However, as the protocol developed, hurdles had begun to develop that technology would have to overcome: namely, establishing trust in the network and preventing statistical compromises that could expose individual data points.

Suggestion. With regard to the first issue, establishing trust in the query network, we adopted Giddens' definition of trust as appropriate for our purposes: the "confidence in the reality of a person or system, regarding a given set of outcomes or events…" (Giddens, 1990, p. 34). Giddens' notions were appropriate for our case; we were not dealing with trust between individual persons, but rather an institutional form of trust, where trust is vested in "abstract capacities characteristic of modern institutions" (Nandhakumar & Baskerville, 2006, p. 189). Such a form of trust is established through confidence in the prevalence of order and routine.

With regard to the second issue, prevention of statistical compromises, considerable work had been done in this area, particularly in the 70–80 s. This work originated with early privacy problems arising in attempts to release census data in electronic form (see "Security of Census Population" Security of census population, CMND. 5365, 1973). A statistical database is compromised whenever it is possible to obtain or deduce previously unknown information about an individual from one or more queries. For example, regression analyses are both an avenue for compromise (Palley & Simonoff, 1987) and as a vehicle for big data analytics (Fule & Roddick, 2004).

Given the use of data streams in developing big data analytics, we reckoned that these compromises were equally applicable to a query network.

Practically every query path into a statistical database can be subverted for compromising queries. These include simple "count" queries and simple statistical means. One major safeguard to prevent statistical database compromise involves the use of sampling fortified by introducing sampling errors. However, the errors can bias the data, and repeated sampling may still compromise the data.

The problem with the collection of large statistical databases, particularly marketing data, census data and research data, is that these can be compromised in various ways. Such compromises involve using statistical operations on the data to determine information about an individual from the database (Palley & Simonoff, 1987). This is a particularly serious problem in small statistical databases which reduce the effectiveness of sampling subfiles as a means to protect the data.

The known techniques to protect against such operations against statistical databases are usually emplaced within the statistical sampling programs themselves. For example, logging can be used to monitor excessive activity into a database. While detective kinds of controls help reveal a rising risk of compromise, the more effective controls involve perturbing or obfuscating the data (Adam & Worthmann, 1989; Traub, Yemini, & Woźniakowski, 1984). These techniques involve inoculating the data with random individual errors that are ultimately processed out of the results (Ahituv & Neumann, 1988). Such techniques have been used effectively for many years (e.g., Hoffman, 1977). For example, these have been used by the US and British Census organizations for ad hoc queries since 1971 (see Security of census population, CMND. 5365, 1973). More recently these database protection techniques have been advanced as a general technique for protecting the security and privacy of data in general, not just databases as a collective (Bakken, Rarameswaran, Blough, Franz, & Palmer, 2004).

In designing the first version of the computer-based prototype, the more thorough awareness of the problems and relevant literature at hand meant that the prototype needed means for establishing trust among members of the network and means for protecting the data streams from statistical compromise. Such a security control means inoculating, obfuscating, or perturbing the data itself.

The design team decided to deal with the trust aspect of the problem by distributing control and power throughout the query network protocols. While a central server would vet admission to the network, the protocol would empower the member nodes and control the power of the central server. Nodes would initiate queries and each node could decide whether or not to participate in any query. For example, a node could decide whether the number of nodes (the query population) was large enough to guarantee randomness in the query node order. If this population was insufficient, the node could withdraw from participating in the query.

The design team decided to deal with the statistical compromise issue using proven approaches to prevent such compromise. As described in Lap 1, the initiating node already was empowered to introduce obfuscating data that could be removed later in the process when n was large enough to prevent detection of individual data points. This is a well-established process known as inoculating the data stream with random individual errors, yet inevitably maintain the statistical integrity of the data (Hoffman, 1977). Further, the computer-based protocol would support multiple passes through the data stream processing. Any node could flag the partial product to reserve a future visit for calculation. This feature permitted any node to introduce its own inoculations and to remove these in a future pass, when the data stream was considered safe against compromise.

The design team decided to otherwise keep this simulation prototype as simple as possible. This first computer-based prototype would only calculate the mean of a data stream. Other known inoculation techniques, such as the rounding of results, the use of random samples from the data stream, and the careful introduction of sampling errors (sampling obfuscation) (Ahituv & Neumann, 1988) would be postponed until more sophisticated calculations are involved.

Similarly, the design team decided to simulate for the time being the query network on a standalone computer system. This eliminated much of the technical overhead in actually operating a network. The "nodes" would be virtual machines that communicate with each other through the host operating system rather than the Internet or other network infrastructure.

Development. Early in the development, we decided on Shibboleth[6] as a technical basis for admission to the query network and participation in query processing. Shibboleth is an open source program that provides access control, while at the same time affording a degree on anonymity to the network nodes. It is described as providing "Single Sign-On capabilities and allows sites to make informed authorization decisions for individual access of protected online resources in a privacy-preserving manner."[6] It provides an ideal platform for distributing trust across a technical network.

3.2.1   Our Solution

Trusted Query Network (TQN), is a distributed and peer-to-peer architecture for risk data generation, aggregation, management and analysis, as shown in Fig. 2. A Trusted Query Network protocol provides the communication mechanism for the architecture. We stress again that participating organizations store their own risk data locally, with complete control over its access and release—indeed, there is no reliance on a third party. Since it is unnecessary for organizations to trust a third party, and there is no data access except where a company chooses to release its data as included in an aggregated data set, we anticipate a high level of organizational participation. We emphasize that inhibition to sharing data is overcome specifically because any data released is only as part of an aggregated set—there is no organizational specific data that can be seen. In turn, any organization that participates by contributing data in turn obtains valuable information from other organizations (in aggregate) quickly (not as a result of a months-long reporting process) and effectively (in response to a

---

[6]Accessed 31 December 2017 https://www.shibboleth.net/.

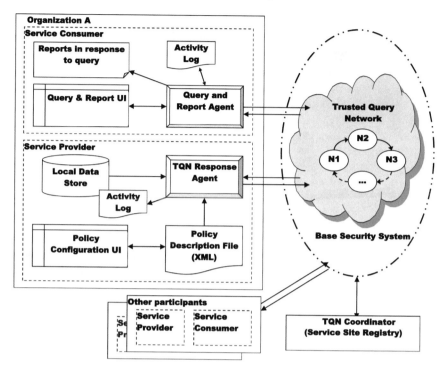

Fig. 2 TQN architecture

direct, specific query of interest) for their emergent decision. The TQN architecture consists of six logical components: (1) TQN Protocol, (2) TQN Message, (3) TQN Response Agent, (4) TQN Coordinator, (5) Base Security System, and (6) Query and Report Agent.

TQN Protocol. The heart of the solution to guaranteed anonymity is the TQN protocol. This protocol is based on the proposition that only the information aggregated on a group basis can be disclosed. In this way, individual data are always embedded in a result that is not directly associated with any one participant; thus, the identity of an information provider is preserved.

Below is a description of the query protocol in its simplest form. Figure 3 and Table 1 present a simple scenario.

1. A query, Q, is requested by any participant node for an aggregated result, R. The query Q is sent to TQN coordinator for pre-processing.
2. Upon receiving the query request Q, the TQN coordinator queries all nodes for their data release policies (see description of "TQN Response Agent" component below) and service availability. Having determined that there are sufficient

Fig. 3 A simple TQN
scenario

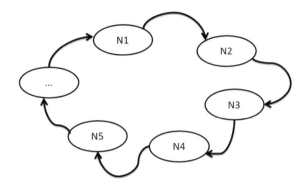

Table 1 A simple scenario: Query "Q0109884": What's the average age? (see Fig. 4)

Nodes	Action	Result R': Numbers in parenthesis are obfuscated data accumulated from initial query Q
Coordinator (after probing all nodes for participation confirmation)	Initiate query Q with obfuscated data; randomize traveling path; send to first node	Total: 40 (40) Respondents Count: 5 (5)
1st responder N1	Add data: 5 Increment count 1	Total: 45 (40)//cumulative Count: 6 (5)//incremented by 1
2nd responder N2	Add data: 15 Increment count 1	Total: 60 (40)//cumulative Count: 7 (5)//incremented by 1
3rd responder N3	Add data: 20 Increment count 1	Total: 80 (40)//cumulative Count: 8 (5)//incremented by 1
…	…	…
Last responder N6	Add data: 20 Increment count 1 Send it back to coordinator	Total: 120 (40)//cumulative Count: 11 (5)//cumulative
Coordinator	Remove obfuscating data;	Total: 80 (0)// = 120−40 Count: 6 (0)// = 11−5
Final result	Broadcast to all responders: N1 to N6	Query "Q0109884": **What's the average age**? Answer: 13 (6 respondents)

participants whose policy permits contributing data to query Q, the TQN Coordinator prepares an initial result R' using randomly generated obfuscating data (Bakken et al., 2004). The TQN Coordinator also establishes a random route among all nodes that agree to respond to Q.

3. Q and R' are passed among participants, in a completely randomized order chosen by the Coordinator in Step 2. The path is randomly varied for each query.

4. Upon receiving a request Q, each participant node releases its data—cumulatively adding its data (query results) to the partial cumulative data, R'.
5. Result R' is accumulated throughout the circulation until all participating nodes respond.
6. R' finally returns to the TQN coordinator. R will be computed from R' by removing the initial obfuscating data.
7. Final result R along with original query Q are wrapped in a TQN message and broadcast to all participants who have contributed data for this query.

TQN Message. The TQN Message is a standard document used to pass information and record communications among nodes. This message is XML standard based and may contain the following elements: original query; query metadata, such as ID, date/time; randomized traveling path; cumulated results and count of respondents.

TQN Response Agent. The TQN Response Agent is responsible for responding to queries within TQN. This agent: (1) Evaluates an incoming query message against the policy; (2) Presents a Policy Configuration user interface; (3) Filters data based on policy established locally by each participant; (4) Transmits the TQN message to the next destination defined in the message; (5) Maintains Activity Logs on all query processing and response activities.

The TQN Response Agent's behavior can be automated based on a data release policy. The policy is described and defined using an XML based Policy Description File and associated language. This file captures the business rules that reflect the organization's policy. Using the policy description file, organizations can flexibly release data based on such factors as query type, characteristics of cumulating query results, or number of responding participants.

TQN Coordinator. The TQN Coordinator provides supporting services that are required to be performed independently (these services do not interfere with the query process/protocol): (1) A Service Site Registry to provide a mapping between a real, networked attached service site (e.g., Uniform Resource Indicators URI) and a unique, pseudonymous identification. This also serves as record of federation participants. The registry join process is handled off-line to ensure that once participants have joined (a process governed by the network organization's policy for member's joining), their identity is subsequently anonymized in the Service Site Registry. (2) A Query Monitor responsible for query processing at the beginning and the end of any query, with functions including traveling path randomization, query result propagation, and query logging.

Base Security System. The Base Security System should provide for authenticated, but privacy preserving, pseudonymous access to the Trusted Query Network. This ideally would leverage the local, autonomous authentication/authorization mechanisms of federated participants, but may optionally be established as a standalone authentication/authorization dedicated to TQN.

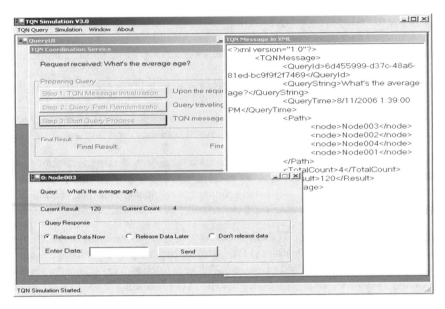

Fig. 4 TQN simulation interface

Query and Report Agent. The Query and Report Agent presents a Query Report user
interface; prepares the query plan and oversees query execution plan; broadcasts the
query result to the network; integrates response data for reports or further analysis;
maintains Activity Logs on all data integration and analysis activities.

Having discussed the Awareness, Suggestion, and Development phases of Lap
2, let us now discuss the rest of the phases of this lap: Evaluation, Conclusion, and
Circumscription.

Evaluation. The prototype demonstrated the TQN protocol through a user interface
(Fig. 4). Any user can specify a query string and initiate a query. The prototype
processes a query by first probing all nodes to assess willingness to participate in
the query, as determined by local policy. Having determined that a quorum of participants is present, the prototype processes the query by establishing a random path
for routing the query to all the participant sites. An appropriate XML message is
generated encapsulating the query id, the query string, the randomly set path, and
the accumulated responses along with the incrementing participant count. Of particular interest is the "obfuscating," random data that is added at query initiation. This
obfuscation is necessary to assure the first participant in the query path of some
protection per The Law of Private Data Disclosure (Vaishnavi et al., 2006). The first
rule followed in our solution is *to Disclose no private data*, which is fulfilled by
the second rule, *to Disclose only aggregate data*. While subsequent participants in
the TQN routing path have some assurance that their responses are hidden amongst
aggregated data and the obfuscating data that they add, the initiator of a query must
be provided a similar assurance. The TQN prototype allows the query initiator to

provide random data, which is corrected after the query has been circulated to all participants (see Table 1).

Other components that remained to be investigated and prototyped at this stage included TQN Coordinator, an implementation for TQN authenticated logins, a data release agent, the Policy Configuration user interface to manage attribute release, a standard for the Policy Description File, and the Query and Report Agent. Full scalability and performance testing were left as future activity, though initial testing could be done once the core prototype components were available.

In addition to the functional evaluation of the software-based prototype, the concepts from the TQN were used as the basis for improving the curriculum in an information assurance bachelor's program (Peltsverger & Zheng, 2012) and as a basis for an free simulation experiment in trust in systems (Sainsbury & Vance, 2007; Vance, 2009).

Conclusion. The work done in this lap developed the simple and powerful idea introduced in Lap 1 into a concrete contribution for the solution of the problem: *How do we enable a distributed power-base of cybersecurity managers to collectively determine their benchmark data without actually disclosing their own data points?*

Circumscription. Full scalability and performance testing were to be future activity, though initial testing could be done once the core prototype components were available.

In conclusion, this lap confirmed the feasibility of the concept developed in Lap 1 and demonstrated that the two hurdles, trust in the network and the prevention of statistical compromises, can be successfully overcome. It also showed that TQN is not limited to collective determination of cybersecurity performance benchmark data but also can be used to find out other needed benchmark data.

3.3 Lap 3—"Network-Based Prototype"

Awareness of Problem. In the third lap, the design team focused on moving toward a fully operational prototype. We realized that we were able to bypass components in a simulation and that many issues that might arise from operating TQN across a network were also bypassed.

Suggestion. Such a more complete prototype would include elements specified in the evaluation at Lap 2: The TQN Coordinator, full implementation of TQN authentication login, a simplified policy specification interface. In addition, Lap 2 would need to operate using a network of workstations rather than just a simulated network on a single workstation (as was the case in Lap 2).

Development. TQN was implemented on a network of six different TQN clients, each running on a different desktop computer. Each client operated with a different IP

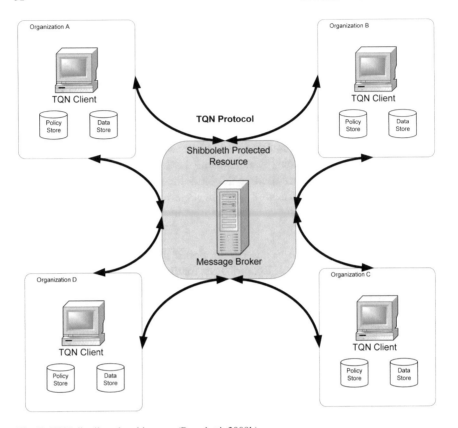

Fig. 5 TQN distributed architecture (Bertolotti, 2009b)

address. The Message Broker were architecturally separated from the TQN Clients. Figure 5 illustrates the architecture of the network-based TQN prototype. The system details are shown in Fig. 6.

The TQN client in Figs. 5 and 6 included a Shibboleth-based Authenticator. This authenticator is designed to provide protection for web resources, which is conducive to a web-based architecture. The client module asks users for credentials and inter-changes with the server module to authenticate the client into the network (i.e., provided a Security Assertion Markup Language SAML certificate). TQN Protocol Client operates the TQN Logic, implements the distributed coordination, handles incoming messages, and creates outgoing messages in a way that is functionally similar to the simulation prototype. Using the unique message identifier, it tracks the history of each TQN Message and controls the different protocol rounds. It also contains a TQN Policy and Data Store using a simple XML file. Finally, a communications component manages message traffic and RSA-based encryption of messages.

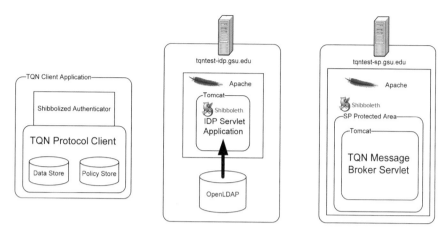

Fig. 6 Details of the Network-Based implementation of TQN (Bertolotti, 2009b)

The TQN Message Broker is implemented as a Java Servlet. It interacts with a web server (Apache in the prototype). It includes a Shibboleth component that runs as a system service both in Windows and in Unix. This component protects the namespace of the server, manages the authorization certificate and blocks unauthentic messages. It stores a Node Repository in which each client node must register and unregister itself. This process reveals unwanted nodes to prevent them from intruding. A keep alive feature in the client-server protocol reveals crashed nodes.

The TQN Shibboleth Identity Provider is another Java Servlet that provides a credential store.

Evaluation. Once fully operational, the network prototype was evaluated both in terms of requirements performance and customer satisfaction. The major technical requirements of the network-based prototype were delivered as follows:

- Anonymity: the physical locations of the TQN Clients were undetectable to other network nodes: Shibboleth split the authentication infrastructure from the network and the TQN Message Broker added client screening.
- Aggregated Data Disclosure: enabled by the data rounds of the TQN Protocol guaranteeing the secrecy of each organization's private data.
- Distributed Coordination: the TQN Protocol follows a series of small decisions taken by discrete TQN Clients. The initiating node for each TQN Query manages coordination, but each TQN Client in the network has a role in determining the TQN Message path in each of the various rounds, preventing any one node from pre-programming a query path.
- Secure Network: TQN enables several layers of encryption between the clients and the Message Broker. The system provides authenticity and confidentiality of every message's contents to every sender and receiver.
- Optional Participation: Policy Rules enable any organization to opt-in or opt-out of a query.

- Automated Operability: the design does not require human intervention to complete a query.
- Scalability: TQN is based on a well-established, federated approach (Shibboleth), an architecture that supports easy scalability.

In terms of customer satisfaction, the network-based prototype was demonstrated to a panel of experts from academia and various commercial sectors from the corporate world. A six-workstation TQN was set up in a laboratory setting and the experts were invited to occupy a workstation and participate in the demonstration. The experts universally expressed interest in seeing the further development of TQN. The strongest interest arose in the financial sector, with banking expressing the strongest satisfaction.

In addition to the functional evaluation of the network prototype, the TQN concepts were also put forward as the basis for a tool for implementing collaborative risk assessment. Tools of this kind can be used to enable a network of organizations to collectively perform risk assessments at the industry level. Such tools have been called for in order to provide risk assessment standards, such as NIST, to operate interorganizationally (Bertolotti, 2009a).

While the goals of the network-based prototype have been achieved, several critical shortcomings were notable. From a business viewpoint, we learned that TQN success would have both technical and business dependencies. Businesses on the network would have to invest in hardware, software, and operations. The cost of the message broker would have to be shared. In addition, participants in the network must trust each other. Organizations could easily game a TQN, launching queries but never sharing their own data. Technically, the presence of a message broker offered a vulnerability point too similar to a centralized repository. It is difficult to protect the network if the message broker is compromised.

Conclusion. The network-based prototype of TQN worked as per expectations. This lap also pointed to the fact that TQN can be used for networks ranging in size from small to large. Also, the use of TQN need not be limited to within a country but can used across countries to get international benchmark data for different sectors of industry.

Circumscription. The platform for TQN was running at its limits. In order to scale it must be rewritten for better code efficiency. In the operating prototype, for example, the IP addresses were hard coded into the server and the clients.

3.4   Lap 4—"Server-Less Trusted Query Network"

This was a specification Lap: goal was to specify requirements

Awareness of Problem. The problem of trust remains somewhat because there is still a central server that would engender suspicions that a single point of confidence failure remained. The next essential problem meant eliminating the need for a single coordinator or server.

Suggestion. This design lap focused on distributing the work of the central coordinator ("server") across the network of "client" machines. We decided to find an existing peer-to-peer network platform that sits at the application layer of the network and did not involve the coordination of a central control computer.

Development. This lap involved an unsuccessful search for a true peer-to-peer operating platform for TQN. All operating peer-to-peer platforms involve dedicated servers to start and control the work. Those that exist include a few experimental platforms.

Evaluation. Since there is no current platform, further development of a server-less version of TQN concluded.

Conclusion. There is need for fundamental work to develop a truly server-less peer-to-peer platform at the application layer of the network in which all network operation work is distributed, such as authentication, access control and workload distribution. This platform has strong potential at the level of the WWW.

Circumscription. The use of blockchain technology (Czepluch, Lollike, & Malone, 2015) as a basis for TQN is a possibility that needs to be explored in further development of this project.

4 The Results

Figure 7 summarizes the four laps and the concomitant iterations of the design science method. This table shows how the evaluation of the development triggers circumscription as feedforward to the problem awareness stage of the subsequent lap. This process continues until both the goals for the artifact had been achieved and subsequent problem awareness did not lead to any further development.

The table helps understand that, when viewed chronologically and row-wise, the design science process is an iterative series of stages: Problem-awareness 1, suggestion 1, development 1, evaluation 1, circumscription 1, problem-awareness 2, suggestion 2, and so forth. However, when viewed functionally (columnwise), the design science process is also a stack of five different kinds of experiences. There is a stack of five different problem-awareness experiences. There is a stack of five different suggestion experiences, and so forth.

The problem-awareness stack is dominated by issues of distrust: keeping mum, distrust in networks and central servers. Only once was the main problem a technical issue. The suggestion stack is dominated by distribution: distributing calculation, control, power across multiple stations and nodes. The development stack

	Awareness of Problem	Suggestion	Development	Evaluation	Circumscription
Lap 1 – Paper-based Prototype	Unwillingness of cybersecurity managers to reveal unpleasant data	Distribute calculation	Slips of paper and rough protocol	Protocol is workable and promising	Aim for computer-based prototype
Lap 2 – Simulation Prototype	Lack of trust in networks	Distribute control and power	Incorporate Shibboleth into TQN	Technical requirements for a digital solution satisfied	Aim for a full (network) prototype
Lap 3 – Network-based Prototype	Components were bypassed or stubbed in simulation	Work prototype into a multi-station Internet-based prototype	Develop separate coordinator & message broker	Both technical requirements and customer satisfaction	Aim for scalable network prototype
Lap 4 – Serverless-TQN	Trust is vested in a central server (coordinator & message broker)	Serverless network: server routines distributed across nodes	No existing platforms available	Serverless TQN project concludes.	Aim for blockchain TQN architecture.

Fig. 7 Summary of the lap iterations

reveals creeping complexity: a simple protocol, adoption of platforms like Shibboleth, purpose-built programming, until platforms options were exhausted. The evaluation stack also reveals a progression of complexity: a protocol check, requirements satisfaction check, customer satisfaction check. Finally, the circumscription stack is a series of increasingly ambitious prototype characteristics: computability, networkability, scalability.

4.1   Presentation of Artifact(S)

In addition to the stack of experiences, there is a stack of artifacts generated during the design journey.

The first artifact in this stack was the simple paper-based prototype and its protocol. The protocol was effectively the only outcome artifact. The use of the protocol was entirely manual, and required a sufficiently sized group (e.g., about a dozen people) to demonstrate both effectiveness and privacy.

In the second lap, a computer-based simulation prototype was created. The essential architecture of a TQN was defined. In this prototype, there were six artifacts added to the stack in this development. Two were data-structure oriented artifacts, and four were computational processes. These artifacts are described in more detail in Sect. 3.2.1.

The two artifacts that were embodied as data structures were the *TQN Protocol* and the *TQN Message.* The TQN Protocol was a specification artifact that defined the basic behavior of the information exchanges in the TQN system. The TQN Message was a standardized specification (XML style) of the contents of any element of communications traffic that was exchanged across the TQN network.

The four computational process artifacts were the *TQN Response Agent,* which responded to queries according to stored policy, *the TQN Coordinator,* which registered network members and managed message traffic, *the Base Security System,* which provided platform-based authentication and privacy, and *the Query and Report Agent,* which embodied the user interface. These artifacts are described in more detail in Sect. 3.2.1.

In the third lap, two additional computational artifacts were added to the stack. *The Message Broker* managed the identity of TQN nodes and routing of authenticated messages to the proper, authenticated nodes. An upgraded *TQN Coordinator* was added to the stack (replacing the previous version) that enabled interoperability with the Message Broker. These artifacts are described in more detail in Sect. 3.3.

4.2 Application of Artifact(S)

The stack of TQN artifacts were each applied in test-and-evaluate sessions against requirements of increasing complexity. The paper-based protocol was exercised interactively with a body that included representatives of the development, the project sponsor, and members of a security ISAC. This exercise is described in Sect. 3.1 and resulted in funding to develop the simulation artifact. The simulation TQN artifact was developed and demonstrated in a technical exercise. It was a measure of technical performance against requirements. This demonstration resulted in continuation of the project to develop a full network-based prototype and was reported in a conference paper (Vaishnavi et al., 2006). Further details are found in Sect. 3.2.1 (also see Figs. 3, 4, and Table 1). The network-based TQN prototype was also demonstrated, but in this case the demonstration not only measured technical performance against technical requirements, but also involved inviting customer representatives (including the ISAC) to participate in the demonstration (Bertolotti, 2009a, b). This enabled interactive customer evaluation of the prototype utility. Further details are in Sect. 3.3 (also see Figs. 5 and 6).

4.3 Evaluation of Artifact(S)

For TQN, the laps explain the progressive evaluation, moving from more formative to more summative evaluations. The evaluations remain generally in the mode of "artificial" type evaluations, such as simulations, where the outcome measures were mainly those of technical performance. In the FEDS design science evaluation frame-work, this evaluation strategy is described as "purely technical" and is appropriate for the development of a software protocol and software artifact like TQN (Venable, Pries-Heje, & Baskerville, 2016). There was a small element of more naturalistic evaluation in the third lap, when the product was demonstrated to a panel of experts; however, the essential evaluations were mainly technical.

Since its origin, TQN has been recognized as one of several different examples of an Anonymizing System (ANS); others include anonymizer.com and the Onion Router (TOR) (Vance et al., 2016). Vance, Lowry and Wilson (2016) investigated the effect of TQN on user's trusting beliefs using a free-simulation experiment. Using TQN as a vehicle, they were unable to conclude that the use of a technology like TQN was sufficient on its own to establish the trust necessary to system use. Rather, it is necessary to establish the trust first; then TQN has more likelihood to attract usage. This critical finding further underscores the results from Lap 4 that there is a need to purge the network of central nodes such as the message broker. The Vance, Lowry and Wilson study did conclude that "ANS are a compelling technology that can help address the need for more open sharing of cyber intrusion information among organizations and nations" (p. 993).

Finally, the TQN protocol and conceptual design were successful in the patent process (Baskerville et al., 2014; Baskerville, Vandenburg, Bertolotti, & Duraisamy, 2014).

4.4 Growth of Design Theory

Rationale for Design Correctness and Effectiveness. The heart of the design is the concept developed in Lap 1 of the design journey. This concept is based on the rather simple intuitive idea that aggregation and similar other statistical computations across a network can be used to maintain anonymity of individual data points. The use of this concept has to overcome hurdles of trust and statistical compromises but existing theory can be used to handle these hurdles.

General Contributions to Knowledge. The design journey demonstrates an inter-esting case of peer-to-peer computing across a network. Here the peer-to-peer computing across a network is used to implement the goal of (Disclose no private data) ˆ (Disclose only aggregate data) to address the Law of Private Disclosure (Vaish-navi et al., 2006). This use of network computing is pointing to other similar uses of peer-to-peer network computing. Such applications seem to form a different class of novel uses of network computing than the common use of networks for computing.

Nascent Design Theory. The design science research project is contributing a nascent design theory. The theory is following the profile of a design theory (Gregor & Jones, 2007; Vaishnavi & Kuechler, 2015) as follows:

Core Components

(1) *Purpose and Scope.* To collectively determine cybersecurity performance benchmark data without actually disclosing individual data.
(2) *Constructs.* TQN (Vaishnavi et al., 2006), Trust (Giddens, 1990; Nandhakumar & Baskerville, 2006), statistical compromises and their prevention (Fule & Roddick, 2004; Hoffman, 1977; Palley & Simonoff, 1987).
(3) *Knowledge of Form and Function.* TQN architecture, TQN protocol (See Sect. 3).
(4) *Abstraction and Generalization.* The theory is at a general level such that the artifacts resulting from the theory can be changed without affecting the theory.
(5) *Evaluation and Validation Propositions.* The relevant evaluation and validation propositions, and the degree to which they have been carried out are discussed in the Evaluation sub-sections of Sects. 3 and 4.3.
(6) *Justificatory Knowledge.* The basic idea of TQN (discussed in the first lap of the design journey (Sect. 3) are based on experience-based insights and intuitions. The theory for overcoming hurdles in developing the idea is from available theories regarding trust and statistical compromises.

Optional Components

(7) *Principles of Implementation.* They are discussed in Sect. 3 (e.g., TQN architecture, TQN protocol).
(8) *Expository Instantiation.* This is described in the third lap of the design journey (Sect. 3.3, Network-based Prototype).

5 Key Learnings

The most central of the key learnings from the TQN project is that distributed processing is a promising ground for inducing trust and privacy into computing networks. This learning provides a kernel theory, to guide future design science studies that deal with privacy and security of information and information systems. By distributing processing of data, rather than distributing data, it is possible to generate information based on private data without sharing, releasing or endangering that data. The principle also helps to understand the importance of blockchain technologies. While blockchains themselves are not intrinsically privacy preserving, they do involve a distributed process. It is possible for every node in a blockchain to be calculated by a different processor. The security arises from the public nature of the results of these calculations.

In addition, the TQN project was an early experience in applying a design science approach to a generalized, real world problem. Much of the body of learning that proceeds from the project was confirmatory. The design science research process model provides an accurate organization for the scholarly development of artifacts as a way of both generating improvements while making discoveries.

Key learnings from this project also included softer learnings, such as the value of group effort, the role of creativity, and the importance of being visionary.

Group Effort. The project was a result of a new research group in the area of cybersecurity. The group members represented expertise in a number of different but complementary areas. The group provided an avenue for broad discussions, cross fertilization of ideas, and brainstorming sessions. It exemplified the fact that in research a group working in a problem area can achieve lot more than what the members of the group can achieve individually in the absence of the group.

Role of Creativity. Creativity is central to all aspects of design science research but particularly in the Suggestion phase of the research (see Fig. 1). The research effort of this project had its basis in a simple 'out of the box' creative idea discussed in Sect. 3.1 (the first lap of the design journey). The rest of the research effort was devoted to realizing this idea and in overcoming the hurdles faced in doing so.

Being Visionary. Being bold and visionary in design science research is key to taking up seemingly impossible research problems and in solving them. It is also key to carrying out research that is impactful. The research group, possibly as a result of diverse expertise of the group members, stayed away from beaten paths and focused on the real issues faced by the private and public enterprises and how they can possibly be addressed. The patents (Baskerville et al., 2014; Baskerville, Vandenburg, et al., 2014) resulting from the research effort show the potential of this 'being visionary' approach.

Acknowledgments This work is partially funded by Georgia State University. An earlier version of this paper appeared in the WITS Workshop on Information Technologies and Systems (Vaishnavi et al., 2006), Milwaukee Wis. Art Vandenburg was a key architect and supervised much of the construction of the TQN prototypes. Other GSU faculty and students who worked with the TQN project included: Michelle Bellard, David Bloomquist, Martin Grace, Mala Kaul, Robert Sainsbury, Detmar Straub, Carl Stucke, Tony Vance, Jack Guangzhi Zheng, Daniele Bertolotti, and Saravanaraj Duraisamy.

The authors are thankful to the anonymous reviewer for providing useful comments that have helped in improving the clarity of the chapter.

References

Adam, N. R., & Worthmann, J. C. (1989). Security-control methods for statistical databases: A comparative study. *ACM Computing Surveys (CSUR), 21*(4), 515–556.

Ahituv, N. L., Y., & Neumann, S. (1988). Protecting statistical databases against retrieval of private information. *Computers and Security, 7*, 59–63.

Bakken, D. E., Rarameswaran, R., Blough, D. M., Franz, A. A., & Palmer, T. J. (2004). Data obfuscation: Anonymity and desensitization of usable data sets. *IEEE Security and Privacy, 2*(6), 34–41. https://doi.org/10.1109/MSP.2004.97.

Baskerville, R., Bellard, M., Bloomquist, D., Grace, M., Sainsbury, R., Straub, D. … & Duraisamy, S. (2014). United States Patent No. 8,775,402. U. S. P. Office.

Baskerville, R., & Vaishnavi, V. (2016). *Pre-Theory Design Frameworks and Design Theorizing* Paper presented at the HICSS 49 Hawaii International Conference on Systems Science, Kauai, HI.

Baskerville, R., Vandenburg, A., Bertolotti, D., & Duraisamy, S. (2014). United States Patent No. 8,910,237 B2 U. S. P. Office.

Bertolotti, D. (2009a). *Trusted Query Network: A Collaborative Approach to Sensitive Data Sharing to Support Risk Analysis Activities.* (MSc Master's Thesis), University of Brescia, Brescia, Italy.

Bertolotti, D. (2009b). *Trusted Query Network: A Collaborative Approach to Support Risk Analysis.* Computer Information Systems. Working Paper. Georgia State University. Atlanta, Ga.

Czepluch, J. S., Lollike, N. Z., & Malone, S. O. (2015). *The use of block chain technology in different application domains.* (BSc Bachelor's Project in Software Development), The IT University of Copenhagen, Copenhagen.

Fule, P., & Roddick, J. F. (2004). *Detecting privacy and ethical sensitivity in data mining results.* Paper presented at the Proceedings of the 27th Australasian conference on Computer science—Volume 26, Dunedin, New Zealand.

Giddens, A. (1990). *The consequence of modernity.* Oxford: Polity.

Gregor, S., & Jones, D. (2007). The Anatomy of a Design Theory. *Journal of the Association for Information Systems, 8*(5), 312–335.

Hoffman, L. (1977). *Modern methods for computer security and privacy.* Englewood Cliffs: Prentice-Hall.

McCarthy, J. (1980). Circumscription—a form of non-monotonic reasoning. *Artificial Intelligence, 13*(1), 27–39.

Nandhakumar, J., & Baskerville, R. (2006). Durability of online teamworking: Patterns of trust. *Information Technology & People, 19*(4), 371–389.

Palley, M. A., & Simonoff, J. S. (1987). The use of regression methodology for the compromise of confidential information in statistical databases. *ACM Transactions on Database Systems, 12*(4), 593–608. https://doi.org/10.1145/32204.42174.

Peltsverger, S., & Zheng, G. (2012). Defining a framework for teaching privacy in information assurance curriculum. In *Proceedings of the 16th Colloquium for Information Systems Security Education.* Lake Buena Vista, Florida.

Rezmierski, V., Rothschild, D., Kazanis, A., & Rivas, R. (2005). *Final report of the computer incident factor analysis and categorization* (CIFAC) project (Volume 2). Retrieved from.

Sainsbury, R., & Vance, A. (2007). The effects of identifiability, Trust, and Deception on Information Sharing Behaviors in an Anonymous System. In *AIS SIGHCI 2007 Proceedings Paper 4.*

Security of census population, CMND. 5365. (1973). London, H.M.S.O.

Traub, J. F., Yemini, Y., & Woźniakowski, H. (1984). The statistical security of a statistical database. *ACM Transactions on Database Systems (TODS), 9*(4), 672–679.

Vaishnavi, V. K., & Kuechler, W. (2015). *Design science research methods and patterns: Innovating information and communication technology* (2nd ed.). New York: CRC Press.

Vaishnavi, V. K., Vandenberg, A., Baskerville, R., & Zheng, G. (2006). *TQN: A novel approach to generating information security data.* Paper presented at the 16th Workshop on Information Technologies and Systems (WITS), Milwaukee Wis.

Vance, A. (2009). *Trusting IT Artifacts: How Trust Affects our Use of Technology.* (Ph.D. Doctoral Dissertation), Georgia State University, Atlanta, Ga.

Vance, A., Lowry, P. B., & Wilson, D. W. (2016). Using trust and anonymity to expand the use of anonymizing systems that improve security across organizations. *Security Journal, 30*(3), 979–999.

Venable, J., Pries-Heje, J., & Baskerville, R. (2016). FEDS: A framework for evaluation in design science research. *European Journal Information Systems, 25*(1), 77–89.

Easier Crowdsourcing Is Better: Designing Crowdsourcing Systems to Increase Information Quality and User Participation

Roman Lukyanenko and Jeffrey Parsons

Abstract Crowdsourcing promises to expand organizational knowledge and "sensor" networks dramatically, making it possible to engage ordinary people in large-scale data collection, often at much lower cost than that of traditional approaches to gathering data. A major challenge in crowdsourcing is ensuring that the data that crowds provide is of sufficient quality to be usable in organizational decision-making and analysis. We refer to this challenge as the Problem of Crowd Information Quality (Crowd IQ). We need to increase quality while giving contributors the flexibility to contribute data based on their individual perceptions. The design science research project produced several artifacts, including a citizen science information system (NLNature), design principles (guidelines) for the development of crowd-sourcing projects, and an instance-based crowdsourcing design theory. We also made several methodological contributions related to the process of design science research and behavioral research in information systems. Over the course of the project, we addressed several challenges in designing crowdsourcing systems, formulating design principles, and conducting rigorous design science research. Specifically, we showed that: design choices can have a sizable impact in the real world; it can be unclear how to implement design principles; and design features that are unrelated to design principles can confound efforts to evaluate artifacts. During the project, we also experienced challenges for which no adequate solution was found, reaffirming that design is an iterative process.

R. Lukyanenko
HEC Montreal, Montreal, Canada
e-mail: roman.lukyanenko@hec.ca

J. Parsons (✉)
Memorial University of Newfoundland, St. John's, Canada
e-mail: jeffreyp@mun.ca

© Springer Nature Switzerland AG 2020
J. vom Brocke et al. (eds.), *Design Science Research. Cases*, Progress in IS,
https://doi.org/10.1007/978-3-030-46781-4_3

1 Introduction: The Crowd IQ Problem

The widespread use of content-creation websites, mobile devices, and smart-phone apps creates the opportunity for organizations to harness people's interests, talent, and availability for organizational decision making and data collection needs. Such developments have fueled the rapid growth of *crowdsourcing*, where work, including data collection and analysis, is performed by members of the general public (typically referred to as "the crowd"), rather than employees or traditional subsidiaries (Howe, 2006).

Crowdsourcing has the potential to expand an organization's knowledge and enhance its "sensor" network, making it possible to engage ordinary people in large-scale data collection, often at much lower cost than traditional data collection approaches (Brabham, 2013; Doan, Ramakrishnan, & Halevy, 2011; Franklin, Kossmann, Kraska, Ramesh, & Xin, 2011; Garcia-Molina, Joglekar, Marcus, Parameswaran, & Verroios, 2016; Li, Wang, Zheng, & Franklin, 2016). In addition, as ordinary people perceive the world through the lenses created by their own perspectives and experiences, which often differ from those of organizational actors, crowdsourcing has unprecedented potential for discovery and innovation (Schuurman, Baccarne, De Marez, & Mechant, 2012).

Data collection opportunities that rely on crowds are diverse and include: customer feedback and product reviews; reports on urban incidents, disasters, crime, and civic issues; observations of nature; hospital and doctor ratings; personal health and wellness stories; and annotations of images. Increasing numbers of organizations seek to obtain such data to support process and product improvement, public policy and e-government initiatives, scientific research, conservation and management of natural resources, disaster response and recovery, and civic planning and municipal services. Crowdsourcing is even considered for use in addressing major societal and technological challenges, such as climate change (Burgess et al., 2017), large-scale natural disasters (Pultar, Raubal, Cova, & Goodchild, 2009), and common-sense reasoning in artificial intelligence (Davis & Marcus, 2015; Quinn & Bederson, 2011).

Despite the promise (and sometimes hype) of crowdsourcing, one challenge stands in the way of unlocking the crowd's full potential: the *problem of Crowd IQ*, that is, ensuring that the data provided by the crowds is of sufficient quality to be usable in organizational decision-making and analysis (Lukyanenko & Parsons, 2015). It is a complex problem with many, often overlapping, dimensions. Online crowds are more disconnected from the organization than traditional employees are, making it harder to train them to provide feedback to content contributors, especially for large projects (Faraj, Jarvenpaa, & Majchrzak, 2011; Hosseini, Phalp, Taylor, & Ali, 2014; Ipeirotis & Gabrilovich, 2014). In addition, casual online users often lack the specialized knowledge (e.g., bird taxonomy, medical expertise, product knowledge) commonly required for organizational use (Lewandowski & Specht, 2015; Lukyanenko, Parsons, & Wiersma, 2014) and may lack the incentive to participate, especially if the process of making contributions is difficult (Ipeirotis, Provost, & Wang, 2010; Kleek, Styke, Schraefel, & Karger, 2011; Nov, Arazy, & Anderson,

2011, 2014). Furthermore, as online technologies are becoming accessible to broad audiences (including elderly, people with disabilities, and those with literacy challenges), contributors may have reduced abilities to use technologies (Tams, Grover, & Thatcher, 2014) and face additional challenges to report their observations if the system is difficult to use (Stevens, Vitos, Lewis, & Haklay, 2013; Vitos, Lewis, Stevens, & Haklay, 2013). Finally, the conditions under which online contributors make observations vary drastically, making it challenging to assess the quality of a given contribution. These and many other aspects of Crowd IQ make it a wicked problem (Lukyanenko, Wiggins, & Rosser, 2019).

We have been developing an innovative solution to the problem of Crowd IQ. Much research in this space has followed traditional approaches to data collection used in organizational settings, resulting in strategies like imposing data-entry controls over the crowd's information production, training crowd members to perform specific data-collection tasks, requiring contributors to pass qualifying tests to participate, and seeking experts in crowds (Kilian, 2008; Kosmala, Wiggins, Swanson, & Simmons, 2016; Ogunseye, Parsons, & Lukyanenko, 2017). While acknowledging the merits of these approaches, we also saw in them a critical limitation—imposing such restrictions can stifle the level of engagement and participation and can come at the cost of inhibiting discoveries and innovation because data-collection restrictions invariably condition crowds on the kinds of data expected and may prevent other relevant information from being reported. Therefore, we embarked on a journey searching for a solution to free the crowd from traditional data collection constraints while ensuring that data produced by crowdsourcing is of high quality.

2 The Context: Online Citizen Science

Citizen science refers loosely to a wide and expanding range of activities, encompassing terms like amateur science, volunteered geographic information, civic science, participatory monitoring, networked science, crowdsourced science, and volunteer monitoring. The practice has a long history, predating conventional science. Until the nineteenth century, most scientific breakthroughs were made by amateurs or self-funded scientists like Descartes, Newton, Leibniz, and Darwin (Ogilvie, 2008). Some even regarded the gradual transition to modern credentialed and institutional science as detrimental to the spirit of openness, daring, and discovery that preceded it (Feyerabend, 1980). The interest in returning to the roots of science by increasing the role of amateurs grew with the explosive development of the Internet and digital technologies in 1990s, when the term "citizen science" was coined by Rick Bonney and Alan Irwin (Bonney, 1996; Irwin, 1995). While the early Internet was mainly static (Web 1.0), scientists were among the first to realize its potential not only as mass media, but also as a tool for two-way information exchange. Online citizen science became one of the early applications of content-producing technologies (Web 2.0) (Bauer, Petkova, & Boyadjieva, 2000; Bonney et al., 2009; Brossard, Lewenstein, &

Bonney, 2005; Goodchild, 2007; Louv, Dickinson, & Bonney, 2012; Lukyanenko, Parsons, & Wiersma, 2011; Osborn et al., 2005; Wiersma, 2010).

Since its inception in the late 1990s, the practice of *online citizen science*–engaging citizens in scientific endeavours via the Internet—has been booming, as evidenced by the ever-increasing number of projects and research papers written about citizen science and with the help of citizen scientists (Burgess et al., 2017; Kullenberg & Kasperowski, 2016; McKinley et al., 2016). Most such projects have been in the field of biology (Kullenberg & Kasperowski, 2016), where ordinary people are typically asked to collect data or assist researchers in analyzing and processing data. An example of this kind of project is eBird.org, launched in 2002 by the Cornell Lab of Ornithology (Sullivan et al., 2009). Since 2002, its database of amateur reports of birds has grown to more than 30 million sightings of more than 10,000 distinct species and has become one of the largest ornithology databases.[1] Based on data generated by projects such as eBird, as of 2019 the closely related fields of Biology, Ecology and Natural Resource Conservation published over 1,000 scientific papers (Lukyanenko, Wiggins, & Rosser, 2019).

For several reasons, citizen science is an ideal setting for a *critical test* (Popper, 2014) of any design purposed to improve Crowd IQ. First, citizen science in biology is a societally important domain, where improvements in information quality contribute to the conservation and preservation of dwindling natural resources (Loos et al., 2011; Seidel, Recker, & Vom Brocke, 2013; Theobald et al., 2015). Second, information quality is a critical concern to scientists who seek to use data in scientific analysis. Third, citizen science is a voluntary type of crowdsourcing in which an inescapable challenge is how to collect high-quality data from ordinary, non-scientist citizens, while keeping participation open and inclusive. Fourth, in the context of citizen science biology, there are established standards for information quality (e.g., biological nomenclature), a well-defined cohort of data consumers (scientists), and relatively well-established information needs (e.g., collection of data at the species level of analysis) (Burgess et al., 2017; Levy & Germonprez, 2017) that make it possible to measure the impact of design interventions more objectively. Finally, the general qualities of citizen science (e.g., open and voluntary participation, heterogeneous data contributors, and a need to facilitate discovery) make the findings from one domain readily transferable to other areas, including other crowdsourcing applications and data collection in corporate settings when flexibility and support for unanticipated uses of data are desirable (for discussion, see Lukyanenko, Wiggins, & Rosser, 2019).

Almost every branch of science now engages with volunteers using online technologies. Successful projects have been conducted in astronomy, oceanography, history, computer science, ethnography and anthropology, political science, geography, and other disciplines (Burgess et al., 2017; Louv et al., 2012). Consider GalaxyZoo (zooniverse.org), which allows online users to classify galaxies based on photos from the Sloan Digital Sky Survey and the Hubble Space Telescope (Fortson et al., 2011; Ponti, Hillman, Kullenberg, & Kasperowski, 2018): The project resulted in several notable scientific discoveries, such as Hanny's Voorwerp–a mysterious

---

[1] https://ebird.org/region/world.

cosmic body described as one of the most exciting recent discoveries in astronomy– and a new type of galaxy (Lintott et al., 2009). GalaxyZoo's host platform, Zooniverse (zooniverse.org), contains more than a dozen other projects (e.g., Planet Hunters) and boasted more than 1.6 million registered users as of August 2018.

As these and other projects demonstrate, citizen science has become a booming hobby for online participants worldwide and a major trend in science. Although its direct impact is difficult to measure, some have estimated that a medium-sized project stands to gain more than $400,000 in in-kind value based on paying research assistants a conservative rate of $12 per hour (Sauermann & Franzoni, 2015). As of 2015, biology projects alone engaged more than two million people, who contributed up to $2.5 billion of in-kind value annually (Theobald et al., 2015).

Beyond their monetary value, citizen science's contributions to society are difficult to overestimate. Citizen science plays a major role in raising public awareness of environmental issues, engaging people in matters of science, and providing them with a forum on which to voice their suggestions and concerns. As ordinary people will experience the direct impact of environmental changes, they are also well-positioned to find creative solutions (Lukyanenko, Parsons, & Wiersma, 2016). Much hope is vested in the potential of citizens to solve humanity's "evil quintet" of climate change, overexploitation, invasive species, changes in land use, and pollution (Theobald et al., 2015). As Light and Miskelly (2014, p. 14) put it, the "urgency of environmental issues draws our attention to the management of finite resources, and the potential of digital tools to help us work with them effectively."

Citizen science has emerged as a major trend in science but is also becoming increasingly ingrained in the broader society as millions of people begin to enjoy being part of science via online tools. Even so, while the promise of modern citizen science is based on leveraging innovative information technologies, much remains to be done to make these technologies more effective in unlocking the full potential of citizens in contributing to science. Among the many technological challenges, those that relate to the quality of data and user engagement are perhaps the most pressing. Scientists require high-quality data to conduct reliable analyses and make sound decisions. To be publishable, research must be rigorous, which requires basing conclusions on solid evidence, a challenge when the data sets are created by amateurs via online technologies that permit little control or oversight.

However, to be successful, citizen science projects must attract interested online users and facilitate their participation and engagement. Given the volitional nature of technology use in online citizen science and the growing number of projects to choose from, if the process of engagement is too arduous, online users can simply abandon one project and switch to another.

Thus, participation and quality may be the two greatest prerequisites for the success of online citizen science. Our research focuses on both information quality and participation in the context of online citizen science in biology.

3   The Journey from Classes to Instances

The case study is based on our direct involvement in developing a citizen science project, NLNature (www.nlnature.com), the mission of which is to record sightings of plants and animals in the province of Newfoundland and Labrador, Canada. The project was conceived in 2009 as a way to capture data over a large and sparsely populated geographic region area of approximately 400,000 km^2 by engaging citizens who are active in their natural environments.

3.1   Lap 1—Class-Based Citizen Science

The original design of NLNature followed a traditional approach to the development of natural-history-based citizen science projects. Specifically, many design decisions focused on the goal of reporting species, so the interface was designed to provide contributors with lists of species from which to choose, an approach consistent with a variety of other projects in similar domains (e.g., eBird).

After the project operated for four years, the project team (a landscape ecologist and information systems researchers) was disappointed with the volume and diversity of the contributions that had been made. For example, most contributions were coming from a small group of "amateur naturalists," citizens with above-average biology knowledge. Coverage was also skewed to a few geographic regions where knowledgeable contributors were concentrated. As a consequence, the team reflected on how design decisions in the original implementation might have inhibited contributions from a broader range of interested citizens and undertook a major redesign of the system. In this redesign effort, the team performed A/B testing with two versions of the site to determine how changes to the philosophy that guided the data collection affected various dimensions of the quality of data collected.

Prior to the interface's redesign, the team considered factors that contributed to the number of contributors being lower than expected. A key factor emerging from this analysis was a possible mismatch between the requirements of the task (reporting observations at the species level) and the capabilities of non-expert contributors, which generally do not include species-level identification. This requirement appeared to force some participants to select a potentially incorrect species just to record a contribution (Fig. 1). Coupled with a theoretical perspective on the impact of classification structures on data collection and information quality (Lukyanenko & Parsons, 2011a, b; Parsons, Lukyanenko, & Wiersma, 2011), these observations by the team precipitated the second design phase of the project.

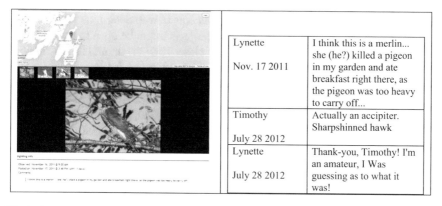

Lynette Nov. 17 2011	I think this is a merlin... she (he?) killed a pigeon in my garden and ate breakfast right there, as the pigeon was too heavy to carry off...
Timothy July 28 2012	Actually an accipiter. Sharpshinned hawk
Lynette July 28 2012	Thank-you, Timothy! I'm an amateur, I Was guessing as to what it was!

Fig. 1 A vignette of an observation classified as a Merlin (*Falco columbarius*), where the contributor admits to guessing

3.2   Lap 2—Instance-Based Citizen Science

The second phase was guided by a theoretical foundation for understanding the Crowd IQ problem. Specifically, we used classification theory from psychology and Bunge's ontology as kernel theories (Hanseth & Lyytinen, 2004; Hevner, March, Park, & Ram, 2004) to guide the new design.

Classification theory (Murphy, 2004; Smith & Medin, 1981) examines the core principles that guide humans in making sense of phenomena in the world by arranging them into categories or classes (Parsons & Wand, 2008a, b). Among the core ideas relevant to information systems design are that a class constitutes a useful abstraction of features shared by its members, and different ways of classifying are possible and valuable because they reflect different manifestations of usefulness (Parsons, 1996). Classification theory also suggests that people are adept at describing entities via their attributes and classifying them into *basic-level categories*—high-level general categories that are first learned in childhood (e.g., *bird*, *tree*, *fish*, *car*, *chair*) for which instances share many attributes (Rosch, Mervis, Gray, Johnson, & Boyesbraem, 1976). Identifying organisms as instances of such categories does not require the specialized domain knowledge generally required to classify at the species level.[2] Based on this observation, we posited that designing citizen science applications to match contributors' capabilities and perceptions of usefulness would lead to higher numbers of contributions and contributions of higher quality.

---

[2] While basic-level categories are among the most researched notions in cognitive psychology (Lassaline, Wisniewski, & Medin, 1992), our realization that this notion lacks operational precision precipitated development of a separate DSR project to formalize the notion of basic-level categories, provide clear and unambiguous principles for discovering and identifying these classes in a domain, and provide practitioners with principles for using these classes in the design, development and use of information systems (Castellanos, Castillo, Lukyanenko, & Tremblay, 2017; Castellanos, Lukyanenko, Samuel, & Tremblay, 2016; Lukyanenko & Samuel, 2017).

However, a problem in crowdsourcing concerns how to determine which classes match contributors' capabilities, given that projects might be open to everyone and there could be considerable variability in the classes that are natural to contributors.

We turned to the philosophical ontology of Mario Bunge for further guidance in addressing this problem. Bunge (1977) postulates that the world consists of "things" (which can also be referred to as instances, objects, or entities) that have "properties." We apply the notion of "instances" to things in the physical, social and mental worlds (Perszyk, 2013). Examples of instances include specific objects that can be sensed in the physical world (e.g., *this chair, a bird sitting in a tree, Mario Bunge*), mental objects humans conceive of (e.g., *a promise, Anna Karenina*), and social objects (e.g., *the European Union, a bank account*) (Bergholtz & Eriksson, 2015; Eriksson & Agerfalk, 2010; March & Allen, 2012, 2014; Searle, 1995). Thus we define an instance as any physical, mental, or social "thing" to which someone ascribes an individual, unique identity (Lukyanenko, Parsons, & Samuel, 2018b).

Following Bunge, we suggested that at least some crowdsourcing systems should move away from the traditional approach of collecting observations using pre-defined classes and instead collect reports of unique instances. Instances can be captures as lists of attributes, lists of classes, textual descriptions, or multimedia content that depicts individuals. After the data are captured, the data's consumers (scientists) may be able to infer classes.

To explore the utility of these ideas, we conducted a series of laboratory experiments (Lukyanenko & Parsons, 2013a; Lukyanenko & Parsons et al., 2014) in which we studied the effect of various data-entry options on data accuracy and information loss. Collectively, these experiments showed that data collection focusing on attributes and basic-level categories produced more accurate and complete observations than data collection that focuses on specialized categories that require a high level of domain knowledge (i.e., species-level categories).

The results of our laboratory experiments, coupled with the kernel theories from psychology and ontology, guided the redesign of NLNature. Our working hypothesis was that incorporating the principles of attribute-based data collection would remove a significant barrier to contribution by non-experts. Accordingly, we revamped the site to allow contributors to report observations by specifying attributes and any categories they deemed relevant, without the need to report species-level categories. Figure 2 depicts the differences in the two data-entry interfaces.

Subsequent to the redesign, we ran an A/B experiment for new members who registered accounts with NLNature over a six-month period. The results (discussed in greater detail below) supported our original conjecture that relaxing the requirement to contribute data based on the needs of the data consumers (scientists) resulted in improvements in information quality and levels of user participation.

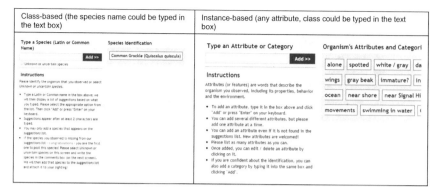

Fig. 2 Data entry interfaces in class-based and instance-based implementations

3.3   Lap 3—Toward Hybrid Intelligence: Combining Crowds and Machines

Despite the benefits of the instance-based approach to crowdsourcing, once the new design was implemented, several new problems emerged. A natural concern related to collecting data in terms of unconstrained attributes and classes instead of predetermined ones is whether the attributes can be useful to scientists in classifying "things" at the desired level. Many observations on the redesigned instance-based NLNature did not include species identification but provided some generic (i.e., basic-level) category (e.g., *bird*) and a list of attributes and/or several sentences describing it (Fig. 3).

In addition, after relaxing the constraints on the structure of the data to be collected, observations had heterogeneous structure–varying sets of classes and attributes–even when they described the same organism (Table 1). Therefore, the new challenge concerned how to ensure that the sparse, heterogeneous, and highly variable data could be made more consistent so it was more usable for scientific analysis.

To address these new challenges, we turned to human experts and machine learning, conducting two additional studies to determine whether and to what extent it is possible to infer classes of interest (e.g., lists of species) automatically based on sparse and heterogeneous instance-based data provided by non-experts.

The results (discussed below) demonstrate the potential for using either human experts or machine learning to classify organisms based on an instance-based model of crowdsourcing. This practical solution can free non-experts from having to comply with the organization's views of reality while allowing them to deliver data that fits the organization's needs.

Fig. 3 Sample observation on NLNature lacking species identification. As this observation demonstrates, the lack of a precise classification (here, species identification) might be caused by the observer's low domain knowledge or by conditions of the observation that prevent even experts from making a positive identification

Table 1 Sample of two real observations about the same kind of organism (Atlantic puffin), each describing the observed individual differently

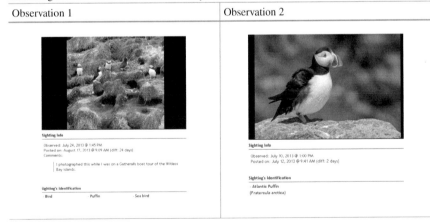

4 The Results

The projects produced several artifacts, including the NLNature system and design principles for the development of crowdsourcing projects. We also contributed a design theory and methodological advances related to the process of design science research and behavioral research in information systems.

4.1 Presentation and Application of the Artifact

A tangible outcome of our project is a real-world artifact, NLNature (www.nlnature. com). Following the iterations discussed above, the interface was designed to be simple (e.g., lean registration form, optional demographic questions, photos), but it emphasized the traditional biological focus of recording observations of biological species. The requirement to classify species was dropped, and participants could simply describe it using an open-ended form. We did not require contributors to list everything they saw; the choice of what to contribute and how often was left to them.

To ensure that the data that contributors provided was in the target domain of scientists, we employed digital nudging (Weinmann, Schneider, & vom Brocke, 2016) by seeding the project's "About Us" page with cues on what we hoped participants would report on (Fig. 4). These cues are "soft targets" (Lukyanenko et al., 2017) in

Fig. 4 The "About Us" page on NLNature Phase 2, describing the focus of the project

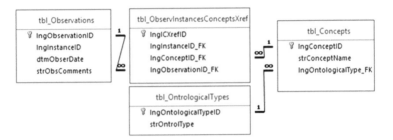

Fig. 5 Simplified database architecture of NLNature

that they do not constrain user input. Consequently, users occasionally reported on sightings outside the domain of biology.

To store user input, we selected a flexible database technology with corresponding functionality. There is a booming market of noSQL databases that provide suitable schema-less databases (Cattell, 2011). Candidate data models included key-value (DeCandia et al., 2007), document-focused (Chang et al., 2008), instance-based (Parsons & Wand, 2000), and graph (Angles & Gutierrez, 2008) data models. Of these, the closest match to our concept of flexible data collection using instances and attributes was the instance-based data model (Parsons & Wand, 2000), as it shares the ontological and cognitive foundations that underlie this research and includes the required modeling constructs.

An instance-based data model can be deployed on top of relational database management software. In Lap 2, we focused on representing individual, unique instances. To capture observations of instances, we created the "Observations" table, which contained the date and time of the instance observation, guided by the assumption that instances are observed at some moment in time.[3] NLNature stored attributes and classes in a generic "Concepts" table that contained a unique identifier, a concept name, and a flag that distinguished classes (e.g., bird) from attributes (e.g., red). In this implementation, we equated Instances with Observations under the assumption that, in a wide-scope natural science project, it may not be feasible to identify instances as unique (i.e., to know that observations x and y refer to the same instance). Nevertheless, we included an InstanceID field in the Observations table (tbl_Observations, see Fig. 5) to permit probabilistic (e.g., based on common descriptions, coordinates, time) links of observations of the same instance.

Over the years, we made changes to the data collection interface, in each case seeking to make it more usable and intuitive for the contributors. Figure 6 presents one of the data-collection pages, which asks participants to report what they have observed. The form does not restrict user input to predefined choices but, following popular practice on social media websites (e.g., Facebook, Twitter, PatientsLikeMe.com), search engines (e.g., Google), and citizen science projects

---

[3]This is a simplified implementation. In the real schema, additional attributes were included in each table, including additional semantic attributes and a variety of system attributes like time stamp, IP address, system properties of the record creator, security, validation, and monitoring keys.

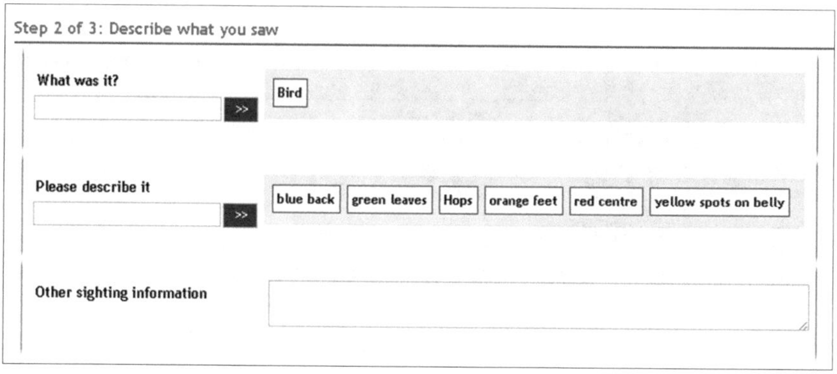

Fig. 6 Current form for collecting sightings

(e.g., www.iSpot.org.uk), we use a prompt-assisted (autocomplete) text field (Kallinikos & Tempini, 2014). Such fields dynamically show recommendations when a participant begins to typing a class or an attribute. This approach has advantages over a traditional constrained-choice mode. That a text field is always initially empty mitigates any adverse ordering and priming effects. When reporting attributes or classes, users are instructed to begin typing in the textbox and to click "add" or press "enter" when they are finished. As soon as the user has entered more than two characters, a suggestion box appears with the classes or attributes that contain the string of characters the user entered. Users then either select an item from the list or provide attributes and classes that do not appear on the list. New attributes and classes are added to the system for future use as they are reported.

Since data collection based on instances is not typical of citizen science projects, instructions for participants are provided on how to report observed instances. Next to the dynamic text field we define attributes (i.e., "attributes (or features) are words that describe the organism you observed, including its properties, behavior and the environment"), which are removed once the user adds attributes. Contributors can also specify classes if they wish, as we prompt data entry using simple questions: (1) "What was *it*?" (for classes; where *it* denotes any instance); (2) "Please describe *it*" (for attributes), and (3) "Other sighting information" (to capture anything else a contributor wishes to report about a sighting using unstructured text). We also ask users to provide photos, if available. Once a user finishes the process by clicking a button, the observation becomes public. The website also contains a dynamic map on the front page of the project that shows the most recent sightings.

Once an observation is recorded, a contributor can view other observations (Fig. 7), search for previous observations using classes or attributes, or communicate with other users via built-in forum.

NLNature remains a popular local citizen science project with more than 3,800 members, more than 9,000 observations of local flora and fauna, and more than 5.5 million views of observations since 2010 (Table 2). All observations posted on NLNature are publicly visible, and any interested organization can extract any subset

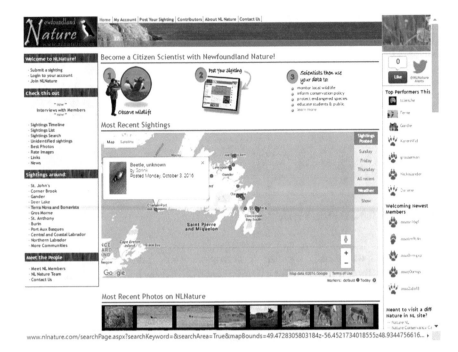

Fig. 7 Front page of NLNature (public view)

Table 2 Usage statistics on NLNature (as of April. 2019)

Members	Sightings	Photos uploaded	Sighting views by other users
3,853	9,390	14,024	5,515,037

for analysis. Typical data consumers of the project are local scientists (mostly biologists), but the data extracted from the project is also delivered to other environmental agencies and project partners. For example, data related to oceans is provided for the OceanViewer.org project. The project also participates in a Canada-wide network of projects that investigate how the public uses the interactive technologies that are available on the internet to work for environmental change. Several nodes of the project are located across Canada, each focused on a different environmental issue (e.g., invasive species, http://ibis.geog.ubc.ca/biodiversity/geoide).

We believe that, through several design iterations, we were able to resolve important aspects of the Crowd IQ problem. The revamped design removed traditional participation barriers that arose from the lack of contributors' species-identification ability, thereby improving the quantity aspect of crowd IQ, while also allowing participants to provide data at their level of comfort, thereby improving the data's accuracy. In addition, with the removal of the requirement that contributors comply with a pre-specified set of categories, the project provided greater support for unanticipated contributions and discoveries. At the same time, with the application of machine learning, the final data can be structured in a way that is more convenient for organizational decision-makers. Thus, the final artifact provides a substantial improvement over other extant approaches to Crowd IQ.

4.2 Evaluation of the Artifact

We conducted multiple evaluations of the artifact at various stages of its development (Baskerville, Kaul, & Storey, 2015; Sonnenberg & vom Brocke, 2012; Venable, Pries-Heje, & Baskerville, 2012) using field and laboratory experiments, along with qualitative interviews.

To compare the original version with the new version of NLNature, we performed A/B testing before converting the entire project to the instance-based approach. In the field experiment, new members who registered during the period of the experiment were randomly assigned to either the new version of the site or to the original version. As hypothesized, the instance-based version resulted in (4.5 times) more contributions than the class-based version did (Lukyanenko, Parsons, Wiersma, & Maddah, 2019). We also found that contributors who used the attribute-based version of the site provided seventeen times more contributions of organisms that the project owner had not anticipated (i.e., organisms that were not in the database of options in the original design), even though the traditional design also allowed unanticipated organisms to be reported.

The laboratory experiment we conducted showed that the accuracy of data was higher in the instance-based version, and that familiarity had a moderating effect on accuracy in the class-based version but not in the instance-based version.

The differences in accuracy and completeness we found in the class-based laboratory condition, depending on familiarity with the stimuli (absent in the instance-based condition), suggest that data quality suffers when non-experts are forced to classify at a level determined by scientific considerations (e.g., the species level). Non-experts can contribute class-based data accurately only when they are highly familiar with the classes in question, so crowdsourcing projects that require contributors to classify at a level required by the project will either have to restrict participation to amateur experts (e.g., skilled birdwatchers) or risk inaccurate or incomplete data even when the participants are confident in the quality of their contributions. This problem is resolved by the instance-based design.

Notwithstanding these gains in Crowd IQ, a limitation of the instance-based approach is low precision of data, as participants are no longer required to classify at the species level. To determine the potential utility of instance-based crowdsourcing for organizations that require data at particular levels of granularity, we used instance-based data in a controlled laboratory setting that simulated the real data created by NLNature.

The dataset was obtained from a laboratory experiment with 390 non-experts in natural history–undergraduate business and engineering students–who reported free-form attributes and classes, consistent with the instance-based model (Lukyanenko, Parsons, et al., 2014). We then interviewed experts in biology (e.g., biology professors, members of natural history societies) to determine whether the classes and attributes provided by the non-experts could be used by experts to identify organisms at the species level (the level typically sought in citizen science crowdsourcing). In one-hour interviews, we asked the experts to provide a "best guess" as to what the organism was after being given, one at a time, each of the most common attributes provided by the non-experts. The experts "thought out loud" while we recorded their comments after each attribute was provided.

In a similar experiment using machine learning, we converted the attributes data set used with the experts into a matrix of attributes, assigning 1 to the attributes provided in Lukyanenko, Parsons, et al. (2014) if a participant used that attribute to describe the species of interest, and 0 otherwise. We then trained machines using a variety of common data-mining algorithms (e.g., neural networks) to classify the organisms in the study at the species level.

The natural history experts were able to identify an average of 59.8% ($\pm 34.0\%$ s.d.) of the organisms at the species level based on the attributes provided by non-experts, which was a significantly larger percentage than the non-experts' percentage of correct species-level classifications (see Lukyanenko et al., 2014). The natural history experts' confidence in their final guesses was also highly correlated with the percentage of times the guess was correct (Spearman's rho $= 0.68$, $p < 0.01$). The result of the machine learning experiment is consistent with that of the experiment with human experts, as using common machine learning methods, we obtained an average of 74.4% species-classification accuracy based on the attributes provided by non-experts.

We also have reason to believe that the introduction of instance-based data collection increased the overall volume of contributions per user. Table 3 demonstrates a doubling of the average number of contributions per user after the switch to the new

Table 3 Average number of contributions per user per year

Year	Average	System used
2010	6.35	Class-based data collection
2011	4.56	
2012	4.88	
2013	N/A*	
2014	11.64	Instance-based data collection
2015	14.14	
2016	13.62	
2017	7.95	

*Note The year 2013 is excluded since the project implemented both the class-based and instance-based approaches in that year. The change to the instance-based system occurred at the beginning of 2014 (a drop in 2017 is possibly due to the rise of mobile Internet browsing, which our platform did not support)

way of collecting observations, which suggests that contributors are able to communicate more of what they observe in the wild when the requirements to comply with an existing observational schema are removed.

With the flexibility in reporting attributes and classes, data contributors gained the ability to report on unanticipated observations. Perhaps the most significant such sighting was contributed by one active member with an enthusiasm for microphotography of insects. When we initially designed NLNature, we presented it to local natural history groups, who suggested that the main focus should be on birds and wildflowers, so our original pre-specified categories focused on these "charismatic" taxa. Because the new version allowed for direct entry of new classes and attributes, one contributor used this opportunity to provide a host of insect sightings. Two professional entomologists follow this contributor's posts closely. In one case, the insect enthusiast reported a particular banding pattern on the legs of a mosquito that he had not seen before, and online research suggested it was a new species to the province. Consultations with entomologists, followed by sample collection in the field, confirmed it (Fielden et al., 2015).

Finally, we got direct feedback from the NLNature's data contributors via a series of interviews and focus groups, which provided additional evidence of the utility of the instance-based NLNature in supporting user engagement while delivering high-quality data. In particular, we saw how the demographics of the project were more diverse and no longer favored "amateur experts" and their comparatively narrow view of biology. Our interview subjects included people who worked in jobs that brought them outdoors (e.g., parks and recreation, fishing, beekeeping, forestry) and people who worked in indoor settings (e.g., politics, computer programming, retail work), most without professional background in biology or ecology. Many listed outdoor pursuits (e.g., hiking, fishing, mountain biking, birding) as hobbies and saw the NLNature website as fitting with their hobbies. However, not all saw themselves as avid outdoor people. As one noted, "I'm not a super-super-nature-fit hiking kind of person, [but] if I'm outside, it's often because I'm observing things or just enjoying nature, going for a walk with my dog—that kind of stuff." Two participants saw the website as a way to enhance intergenerational relationships. One woman, who contributed sightings with her father, said that participating in NLNature "definitely improved and enhanced our relationship, because it gives us something to do [together]." Another participant noted that they "want to provide a nurturing environment for [their four granddaughters] socially and physically" and that a website like NLNature helped "nurture [their] curiosity about the world."

A key barrier to potential contributors' use of the original NLNature design was the focus on species-level identification. Our lab experiments showed that casual, non-expert contributors were often unable to perform this task, with the exception of a few well-known species. This mismatch between the project owners' goals and requirements and most of the potential contributors' capabilities was a significant barrier to achieving a large number of high quality contributions.

The switch to an instance-based data-entry interface led to a surge in the number of contributions and the diversity in the organisms represented in sightings and a

Table 4 Key lessons learned during each project lap

Lap	Design approach	Key design objective	Evaluation setting	Lessons learned
1	• Traditional (practice-based) • Class-based	Satisfying the data-consumers' predefined need (species identification)	(a) Field (b) Interviews with users	• Only experts could provide high quality data • Non-experts resort to guessing or abandon data entry
2	• Innovation (kernel-theory-driven) • Instance-based	Focusing on data contributors' capabilities (via attributes, basic-level categories)	(a) Lab (controlled experiments) (b) Field (c) Interviews with users	• Novices can contribute more accurate and complete data using instances (vs. classes) • An instance-based approach leads to greater diversity of data and discoveries
3	• Innovation (exploratory) • Instance-based • Application of machine learning	Satisfying data-consumers' need (species identification), while keeping the project instance-based	(a) Expert classification (b) Machine learning	• Instance and attribute data can often be classified post hoc to the desired level of precision to support the needs of data-consumers

notable broadening of the projects' audience. Table 4 summarizes the key lessons learned during each project lap.

4.3 Growth of Design Theory

Throughout the design cycles, we were gradually developing a design theory to capture the essential design elements of the NLNature artifact and contribute to design knowledge (Gregor & Jones, 2007), while also providing a theoretical explanation for the impact of these design elements on our core variable of interest–information quality.

The re-design of NLNature was driven by the kernel theories of classification and general ontology (Sect. 3.2). From these theories, we formulated six design principles (guidelines) for practitioners to follow:

Guideline 1. Assume the representational uniqueness of observations.
Guideline 2: Represent crowd data based on unique instances unconstrained by any pre-defined classes or attributes.

Guideline 3: Use attributes to represent individual instances.
Guideline 4: Use classes to represent individual instances.
Guideline 5: Use additional mechanisms (e.g., unstructured text, videos, photos) to represent individual instances.

We referenced the two kernel theories to derive the consequences of adopting these guidelines. The theoretical guidance from both psychology and ontology suggested that we can expect a positive effect of adopting these guidelines on the accuracy and completeness of crowd data (the key elements of Crowd IQ). The same theoretical foundation suggested a negative impact of these guidelines on the level of granularity/precision since non-experts would usually avoid providing specific classes, such as species. Therefore, we introduced Guideline 6–reconcile instances with a target organizational model. As we demonstrated, this can be accomplished by conducting additional processing of the resulting instance-based data (e.g., using machine learning)—to create final structures (e.g., a list of species) that match the data-consumers' original information needs and those of the organizations that sponsor and develop crowdsourcing projects. Figure 8 summarizes the *Instance-based crowdsourcing design theory* graphically.

Guideline 6: Using traditional conceptual modeling methods, develop a target organizational model elicited from data-consumers to capture their information requirements; provide model cues and a target for automatic reconciliation of the instance-based data obtained from using previous guidelines.

These six principles or guidelines formed the antecedent component of our design theory; that is, implementing these guidelines results in the creation of an instance-based IS artifact like NLNature.

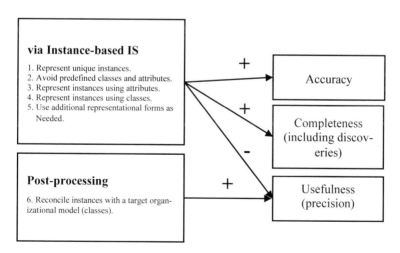

Fig. 8 Instance-based crowdsourcing design theory

Finally, by referencing the theoretical foundations of philosophy and psychology, we formulated the boundary conditions of the instance-based crowdsourcing design theory. Specifically, we argued that the six guidelines are most effective when projects seek to engage heterogeneous audiences, including amateurs and non-experts. These guidelines are also useful when the project's domain is large and is not fully understood by the expert community (e.g., plants and animals in a large geographic area, emerging consumer markets, healthcare). In such scenarios, organizations may be particularly interested in harnessing the crowd's creativity and ingenuity to discover something new or gain unanticipated insights from crowdsourced data. In addition, as our approach does not require the crowd to have domain expertise, it can be applied in situations where training is either expensive or ineffective, as is the case in many online scenarios). Table 5 summarizes the scenarios when our instance-based approach works best (and contrasts it with the traditional class-based approach).

Each element of this design theory (e.g., impact on accuracy and completeness) has been evaluated by quantitative (e.g., field and laboratory experiments) and qualitative (e.g., interviews with users) methods. The results are consistent and strongly support the causal mechanisms predicted by the design theory, suggesting that the application of the instance-based design guidelines can be a powerful tool for harnessing crowdsourcing as an organizational resource.

In addition to the domains of crowdsourcing and user-generated content in citizen science, our project made a number of theoretical contributions to other areas of research. The project formulated the "Problem of Crowd IQ" and helped to clarify the nature of information quality. One common assumption is that low information quality is caused by contributors' low domain expertise and low motivation, but the project suggested that low-quality information may result from the approaches to modeling and IS development that are currently used in practice.

This project established a connection between modeling approaches and information quality. Traditionally, conceptual modeling and information quality have been considered quite different domains, but new challenges suggest that modeling can play a critical role in information quality that is likely to be applicable in corporate settings and online environments.

5 Key Lessons

While developing NLNature, we arrived at a number of insights related to the design of crowdsourcing systems, theoretical issues and challenges in formulating design principles, and uncertainties in conducting rigorous design science research.

Design Decisions Matter in Crowdsourcing. A key lesson learned from developing the project is that design decisions play an important role in improving Crowd IQ. Much has been written on strategies and techniques to improve information quality and foster participation in crowdsourcing projects (Haklay, 2013; Kosmala et al., 2016; Lewandowski & Specht, 2015). Among the approaches suggested

Table 5 Data collection scenarios for Instance versus Class-based approaches (from Lukyanenko, Parsons, Wiersma, & Maddah, 2019)

Project dimension	Sub-dimension	Open with many unknowns	Closed with few unknowns
Project nature	Domain Scope	*Large, unbounded* (e.g., entire natural history of a region)	*Small, bounded* (e.g., tufted puffins in an area)
	Task	*Open-ended* (e.g., tell me anything about an object)	*Close-ended* (e.g., tag all pedestrians in a photo, transcribe text using finite symbols)
Data contributors	Skills and abilities	*Open participation: non-experts and experts in project domain* (e.g., ability to observe phenomena and describe it using own vocabulary)	*Closed Participation: experts in domain* (e.g., ability to identify instances of birds at species level of precision)
	Training	*Not required* (e.g., anyone can contribute data)	*Might sometimes be required* (e.g., users must pass tutorial to contribute data)
Data consumers	Uses	*Unknown, evolving, some known* (e.g., CitySourced.com collects civic reports; municipalities access data and use it in own ways)	*Known and well-understood* (e.g., detect occurrence of specific invasive species in a given area)
Suggested IQ Management and IS Design	IQ Management	*Contributor-centric*	*Consumer-centric (fitness-for-use)*
	Data collection	Proposed, Instance-***based***	Traditional, Class-***based***
	Post-processing	*Significant and advanced post-processing may be required* (e.g., machine learning may help infer species from contributed attributes of instances)	*Significant and advanced post-processing is generally not required* (e.g., classifications of galaxies may be aggregated by type)
Exemplar project		*iSpotNature* (www.ispotnature.org)—observations of wildlife worldwide	*eBird* (www.ebird.org)—classification of birds primarily into pre-specified species

(e.g., training, protocols, tutorials, instructions, attracting experts in crowds), design choices are understudied, poorly understood, and underused. This is somewhat surprising. While organizations have weak controls over citizen volunteers, they retain complete control over how crowdsourcing projects are developed. Our experience in redesigning NLNature revealed substantial improvement in the accuracy and completeness of data and the level of user engagement (e.g., in the number of observations, reports on unanticipated phenomena, rates of observations per user) as a consequence of the redesign. These findings can motivate future studies on how to design data-collection processes and user interfaces in crowdsourcing and other domains.

More Flexibility Can Lead to Better Quality. A common-sense assumption that permeates crowdsourcing research is that crowds must be guided and constrained if they are to produce high-quality data. Indeed, the very essence of the "wisdom of crowds" lies in strengthening what are otherwise highly unreliable signals by aggregating data (Surowiecki, 2005). Researchers often argue that online crowds produce "noisy data," so constraints are needed to reduce the noise and improve data quality (Ipeirotis & Paritosh, 2011). Our work shows the opposite. We also demonstrated the benefit of adopting a new, instance-based approach to data collection in citizen science. The flexibility of this approach allows non-experts to report interesting observations that would otherwise not be captured and to engage more effectively with the project without having to face the barrier of having to produce data in the format that scientists prefer. The measurable success of adopting this approach suggests a promising direction for citizen science research and practice: exploring additional design decisions that remove participation barriers by making the process more flexible and easier for contributors to use.

There is Considerable Ambiguity (Theoretical Indeterminacy) in Design Science Research. As part of the project, we formulated and implemented a set of design guidelines and a design theory that capture the essence of our new approach to crowdsourcing. In doing so, we encountered a peculiar challenge that has not received much research attention: since design theories are formulated in terms of linguistic or mathematical concepts, there is a gap between theoretical propositions and the concrete issues faced in practice, a challenge we refer to as *design theory indeterminacy*. Consequently, it is possible that the effects of instantiating an artifact may result in part from capricious design decisions rather than from features that are included based on theoretical considerations.

Part of the issue in our case is that Bunge's (1977) ontology and classification theory were developed outside the context of information systems, and our design theory itself was more general than the context of citizen science. As a result, neither the design theory nor the kernel theory that underlies it operated with concepts like web servers, programming languages, Internet connection speeds, or types of client devices, nor did they cover constructs like citizens, scientists, and species. As a result, answers to a number of design questions cannot be justified based on theoretical prescriptions. For example, how should the first (landing) and subsequent pages look? Do the landing page and other pages have to behave differently each time?

Does the file structure become dynamic and personalized for each user? Furthermore, personalization is possible once users' profiles are known, suggesting that, at least for new users, some of the dynamic elements should initially be static, so at what point in the user's interaction should the switch to personalized content occur? In summary, while the proposed design theory supports flexible design, it is unclear to what degree and what elements should be made dynamic *to ensure that Crowd IQ is improved in a given project*.

One way to address this problem is to formulate design principles (guidelines) in a way that supports their reuse in other situations. Research on this issue is ongoing (Chandra Kruse & Seidel, 2017; Chandra Kruse, Seidel, & Purao, 2016; Chandra, Seidel, & Gregor, 2015; Lukyanenko & Parsons, 2013b); in future work, we hope to consider emerging ideas about the presentation of design science knowledge to improve communication on the design essence of the instance-based approach to crowdsourcing to practitioners.

Pay Attention to Instantiation Validity. Design theory indeterminacy leads to another challenge in design science research. One element of design science and rigor is evaluation of the artifact, which means rigorously demonstrating that the artifact produces the hypothesized outcomes (i.e., increases the quality of the dimensions of interest to organizations). To undertake this demonstration, we used the proposed design guidelines to create real artifacts with varying levels of structure (i.e., class-based vs. instance-based) and asked human participants to use them in hopes of draw statistical inferences from their use.

However, when a particular theoretical construct or design guideline is instantiated, there are virtually unlimited ways to operationalize (i.e., design) the feature in the corresponding artifact, with no clear guidance for choosing the most appropriate one because of design theory indeterminacy. Further, while a researcher may be interested in only one construct (e.g., level of structure), the artifact that instantiates that construct must often include a variety of features (e.g., navigation/help buttons, actual data from past users) to provide real-world functionality and usability. These features are not chosen based on instantiating the construct of interest but may interact with this construct in unpredictable ways, affecting results and diminishing internal validity.

These concerns resulted in a proposal for a new kind of research validity, ***instantiation validity***, defined as the extent to which inferences and conclusions are warranted from observations of IT features as instantiations of theoretical constructs or design principles (Lukyanenko, Evermann, & Parsons, 2014; Lukyanenko, Parsons, & Samuel, 2019).

There is no perfect solution to the problem of instantiation validity. (For a discussion, see Lukyanenko, Evermann, & Parsons (2015).) As Iivari (2007) noted, it is usually impossible to derive specific design guidance from more general (e.g., kernel or design) theories. We contribute to research on instantiation validity by proposing a series of guidelines for researchers to follow (Lukyanenko et al., 2015) and an innovative methodological practice of using multiple artifacts, which we call ***artifact sampling***, to complement existing ways of establishing the artifacts' validity

(Lukyanenko et al., 2018). We hope to pursue this problem in future studies and call on the research community to address this serious issue.

Design Never Ends. Throughout the project, we experienced challenges for which we found no adequate solution. One such challenge was how to engage prospective contributors effectively in participatory design given the diversity of users and the geographic distance between the developers and the contributors. We documented the challenges we faced in engaging prospective users, but a survey of the extant research on participatory design does not offer much guidance, as most of that work was conducted in organizational settings (Lukyanenko, Parsons, Wiersma, Sieber, & Maddah, 2016).

Another challenge lies in ensuring that, once participants provide data using instance-based IS, the data can be integrated effectively into scientific decision-making and analysis. We have been exploring the potential of artificial intelligence (e.g., natural-language-processing, machine learning) to infer species of interest to scientists automatically from non-experts' observations that contain rich descriptions but lack definitive species identification. More generally, we observe a wealth of research in citizen science on ways to capture contributions, but there is little design knowledge on how to make effective use of the data produced by volunteers, opening a new opportunity for future research.

Many unaddressed issues relate to the effective use of machine learning in crowdsourcing. For example, machine learning requires training based on the same data it is required to score, so one must obtain known answers from the crowd (e.g., correct species). Among the many challenges is mitigating the effect of the framing bias: It is reasonable to posit that volunteers who provide species identification along with attributes would provide sets of attributes that differ from those of crowd members who do not provide species identification and report only attributes—paradoxically, exactly the scenario that machine learning intends to support.

Another challenge of machine learning is creating the ability to train on and infer large number of classes. Most successful applications of machine learning operate on a small set of target classes; many analytics/machine learning tools have an upper bound on the number of classification targets (e.g., SAS Enterprise Miner currently limits neural networks to 512 targets). However, in a large domain like ornithology, the number of classification targets could be in the thousands (e.g., about 10,000 species of birds).

Another issue is the closed-world assumption of the currently popular supervised machine learning algorithms. Supervised learning typically has finite targets, and the objective function is to maximize fit between data and those targets. However, crowdsourcing offers a unique opportunity for organizations to discover something new or to draw unanticipated insights from the data. Therefore, a specific challenge of machine learning is to create the ability to detect and flag observations that do not fit the predefined classification schema and so could be instances of unanticipated or unknown classes.

In the next phase of design, we hope to address some of the challenges to hybrid intelligence, such as improving the ability of machines and crowds to complement one another.

Design science research is hard! We conclude with a few words of reflection on the design science research methodology. Design science research has a number of unique features, the most notable of which are its twin objectives of producing knowledge while solving real-world problems with innovative artifacts. Design science shares many of the features of conventional research, especially during the evaluation phase, but what sets it apart is its deeper engagement with practice (Iivari, 2007; Sein, Henfridsson, Purao, Rossi, & Lindgren, 2011). In our experience, we had to wear the hats of developer, IT support, analyst, project manager, public relations officer, marketer, entrepreneur, accountant, lawyer, and strategist.

To illustrate, project sustainability has emerged as a serious concern. As the project attracted more potential contributors, we had to deal with a variety of issues, such as how to keep people engaged with and excited about the project, how to handle potentially abusive users, and how to facilitate information exchange between users in the context of anonymity (i.e., when one user wishes to contact the other). Not least of our challenges concerned where to obtain the funds necessary for the ongoing development, maintenance, upgrade, and operation of NLNature. While other research initiatives require funding, running a real-world project like NLNature requires continuous and uninterrupted funding that is sufficient to ensure the online platform is always available and responsive enough to provide a smooth and effective user experience.

Other unique challenges included maintaining sufficient consistency to make comparisons and reach scientifically valid conclusions by testing hypotheses. For example, many online users are accustomed to constant changes and upgrades of technologies. However, in a project that seeks to test scientific hypotheses, change is an obstacle. Therefore, many features we thought would be good to include in NLNature could not be implemented during the research without creating confounds or jeopardizing the ability to compare users' performance across time. For example, the project lacks a mobile version because we are yet to conceptualize fully the design of a mobile platform that is consistent with our theories. The second reason for not having a mobile platform is more mundane: we were not able to attract sufficient funding to retain a skilled mobile developer.

While these concerns are not typically discussed in scientific papers, without adequate funding, effective user management, and a sustainability strategy, one cannot engage citizens effectively and assemble the data sets needed to test theoretical propositions. Our final lesson learned is that design science research is more than just research, and its non-research component is just as important as and perhaps more difficult to manage than its scientific one!

References

Angles, R., & Gutierrez, C. (2008). Survey of graph database models. *ACM Computing Surveys, 40*(1), 1–39.

Baskerville, R. L., Kaul, M., & Storey, V. C. (2015). Genres of inquiry in design-science research: Justification and evaluation of knowledge production. *MIS Quarterly, 39*(3), 541–564.

Bauer, M. W., Petkova, K., & Boyadjieva, P. (2000). Public knowledge of and attitudes to science: Alternative measures that may end the "science war". *Science, Technology and Human Values, 25*(1), 30–51.

Bergholtz, M., & Eriksson, O. (2015). Towards a socio-institutional ontology for conceptual modelling of information systems. In *Advances in Conceptual Modeling* (pp. 225–235). Springer.

Bonney, R. (1996). Citizen science: A lab tradition. *Living Bird, 15*(4), 7–15.

Bonney, R., Cooper, C. B., Dickinson, J., Kelling, S., Phillips, T., Rosenberg, K. V., et al. (2009). Citizen science: A developing tool for expanding science knowledge and scientific literacy. *BioScience, 59*(11), 977–984.

Brabham, D. C. (2013). *Crowdsourcing*. Cambridge, MA: MIT Press.

Brossard, D., Lewenstein, B., & Bonney, R. (2005). Scientific knowledge and attitude change: The impact of a citizen science project. *International Journal of Science Education, 27*(9), 1099–1121.

Bunge, M. (1977). *Treatise on basic philosophy: Ontology I: the furniture of the world*. Boston, MA: Reidel.

Burgess, H., DeBey, L., Froehlich, H., Schmidt, N., Theobald, E., Ettinger, A., … Parrish, J. (2017). The science of citizen science: Exploring barriers to use as a primary research tool. *Biological Conservation*, 1–8.

Castellanos, A., Castillo, A., Lukyanenko, R., & Tremblay, M. C. (2017). Understanding Benefits and Limitations of Unstructured Data Collection for Repurposing Organizational Data. In S. Wrycza & J. Maślankowski (Eds.), *Information Systems: Research, Development, Applications, Education: 10th SIGSAND/PLAIS EuroSymposium 2017, Gdansk, Poland, September 22, 2017, Proceedings* (pp. 13–24). Cham: Springer International Publishing.

Castellanos, A., Lukyanenko, R., Samuel, B. M., & Tremblay, M. C. (2016). Conceptual modeling in open information environments. In *AIS SIGSAND Symposium* (pp. 1–7). Lubbock, TX.

Cattell, R. (2011). Scalable SQL and NoSQL data stores. *ACM SIGMOD Record, 39*(4), 12–27.

Chandra Kruse, L., & Seidel, S. (2017). Tensions in design principle formulation and reuse. In *DESRIST 2017*.

Chandra Kruse, L., Seidel, S., & Purao, S. (2016). Making Use of Design Principles. *LNCS 9661* (pp. 37–51). Berlin, Heidelberg: Springer.

Chandra, L., Seidel, S., & Gregor, S. (2015). prescriptive knowledge in is research: conceptualizing design principles in terms of materiality, action, and boundary conditions. *Hawaii International Conference on System Sciences*, pp. 4039–4047.

Chang, F., Dean, J., Ghemawat, S., Hsieh, W. C., Wallach, D. A., Burrows, M., … & Gruber, R. E. (2008). Bigtable: A distributed storage system for structured data. *ACM Transactions on Computer Systems, 26*(2), 4–23.

Davis, E., & Marcus, G. (2015). Commonsense reasoning and commonsense knowledge in artificial intelligence. *Communications of the ACM, 58*(9), 92–103.

DeCandia, G., Hastorun, D., Jampani, M., Kakulapati, G., Lakshman, A., Pilchin, A., … & Vogels, W. (2007). Dynamo: amazon's highly available key-value store. In *ACM SIGOPS Operating Systems Review* (Vol. 41, pp. 205–220). ACM.

Doan, A., Ramakrishnan, R., & Halevy, A. Y. (2011). Crowdsourcing systems on the World-Wide Web. *Communications of the ACM, 54*(4), 86–96.

Eriksson, O., & Agerfalk, P. J. (2010). Rethinking the meaning of identifiers in information infrastructures. *Journal of the Association for Information Systems, 11*(8), 433–454.

Faraj, S., Jarvenpaa, S. L., & Majchrzak, A. (2011). Knowledge collaboration in online communities. *Organization Science, 22*(5), 1224–1239.

Feyerabend, P. (1980). Science in a free society. *Philosophical Quarterly, 30*(119), 172–174.

Fielden, M. A., Chaulk, A. C., Bassett, K., Wiersma, Y. F., Erbland, M., Whitney, H., et al. (2015). Aedes japonicus japonicus (Diptera: Culicidae) arrives at the most easterly point in North America. *The Canadian Entomologist, 147*(06), 737–740.

Fortson, L., Masters, K., Nichol, R., Borne, K., Edmondson, E., Lintott, C., ... & Wallin, J. (2011). Galaxy Zoo: Morphological classification and citizen science. *Advances in Machine Learning and Data Mining for Astronomy*, 1–11.

Franklin, M. J., Kossmann, D., Kraska, T., Ramesh, S., & Xin, R. (2011). CrowdDB: Answering queries with crowdsourcing. In *Proceedings of the 2011 ACM SIGMOD International Conference on Management of data* (pp. 61–72). Athens, Greece: ACM.

Garcia-Molina, H., Joglekar, M., Marcus, A., Parameswaran, A., & Verroios, V. (2016). Challenges in data crowdsourcing. *IEEE Transactions on Knowledge and Data Engineering, 28*(4), 901–911.

Goodchild, M. (2007). Citizens as sensors: The world of volunteered geography. *GeoJournal, 69*(4), 211–221.

Gregor, S., & Jones, D. (2007). The Anatomy of design theory. *Journal of the Association for Information Systems, 8*(5), 312–335.

Haklay, M. (2013). Citizen science and volunteered geographic information: Overview and typology of participation. In *Crowdsourcing geographic knowledge* (pp. 105–122). Springer.

Hanseth, O., & Lyytinen, K. (2004). Theorizing about the design of Information Infrastructures: design kernel theories and principles. *Sprouts: Working papers on information environments, systems and organizations, 4*(4), 207–241.

Hevner, A., March, S., Park, J., & Ram, S. (2004). Design science in information systems research. *MIS Quarterly, 28*(1), 75–105.

Hosseini, M., Phalp, K., Taylor, J., & Ali, R. (2014). The four pillars of crowdsourcing: A reference model (pp. 1–12). Presented at the 2014 IEEE Eighth International Conference on Research Challenges in Information Science (RCIS), IEEE.

Howe, J. (2006). The rise of crowdsourcing. *Wired, 14*(6).

Iivari, J. (2007). A paradigmatic analysis of information systems as a design science. *Scandinavian Journal of Information Systems*, 39–64.

Ipeirotis, P. G., & Gabrilovich, E. (2014). Quizz: Targeted crowdsourcing with a billion (potential) users (pp. 143–154). Presented at the Proceedings of the 23rd international conference on World wide web, International World Wide Web Conferences Steering Committee.

Ipeirotis, P. G., & Paritosh, P. K. (2011). Managing crowdsourced human computation: a tutorial. In *Proceedings of the 20th international conference companion on World wide web*. ACM.

Ipeirotis, P. G., Provost, F., & Wang, J. (2010). Quality management on amazon mechanical turk. In *Proceedings of the ACM SIGKDD workshop on human computation* (pp. 64–67). ACM.

Irwin, A. (1995). *Citizen science: A study of people, expertise and sustainable development*. Psychology Press.

Kallinikos, J., & Tempini, N. (2014). Patient data as medical facts: Social media practices as a foundation for medical knowledge creation. *Information Systems Research, 25*(4), 817–833.

Kilian, D. (2008). *When it absolutely has to be accurate, don't trust the crowd*. ECT News Network.

Kleek, M. G. V., Styke, W., Schraefel, M., & Karger, D. (2011). Finders/Keepers: A longitudinal study of people managing information scraps in a micro-note tool. In *Proceedings of the SIGCHI Conference on Human Factors in Computing Systems* (pp. 2907–2916). Vancouver, BC, Canada: ACM.

Kosmala, M., Wiggins, A., Swanson, A., & Simmons, B. (2016). Assessing data quality in citizen science. *Frontiers in Ecology and the Environment, 14*(10), 551–560.

Kullenberg, C., & Kasperowski, D. (2016). What is citizen science?–A scientometric meta-analysis. *PLoS ONE, 11*(1), e0147152.

Lassaline, M. E., Wisniewski, E. J., & Medin, D. L. (1992). Basic levels in artificial and natural categories: Are all basic levels created equal? In B. Barbara (Ed.), *Percepts, Concepts and Categories: The Representation and Processing of Information* (Vol. Volume 93, pp. 328–378). North-Holland.

Levy, M., & Germonprez, M. (2017). The potential for citizen science in information systems research. *Communications of the Association for Information Systems, 40*(1), 2.

Lewandowski, E., & Specht, H. (2015). Influence of volunteer and project characteristics on data quality of biological surveys. *Conservation Biology, 29*(3), 713–723.

Li, G., Wang, J., Zheng, Y., & Franklin, M. (2016). Crowdsourced data management: A survey. *IEEE Transactions on Knowledge and Data Engineering,* 1–23.

Light, A., & Miskelly, C. (2014). Design for sharing. *Northumbria University/The Sustainable Society Network.*

Lintott, C. J., Schawinski, K., Keel, W., Arkel, H. V., Bennert, N., Edmondson, E., ... & Vandenberg, J. (2009). Galaxy Zoo: Hanny's Voorwerp, a quasar light echo? *Monthly Notices of the Royal Astronomical Society, 399*(1), 129–140.

Loos, P., Nebel, W., Gómez, J. M., Hasan, H., Watson, R. T., vom Brocke, J., ... & Recker, J. (2011). Green IT: a matter of business and information systems engineering? *Business & Information Systems Engineering, 3*(4), 245–252.

Louv, R., Dickinson, J. L., & Bonney, R. (2012). *Citizen science: Public participation in environmental research.* Ithaca, NY: Cornell University Press.

Lukyanenko, R., Evermann, J., & Parsons, J. (2014). Instantiation validity in IS design research. In *DESRIST 2014, LNCS 8463* (pp. 321–328). Springer.

Lukyanenko, R., Evermann, J., & Parsons, J. (2015). Guidelines for Establishing Instantiation Validity in IT Artifacts: A Survey of IS Research. In *DESRIST 2015, LNCS 9073.* Berlin/ Heidelberg: Springer.

Lukyanenko, R., & Parsons, J. (2011a). *Rethinking data quality as an outcome of conceptual modeling choices* (pp. 1–16). Adelaide: Australia.

Lukyanenko, R., & Parsons, J. (2011b). Unintended consequences of class-based ontological commitment. In O. De Troyer, C. Bauzer Medeiros, R. Billen, P. Hallot, A. Simitsis, & H. Van Mingroot (Eds.), (Vol. 6999, pp. 220–229). Berlin, Heidelberg: Springer.

Lukyanenko, R., & Parsons, J. (2013a). Is traditional conceptual modeling becoming obsolete? In *Conceptual Modeling* (pp. 1–14).

Lukyanenko, R., & Parsons, J. (2013b). Reconciling theories with design choices in design science research. In *DESRIST 2013, LNCS 7939* (pp. 165–180). Springer Berlin, Heidelberg.

Lukyanenko, R., & Parsons, J. (2015). Information quality research challenge: Adapting information quality principles to user-generated content. *ACM Journal of Data and Information Quality, 6*(1), 1–3.

Lukyanenko, R., Parsons, J., & Samuel, B. M. (2018). Artifact sampling: using multiple information technology artifacts to increase research rigor. In *Proceedings of the 51st Hawaii International Conference on System Sciences (HICSS 2018)* (pp. 1–12). Big Island, Hawaii.

Lukyanenko, R., Parsons, J., & Samuel, B. M. (2019a). Representing instances: The case for reengineering conceptual modeling grammars. *European Journal of Information Systems, 28*(1), 68–90.

Lukyanenko, R., Parsons, J., & Wiersma, Y. (2011). Citizen Science 2.0: Data management principles to harness the power of the crowd. In H. Jain, A. Sinha, & P. Vitharana (Eds.), (Vol. 6629, pp. 465–473). Springer Berlin, Heidelberg.

Lukyanenko, R., Parsons, J., & Wiersma, Y. (2014b). The IQ of the crowd: Understanding and improving information quality in structured user-generated content. *Information systems Research, 25*(4), 669–689.

Lukyanenko, R., Parsons, J., & Wiersma, Y. (2016a). Emerging problems of data quality in citizen science. *Conservation Biology, 30*(3), 447–449.

Lukyanenko, R., Parsons, J., Wiersma, Y. F., Wachinger, G., Huber, B., & Meldt, R. (2017). Representing crowd knowledge: Guidelines for conceptual modeling of user-generated content. *Journal of the Association for Information Systems, 18*(4), 297–339.

Lukyanenko, R., Parsons, J., Wiersma, Y., & Maddah, M. (2019b). Expecting the unexpected: effects of data collection design choices on the quality of crowdsourced user-generated content. *MIS Quarterly, 43*(2), 634–647.

Lukyanenko, R., Parsons, J., Wiersma, Y., Sieber, R., & Maddah, M. (2016b). Participatory design for user-generated content: understanding the challenges and moving forward. *Scandinavian Journal of Information Systems, 28*(1), 37–70.

Lukyanenko, R., & Samuel, B. M. (2017). Are all classes created equal? Increasing precision of conceptual modeling grammars. *ACM Transactions on Management Information Systems (TMIS), 40*(2), 1–25.

Lukyanenko, R., Wiggins, A., & Rosser, H. K. (2019). Citizen science: An information quality research frontier. *Information Systems Frontiers*, 1–23.

March, S., & Allen, G. (2012). Toward a social ontology for conceptual modeling. In *11th Symposium on Research in Systems Analysis and Design* (pp. 57–62). Vancouver, Canada.

March, S. T., & Allen, G. N. (2014). Toward a social ontology for conceptual modeling. *Communications of the AIS, 34*.

McKinley, D. C., Miller-Rushing, A. J., Ballard, H. L., Bonney, R., Brown, H., Cook-Patton, S. C., … & Phillips, T. B. (2016). Citizen science can improve conservation science, natural resource management, and environmental protection. *Biological Conservation*.

Murphy, G. (2004). *The big book of concepts*. Cambridge, MA: MIT Press.

Nov, O., Arazy, O., & Anderson, D. (2011). Dusting for science: Motivation and participation of digital citizen science volunteers. *2011 iConference*, 68–74.

Nov, O., Arazy, O., & Anderson, D. (2014). Scientists@ home: what drives the quantity and quality of online citizen science participation. *PLoS ONE, 9*(4), 1–11.

Ogilvie, B. W. (2008). *The science of describing: Natural history in Renaissance Europe*. Chicago, IL: University of Chicago Press.

Ogunseye, S., Parsons, J., & Lukyanenko, R. (2017). Do crowds go stale? Exploring the Effects of Crowd Reuse on Data Diversity. In *WITS 2017*. Seoul, South Korea.

Osborn, D. A., Pearse, J. S., Roe, C. A., Magoon, O., Converse, H., Baird, B., … & Miller-Henson, M. (2005). Monitoring rocky intertidal shorelines: a role for the public in resource management (pp. 624–636). Presented at the California and the World Ocean '02, conf. proc. American Society of Civil Engineers, Reston, VA.

Parsons, J. (1996). An information model based on classification theory. *Management Science, 42*(10), 1437–1453.

Parsons, J., Lukyanenko, R., & Wiersma, Y. (2011). Easier citizen science is better. *Nature, 471*(7336), 37.

Parsons, J., & Wand, Y. (2000). Emancipating instances from the tyranny of classes in information modeling. *ACM Transactions on Database Systems, 25*(2), 228–268.

Parsons, J., & Wand, Y. (2008a). A question of class. *Nature, 455*, 1040–1041.

Parsons, J., & Wand, Y. (2008b). Using cognitive principles to guide classification in information systems modeling. *MIS Quarterly, 32*(4), 839–868.

Perszyk, K. J. (2013). *Nonexistent objects: Meinong and contemporary philosophy*. Netherlands: Springer.

Ponti, M., Hillman, T., Kullenberg, C., & Kasperowski, D. (2018). Getting it right or being top rank: Games in citizen science. *Citizen Science: Theory and Practice, 3*(1).

Popper, K. (2014). *Conjectures and refutations: The growth of scientific knowledge*. Cambridge, Mass: Routledge.

Pultar, E., Raubal, M., Cova, T. J., & Goodchild, M. F. (2009). Dynamic GIS case studies: Wildfire evacuation and volunteered geographic information. *Transactions in GIS, 13*(s1), 85–104.

Quinn, A. J., & Bederson, B. B. (2011). Human computation: a survey and taxonomy of a growing field (pp. 1403–1412). Presented at the Proceedings of the SIGCHI conference on human factors in computing systems, ACM.

Rosch, E., Mervis, C. B., Gray, W. D., Johnson, D. M., & Boyesbraem, P. (1976). Basic objects in natural categories. *Cognitive Psychology, 8*(3), 382–439.

Sauermann, H., & Franzoni, C. (2015). Crowd science user contribution patterns and their implications. *Proceedings of the National Academy of Sciences, 112*(3), 679–684.

Schuurman, D., Baccarne, B., De Marez, L., & Mechant, P. (2012). Smart ideas for smart cities: investigating crowdsourcing for generating and selecting ideas for ICT innovation in a city context. *Journal of Theoretical and Applied Electronic commerce Research, 7*(3), 49–62.

Searle, J. R. (1995). *The construction of social reality.* Simon and Schuster.

Seidel, S., Recker, J. C., & Vom Brocke, J. (2013). Sensemaking and sustainable practicing: functional affordances of information systems in green transformations. *Management Information Systems Quarterly, 37*(4), 1275–1299.

Sein, M., Henfridsson, O., Purao, S., Rossi, M., & Lindgren, R. (2011). Action design research. *MIS Quarterly, 35*(1), 37.

Smith, E., & Medin, D. (1981). *Categories and concepts.* Cambridge, Mass: Harvard University Press.

Sonnenberg, C., & vom Brocke, J. (2012). Evaluations in the science of the artificial–reconsidering the build-evaluate pattern in design science research. In *Design Science Research in Information Systems* (pp. 381–397). Springer.

Stevens, M., Vitos, M., Lewis, J., & Haklay, M. (2013). Participatory monitoring of poaching in the Congo basin. Presented at the 21st GIS Research UK Conference.

Sullivan, B. L., Wood, C. L., Iliff, M. J., Bonney, R. E., Fink, D., & Kelling, S. (2009). eBird: A citizen-based bird observation network in the biological sciences. *Biological Conservation, 142*(10), 2282–2292.

Surowiecki, J. (2005). *The wisdom of crowds.* New York, NY: Anchor Books.

Tams, S., Grover, V., & Thatcher, J. (2014). Modern information technology in an old workforce: toward a strategic research agenda. *The Journal of Strategic Information Systems, 23*(4), 284–304.

Theobald, E. J., Ettinger, A. K., Burgess, H. K., DeBey, L. B., Schmidt, N. R., Froehlich, H. E., … & Harsch, M. A. (2015). Global change and local solutions: Tapping the unrealized potential of citizen science for biodiversity research. *Biological Conservation, 181*, 236–244.

Venable, J., Pries-Heje, J., & Baskerville, R. (2012). A comprehensive framework for evaluation in design science research. In *DESRIST 2012, LNCS 7286* (pp. 423–438). Springer.

Vitos, M., Lewis, J., Stevens, M., & Haklay, M. (2013). Making local knowledge matter: Supporting non-literate people to monitor poaching in Congo (pp. 1–10). Presented at the ACM Symposium on Computing for Development, ACM.

Weinmann, M., Schneider, C., & vom Brocke, J. (2016). Digital nudging. *Business & Information Systems Engineering, 58*(6), 433–436.

Wiersma, Y. F. (2010). Birding 2.0: Citizen science and effective monitoring in the Web 2.0 world. *Avian Conservation and Ecology, 5*(2), 13.

DSR in Information Systems Development

Designing Evolution Paths
for Enterprise-Wide Information Systems

Robert Winter and Stephan Aier

Abstract Because of heterogeneous stakeholder requirements, highly diverse tasks, and the massive investment required, enterprise-wide information systems (e-wIS) are often developed through multiple projects over long time periods. In this context, choosing the "right" evolution path is essential, although doing so is not straightforward because e-wIS comprise technical, organizational, and use-related issues that require development stages to be aligned over heterogeneous dimensions. Although maturity models (MM) are an established instrument with which to devise development paths, their development processes often lack transparency and theoretical and empirical grounding. Moreover, extant MM often focus on the control of certain capabilities (doing things right) rather than on providing the necessary capabilities in a sequence appropriate to the type of organization (doing the right things). We propose an empirically grounded design method for MM that devises capability-development sequences rather than control levels. We instantiate the proposed method twice—once in developing a Business Intelligence (BI) MM and once in developing a Corporate Performance Management (CPM) MM, as two exemplary types of e-wIS. The artifacts are developed over three laps to enhance successively their projectability in the problem space and their tangibility in the solution space.Lessons learned: (1) In conducting DSR projects, it often proves valuable to be open to diverse research approaches like classical qualitative or quantitative approaches since they may purposefully ground and guide design decisions. (2) Complex artifact design processes may not be carried out by a single Ph.D. student or published in a single paper, as they require adequate decomposition and organizational integration. (3) Complex and emergent artifact design processes require a reliable network of practice organizations rather than a project contract with a single organization.

R. Winter (✉) · S. Aier
Institute of Information Management, University of St. Gallen, St. Gallen, Switzerland
e-mail: robert.winter@unisg.ch

S. Aier
e-mail: stephan.aier@unisg.ch

© Springer Nature Switzerland AG 2020
J. vom Brocke et al. (eds.), *Design Science Research. Cases*, Progress in IS,
https://doi.org/10.1007/978-3-030-46781-4_4

1 Introduction

In addition to focused information systems (IS), such as those that provide specific customer touchpoints or support specific products, organizations also need complex IS that provide standardized business functionality or integration services on an enterprise-wide level. We refer to such IS as enterprise-wide IS (e-wIS) (Haki, Aier, & Winter, 2016). Examples of e-wIS may be found among enterprise resource planning (ERP) systems, data warehouse (DWH) and business intelligence (BI) systems, or among corporate performance management (CPM) systems.

Because of their integrative character, e-wIS usually cover a wide set of functionalities and provide many services for a diverse and heterogeneous set of stakeholders. Developing, introducing, and continuously evolving such e-wIS is challenging because they must be understood on multiple levels (e.g., the individual, group, and organizational levels), from multiple perspectives (e.g., the business and technology perspectives), and over a lifecycle that is much longer than that for focused applications because of the significantly higher investment and the greater stability of shared functionalities.

To guide organizations through the evolution of their IS and related processes, research and practice have developed a multitude of maturity models (MMs) that focus on a variety of concerns. A widely adopted and well-known example of such MMs is CMMI (*Capability Maturity Model Integrated*, later renamed *Capability Maturity Model Integration*). What CMMI shares with many other MMs is that they impose a governance perspective on a set of core capabilities in a certain domain, such as software development. As a consequence, MMs do not help to identify which capabilities should be developed in which sequence (doing the right things); instead they focus on systematically improving control of all capabilities that are regarded as essential (doing things right).

Our perspective in this discussion is that MMs for e-wIS should cover a large and diverse set of capabilities as well as a potentially long and expensive evolution path, and that "doing the right things" is much more important than achieving a desired level of control. In addition, e-wIS are characterized by their large and potentially heterogeneous groups of stakeholders, which may have conflicting goals and which change their perspectives only in *long-running sensemaking processes.* Conflicts between business and IT perspectives and between local and global perspectives often arise (Haki et al., 2016), so understanding the development paths and potential path-dependencies is important in such scenarios. Therefore, a meaningful sequence of capabilities to be developed corresponds much better to systematic maturity development than it does to a certain level of heterogeneous capabilities that share only the same level of control maturity.

Such sensemaking processes are inevitably also processes of organizational learning. Guidance for such e-wIS learning processes should be based on an empirical understanding that captures the complex interactions in such IS.

To illustrate these arguments, let us consider BI as an example of an e-wIS: BI often has many stakeholders, such as financial and risk reporting, sales, and business development. BI stakeholders have many and diverse needs that can be served only by integrated data and harmonized toolsets. Longitudinal analyses of BI adoption in complex organizations show that it is reasonable to assume that BI development phases are not characterized by maturing process control, but by adoption episodes and learning processes that lead to the continuous use of these BI systems (Audzeyeva & Hudson, 2015; Deng & Chi, 2013).

The design ambition of the journey reported in this paper is to propose artifacts that support the systematic maturity development in e-wIS and meet three general requirements: (i) all important perspectives are covered, (ii) artifacts are based on empirical accounts of organizational learning, and (iii) application of artifacts focuses on capability development sequences instead of on developing control maturity.

2 The Context: Maturity Model Development for Business Intelligence

Since e-wIS is an abstract class of IS and we seek an empirical grounding for our design, we illustrate artifact development by focusing on BI systems as an instance of e-wIS. In this section, we first discuss concepts of maturity and MM development for e-wIS. Then we introduce BI as an example of e-wIS, followed by a discussion of BI MMs' state of the art as the starting point and foundation for our design journey.

2.1 Maturity Concepts and Maturity Model Development

Maturity is commonly defined as a means by which "to evaluate the capabilities of an organisation in regard to a certain discipline" (Rosemann & De Bruin, 2005, p. 2). MMs are conceptual models that depict evolution paths toward maturity (Becker, Knackstedt, & Pöppelbuß, 2009), so they are accepted instruments for systematically documenting and guiding the development and transformation of organizations on the basis of best or common practices (Paulk, Curtis, Chrissis, & Weber, 1993). The concept of MMs was first proposed during the 1970s (Gibson & Nolan, 1974), and driven by the success of prominent examples (e.g. Ahern, Clouse, & Turner, 2003; Crawford, 2006; Humphrey, 1988), academics and practitioners have developed numerous MMs since then. In the field of IS alone, more than a hundred MM instantiations had been published by 2009 (Mettler & Rohner, 2009), with particular emphasis on the Capability Maturity Model (CMM) for software development (Paulk et al., 1993), which was developed by the Software Engineering Institute of Carnegie Mellon University (Jiang et al., 2004; Phan, 2001; Ramasubbu, Mithas, Krishnan, & Kemerer, 2008). Table 1 summarizes the fundamental MM concepts.

Because of their infrastructure-like character, e-wIS are subject to continuous evolution, comprise a large number of components, and reflect diverse stakeholder

Table 1 Fundamental MM concepts

Element	Description
Capability	At the heart of MMs are capabilities that are related to objects like technologies/systems (Popovic, Coelho, & Jaklič, 2009), processes (Chrissis, Konrad, & Shrum, 2003; Paulk et al. 1993), people/workforce (Curtis, Hefley, & Miller, 2010), and management abilities like project and knowledge management (Crawford 2006; Paulzen, Doumi, Perc, & Cereijo-Roibas, 2002)
Dimension	Dimensions are capability domains or categories—that is, sets of related capabilities. Dimensions should be both exhaustive and mutually exclusive (Mettler & Rohner, 2009)
Level	Levels represent archetypal stages of maturity, with each level related to a specific set of capabilities that should be empirically testable (Nolan, 1973)
Core model	The core (maturity) model captures the relationships among capabilities, dimensions, and levels
Assessment instrument	Based on the core model, the assessment instrument assigns testable assessment criteria to each of the dimensions and levels

concerns. MMs were proposed to address exactly this challenge. Since capabilities are a MM's common denominator for all relevant problem dimensions and issues, an MM is well able to outline anticipated, typical, and/or logical evolution paths from an initial to a desired target stage in a coherent way, even for complex, multi-faceted problems (Kazanjian & Drazin, 1989). Over time, MMs have become an established means to identify and explore the strengths and weaknesses of organizations as a whole (e.g. Benbasat, Dexter, & Mantha, 1980; Galbraith, 1982; Kazanjian & Drazin, 1989) or of certain domains thereof (e.g. software development, cf. Paulk et al., 1993; Ramasubbu et al., 2008).

2.2 Business Intelligence Systems as Enterprise-Wide IS

BI is a "broad category of technologies, applications, and processes for gathering, storing, accessing, and analysing data to help its users make better decisions" (Wixom & Watson, 2010, p. 14). The importance of BI to management has been increasing over the last two decades, and its contribution to overall organizational success is undisputed (Davenport, Harris, & Morison, 2010, p. 3; Wixom & Watson, 2010, p. 14). Over time, the role of BI has changed from a "single analytical applica-tion" view to an organizational capability of strategic importance (Negash & Gray, 2008, p. 175). Technological challenges are increasingly accompanied by questions about the organizational implementation of an enterprise capability (e.g., crafting of an enterprise-wide data-management strategy), IT/business alignment, and compe-tence in the use, operation, and further development of a broad solution architecture

(Richardson & Bitterer, 2010, p. 2; Williams & Williams, 2007, p. 11). As a consequence, the initial significance of BI as a top technology priority for chief information officers has grown into a top business priority as well (Luftman et al., 2013; McDonald & Aron, 2010; Richardson & Bitterer, 2010). In addition to the need to increase excellence in the IT deployment of BI, organizations have to establish adequate processes (Davenport, Barth, & Bean, 2012) and ensure sufficient acceptance and continuous us of BI (Bischoff, Aier, Haki, & Winter, 2015) to create maximum business value.

Despite its widely acknowledged importance, putting BI into place is challenging from both a technological perspective and an organizational one (Luftman & Ben-Zvi, 2010, p. 54). Existing approaches often reveal a strong but isolated focus on either technical, organizational, or cultural issues, and a focus on individual design projects rather than on the systematic evolution of an e-wIS.

In this regard, the challenge of putting BI systems into place is comparable to other e-wIS, such as ERP and CPM systems. In all of these cases, a large spectrum of technical, organizational, and cultural issues has to be addressed, while the IS itself is a complex composite artifact, rather than a single piece of software, and its evolution is a long-term initiative and an organizational learning process, rather than a software development and adoption project.

2.3 Business Intelligence Maturity Models

Various MMs have been proposed in the BI field (Wixom & Watson, 2010). Literature reviews have identified multiple BI MMs and analyzed them with respect to their methodology and content (Chuah & Wong, 2011; Lahrmann, Marx, Winter, & Wortmann, 2010). Table 2 presents an updated overview of these models. With the popularity of MMs increasing, several aspects of existing MMs have been criticized, so these challenges should be acknowledged as design requirements.

MMs for e-wIS should focus on the *organizational learning process* (doing the right things) rather than on optimizing control of a certain set of capabilities (doing things right) (requirement R1). As all of the BI MMs that have been analyzed are CMMI cousins, none of them meets this requirement (R1).

In respect to the *development process*, a transparent and well-documented MM development process (Becker et al., 2009; Mettler & Rohner, 2009) is ensured by nine BI MMs (nos. 1,7,11,12,14,15,16,17,18). BI MMs from practice typically do not disclose their development or construction process, so the lack of empirical foundation is another challenge of existing MMs (Solli-Sæther & Gottschalk, 2010, p. 280). In the BI domain only three models have revealed an empirical foundation: a Delphi study was conducted for the development of the EBI2M (no. 1); Lukman et al. (no. 14) employed a cluster analysis; And Tan et al. (no. 16) used a factor analysis. Therefore, we acknowledge that existing BI MMs still "rely mainly upon anecdotal evidence and case studies describing success stories" (McCormack et al., 2009, p. 793). For the proposed e-W IS MM, development will be transparent, well documented, and empirically grounded (requirement R2).

Table 2 Overview of existing BI MMs

No.	Name	Source	Origin
1	Watson et al.	(Watson et al., 2001)	Practice
2	SAS	(Hatcher & Prentice, 2004; Sas Institute, 2009)	Practice
3	TDWI	(Eckerson, 2004, 2009)	Practice
4	SMC	(Chamoni & Gluchowski, 2004; Schulze et al., 2009)	Academia
5	Cates et al.	(Cates, Gill, & Zeituny, 2005)	Practice
6	Dataflux	(Fisher, 2005)	Academia
7	Sen et al.	(Sen, Sinha, & Ramamurthy, 2006; Sen, Ramamurthy, & Sinha, 2011)	Practice
8	HP	(Henschen, 2007; Hewlett, 2009)	Practice
9	Gartner	(Rayner & Schlegel, 2008)	Practice
10	Teradata	(Töpfer, 2008)	Academia
11	EBI2M	(Chuah, 2010; Chuah & Wong, 2012)	Academia
12	DW CMM	(Sacu, 2010)	Academia
13	BIDM	(Sacu & Spruit, 2010)	Academia
14	Lukman et al.	(Lukman, Hackney, Popovic, Jaklic, & Irani, 2011)	Academia
15	Ong et al.	(Ong, Siew, & Wong, 2011)	Academia
16	Tan et al.	(Tan, Sim, & Yeoh, 2011)	Academia
17	Cosic et al.	(Cosic, Shanks, & Maynard, 2012)	Academia
18	Brooks et al.	(Brooks, El-Gayar, & Sarnikar, 2013)	Academia
19	OCU	(Ocu, 2013)	Practice

As our analysis reveals, MM *evaluation* (requirement R3) is a general deficit of MM proposals (Conwell et al., 2000) and a major weakness of many BI MMs. Six BI MMs (nos. 1,4,5,7,12,16) are assessed in respect to reliability, but in all six cases, only minor validation activities were conducted on the basis of qualitative feedback from experts, and none has been subject to a thorough empirical validation.

Overall, the developed models lack a *comprehensive scope* (requirement R4), as Lahrmann et al. (2010) discussed. Traditional IT topics like applications, data, and infrastructure are dominant, whereas topics like BI organization, BI strategy, and BI use/impact are widely neglected. This neglect is in contrast to the current IS literature, where the latter topics have high visibility (e.g. Boyer, Frank, Green, Harris, & Van De Vanter, 2010; Vierkorn & Friedrich, 2008).

Most models provide some form of *assessment instrument* to enable maturity measurement (requirement R5) for either self-assessment or assessment by a third party (Mettler, 2010), although, the mechanisms and calculations behind MMs that provide third-party assessments are generally not revealed by any of the BI MMs we analyzed.

Grounding is a major issue with existing MMs (McCormack et al., 2009, p. 793; Poeppelbuss, Niehaves, Simons, & Becker, 2011, p. 510), as only two of the nineteen

BI MMs we analyzed feature a theoretical foundation (requirement R6): Watson et al. (no. 1) based their model on the stages-of-growth approach (Gibson & Nolan, 1974), and Cosic et al. (no. 17) referred to the resource-based view (Barney 1991).

Since all of the BI MMs discussed here adopted the CMMI-style "doing things right" focus, these models are also susceptible to criticisms of the MM concept in general (e.g. Benbasat, Dexter, Drury, & Goldstein, 1984; de Bruin, Rosemann, Freeze, & Kulkarni, 2005; McCormack et al., 2009). Reliable artifacts for describing and measuring the BI maturity level of organizations and for guiding their BI evolution from the perspective of organizational learning (and, thus, "doing the right things,") are not available. Therefore, our design journey seeks to design a method for developing e-wIS MMs that meet requirements R1 through R6, which (at least for BI) were not met by any of the nineteen MMs we analyzed.

3 The Journey

As we propose a designed and evaluated method for guiding the evolution of e-wIS, we mainly follow Peffers, Tuunanen, Rothenberger, and Chatterjee's (2007) process model for design science research. While the present article reports on all steps in Peffers et al.'s process, this section primarily reports on the design/development and demonstrate/evaluate laps, which iteratively extended and deepened our view of the problem and its solution.

In the first and most comprehensive lap, we developed our foundational conceptualization and adapted the techniques for MM development accordingly. Then we instantiated the resulting method for developing a BI MM that satisfies the requirements discussed in Sect. 2.3.

In the second lap, we went beyond these basic requirements since we understood that our BI MM was not equally projectable to all cases. Therefore, we sought to understand the structural differences among situations and their consequences for situating our BI MM. The method was extended by situation identification and MM configuration.

In the third lap we leveraged our understanding of the BI MM problem and solution to develop MMs for e-wIS beyond BI. To demonstrate and evaluate this even wider projectability of our approach to MM development, we re-instantiated it for the CPM domain and fed the re-instantiation experience back into the method design.

These laps do not represent elementary build-evaluate iterations but aggregate the stages of purposeful development of design knowledge along the two dimensions of *increasing projectability* (of design knowledge in the problem space) and *increasing tangibility* (of design knowledge in the solution space). This journey is illustrated in Fig. 1 and described in the following sub-sections.

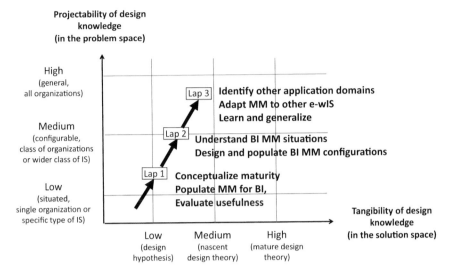

Fig. 1 Laps of the design journey

3.1 Lap 1: A Method for Developing E-WIS MMs and Its Instantiation for BI

In the first lap, our problem understanding was driven by the analysis of requirements for MM development in general and BI MM development in particular. As discussed in Sect. 2.3, the state of the art does not meet the following core requirements:

R1   Maturity focuses on organizational learning (doing the right things), not on governance and control (doing things right).
R2   The MM's development is transparent, well documented, and empirically grounded.
R3   The MM's quality and utility is evaluated.
R4   The MM's scope is comprehensive (i.e., not based only on the resource-based view but also on impact/use).
R5   The MM is accompanied by an assessment instrument.
R6   The MM is grounded in (domain-specific success) theory.

Taking these six requirements into account, we designed a (meta-level) MM development method and instantiated this method for BI.

On the meta level, the design process starts with developing a metamodel that covers all perspectives that are relevant to a given domain. This development can often be based on respective theory (e.g., IS success models) or on practices and capabilities that can be observed in practice, and/or can be condensed from empirical research in the respective domain. In developing our BI MM, we developed and validated a *BI success model*, a "theory-building" (Nunamaker Jr, Chen, & Purdin, 1991) activity that might seem unusual in a DSR project. However, it is common to differentiate two types of DSR knowledge (Mokyr, 2002) and their interactions (Gregor & Hevner, 2013): descriptive knowledge (Ω), which regards natural phenomena and the regularities among them, and prescriptive knowledge (Λ), which is the "how" knowledge of artifacts. Whereas the deep interaction between Ω and Λ is widely acknowledged, most researchers have focused either on Ω or Λ—often for good reason, such as in the service of clarity and simplicity. However, it is often necessary and appropriate to balance such contributions. Therefore, we first contribute to Ω to create an appropriate foundation for rigorously designing and contributing to Λ.

The BI success model is based on key IS/IT capabilities (Lahrmann, Marx, Winter, & Wortmann, 2011b). In the context of our work, these capabilities are defined as managerial, methodological, and technological capabilities that are involved in planning, designing, constructing, and implementing IT artifacts (Benbasat & Zmud, 2003). Capabilities are the skills, competencies, and abilities on which the value of the physical IT resource can be leveraged (Doherty & Terry, 2009). By validating the means-end relationships between key BI IS/IT capabilities and organizational performance, we set the basis for developing an effective BI MM. More specifically, our BI success model grounds use of the BI MM in value (Goldkuhl, 2004); that is, it provides evidence that a certain set of BI-related capabilities have a positive impact on business value. Ultimately, the BI success model acts as a theoretical justification for the BI MM and is transformed into a set of prescriptive statements (Goldkuhl, 2004; Kuechler & Vaishnavi, 2008) captured by the BI MM.

In the second step on the meta level, we require a MM population technique that appropriately clusters capabilities and assigns these clusters to certain maturity levels. To capture the organizational learning processes (and the relative difficulties of its stages) adequately in the context of e-wIS and their complex sociotechnical environments, we chose an empirically grounded, quantitative approach (Lahrmann, Marx, Mettler, Winter, & Wortmann, 2011a). We used the proposed Rasch algorithm, as an Item Response Theory (IRT)-based approach, in combination with cluster analysis. IRT in general and its Rasch operationalization in particular measure the difficulty of the capabilities (each represented by a measurement item) of organizations on the same scale based on quantitative (e.g., questionnaire) data. Thus, the Rasch algorithm provides an empirically grounded list of capabilities, ordered by their perceived difficulty. The capabilities on this list can then be clustered and assigned to maturity levels based on their position on the list. For our BI MM we collected empirical BI maturity data and ran it through the Rasch algorithm, finding an array of relevant capabilities sorted by difficulty from the least difficult (capabilities that all organizations can achieve) to the most difficult (capabilities that only the most successful organizations can achieve). The capabilities are then clustered into sets of similar difficulty. The optimal number of sets can be determined quantitatively, but to comply with the general expectations of MMs, we created five clusters of capabilities analogous to the five maturity levels in all widely used MMs. These five clusters of capabilities represent the organizational learning stages of BI, starting from an initial stage of "low-hanging fruit" all the way to the final stage that comprises the most difficult capabilities.

To serve as practical guidance for organizations, the MM should be provided along with a maturity assessment instrument, so we derived a pragmatic (short and simple) questionnaire from the BI MM and defined a procedure for calculating an organization's BI maturity level based on the questionnaire (Raber, Wortmann, & Winter, 2013b). As part of a design science research project, we also developed a MM evaluation technique to test whether an empirically assessed maturity level of a set of organizations is statistically significantly correlated to the defined success measures (Raber, Epple, Rothenberger, & Winter, 2016).

This first lap was "technically" driven. Based on an analysis of extant (BI) MMs, their documentation, and (as far as available) their development processes, we derived a set of requirements that led to am MM design method that is characterized in all of its steps by a strong focus on theoretical and empirical justification. By comparing real-life BI maturity assessments using the proposed BI MM with an alternative evaluation (qualitative case studies), we showed that our MM development process analytically satisfies our design requirements and creates assessments that correspond to traditional maturity evaluations (Raber et al., 2016).

3.2   Lap 2: The Need for a Situated Maturity Assessment

In lap 1, the BI MM population was based on a data set of more than 100 companies, allowing our method to create a "one size fits all" organizations MM. We discovered a generic organizational learning reference process for BI, although it may vary in certain companies because of their specific goals or contexts. This exception led to the idea that the BI MM may be further configured to fit the specific situation of any organization. Still, the goal was to provide a somewhat generic BI MM, not to end up with an infinite set of individual BI MMs, so we went back to the empirical data collected in lap 1 to determine whether we would achieve different clusters of capabilities assigned differently to maturity levels if we ran the Rasch algorithm with certain subsets of cases. From a design perspective, we extended the designed method with components for identifying situations and for configuring results (MMs) to specific situations.

For a foundation of a situational BI MM, we identified contingencies that are relevant moderators of the definition of maturity levels. After testing several hypotheses in our data set, the *size of the organization* and its *environment* (service or non-service industry) were selected as contingencies because they significantly moderate the definition of maturity levels. Thus, on the meta level, we extended our process of MM model development by a step. On the instance level, we built size- and environment-dependent data subsets, re-populated situated BI MMs from these subsets, and re-evaluated the situational BI MM based on the evaluation approach used in lap 1. As a result, the correlations between the BI maturity level and success improved (Raber, Wortmann, & Winter, 2013a).

Lap 2 contributed an option with which to customize learning paths for specific types of organizations by reflecting specific challenges and opportunities. Because the method's output is adaptable to more situations (no longer "one size fits all"), its projectability is enhanced, and because the method is extended (by configuration mechanisms) and more diverse evaluation experience is available, its tangibility also increased.

3.3 Lap 3: The Opportunity to Reuse Maturity Development Knowledge in Other Domains

Laps 1 and 2 focused on conceptualizing maturity and populating, situating, and evaluating MMs in BI. To increase the method's projectability and tangibility, related problem domains for organizational learning had to be identified, and the method eventually had to be adapted to and evaluated in these domains.

On the meta level, the domain-specific BI success model had to be generalized to cover related domains where technical, organizational, individual, and business value creation aspects are interrelated and where these aspects are not masked by specific market, product, or functional specifics. We identified the domain of CPM as appropriate (Marx, Lahrmann, & Winter, 2010), as it shares many properties with BI. We collected a dataset based on the generalized success model and populated a CPM MM (Marx, Wortmann, & Mayer, 2012). In collaboration with a large consultancy company, the CPM MM was implemented for consulting purposes (KPMG AG, 2011).

Since the coverage of CPM required only marginal amendments on the meta level and, as a product of a big consulting company, the CPM appeared to be useful for practical purposes, lap 3 demonstrated the artifact's potential as a nascent design theory. The proposed design knowledge is a MM construction method that identifies situated learning paths for organizations in e-wIS domains that require a coherent development of heterogeneous (technology, organization, use) capabilities.

4 The Results

This section presents the designed artifacts. Section 4.1 presents the e-wIS success model, the MM population technique, and the evaluation technique as artifacts on the meta level. Section 4.2 presents the (BI) MM and the (BI) maturity assessment instrument as artifacts on the (BI) instance level.

We claim that, for every type of e-wIS, an appropriate (scope of cases, number of cases) e-wIS-success-model-based survey will create a dataset that, using the Rasch-based MM population technique, can be used to create am MM and a maturity assessment instrument for the respective domain that meets the requirements stated in Sect. 2.3.

4.1   Meta-Level Artifacts

Techniques for success model construction and capability identification

Not only BI (Wixom & Watson, 2010, p. 14), but also other e-wIS must be addressed in their entire scope, ranging from strategic questions to organizational questions to questions of a technical nature. These ideas have been formalized in various IS success models on a general IS level, so we develop the theoretical foundation of our MMs based on established IS theories. However, BI has unique characteristics that may require adaptations and/or extensions of existing theory (Wixom & Watson, 2001). For example, BI supports unstructured, ad hoc decision processes, while general-transaction-processing IS enable well-structured processes like order processing and accounting. Hence, these theories might not be valid or have to be adapted and extended to address the causes and effects in the BI domain and their impact on organizational performance. To address this challenge, we follow an approach similar to that of Gable, Sedera, and Chan (2008) and draw on IS success models and their underlying theory (Petter, DeLone, & McLean, 2008; Sabherwal, Jeyaraj, & Chowa, 2006) and on the IS nomological net (Benbasat & Zmud, 2003) to develop and validate an e-wIS success model (cf. Fig. 2). The model (with its terminology adapted to the BI context) nicely supports our understanding of BI as a comprehensive and multifaceted concept.

Only a few studies have examined BI capabilities in depth. In their stages-of-growth model for DWH success (Watson, Ariyachandra, & Matyska, 2001) and their empirical investigation of factors that affect DWH success, Wixom and Watson

Fig. 2 BI success model (Lahrmann et al., 2011b)

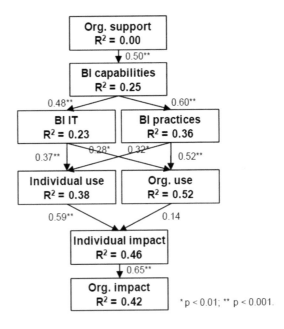

(2001) identified *individual BI capabilities* (i.e., BI team skills as a first set of key IS/IT capabilities). A second set of IS/IT capabilities are *BI practices,* which spans all managerial, methodological, and operations activities involved in planning, designing, constructing, and implementing BI artifacts (Benbasat & Zmud, 2003)— in fact, all of the organizational processes, guidelines, and knowledge concerned with the IT artifact (Wixom & Watson, 2010). Measurement items for both constructs were adapted from existing research (Sen et al., 2006; Watson et al., 2001). To conceptualize the IT artifact in the context of IS success, two major perspectives have to be captured: system quality and information quality (e.g. DeLone & McLean, 1992; Gable et al., 2008). To measure the BI IT artifact using these perspectives, we included items from (Sen et al., 2006; Watson et al., 2001) in our instrument. The *use* construct has frequently been deployed as an IS success measure (DeLone & McLean, 1992). Although it has been criticized as inappropriate for measuring IS success (e.g. Seddon, 1997), following DeLone and McLean (2003) and other researchers, we believe that the use construct is an important mediator between the three IS/IT sets of BI capabilities and BI impact on individual decision quality and organizational performance. In our instrument, BI use is measured with items from existing studies (Chin, Johnson, & Schwarz, 2008; Petter et al., 2008; Sabherwal et al., 2006). BI impact on individual decision quality and organizational performance is a consequence of using IS applications (Benbasat & Zmud, 2003). In the context of BI, *BI impact* was operationalized on an individual level—that is, BI value is created by improving individual decisions (Davenport et al., 2010; Wixom & Watson, 2001, 2010), as well as on an organizational level, where BI value is created by improving overall organizational performance (Elbashir, Collier, & Davern, 2008).

While the *success model* and candidates for capabilities are derived from general IS models and their construct definitions by adapting them to the e-wIS type at hand, relevant *capabilities* are derived from related work in the specific domain (e.g., BI) and assigned to the best-fitting construct.

The hypothesis development, data collection, analysis, and validation of our BI success model are described in Lahrmann et al. (2011b). Figure 2 illustrates its top-level constructs and their dependencies. The model appears to be a valid foundation for maturity measurement, so served as a justifying foundation for the subsequent design steps. Constructs are candidates for dimensions of the MM, and assigned capabilities are candidates for measurement items, which are used later for sorting and clustering the capabilities based on their level of difficulty for the respective organization.

Using the approach presented in this sub-section, we generated the BI success model in lap 3 to be also applicable in CPM (Marx et al., 2010).

MM population technique

All generic and situated MMs were constructed in three key steps: (1) definition and refinement of maturity dimensions, (2) questionnaire development and corresponding data collection, and (3) determination of maturity levels and their corresponding IS capabilities.

We defined maturity dimensions based on the success model. In the case of BI, our success model provided evidence that IS capabilities related to *individual BI capabilities, BI practices*, and *BI IT*—which influence *BI impact* via *BI use*—should be covered by the MM, so these constructs serve as MM dimensions. For all MM dimensions, the identified capabilities, along with the success model, formed the basis from which to identify measurement items. The process was conducted with practitioner focus groups and informed by existing MMs. (For BI, see Table 2.)

The capabilities are assumed to be progressively more difficult to acquire as indicators of maturity. To populate the MM we conducted a questionnaire-based survey in a second step. For each capability one questionnaire item was generated, and the respondents specified the as-is situation as well as the desired to-be situation on a five-point Likert scale. Data was collected from experts, managers, and executives using questionnaires that were distributed at practitioner events on paper and online.

Following Lahrmann et al.'s (2011a) quantitative design approach, we used the Rasch algorithm (RA), an IRT-based approach, in combination with cluster analysis in a third step. This approach adapts and extends the work of (Dekleva & Drehmer, 1997) for MMs in the IS domain. The RA assumes that highly capable organizations have a high probability of having successfully implemented difficult capabilities, while immature organizations have implemented only basic capabilities. Therefore, the algorithm calculates a score for the capabilities' difficulty and the organization's capabilities. Both scores are measured on the same scale such that, on the basis of the actual and desired values, the RA yields a single ordinal scale that represents the logit measure of each capability and organization, but no distinct maturity levels (Fig. 3).

To overcome subjectivity in defining maturity levels, we employed hierarchical clustering (squared Euclidean distance, Ward's cluster method) to assign capabilities to levels. In early MM research, various numbers of maturity levels were used, so lengthy discussions about the appropriate number of maturity levels ensued. Because of the prominence of the various CMM-based MMs (e.g. Curtis et al., 2010; Ramasubbu et al. 2008; Sen et al. 2006), the use of five maturity levels has become standard, so we adopted five maturity levels as a working hypothesis.

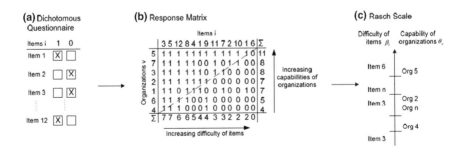

Fig. 3 Schematic principle of the Rasch algorithm (Lahrmann et al., 2011a)

MM evaluation technique

While the success model's validity can be tested empirically by employing quantitative techniques, the MM, as a designed artifact, requires a utility evaluation. An MM is useful if it allows one to measure an organization's maturity in a specific field correctly (necessary condition) and more precisely, more comprehensively, or more efficiently (sufficient conditions) than existing artifacts can. In this section, we discuss whether we met the necessary condition, that is, whether the instrument's assessment is linked to actual organizational performance. For the BI MM, evaluation data was collected using a questionnaire distributed to a community of BI practitioners, and 92 out of 197 participants returned it, for a response rate of 45.7%. We used the data to compute each organization's BI maturity level. We employed a structural equation model to analyze the link between the computed maturity levels and organizational performance. The model relates the output of our BI MM (i.e., the BI maturity level) as an independent variable and three business benefits of BI that we derived from the literature as dependent variables. We used as a basis for our research model a proven instrument for assessing BI's organizational performance that Elbashir et al. (2008) proposed. According to their instrument, the business benefits of BI can be measured on the basis of three key concepts: (1) internal process efficiency benefits, (2) business supplier/partner relationship benefits, and (3) customer intelligence benefits that arise from improved understanding of the customer and the market. These three concepts were also incorporated in our questionnaire. The corresponding items are listed in Table 3.

Using Partial Least Squares (PLS) analysis using the SmartPLS software to validate the model (Ringle, Wende, & Will, 2005), we verified that reliability and validity criteria have been met.[1] We also tested the structural model for the hypothesized paths and found that the research model explained 24.8% of the variance in the dependent variable "internal process efficiency," 15.2% of the variance in "business supplier/partner relations," and 16.0% of the variance in "customer intelligence." All three path coefficients are positive (0.498, 0.390, 0.400, respectively) and significant at $p < 0.001$. Thus, the analysis confirmed that the proposed BI MM, which measures BI maturity in a non-traditional way, is a valid predictor of organizational performance.

---

[1]Cronbach's α exceeds 0.80 for every latent variable, and all composite reliability values are higher than 0.87, which exceeds the requested value of 0.7 (Nunnally & Bernstein, 1994), thus providing strong support for our model's internal consistency and reliability. Furthermore, the item loadings of the indicators are larger than 0.7 (Nunnally & Bernstein, 1994) in all but one case, although the loading of CB4 (0.691) is larger than 0.6 (Bradley, Pridmore, & Byrd, 2006; Hair Jr, Anderson, Tatham, & Black, 1998). Our model exhibits an AVE for at least 0.6 for every latent variable, which satisfies the 0.5 threshold (Chin, 1998) and, together with the item loadings, establishes the research model's convergent validity. As each AVE value is higher than the squared correlations with all other latent variables, the Fornell-Larcker criterion is also met, showing discriminant validity (Fornell & Larcker, 1981). The cross-loadings support this observation, as the correlation of every indicator with its respective latent variable is significantly higher than its correlation with any other latent variable (Chin, 1998; Götz, Liehr-Gobbers, & Krafft, 2010).

Table 3 Measurement instrument for business benefits (Raber et al., 2013b)

Construct	Label	Item (five-point Likert scale: "strongly disagree" to "strongly agree")	Loadings
BI maturity	BIM	BI maturity level based on computations from step 2	1.000
Benefits to internal processes' efficiency	IB1	Improved efficiency of internal processes	0.786
	IB2	Increased staff productivity	0.837
	IB3	Reduction in the cost of effective decision-making	0.794
	IB4	Reduced operational costs	0.742
Benefits to business supplier/partner relationship	SB1	Reduction in the cost of transactions with business partners/suppliers	0.766
	SB2	Improved coordination with business suppliers/partners	0.949
	SB3	Increased responsiveness to/from suppliers	0.924
Benefits to customer intelligence	CB1	Increased revenues	0.787
	CB2	Reduction in lost sales	0.836
	CB3	Increased geographic distribution of sales	0.849
	CB4	Reduced marketing costs	0.691
	CB5	Reduced time-to-market for products/services	0.721

While the underlying measurement instrument is derived from related work in BI and is applicable only in the context of BI, the technique of quantitative analysis of the correlation between "computed" maturity and organizational performance is projectable to all kinds of MMs.

4.2 Instance-Level Artifacts (for the BI Domain)

BI maturity model

The BI MM items, which result from applying the population technique on the basis of the BI success model, are presented in Table 4. Each item is assigned to a maturity level (L), a maturity dimension (individual BI capabilities, operational BI practices, strategic BI practices, BI IT artifact), and an RA score value (logit measure).

By arranging items according to dimension and maturity level, the traditional MM visualization can be derived (Table 5).

Table 4 BI MM items

L	D	Measure	Measurement Item for Capability
5	OP	1.04	Proactive management of data quality
	SP	1.03	Balanced Scorecard for BI management, including quality, cost, and user satisfaction
	SP	1.02	Systematic and comprehensive measurement/management of actual BI use
	SP	0.82	BI steering committee
	SP	0.79	BI strategy updated on a regular basis
4	IC	0.36	Role of IT: Business partner with business lines
	IT	0.53	BI systems provide flexible, proactive analytics functionalities
	OP	0.56	Defined governance and standards for content
	OP	0.55	Development of BI solutions based on a standardized BI-specific process
	OP	0.41	Defined and documented roles for management of data quality
	SP	0.6	Portfolio management for systematic development of BI
	SP	0.4	Value-oriented development of BI (e.g., using business cases)
3	IT	0.2	Standardized definitions of key performance indicators
	IT	0.13	BI systems provide functionalities for ad hoc analyses (OLAP)
	IT	0.13	BI systems provide integration of different frontends, e.g. 'drill-through' from standard reports into OLAP cubes
	OP	0.29	Defined governance and standards for management
	OP	0.21	Central operation of BI applications based on ITIL
	OP	0.18	Defined processes for management of data quality
	OP	0.12	Cost-efficient BI operations
	OP	0.12	BI operations based on well-defined service-level agreements (SLAs)
	OP	0.07	Standardized cost and profit calculation for BI
	SP	0.12	Central, influential sponsor from business
	SP	0.11	BI strategy with focus on technology and tools
	SP	0.04	BI steering committee in IT
	IC	−0.07	Role of IT: Provider of standardized services
	IC	−0.1	Decentralized BI organization in central CIO organization
	IC	−0.13	Centralized BI organization and responsibilities
	IC	−0.26	Balanced mix of central and decentralized organizational units

(continued)

Table 4 (continued)

L	D	Measure	Measurement Item for Capability
	IC	−0.4	Role of IT: Operator of infrastructure
	IT	−0.06	Core business objects are consistently defined for the whole enterprise
	IT	−0.09	Balanced mix of central and decentralized systems based on organizational structure
	IT	−0.11	Standardized definitions for master data
	IT	−0.2	Homogeneity: Use of a few coherent BI tools
	IT	−0.4	BI systems provide static reporting functionalities
	OP	−0.01	Development of BI solutions using agile development methods (e.g., SCRUM)
	OP	−0.05	Defined governance and standards for development
	OP	−0.19	Hybrid development of BI solutions that combine agile development and waterfall methods
	OP	−0.37	Defined governance and standards for operations
	OP	−0.46	Defined governance and standards for tools and applications
	OP	−0.46	Development of BI solutions based on standardized IT process
1	IC	−1.15	Decentralized BI organization and responsibilities
	IT	−0.67	High system availability: No breakdowns, maintenance in well-defined, short time periods
	IT	−0.91	Decentralized, but harmonized systems (e.g., standardized master data)
	IT	−1.1	Decentralized DWH and central enterprise DWH
	OP	−0.84	Central operation of BI applications
	SP	−0.63	Central, influential sponsor from IT
	SP	−1.18	Many decentralized sponsors from IT

IC: individual BI capabilities, OP: operational BI practices, SP: strategic BI practices, IT: BI IT artifact; capabilities are sorted in a descending order according to maturity level, dimension, and logit measure

The evolution of the BI MM takes a clear: Level 1 is characterized by a high degree of decentralism with regard to organization and infrastructure, as there are almost no standardization efforts; the only BI operations that are emphasized are those that represent an early and immature state of BI. Thus, level 1 is titled *initiate*.

Organizations that achieve level 2 are clearly oriented to centrally managed BI in terms of governance and organizational setup. Standardization efforts regarding operations, development, tools, processes, and applications support this development by providing consistent policies and transparency beyond functional borders. The BI infrastructure at this level of maturity is still mainly decentralized but is on the way to a harmonized system landscape. Therefore, we label level 2 *harmonize*.

Table 5 BI MM (traditional representation) (Raber et al. 2012)

	Level 1	Level 2	Level 3	Level 4	Level 5
	Initiate	*Harmonize*	*Integrate*	*Optimize*	*Perpetuate*
Strategy	Decentralized IT-driven BI	Centralized IT-driven BI	Business sponsor, initial BI strategy	BI portfolio management and BI business cases	Comprehensive BI strategy and BI performance management
Social system (organization)	Decentralized, individually acting BI organization	Standardization of operations, tools, applications and development	Centralized with respect to the business model	Well-defined governance and business content	
Technical system (IT)	Decentralized, non-standardized BI infrastructure	Decentralized but harmonized systems	Centralized with respect to the business model	Flexible, proactive analytics	
Quality of service		High availability and proper maintenance	Data and system quality is guaranteed	Cost-efficient BI operations	Proactive management of data quality
Use/impact		Top management and operational use	Specialized analysts	Middle management	

Level 3 of the model is the final step to centralization and integration and an intermediate stage with respect to optimization, so this level is designated *integrate*. A BI steering committee located in IT centrally defines an initial BI strategy that is focused on technology and tools. An enhanced system and data integration, along with standardized definitions of key performance indicators, achieve consistency across functional and system boundaries.

On level 4, organizations realize the full potential of BI and drive advanced topics like BI portfolio management and business cases for BI. Governance is now well-defined, also with regard to content. On the technical side, flexible and proactive analytics are provided to achieve business impact, and management of data quality is improved. We designate this level as *optimize*.

To achieve the highest level of BI maturity, level 5, sustainable and continuous management of BI must be established. This stage of maturity requires that a comprehensive BI strategy be specified and regularly updated and that BI performance management and pro-active data quality management be established. Hence, this stage is designated *perpetuate*.

The five levels describe a learning process that most companies must work through when establishing BI as an organizational capability. Industry- and size-specific variations of this organizational learning process have been designed using the Raber et al.'s (2013a) same meta-level techniques. Using these BI MMs allows the business to assess its current maturity state, to identify a desired state, and to derive capability development paths, thus focusing on "doing the right things" in an appropriate sequence.

BI assessment instrument

The BI maturity assessment instrument is depicted in Table 6.

In a second step, to measure the survey responses against the maturity levels in the core model, ideal maturity profiles—that is, characteristic values—were defined for each maturity level, so we follow a theoretical approach developed by Sabherwal and Chan (2001), which was later adapted by Joachim, Beimborn, and Weitzel (2011) to the context of service orientation. These characteristic values are based on the assumption that BI maturity increases in a linear manner in equidistant steps and on the fact that items are measured using a five-point Likert scale. For example, the ideal maturity profile for level 1 is represented by all items having a rating of 1. In a first application of the Euclidean distance metric, maturity levels for each of an organization's maturity dimensions are calculated. Applying the Euclidean distance metric once more on the basis of dimensional maturity levels yields the organization's overall BI maturity level.

Figure 4 illustrates the results of three exemplary BI maturity assessments using the proposed BI MM and the results of an alternative maturity assessment using in-depth qualitative interviews. The three cases were not chosen arbitrarily but represent companies that have representative characteristics for a very low (1–2), medium (2–4), and high (4–5) BI maturity level, respectively. Not unlike polar sampling, these three cases were chosen to allow for a complementary evaluation of the proposed approach.

In summary, we instantiated our proposed MM construction method and its techniques for two examples of e-wIS—that is, BI and CPM—resulting in two MMs. Only the BI MM has been extended by situational configuration. By providing five distinct levels of BI maturity, our model can help practitioners to focus on "doing the right things" when they work to develop their BI function toward a more mature level by addressing important, dominant problems (Kazanjian, 1988) and temporarily ignoring problems that will become important only in the distant future. In practice, bypassed stages and reverse evolution, though observed, are uncommon (Teo & King, 1997, p. 185). Therefore, the BI MM may enable practitioners to address the multi-faceted design challenges that are inherent in BI and to create realistic plans for the successful evolution of their organization's BI function. This contribution becomes especially valuable in light of recent trends like big data analytics that require a baseline BI organization (i.e., continuous processes for gathering, analyzing, and interpreting data) (Davenport et al., 2012) to be in place. Large organizations in particular often have large amounts of data, but making it available for analytic

Table 6 BI assessment instrument (Raber et al. 2013b)

Maturity Dimension	Item	Five-point Likert scale from (1) "strongly disagree" to (5) "strongly agree"
Strategy	S1	BI is financially supported/led by influential persons from business
	S2	Significant BI decisions are made by a BI steering committee
	S3	BI is based on a comprehensive BI strategy that is regularly updated
IT	I1	Standard reports and dashboards ensure the supply of high-quality information
	I2	Advanced analytical requirements are addressed on the basis of existing OLAP tools and software for proactive analyses
	I3	State-of-the-art BI frontends are used
	I4	BI backend systems are centralized and standardized
	I5	Information is integrated across departmental borders

Clearly defined standards and principles exist in the following areas of BI (average of these five items is used):

Organization	O1	Tools and applications
	O2	Business content (i.e., KPIs and dimensions)
	O3	Management and sourcing processes
	O4	Development processes
	O5	Operations processes

BI applications are used by the following groups of people:

Use	U1	Top management
	U2	Middle management
	U3	Analysts, data scientists
	U4	Operative users

Data quality is ensured by the following means:

Quality	Q1	Roles, tasks, and responsibilities are clearly defined and documented in the context of data quality
	Q2	Core business objects, performance indicators, and dimensions are consistently defined
	Q3	Data quality is continuously measured to manage data quality proactively

BI systems have the following properties:

Quality	Q4	Operation of BI systems is based on defined service-level agreements

(continued)

Table 6 (continued)

Maturity Dimension	Item	Five-point Likert scale from (1) "strongly disagree" to (5) "strongly agree"
	Q5	BI applications are operated on the basis of standards like ITIL

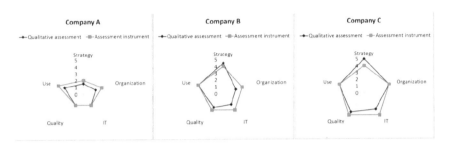

Fig. 4 BIMM-based maturity assessment versus traditional maturity assessment (Raber et al., 2016)

purposes is not a one-off exercise but an organizational learning process that may be guided by the BI MM presented here.

The CPM instantiation was developed in an academic context and in a professional consulting context of providing a KPMG consulting product (KPMG AG, 2011). Beyond the instantiation of the construction method, we also applied the resulting MMs and their assessment instruments in several cases of assessing and benchmarking real-world organizations. Beyond providing insights on the current state of an organization's maturity, these assessments also provide insights on the balance or imbalance of the maturity levels of certain capabilities. Such analysis allowed us to identify *capability gaps*, that is, relatively immature capabilities, as well as *capability profusion*, that is, capabilities that are too mature in the sense that the organization cannot exploit them because it lacks maturity in related capabilities. An example may be a gap between the maturity level of a firm's IT system and its social system. Based on these analyses, we derived recommendations for further development steps of the respective e-wIS.

However, we have not yet validated the utility of the proposed evolution guidance over time.

4.3   Growth of Design Theory

The laps of our design journey took us through several areas in the projectability and tangibility dimensions of design knowledge (Fig. 1) and combined general methods and techniques (MM development method) with multiple levels of instantiation (BI/CPM MM development, BI/CPM MM application/assessment). This multilevel

DSR process was not a linear process since it often focused on the meta level and the instance level in parallel. This data-driven parallel reasoning allowed for a successive extraction of design knowledge that represents a nascent design theory (Gregor & Hevner, 2013)—that is, knowledge as operational principles. While we consistently followed this multilevel approach to DSR, our contribution remains limited to the domains of BI and CPM, as we have not yet fully leveraged the promise of MMs as proven, powerful, and well-accepted tools for IS practitioners (e.g., Benbasat et al., 1980; Galbraith, 1982; Kazanjian & Drazin, 1989) in general. However, by overcoming some of the existing challenges in the context of MM research (cf. Sect. 2.1), we advance the existing state of the art in MM development, especially in respect to grounding (R2 and R6). The BI MM is based on well-established literature on IS success models. Constructs and measures were adapted to the respective domain to serve as a theoretical foundation that is comprehensive and value-oriented. Hence, we leverage theory to develop tools and techniques—that is, the BI MM—for relevant practices. We facilitate empirical MM grounding by pursuing a Rasch-based quantitative MM construction approach.

Going forward, methods for constructing and applying MMs may serve as the foundation for a design theory for the systematic evolution of e-wIS. A key design challenge of e-wIS is the integration of diverse improvement activities into a coherent evolution process (Ward, 2012). MMs have the potential to be a viable means by which to address this challenge. Therefore, we encourage the IS community to investigate methods for the rigorous construction of MMs further that (1) are applicable to a broad class of phenomena (e-wIS), (2) leverage existing theory that describes how IS/IT capabilities contribute to organizational performance, (3) integrate relevant perspectives (based on, e.g., organizational, technical, use-related, and value aspects) into a coherent framework, (4) are designed for a system of IS rather than a single IS, and (5) focus on improvement paths that span a project portfolio rather than on a single project. Selected core components of such a design theory for the systematic evolution of strategic IS based on Gregor and Jones (2007) are shown in Table 7.

Finally, our work reveals a more fundamental DSR question that may need attention. Whereas the deep interaction between Ω and Λ is widely acknowledged, and interrelationships between various types of theory (Gregor, 2006) are discussed in the IS literature, most researchers focus on either Ω or Λ. Peffers et al.'s (2007) widely adopted DSR process illustrates this observation, as it is geared to contributions to Λ on the basis of Ω. However, our work contributes to Ω to provide a basis for contributing to Λ, so we strive for a more balanced contribution to Ω and Λ. The questions concerning whether more balanced contributions may be a fruitful way to advance DSR and whether existing DSR processes should reflect this idea remain. This discussion is not limited to the role of Ω and Λ knowledge in general; it also relates to the use of what may be considered traditional quantitative empirical research methods as parts of a well-grounded, data-driven design process. While the intense use of quantitative techniques to analyze empirical data may blur the lines between descriptive and prescriptive research, we found their application to contribute significantly to the quality of our research outcomes.

Table 7 Selected core components of a design theory for the systematic evolution of e-wIS

Type	Component
Purpose and scope	Provide guidance for the systematic evolution of e-wIS
Constructs	IS capability, organizational performance, maturity level, maturity dimension, assessment instrument
Principle of form and function	A method for the construction of MMs that provide prescriptive information to clarify and advance the evolution of a specific type of e-wIS ("organizational learning")
Testable propositions	By following the prescriptive statements of the method, the approach suggests that MMs for the evolution of e-wIS can be developed that depict evolution paths that, if implemented, will improve organizational performance
Justifying knowledge	The approach can be grounded in existing theory and approaches like the resource-based view (Barney, 1991), stages of growth (Gibson & Nolan, 1974), and IS success models and their underlying theory (Gable et al., 2008; Petter et al., 2008; Sabherwal et al., 2006) The models are based on empirical accounts to calibrate them using current practice in the e-wIS domain
Expository instantiation	Method presented in this paper, artifacts created by the presented methods

5   Key Lessons

Lesson 1: Be open to a composite research methodology. Building and evaluating a complex artifact usually requires a diverse set of activities that use a variety of research approaches. In our experience, a "pure" DSR approach rarely works because, for example, explanatory foundations were insufficient, or descriptive knowledge of use situations was missing. In the case described here, we extended existing (descriptive) success models, applied core solution components (RA) from another domain, used quantitative analyses to populate the MM and to identify maturity levels, and used qualitative analysis to validate our maturity assessments. A dogmatic application of DSR methodology would not have allowed us to cover such diverse research activities. Although the overall research concerns artifact design, a multi-method approach is often needed to cover all relevant research tasks. As a consequence, DSR methodology must often be integrated into descriptive research methods to satisfy a complex design problem, not applied dogmatically.

   Lesson 2: Research components of complex artifacts should be decomposed and integrated. Another challenge of designing complex artifacts in complex organizational settings is that one cannot (and should not) present the entire research process (or even the entire "journey") in a single publication. A single publication in which a complex design process is forced would either exceed reasonable length or be too superficial. A complex artifact design process may even exceed the time and space limitations of a Ph.D. thesis. In fact, design research processes that seek to develop artifacts in complex organizational settings are often emergent.

While cumulative dissertations can help to decompose the overall process into self-contained research components, an overarching structure should be in place to link these projects, contributions by different author teams, and/or research work carried out over long periods of time and over multiple and emerging iterations. We learned that ambitious design projects in real-life settings require a suitable organizational foundation, an appropriate publication strategy, and efficient management of design knowledge to be defined and implemented by the contributing researchers.

Lesson 3: Establish an infrastructure for collaboration with practice. Our third lesson relates to the practice collaboration challenge. Not only does design research need real-life organizations if it is to understand design problems, justify problems' relevance, and evaluate the utility of artifacts, but in complex DSR projects or programs, collaborations with real-life organizations must go far beyond gaining project support or winning a consulting contract with some company. Lengthy preparatory and justificatory activities, emergent iterations, polar design instantiations, and impact/utility assessments usually exceed what a single organization is willing to commit in a letter of intent or even a contract. Not unlike the overarching research-management infrastructure mentioned above, the structure of a collaboration with practice should be in place that ensures, even across organizations and over longer periods of time, sufficient access to data and feedback for complex design projects. It can be helpful to collaborate with a (research) consortium of organizations instead of individual organizations, to work with a consultancy or an industry association, which can provide access to multiple organizations, or to join a network of researchers to address the challenge of collaboration with practice.

References

Ahern, D. M., Clouse, A., & Turner, R. (2003). *Cmmi distilled: A practical introduction to integrated process improvement* (2nd ed.). Boston: Addison-Wesley.

Audzeyeva, A., & Hudson, R. (2015). How to get the most from a business intelligence application during the post implementation Phase&Quest; deep structure transformation at a Uk Retail Bank. *European Journal of Information Systems* (advance online publication), pp. 1–18.

Barney, J. B. (1991). Firm ressources and sustained competitive advantage. *Journal of Management, 17*(1), 99–120.

Becker, J., Knackstedt, R., & Pöppelbuß, J. (2009). Developing maturity models for it management—A procedure model and its application. *Business & Information Systems Engineering, 1*(3), 213–222.

Benbasat, I., Dexter, A. S., Drury, D. H., & Goldstein, R. C. (1984). A critique of the stage hypothesis: Theory and empirical evidence. *Communications of the ACM, 27*(5), 476–485.

Benbasat, I., Dexter, A. S., & Mantha, R. W. (1980). Impact of organizational maturity on information system skill needs. *MIS Quarterly, 4*(1), 21–34.

Benbasat, I., & Zmud, R. W. (2003). The identity crisis within the is discipline—Defining and communicating the discipline's core properties. *MIS Quarterly, 27*(2), 183–194.

Bischoff, S., Aier, S., Haki, K., & Winter, R. (2015). Understanding continuous use of business intelligence systems: A mixed methods investigation. *Journal of Information Technology Theory and Application, 16*(2), 5–38, Article 32.

Boyer, J., Frank, B., Green, B., Harris, T., & Van De Vanter, K. (2010). *Business intelligence strategy—A practical guide for achieving Bi excellence.* Ketchum, ID: MC Press Online.

Bradley, R. V., Pridmore, J. L., & Byrd, T. A. (2006). Information systems success in the context of different corporate cultural types: An empirical investigation. *Journal of Management Information Systems, 23*(2), 267–294.

Brooks, P., El-Gayar, O., & Sarnikar, S. (2013). Towards a Business Intelligence Maturity Model for Healthcare. In *HICSS 46.* Kuala Lumpur, Malaysia: IEEE Computer Society.

Cates, J. E., Gill, S. S., & Zeituny, N. (2005). The ladder of business intelligence (Lobi): A framework for enterprise it planning and architecture. *International Journal of Business Information Systems, 1*(1–2), 220–238.

Chamoni, P., & Gluchowski, P. (2004). Integrationstrends Bei Business-Intelligence-Systemen - Empirische Untersuchung Auf Basis Des Business Intelligence Maturity Model. *Wirtschaftsinformatik, 46*(2), 119–128.

Chin, W. W. (1998). The partial least squares approach to structural equation modeling. In G. A. Marcoulides (Ed.), *Modern methods for business research* (pp. 295–336). Mahwah, NJ: Lawrence Erlbaum Associates.

Chin, W. W., Johnson, N., & Schwarz, A. (2008). A fast form approach to measuring technology acceptance and other constructs. *MIS Quarterly, 32*(4), 687–703.

Chrissis, M. B., Konrad, M., & Shrum, S. (2003). *Cmmi: Guidelines for process integration and product improvement* (2 ed.). Addison-Wesley.

Chuah, M.-H. (2010). An enterprise business intelligence maturity model (Ebimm): Conceptual framework. In *Fifth International Conference on Digital Information Management* (pp. 303–308). IEEE.

Chuah, M.-H., & Wong, K.-L. (2011). A review of business intelligence and its maturity models. *African Journal of Business Management, 5*(9), 3424–3428.

Chuah, M.-H., & Wong, K.-L. (2012). A framework for accessing an enterprise business intelligence maturity model (Ebi2m): Delphi study approach. *African Journal of Business Management, 6*(23), 6880–6889.

Conwell, C. L., Enright, R., & Stutzman, M. A. (2000). Capability Maturity Models Support of Modeling and Simulation Verification, Validation, and Accreditation. In *2000 Winter Simulation Conference* (pp. 819–828). Orlando, FL.

Cosic, R., Shanks, G., & Maynard, S. (2012). Towards a business analytics capability maturity model. In *ACIS 2012.* Geelong, Australia.

Crawford, J. K. (2006). The project management maturity model. *Information Systems Management, 23*(4), 50–58.

Curtis, B., Hefley, W. E., & Miller, S. A. (2010). *The people capability maturity model—Guidelines for improving the workforce* (2nd ed.). Boston, MA: Addison-Wesley.

Davenport, T. H., Barth, P., and Bean, R. 2012. "How 'Big Data' Is Different," *MIT Sloan Management Review, 54*(1).

Davenport, T. H., Harris, J. G., & Morison, R. (2010). *Analytics at work: Smarter decisions, better results.* Boston: Harvard Business Press.

de Bruin, T., Rosemann, M., Freeze, R., & Kulkarni, U. (2005). Understanding the Main Phases of Developing a Maturity Assessment Model. In B. Campbell, J.-Underwood, & D. Bunker (Eds.), *16th Australasian Conference on Information Systems (ACIS 2005)* (pp. 1–10). Sydney, Australia: University of Technology Sydney.

Dekleva, S., & Drehmer, D. (1997). Measuring software engineering evolution: A Rasch calibration. *Information Systems Research, 8*(1), 95–104.

DeLone, W. H., & McLean, E. R. (1992). Information systems success—The quest for the dependent variable. *Information System Research, 3*(1), 60–95.

DeLone, W. H., & McLean, E. R. (2003). The Delone and Mclean model of information systems success—A ten-year update. *Journal of Management Information Systems, 19*(4), 9–30.

Deng, X., & Chi, L. (2013). Understanding postadoptive behaviors in information systems use: A longitudinal analysis of system use problems in the business intelligence context. *Journal of Management Information Systems, 29*(3), 291–325.

Doherty, N. F., & Terry, M. (2009). The role of is capabilities in delivering sustainable improvements to competitive positioning. *The Journal of Strategic Information Systems, 18*(2), 100–116.

Eckerson, W. W. (2004). Gauge your data warehouse maturity. *DM Review, 14*(11), 34.

Eckerson, W. W. (2009). Tdwi's business intelligence maturity model. In Chatsworth.

Elbashir, M. Z., Collier, P. A., & Davern, M. J. (2008). Measuring the effects of business intelligence systems: The relationship between business process and organizational performance. *International Journal of Accounting Information Systems, 9*(3), 135–153.

Fisher, T. (2005). How mature is your data management environment? *Business Intelligence Journal, 10*(3), 20–26.

Fornell, C., & Larcker, D. (1981). Evaluating structural equation models with unobservable variables and measurement error. *Journal of Marketing Research, 18*(1), 39–50.

Gable, G. G., Sedera, D., & Chan, T. (2008). Re-conceptualizing information system success: The Is-impact measurement model. *Journal of the Association for Information Systems, 9*(7), 377–408.

Galbraith, J. (1982). The stages of growth. *Journal of Business Strategy, 3*(1), 70–79.

Gibson, C. F., & Nolan, R. L. (1974). Managing the four stages of Edp growth. *Harvard Business Review, 52*(1), 76–88.

Goldkuhl, G. (2004). Design theories in information systems—A need for multi-grounding. *Journal of Information Technology Theory and Application, 6*(2), 59–72.

Götz, O., Liehr-Gobbers, K., & Krafft, M. (2010). Evaluation of structural equation models using the partial least squares (Pls) approach. In V. E. Vinzi, W. W. Chin, J. Henseler, & H. Wang (Eds.), *Handbook of partial least squares: Concepts, methods and applications* (pp. 691–711). Heidelberg: Springer.

Gregor, S. (2006). The nature of theory in information systems. *MIS Quarterly, 30*(3), 611–642.

Gregor, S., & Hevner, A. R. (2013). Positioning and presenting design science research for maximum impact. *MIS Quarterly, 37*(2), 337–355.

Gregor, S., & Jones, D. (2007). The anatomy of a design theory. *Journal of the Association for Information Systems, 8*(5), 312–335.

Hair, J. F., Jr., Anderson, R. E., Tatham, R. L., & Black, W. C. (1998). *Multivariate data analysis.* Upper Saddle River: Prentice Hall.

Haki, M. K., Aier, S., & Winter, R. (2016). A stakeholder perspective to study Enterprisewide is initiatives. In *24th European Conference on Information Systems (ECIS)*. Istanbul, Turkey.

Hatcher, D., & Prentice, B. (2004). The evolution of information management. *Business Intelligence Journal, 9*(2), 49–56.

Henschen, D. (2007). Hp Touts Neoview win, banking solution, Bi maturity model. *Intelligent Enterprise, 10*(10), 9.

Hewlett, P. (2009). *The Hp business intelligence maturity model: Describing the Bi journey.* Hewlett-Packard Development Company L.P.

Humphrey, W. S. (1988). Characterizing the software process: A maturity framework. *IEEE Software, 5*(2), 73–79.

Jiang, J., Klein, G., Hwang, H.-G., Huang, J., & Hung, S.-Y. (2004). An exploration of the relationship between software development process maturity and project performance. *Information and Management, 41*(3), 279–288.

Joachim, N., Beimborn, D., & Weitzel, T. (2011). An instrument for measuring Soa maturity. *ICIS 2011*.

Kazanjian, R. K. (1988). Relation of dominant problems to stages growth in technology-based new ventures. *Academy of Management Journal, 31*(2), 257–279.

Kazanjian, R. K., & Drazin, R. (1989). An empirical test of a stage of growth progression model. *Management Science, 35*(12), 1489–1503.

KPMG AG. (2011). *Reifegradmodelle Im Corporate Performance Management.* Zurich.

Kuechler, B., & Vaishnavi, V. K. (2008). Theory development in design science research: Anatomy of a research project. In V. K. Vaishnavi & R. Baskerville (Eds.), *Third International Conference on Design Science Research in Information Systems and Technology* (pp. 1–15). Atlanta.

Lahrmann, G., Marx, F., Winter, R., & Wortmann, F. (2010). Business intelligence maturity models: an overview. In A. D'Atri, M. Ferrara, J. F. George & P. Spagnoletti (Eds.), *VII Conference of the Italian Chapter of AIS (itAIS 2010)*. Naples, Italy: Italian Chapter of AIS.

Lahrmann, G., Marx, F., Mettler, T., Winter, R., & Wortmann, F. (2011a). Inductive design of maturity models: Applying the Rasch algorithm for design science research. In H. Jain, A. P. Sinha & P. Vitharana (Eds.), *Proceeding DESRIST 2011* (pp. 176–191). Springer.

Lahrmann, G., Marx, F., Winter, R., & Wortmann, F. (2011b). Business intelligence maturity: development and evaluation of a theoretical model. In R. H. Sprague (Ed.), *Forty-Forth Annual Hawaii International Conference on System Sciences (HICSS-44)*. Koloa, Kaua'i, Hawaii: IEEE Computer Society.

Luftman, J. N., & Ben-Zvi, T. (2010). Key issues for it executives 2009. *MISQ Executive, 9*(1), 49–59.

Luftman, J., Zadeh, H. S., Derksen, B., Santana, M., Rigoni, E. H., & Huang, Z. D. (2013). Key information technology and management issues 2012–2013: An international study. *Journal of Information Technology, 28*(4), 354–366.

Lukman, T., Hackney, R., Popovic, A., Jaklic, J., & Irani, Z. (2011). Business intelligence maturity: The economic transitional context within slovenia. *Information Systems Management, 28*(3), 211–222.

Marx, F., Lahrmann, G., & Winter, R. (2010). Aligning corporate planning and Bi: Towards a combined maturity model. In A. D'Atri, M. Ferrara, J.F. George & P. Spagnoletti (Eds.), *VII Conference of the Italian Chapter of AIS (itAIS 2010)*. Naples, Italy.

Marx, F., Wortmann, F., & Mayer, J. H. (2012). A maturity model for management control systems—Five evolutionary steps to guide development. *Business & Information Systems Engineering, 4*(4), 193–207.

McCormack, K., Willems, J., van den Bergh, J., Deschoolmeester, D., Willaert, P., Štemberger, M. I., et al. (2009). A global investigation of key turning points in business process maturity. *Business Process Management Journal, 15*(5), 792–815.

McDonald, M. P., & Aron, D. (2010). *Leading in times of transition: The 2010 Cio agenda.* Stamford: Gartner.

Mettler, T. (2010). *Supply Management Im Krankenhaus: Konstruktion Und Evaluation Eines Konfigurierbaren Reifegradmodells Zur Zielgerichteten Gestaltung.* Gallen: Institut für Wirtschaftsinformatik/Universität St.

Mettler, T., & Rohner, P. (2009). Situational maturity models as instrumental artifacts for organizational design. In *4th International Conference on Design Science Research in Information Systems and Technology (DESRIST 2009)*, Philadelphia, PA: Association for Computing Machinery, p. 9.

Mokyr, J. (2002). The gifts of athena: Historical origins of the knowledge economy. Princeton, NJ: Princeton University Press.

Negash, S., & Gray, P. (2008). Business Intelligence. In F. Burstein & C. W. Holsapple (Eds.), *Handbook on decision support systems 2* (pp. 175–193). Berlin, Heidelberg: Springer.

Nolan, R. L. (1973). Managing the computer resource: A stage hypothesis. *Communications of the ACM, 16*(7), 399–405.

Nunamaker, J. F., Jr., Chen, M., & Purdin, T. D. M. (1991). Systems development in information systems research. *Journal of Management Information Systems, 7*(3), 89–106.

Nunnally, J. C., & Bernstein, I. H. (1994). *Psychometric theory* (3rd ed.). New York: McGraw-Hill.

Ocu. (2013). *Maturity model for institutional intelligence V1.0.* Madrid, Spain: Oficina de Cooperación Universitaria.

Ong, I. L., Siew, P. H., & Wong, S. F. (2011). Assessing organizational business intelligence maturity. In *ICIMU 2011*. Kuala Lumpur, Malaysia.

Paulk, M. C., Curtis, B., Chrissis, M. B., & Weber, C. V. (1993). Capability maturity model, Version 1.1. *IEEE Software, 10*(4), 18–27.

Paulzen, O., Doumi, M., Perc, P., & Cereijo-Roibas, A. (2002). A maturity model for quality improvement in knowledge management. In *ACIS 2002*. Melbourne, Australia.

Peffers, K., Tuunanen, T., Rothenberger, M., & Chatterjee, S. (2007). A design science research methodology for information systems research. *Journal of Management Information Systems, 24*(3), 45–77.

Petter, S., DeLone, W., & McLean, E. (2008). Measuring information systems success: Models, dimensions, measures, and interrelationships. *European Journal of Information Systems, 17,* 236–263.

Phan, D. (2001). Software quality and management: How the world's most powerful software makers do it. *Information Systems Management, 18*(1), 56–67.

Poeppelbuss, J., Niehaves, B., Simons, A., & Becker, J. (2011). Maturity models in information systems research: Literature search and analysis. *Communications of the Association for Information Systems, 29*(1), 505–532.

Popovic, A., Coelho, P. S., & Jaklič, J. (2009). The impact of business intelligence system maturity on information quality. *Information Research, 14,* 4).

Raber, D., Epple, J., Rothenberger, M., & Winter, R. (2016). Closing the Loop: Evaluating a Measurement Instrument for Maturity Model Design. In T. X. Bui & R. H. Sprague (Eds.), *49th Hawaii International Conference on System Sciences* (pp. 4444–4453). IEEE.

Raber, D., Winter, R., & Wortmann, F. (2012). *Using quantitative analyses to construct a capability maturity model for business intelligence* (pp. 4219–4228). Grand Wailea, Maui: IEEE Computer Society.

Raber, D., Wortmann, F., & Winter, R. (2013a). *Situational business intelligence maturity models: An exploratory analysis* (pp. 3797–3806). Wailea, HI: IEEE Computer Society.

Raber, D., Wortmann, F., & Winter, R. (2013b). Towards the measurement of business intelligence maturity. In *European Conference on Information Systems 2013*. Utrecht.

Ramasubbu, N., Mithas, S., Krishnan, M. S., & Kemerer, C. F. (2008). Work dispersion, process-based learning, and offshore software development performance. *MIS Quarterly, 32*(2), 437–458.

Rayner, N., & Schlegel, K. (2008). *Maturity model overview for business intelligence and performance management*. Stamford: Gartner.

Richardson, J., & Bitterer, A. (2010). *Findings: The risks of losing faith in Bi*. Stamford: Gartner.

Ringle, C., Wende, S., & Will, A. (2005). *Smartpls 2.0*. Hamburg: University of Hamburg.

Rosemann, M., & De Bruin, T. (2005). Towards a business process management maturity model. In D. Bartmann, F. Rajola, J. Kallinikos, D. Avison, R. Winter, P. Ein-Dor, J. Becker, F. Bodendorf, & C. R. G. Weinhardt (Eds.), *Thirteenth European Conference On Information Systems (Ecis2005)*. Regensburg.

Sabherwal, R., & Chan, Y. E. (2001). Alignment between business and is strategies: A study of prospectors, analyzers, and defenders. *Information Systems Research, 12*(1), 11–33.

Sabherwal, R., Jeyaraj, A., & Chowa, C. (2006). Information system success: Individual and organizational determinants. *Management Science, 52*(12), 1849–1864.

Sacu, C. (2010). *Dwcmm: The data warehouse capability maturity model*. Utrecht University.

Sacu, C., & Spruit, M. (2010). Bidm—The business intelligence development model. In *12th International Conference on Enterprise Information Systems*. SciTePress.

Sas Institute. (2009). Information evolution model. Retrieved May 2, 2013, from http://www.sas.com/software/iem/.

Schulze, K.-D., Besbak, U., Dinter, B., Overmeyer, A., Schulz-Sacharow, C., & Stenzel, E. (2009). *Business intelligence-studie 2009*. Hamburg: Steria Mummert Consulting AG.

Seddon, P. B. (1997). A respecification and extension of the Delone and Mclean model of is success. *Information Systems Research, 8*(3), 240–253.

Sen, A., Ramamurthy, K., & Sinha, A. P. (2011). A model of data warehousing process maturity. *IEEE Transactions on Software Engineering* (99).

Sen, A., Sinha, A. P., & Ramamurthy, K. (2006). Data warehousing process maturity: an exploratory study of factors influencing user perceptions. *IEEE Transactions on Engineering Management, 53*(3), 440–455.

Solli-Sæther, H., & Gottschalk, P. (2010). The modeling process for stage models. *Journal of Organizational Computing and Electronic Commerce, 20*(3), 279–293.

Tan, C.-S., Sim, Y.-W., & Yeoh, W. (2011). A maturity model of enterprise business intelligence. *Communications of the IBIMA, 2011,* 1–11.

Teo, T. S. H., & King, W. R. (1997). Integration between business planning and information systems planning: An evolutionary-contingency perspective. *Journal of Management Information Systems, 14*(1), 185–214.

Töpfer, J. (2008). Active Enterprise Intelligence. In J. Töpfer & R. Winter (Eds.), *Active enterprise intelligence* (pp. 1–28). Berlin, Heidelberg: Springer.

Vierkorn, S., & Friedrich, D. (2008). *Organization of business intelligence.* Würzburg: BARC Institute.

Ward, J. M. (2012). Information systems strategy: Quo Vadis? *Journal of Strategic Information Systems, 21*(2), 165–171.

Watson, H. J., Ariyachandra, T. R., & Matyska, R. J., Jr. (2001). Data warehousing stages of growth. *Information Systems Management, 18*(3), 42–50.

Williams, S., & Williams, N. (2007). *The profit impact of business intelligence.* San Francisco, CA: Morgan Kaufmann.

Wixom, B. H., & Watson, H. J. (2001). An empirical investigation of the factors affecting data warehousing success. *MIS Quarterly, 25*(1), 17–41.

Wixom, B. H., & Watson, H. J. (2010). The Bi-based organization. *International Journal of Business Intelligence Research, 1*(1), 13–28.

A Design Science Approach to Implementing Flow-Based Information Systems Development (ISD)

Kieran Conboy, Denis Dennehy, and Rob Gleasure

Abstract While organizations are seeking new approaches to improving system development, methods are often designed and tailored in a less than rigorous manner. There is a tendency to blindly adopt the latest fad in methodology and to measure success in terms of adherence to these methods without understanding why they are better or how they create value. Principles, practices, and tools are often introduced without explaining what to expect from these new methods or considering their limits. The project's over-arching goal was to use a design science research (DSR) approach to systems development design to encourage a move toward a more evidence-based assessment of these methods. The study's artifacts were flow tools and practices customized and redesigned in TechCo, rather than new artifacts that were develop and are unavailable elsewhere. We found that DSR addressed the problem, at least in part, by forcing academic and industry participants to expand on 'satisficed' secondary knowledge and engage with ambiguities head on. (i) Apply DSR-appropriate standards of rigour to evaluating information systems development (ISD) methods; (ii) design and evaluate ISD methods before ISD method components; (iii) design clear and discriminatory metrics for ISD methods; (iv) consider temporal issues when designing and evaluating ISD methods; and (v) be wary of self-referencing metrics when evaluating ISD methods. More fundamentally, we found that both academic and industry participants were operating under evolving conditions of bounded rationality.

K. Conboy (✉) · D. Dennehy
Lero | Irish Software Research Centre, NUI Galway, Galway, Ireland
e-mail: kieran.conboy@nuigalway.ie

D. Dennehy
e-mail: denis.dennehy@nuigalway.ie

R. Gleasure
Copenhagen Business School, Frederiksberg, Denmark
e-mail: rg.digi@cbs.dk

© Springer Nature Switzerland AG 2020
J. vom Brocke et al. (eds.), *Design Science Research. Cases*, Progress in IS,
https://doi.org/10.1007/978-3-030-46781-4_5

1 Introduction

Information systems research in recent years has seen an elevated focus on design science research (DSR) (Akoka, Comyn-Wattiau, Prat, & Storey, 2017; Hevner & Chatterjee, 2010; Rai, 2017; Tremblay, Hevner, & Berndt, 2010; Venable, Pries-Heje, & Baskerville, 2016), e.g. DESRIST (Goldkuhl, Ågerfalk, & Sjöström, 2017), EDSS Design Science Symposium (Helfert, Donnellan, & Kenneally, 2014; Helfert & Donnellan, 2013), and journal publications (Gill & Hevner, 2013; Gregor & Hevner, 2013; Hevner & Chatterjee, 2010) on the topic.

DSR's technical focus means artifacts are often studied in highly controlled environments, such that the behavioural impact of different configurations can be reliably isolated (Rothenberger & Kuechler, 2012; Sonnenberg & vom Brocke, 2012; Venable et al., 2016). However, this tendency threatens to obscure the practical learning that occurs when seemingly robust and standardized artifacts are introduced into complex real-world environments. This study examines the large-scale deployment of one such set of robust and standardized artifacts—specifically 'flow'-based systems-development tools–extending the design science perspective deeper into the practical integration process. Several motivations led to this choice of topic.

A move toward a more evidence-based assessment of systems-development methods generally:

In essence, DSR helps designers (a) know why they expect a design to work and (b) evaluate whether that design actually works (McKay, Marshall, & Hirschheim, 2012). These tenets are particularly relevant to information systems development (ISD), where there is a well-established to ignore both and blindly adopt the latest fad methods instead, without understanding why they are better or how they add value (Agerfalk et al., 2005; Conboy, 2009), success is measured as adherence to the method (Conboy, 2009). This cycle has been evident over the last forty years, from waterfall methods to RAD to lean to a whole family of agile methods, including Scrum, XP, and more recently continuous development and flow.[1] However, reporting on the effectiveness of these methods has relied largely on anecdotal evidence and rhetorical arguments (Lee & Xia, 2010; Vidgen & Wang, 2009). One problem of such blind adherence is the potential to discourage ISD process improvement (Conboy, 2009).

An alternative to blind adoption of a method based on anecdotal evidence is one that is more evidence- and value-based (Agerfalk and Fitzgerald, 2005; Lindstrom and Jeffries, 2004). Rather than assessing adherence to a pre-defined commercial method, one assesses the value afforded by any practice or set of practices whether the practice adheres to a commercially labelled method or not. A DSR approach can

---

[1]The term 'flow' is distinct from the psychological state of flow identified by Csikszentmihalyi (1975, 1991), as the former is rooted in lean manufacturing and the latter is associated with an optimal balance between challenge and competence. In this study, flow refers to how work progresses through a system such that 'good' flow describes a system in which work moves through steadily and predictably, and 'bad' flow describes a system in which work stops and starts frequently.

provide such a structured, rigorous, and evidence-based analysis. In fact, one of the rationales that underpinned the emergence of DSR was the desire to move design knowledge beyond the level of a 'craft' without more deliberate theoretical analysis (Gregor and Jones, 2007).

An evaluation of flow methods specifically:

Flow methods are widely regarded as the next generation of agile methods. While there is evidence to suggest that the use and effectiveness of flow methods is becoming prevalent in practice (Anderson, 2013; Dennehy & Conboy, 2017; Nord, Ozkaya, &Sangwan, 2012; Petersen & Wohlin, 2011; Power & Conboy, 2015; Reinertsen, 2009), they suffer from many of the issues described above, and whether the deeper motivations for using flow tools are well understood and whether flow tools are being leveraged effectively toward that deeper motivation is not clear:

- *Rarely do any two flow papers adopt the same definition of flow or flow methods:* People use 'flow' to refer to very different phenomena (e.g. Anderson & Roock, 2011; Leffingwell, 2010; Shalloway, 2011). To state that a particular method does or does not induce flow is almost meaningless, given the lack of consensus regarding what the term refers to.
- *Flow has many methods, variants, and derivatives*: It is not the number of methods that causes a problem but that they are so disparate. Some represent prescriptive operational instructions for developers (i.e. Ahmad, Dennehy, Conboy and Oivo, 2018; Al-baik & Miller, 2015), some bear closer resemblance to project management methods than to ISD methods, and some can best be described as sets of philosophical principles (i.e. Poppendieck's Lean Software Development). These methods can even be contradictory. For example, Orzen and Bell (2016) advocate the "elimination of variation," while Reinertsen (2009) requires "variation exploitation." While it is inevitable that those who create methods will have their own ideas on how flow can be achieved, completely conflicting, polar opposite advice given to ISD teams can be challenging and confusing (Harb, Noteboom, & Sarnikar, 2015).
- *Focus on single flow artifacts:* The existing body of knowledge on flow is limited because most studies only focus attention on a specific flow artifact or do not consider that the flow artifacts must operate in an unpredictable, multifaceted, social, and context-laden environment (Dennehy & Conboy, 2017; Lyytinen & Rose, 2006; Olerup, 1991; Wastell & Newman, 1993). This limitation is particularly concerning in this study, as flow practices are not isolated activities but are influenced by other activities and other changes in their environment.

Therefore, an evidence-based DSR approach can help designers evaluate the design and impact of flow methods. The next section, which describes the context of the design research in more detail, is followed by a description of the 'journey' and the results. The chapter then concludes with the lessons learned from the study.

2 The Context

Flow is part of the next generation of agile methods and is proving to be a catalyst for increasing agility and scale, especially in knowledge-intensive work activities like software project management (Anderson, 2010; Petersen & Wohlin, 2011; Power & Conboy, 2015; Reinertsen, 2009). Flow refers to managing a continuous and smooth flow of value-creating activities throughout the software-development process (Anderson, 2010; Petersen & Wohlin, 2011; Poppendieck and Poppendieck, 2003; Reinertsen, 2009) and emphasizes the continuous movement of valuable work, rather than a sequence of discrete activities performed by distinct teams or departments (Fitzgerald & Stol, 2014). That flow focuses on managing queues, rather than managing timelines and project phases or simple waste elimination, makes it distinct from traditional project management (Anderson, 2013; Anderson, Concas, Lunesu, & Marchesi, 2011; Power & Conboy, 2015). While cognizant of the limitations of drawing comparisons between methods, previous analysis by Kniberg and Skarin (2010) lends to a list of the differences between flow and Scrum methods (Table 1).

Although use of the flow method is gaining momentum in the IS community, it is important to establish how flow brings agile methods to the next level, as the need for a rigorous research approach to understanding the adaptability and extension of agile methods like flow is cited as a significant gap in the current body of knowledge (Conboy, 2009; Dybå & Dingsøyr, 2008).

Case Exemplar

The context of this study is the European headquarters for TechCo,[2] Ireland. TechCo is an industry leader in technology solutions services and support; its global workforce exceeds 140,000 people, of which 1,300 are located at the European headquarters. In response to the competitive global IT market, customers' continuously changing needs, and a commitment to a continuous software delivery process while also reducing waste in the software development life-cycle, directors at the Irish campus were keen to demonstrate that the IT division was delivering value to the organization and its customers. This response required TechCo to undertake a planned digital transformation and modernization of infrastructure, along with a workforce transformation. As part of this transformation, the company decided in 2015 to introduce flow-based systems development tools to assist ISD processes in the European headquarters. The introduction of flow tools and metrics took place over an eighteen-month period, from March 2016 to September 2017. To be clear, the artifacts in this study were customized versions of flow tools that were available and used in other organizations, rather than having been developed as new tools. The roles and experience of the management and four software teams that participated are shown in Table 2.

---

[2]TechCo is a pseudonym used to protect the organization's anonymity.

Table 1 Differences between flow and scrum

Flow	Scrum	Literature sources
Work is pulled through the system as individual work items	Work is pulled through the system in small batches	Power and Conboy (2015, p. 2)
The cadence is continuous flow (with time-boxed iterations optional)	Cadence is based on time-boxed iterations (2–4-week sprints)	Kniberg and Skarin (2010)
Work-in-progress limits are explicit	Work-in-progress limits are implicit	(Reinertsen, 2009; Versionone, 2016)
Roles are required but roles, rather than the method, are prescribed by the team	Prescribed roles: product owner, Scrum master, development team	(Kniberg and Skarin, 2010; Versionone, 2016)
Kanban board is used to visualize work states and is in continuous use	Scrumban board is optional and is reset at the end of a sprint	(Birkeland, 2010; Reinertsen, 2009)
A cross-functional team is optional (Specialist teams are permitted)	Cross-functional teams are prescribed	(Kniberg and Skarin, 2010; Versionone, 2016)
The size of work items can vary, as there is no rule that items must be completed within specific time boxes	The size of work items is based on the size that will fit a sprint (i.e. two-week sprint)	(Birkeland, 2010; Kniberg and Skarin, 2010)
The release methodology is at the team's discretion	The release methodology is to release at the end of each sprint, if approved by the product owner	(Kniberg and Skarin, 2010)
Lead time is the default metric for planning and process improvement	Velocity is the default metric for planning and process improvement	(Birkeland, 2010)
No specific chart is prescribed (A cumulative flow diagram is usually the default chart)	Burndown chart is prescribed	(Cocco, Mannaro, Concas, & Marchesi, 2011; Versionone, 2016)

TechCo had been using the Waterfall software development method but had recently adopted an agile approach by using the Scrum methodology in two-week sprints. However, management viewed flow as a catalyst for continuous software delivery.

3 The Journey

This chapter begins by examining the use of design science in an uncertain, turbulent environment. The 'journey' described in this study is then presented in two distinct 'laps', the first of which presents the management view of the problem and solution

Table 2 Users of flow artifacts

Group	Role	Years of ISD experience
Management	IT director	25
	Portfolio manager	30
	Financial controller	21
	Systems integration manager	20
	Software developer/consultant	18
	IT delivery manager	16
	Senior business analyst	12
Team 1	Project manager	15
	Software developer	12
	Software developer	2
Team 2	Project manager	15
	Software developer	2
	Software tester	3
Team 3	Project manager	21
	Software tester	2
Team 4	Project manager	12
	Software developer	15
	Software developer	2

regarding the use and effectiveness of the flow method applied in TechCo. The second then provides the 'shared' view and understanding.

The rapid emergence and evolution of design science discourse coincides with a time in which technology itself is rapidly changing more quickly than ever before. As a result, there is an insatiable appetite for technology that not only responds to change but can predict such change and shape the future environment around it (Fan & Gordon, 2014; Gleick, 1999; Kamel, Boulos, Sanfilippo, Corley, & Wheeler, 2010; Siegel & Davenport, 2013). This rapid pace of change makes it impossible to maintain an understanding of contemporary technological developments that is both broad and deep. Instead, individuals are increasingly pushed to balance deep specialized knowledge with an ability to collaborate with others who have complementary specializations (Malone, Laubscher, & Johns, 2011; Narayanan, Balasubramanian, & Swaminathan, 2009). This specialization creates conditions in which individuals' information searches are limited by the practical constraints of time, cognitive ability, and information availability that typically lend themselves to a 'bounded rationality' (Arthur, 1994; Simon, 1991).

Bounded rationality describes the scenario in which individuals do not look for optimal solutions based on complete understanding but look for solutions or levels of understanding that are 'good enough' to allow some other problem to become a

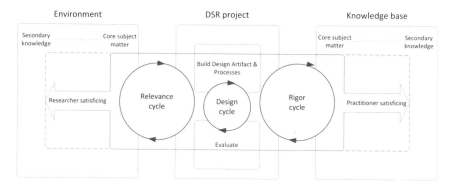

Fig. 1 Three-cycle view of 'saticificing' (Hevner, 2007)

priority (Simon, 1972, 1982). Thus, the goal is often to 'satisfice' during problem-solving, rather than to spend excessive time and effort optimizing some subset of the problems faced, with diminishing returns (Gigerenzer & Goldstein, 1996; Kahneman, 2003). This approach has meaningful implications for both design science researchers and the practitioners with whom they collaborate. For design science researchers, the speed of technological change creates a practical cut-off in terms of the technical and operational details of new tools and practices, yet they must maintain sufficient knowledge to add meaningful value to projects and create insightful, reusable abstractions. For practitioners, the increasing depth and breadth of methodological development in DSR means they cannot stay up to date with the entire spectrum of the growing literature, but they must maintain sufficient knowledge to understand the role of the researchers and what is needed to accommodate them and generate value from their participation. Thus, each must balance a keen interest in core subject matter with incomplete but sufficient grasp of supporting operational/technical knowledge (for design science researchers) and supporting theoretical/methodological knowledge (for practitioners), see Fig. 1.

3.1 Lap 1—Management View of the Problem and Solution

Understanding the problem: The motivation for adopting a new ISD method was based on recurring issues in the ISD process. The initial problems, as management understood them, included: (i) lack of operational visibility of the work being conducted by project teams; (ii) lack of resource visibility for managers; (iii) a perception that project estimating, particularly when planning sprints, was ad hoc and frequently inconsistent; (iv) excessive, unplanned overtime in advance of the monthly release of software; and (v) a 'corrupted' use of the Scrum method.

Understanding the solutions: The initial solution set required designing and developing flow artifacts that would enable managers and project teams to understand and manage flow across projects. These flow artifacts consisted of four commonly known tools: value stream maps, Kanban boards, cumulative flow diagrams (CFDs), and burndown charts (Petersen, Roos, Nyström, & Runeson, 2014).

Value stream mapping: Value stream mapping is used to follow a specified item of work through the ISD process to establish the value added in each processing step (Petersen et al., 2014). Value stream maps have been applied to the context of software development to reduce lead time (Mujtaba, Feldt, & Petersen, 2010) and identify value from the financial perspective and those of the customer, the internal business process, and innovation and learning (Khurum, Petersen, & Gorschek, 2014). The value stream map is the starting point in understanding the ISD flow process.

Kanban board: The Kanban board uses a coded card system to represent the states of workflow (Planned, In Progress, Done) as work (i.e. software code) moves through the ISD process (Anderson, 2013; Petersen et al., 2014; Power & Conboy, 2015). These cards enable team members to observe work in progress, to assign their own tasks, and to complete work without direction from a manager (Anderson, 2010). Explicit work-in-progress (WIP) limits are used to manage the quantity of work in progress at any stage in the workflow, and explicit policies, frequently called 'entry criteria' and 'exit criteria,' determine when a work item can be pulled from one state to another (Power, 2014). Kanban boards can be physical (e.g. mounted on a wall) or digital (e.g. embedded within a code management tool). The work states represented on the Kanban board are based on the processes identified in the value stream map.

Cumulative Flow Diagram (CFD): CFDs, which show the amount of work in each of the work states, are useful in understanding the behaviour of queues and diagnosing problems (Power, 2014; Reinertsen, 2009). Rooted in queuing theory, CFDs are another tool that is used to visualize and manage workflow states, as they represent the same work states that are represented in the Kanban board.

Burndown chart: A burndown chart is used to show the amount of work that was planned to be completed within a certain time period (i.e. one month) and the work that has actually been completed (Kniberg & Skarin, 2010; Petersen et al., 2014). Embedded in a code-management tool, the burndown chart provides an aggregated view of the combined work states.

Complementary to the flow artifacts are three key metrics that are used to understand and manage the flow of work in ISD practices (see Table 3).

Metrics in flow-based product development are used to understand the inputs, processes, outputs, and outcomes that are related to the flow of work and its impediments.

Table 3 Metrics used to manage flow (Power & Conboy, 2015; Reinertsen, 2009)

Metrics	Description
Cycle time	Shows how long individual work items spend in each workflow state. Used to determine how work flows through individual work states or combinations of work states
Lead time	Shows how long it takes for individual work items to move through a system, from initial request to delivery to the end-user
Throughput rate	Reveals the rate of work through the system over time and, when combined with demand analysis, shows how much work is value demand (e.g. customer requests something new, such as a new product feature) versus failure demand (e.g. when a product or product feature does not meet the customer's needs and generates additional work)

3.2 Lap 2—A Shared Understanding of the Problem and Solution

Understanding the problem: Unforeseen problems that emerged from the initial engagements with management included: (i) a need to create mutual understanding between software teams and business units; (ii) a lack of value-based understanding of ISD methods, which resulted in over-emphasis on adherence; (iii) a lack of competency to shift from textbook, 'vanilla' versions of flow tools to customized artifacts that fit the needs of management and project teams; and (iv) a lack of in-depth understanding of how to use and interpret flow tools and metrics in their natural context.

Understanding the solutions: Unforeseen problems emerged from the research team's more than 200 h of direct observations (i.e. daily stand-up meetings, project reviews) and participant observations (i.e. design and use of flow tools) with the four teams during the same period. These observations enabled the researchers to determine whether there was any misalignment between the 'official' view of flow artifacts and the actual case (Robinson, Segal, & Sharp, 2007) and to reflect on the use of DSR given these observations. The research team also facilitated five days of flow-oriented workshops for members of the management and software teams in which the implementation challenges and existing or potential congruencies were discussed and evaluated. Attendees from TechCo were also able to engage with practitioners from organizations of similar size that were more advanced in the use of flow tools. This engagement was particularly useful, as there was a mindset among project team members that TechCo was too large and complex for ISD flow to work effectively.

4 The Results

4.1 Presentation of Artifact(S)

Two sets of tools were introduced to satisfy the interrelated demands for customized tools and shared understanding. For the shared understanding, five discussion canvases were introduced to encourage participants to address the nature of the social and technical changes being proposed. As for the customized tools, the four interrelated flow tools were developed: the value stream map, the Kanban board, the cumulative flow diagram, and the burndown chart.

Value stream map: The project teams initially designed value stream maps (Fig. 2) that were unique to TechCo, which enabled both management and project teams to identify: (i) the various work states of the ISD process, (ii) the value-added and non-value-added activities in each work state (i.e. testing), and (iii) the non-value-added activities between work states (e.g. waiting time, which cannot be billed to the customer).

The value stream map represents the current state of the ISD process, not the future state. To move to the desired state, project teams had to create a Kanban board.

Kanban board: The Kanban board provides a method for managing the flow of work (e.g. story points) with an emphasis on continual delivery without overloading the project team. Having identified the work states, value-added and non-value-added activities, management and project teams created Kanban boards to represent the various work states (see Fig. 3). The teams initially created physical Kanban boards and, after several iterations, migrated to a digital platform, which is critical in a distributed environment. The Kanban board at TechCo allowed project teams to visualize work in progress, observe individual and team-level effort, and quickly identify potential bottlenecks or delays (e.g. non-value-added activities) during or between work states.

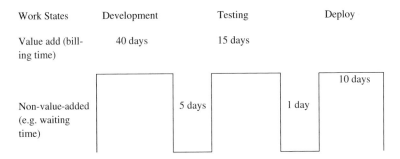

Fig. 2 Value stream map

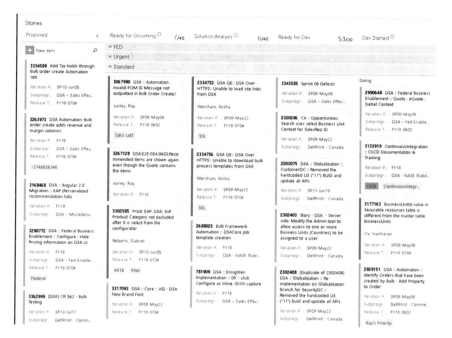

Fig. 3 Digital Kanban board

In this instance, the Kanban board at TechCo represents thirteen work states through which all work items progress: proposed, ready for grooming, solution analysis, ready for development, development started, development complete, ready for development integration testing (DIT), DIT started, DIT complete, system integration started, ready for user-acceptance testing, ready to deploy, and deployed.

After representing the various work states on a Kanban board, the project teams needed to monitor the quality of flow through the ISD process using a cumulative flow diagram.

Cumulative flow diagram (CFD): The CFD visually represents each work state from the Kanban board (Fig. 4), so TechCo's CFD represents the thirteen work states unique to the ISD flow process at TechCo. Each work state is color-coded, allowing management and project teams to check the current status of the entire ISD flow process, how much work has been done (e.g. deployed), work in progress, work waiting to be done (e.g. backlog), impediments to flow, and cycle time and lead time.

Having visibility of workflows across the work states and being able to identify and remove impediments to flow quickly, project teams can then create a burndown chart.

Burndown chart: The burndown chart is a visual measurement tool that enables management and project teams to determine the volume of work being completed per day/week against the projected rate of completion for the current project release (see Fig. 5).

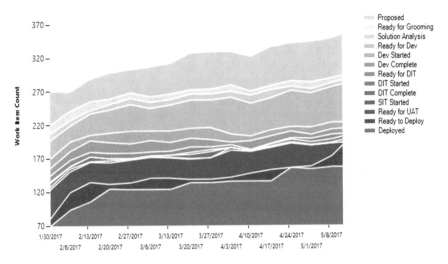

Fig. 4 Cumulative flow diagram

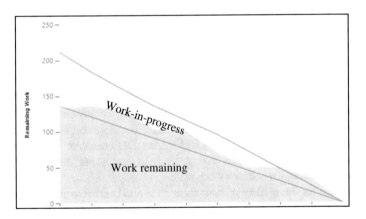

Fig. 5 Burndown chart

Collectively, the four flow artifacts create a common platform for with which management and project teams can enhance the dialogue around the problems in and solutions to current and emergent issues in the ISD flow process.

4.2 Application of Artifacts

As a visualization tool, Kanban created a common platform management and project teams could use to enhance the dialogue around software-development-related problems and solutions. For example, prior to using Kanban, all teams used the term 'done' to confirm that a Product Backlog Item (PBI) had been delivered. Such an approach can be problematic if the acceptance criteria of the work item are not well defined, not agreed upon, or open to interpretations, which is not uncommon in software development because of the complex nature of the work.

From the perspective of a software engineer, 'done' might mean code is completed to satisfy a user story requirement, code reviews and other quality engineering tasks have been signed off, code has been merged into code master repositories, or code has been deployed to a testing system or to production, depending on the work stream. However, if the requirements are confusing or poorly written, from the software engineer's perspective it will be confusing to determine that the work item is really 'done,' thereby creating tensions in the project team and impediments to the flow of work.

Using Kanban enabled the project teams to create a new term called 'done-done,' which comes into play when software engineers (developers and testers) can assure others that an item is completed because they were able to code, test, and deploy it have no change requests for it.

Kanban become a central artifact in the daily interactions between project team leads and team members. It was a focal point for discussion during the daily stand-up meeting and throughout the day, as well as for management's and project team leads' decision-making. Kanban enabled the project teams to visualize the work, limit the amount of work in progress (WIP limit), focus on flow, and strive for continuous improvement.

By matching the amount of work in progress to the team's capacity, Kanban gave project teams more flexible planning options, faster and better outputs, clearer focus on completing work, and more transparency throughout the development cycle. A mindset of 'stop starting and start finishing' developed among the team members, and a culture of 'leadership at all levels' empowered them to be more proactive when issues with the development process emerged. Kanban promoted a culture that encouraged active, ongoing learning and improving by defining the best possible flow throughout the entire software-development process at TechCo.

4.3 Evaluation of Artifacts

Although flow tools and metrics can be implemented quickly, using them as a mental model of how TechCo works required incremental changes in the company's culture over time. These changes were achieved via the flow workshops and presentations to both management and project teams that highlighted the importance of leadership at all levels, two-way communication, and double-loop learning to use flow tools and metrics successfully.

As part of a major project review of ISD flow at TechCo, a technical project manager reported, "After being exposed to flow tools like Kanban and CFDs, we started refocusing the teams' mindset toward a more agile approach. We rebuilt the entire ISD lifecycle tool with queries and dashboards, which has helped teams to focus on priorities rather than just delivering work. This weekend we delivered fifty-eight work items produced in four sprints, which is almost three times our productivity before we adopted flow.".

A similar view was shared by an experienced software tester who reported, "Visualization was the biggest improvement, especially with Kanban, as it allowed us to see priorities and blockers quickly so we could react and make decisions faster."

The benefits of implementing flow had a positive impact beyond the project teams. The view of the manager responsible for regional operational excellence was that "this is really great. This went from being a very focused legacy services project to broadening out to a cross-functional TechCo project with cross-regional interest and collaboration with our customers."

As flow tools created a shared understanding for both management and project teams, they reassured the project teams that flow tools and metrics were not just another management 'control mode' but an opportunity to communicate their strengths as a team while also identifying impediments to achieving their project outputs. Similarly, management teams learned that flow metrics should be interpreted in context and be used to monitor the work, not the person.

Table 4 provides evidence of quantitative and qualitative benefits that were reported across the four software project teams. The quantitative benefits were extracted from the code management tool, which consisted of stories (e.g. work items) that were completed by the project teams before and after the flow tools were implemented. The qualitative data was collected via interviews with management and software teams.

When new flow-based systems development tools designed to change both ISD practices and the mindset underpinning them are introduced, which existing tools and practices will become obsolete and which ones must adapt to complement the new ISD flow tools and practices should be considered.

Table 4 Benefits of flow-based software project management

Stories and defects	Visibility and quality	Planning and allocation
100% of stories were compliant with Team Foundation Server work states Average lead time declined from 109 to 39 days Average cycle time declined from 31 to 24 days 1 in 8 stories had a defect, while previously 1 in 5 stories had a defect	The team took greater ownership of defects Defects were visible during daily stand-ups Quality control checks were integrated throughout each sprint Defects that were not being closed promptly had more visibility	Teams proactively resolved defects rather than waiting to be assigned Planning and resource allocations were improved to ensure defects were closed promptly Communication between management team and project teams, as well as within teams, improved

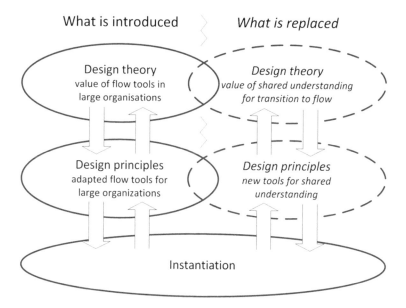

Fig. 6 Levels of theorizing—planned (left) and serendipitous (right)

4.4 *Growth of Design Theory*

The growth in design theory took place in terms of both core knowledge (how new flow tools should work) and secondary knowledge (how users understood the transition to new flow tools). The growth in design theory spanned the three recognized levels of design knowledge (c.f. Gregor & Hevner, 2013; Purao, 2002), as illustrated in Fig. 6.

At the first level, new customized flow tools were introduced, amended, and integrated into the existing technical architecture. The customized tools created refined and reusable software and hardware objects that were specialized to the particular needs of a large, multinational, and geographically distributed systems vendor. These objects demonstrated utility according to a variety of metrics, creating immediate, measurable value for the industry partners.

At the second level of design/operational principles, how the flow tools were used built on design knowledge that transcended the specific tools in question. Instead, the tools' make-up demonstrated some abstract design qualities that could be carried over to other customized flow tools in the future, such as the combination of digital and physical representations to address contrasting motivations. This principle, how it can be implemented, the trade-offs it presents, and the evidence for its utility inform future design across a range of digital/physical flow tools.

At the third level of emergent mid-range theory, the articulation of flow tools against common metrics showed the impact of an organizational move from agile to flow, adding to our understanding of flow tools and the software-development outcomes with which they are associated. Changes like the reduced number of defects show organizations why they should consider flow tools, not just how they should implement specific new practices.

These initial core-subject-matter-specific steps forward in design theory may have been sufficient to meet the project remit. However, the practical demands of introducing customized flow tools into the organization dragged the researchers into multiple ancillary organizational practices and structures, which forced them to learn more about aspects of TechCo that were not initially of scholarly interest, such as specific relationships between individuals, legacy systems, and the historic conditions that gave rise to certain behaviours and attitudes. As the researchers' knowledge grew, it became clear that much of it, learned by necessity, was not known to other parties in the organization. Emergent mid-range design theory then formed as we observed the impact of individuals' lack of awareness regarding their larger, shared activity system. Equally important, the impact of sharing this awareness was demonstrated as the researchers began to pay it more attention.

Design theory at the second level of design/operational principles also emerged in the form of principles that dictated how appropriate shared awareness could be nurtured. Once the problem came into theoretical focus, the researchers formalized design principles based on the need to share visualizations and metrics, recognize systemic tensions, and integrate management and developers more closely. These principles grounded operational changes and outcomes in higher-level reconceptualization of the project and vice-versa.

Finally, new transition-based communication tools were created at level one, that is, the level of situated instantiation. These communication tools created a way to actualize shared awareness of customized flow tools. Most notable among these tools was a set of visual canvases with which practitioners from different backgrounds and with differing interests could make sense of the social, technical, and practical transition being proposed and how it would affect them (for better or worse). These tools encouraged practitioners to expand their knowledge of neighbouring practices in the organization but also to expand their knowledge in the broader academic sense, to ask questions, and to consider how and why different practices had emerged in the first place.

It became increasingly obvious that these two aspects of design theory were related and complementary. On one hand, the growth in design theory for using flow tools is necessary, as this theory ensures the customized flow tools that are introduced are fit for the purpose, without which assurance there would be limited benefit in the transition. On the other hand, the growth in design theory for creating shared understanding is necessary, as it ensures that older tools and practices are replaced selectively and mindfully, without which assurance the benefits of customized flow tools could be offset by losses elsewhere.

As one design theory was refined and became more effective, so did the other. Better flow tools created improved metrics and reporting, strengthening shared understanding and allowing the tools to be used as others in the organization intended so they became more institutionally effective. Therefore, the two problems had to be addressed in tandem, even if the latter was not originally recognized in the core subject matter. Perhaps more importantly, the serendipitous discovery of this hidden aspect of the design problem created more nuanced, novel, and practically useful design knowledge around the new customized tools.

5 Key Lessons

The over-arching goal of this study was to use a DSR approach to systems development design to encourage a move toward a more evidence-based assessment of these methods. While organizations are increasingly seeking new approaches to improving ISD processes and increase agility and scale, methods are often designed and tailored in a less than rigorous manner. Proponents of a particular method make exaggerated claims about its utility but rarely support those claims with empirical evidence, so they put pressure on organizations to adopt these methods quickly with limited explanation, instruction, or clarity of purpose.

Our experience was that DSR addressed these issues, at least in part. Clear benefits included a more lucid rationale and evidence-based reflection on the flow method and its constituent practices and tools. This result is not that surprising, given that DSR is helps developers understand why they expect a design to work and evaluate whether it actually does (McKay et al., 2012). We found support for a 'satisficing'-based model of learning among both academic and industrial participants. As researchers, we strayed beyond core subject matter and into secondary operational practices or institutional structures only when doing so was unavoidable. Similarly, most practitioners strayed into secondary practices, structures, theories, and methods only when they affected the project at hand. While many of these interactions created negligible long-term value, several produced new, serendipitous, and mutually valuable design opportunities that would otherwise have gone undetected. Therefore, the question becomes: *under what conditions should researchers extend their secondary environmental knowledge to improve the quality of DSR outputs?*

Developers can have dual personalities regarding method and product: A stark outcome was that many developers adopted dual personalities when they engaged in DSR: a rigorous, cold, evidence-based approach to the development and evaluation of their software artifact, and a loose, emotionally attached, 'blind' perspective on the flaws and inconsistencies of the method or process they are using. If building the method was their final product, would they adopt such contrasting approaches?

Apply DSR-appropriate standards of rigour to evaluating ISD methods: DSR encourages researchers to adopt a rigorous, evidence-based approach to the development and evaluation of their software artifacts. However, the method used to design and develop software artifacts is often given the liberty of a 'creative process' for which only loose, emotional justifications are sufficient, and researchers can remain blind to the flaws and inconsistencies of the method or process they are using. After all, as the argument goes, if it works, what's the problem? This viewpoint jars against the core assumptions of DSR, which demand clarity in how 'work' is defined and measured. Many DSR studies focus on the development and evaluation of new methods, typically for niche problems or domains, but the surrounding industry-standard methods receive far less scrutiny. Most studies of agile, flow, design thinking, and the like are case studies, rather than research-driven DSR studies in which assumed core benefits are tested against alternatives.

Design and evaluate ISD methods instead of ISD methods' components: Another lesson lies in the appreciation of the difficulty of designing and evaluating at the method level, rather than the individual principle, practice or tool level, particularly with the level of rigor and consideration one typically associates with DSR. A motivation for designing and evaluating at the method level was that the existing body of knowledge on flow is limited by the fact that most studies focus only on a specific flow artifact or do not consider that the flow artifacts must work together to achieve an over-arching method goal and must operate in an unpredictable, multifaceted, social, and context-laden environment (Dennehy & Conboy, 2017; Lyytinen & Rose, 2006; Olerup, 1991; Wastell & Newman, 1993). This motivation again resonates with the bounded rationality perspective, as researchers limit complexity by declining to extend their secondary environmental knowledge. This study shows the perils of such an approach, as interdependencies between methods' practices and tools emerged as key to the design problem. Identifying the impact of each practice/tool, the synergistic effect between two tools, and then the over-arching impact of all practices and tools and their combined and compounded inter-relationships and synergies is challenging. To compound this problem, the strengths of some artifacts are designed to address the shortcomings of others. Using a Kanban board without a clear definition of 'done' will render the activity almost useless or even result in a negative net impact, so a rational deconstructionist approach to designing and evaluating may not solve the problem.

Design clear and discriminate metrics for ISD methods: Another significant challenge is that, even if a method like flow can be evaluated as a cohesive unit, it is difficult to determine what part of the improved metrics, if any, we can attribute to that method. How much of the improvement would have happened anyway? This point alone has implications for the research method's design. Of course, no two systems-development projects are identical and comparing a project to a 'control' project is not possible. As is likely to have been the case in this study, part of the improved metrics is attributable to implementing the flow method, part is attributable to improvements and learning by the team members, and part is attributable to organization-specific culture and knowledge that predates the project. Studying any of these in isolation tempts researchers to limit complexity by declining to extend their secondary environmental knowledge. Therefore, the design of the research should consider and compare two interrelated but distinct sources of improvement–the ISD method and the environment and context within which the ISD method resides. Perhaps the same method should be employed but tailored to study both sources, or perhaps two distinct research methods are required. Either way, subsequent comparison between the two must be feasible and meaningful.

Consider temporal issues when designing and evaluating ISD methods: Limitations of time are key triggers of satisficing, as designers do not have the resources to explore and compare options at length (Arthur, 1994; Simon, 1991). Therefore, just as the collaboration in this study was fuelled by extensions to satisficing, it was clear that the flow implementation's timing had a bearing on the method's design and evaluation. In fact, the timing of the various implementation components—the pace at which the team learned the method, the pace at which they applied the flow knowledge to the design context, and, at the most basic level, the timing at which each of the flow components themselves was implemented—each had a bearing. The timing of this design project in the overall time horizon of the broader development project was also an issue. For example, many variables could have been identified, if not more effectively controlled, if the flow implementation had occurred at the start of the development project. That the flow-specific element occurred after the start of the development project meant that many variables were embedded, not adjustable, and difficult to remove or manage. For example, some developers had built a preconceived notion of what the flow method was and the 'true' agenda that underpinned its use, so correcting these preconceptions was difficult, as was identifying their impact. An obvious solution is to identify suitable development projects at their commencement so a rigorous and effective DSR project can be undertaken. Of course, opportunities to study an ISD project from 'zero' is rare, but the research team could establish a clear point 'zero' at which preconceived notions and levels of training can be identified. While perhaps artificial, such a clear point of reference to 'baseline' skills, preconceptions, and performance metrics on which to measure improvements going forward would be useful.

Be wary of self-referencing metrics when evaluating ISD methods: Another lesson is that part of the improvements in a method design and implementation may be related to how we measured things. Cycle time and throughput rate are specific to the flow method, so it is not surprising that we see improvements in those flow-specific metrics by implementing a flow method. Doing so is analogous to comparing modes of transport by how many nautical miles they can travel over water. A recommendation for future DSR projects on method design may be to identify a set of process-independent measures on which one can judge flow—or, indeed, any method. Such an approach would allow us to compare and contrast practices and tools from across methods or practices and tools that may not belong to any pre-defined method.

In terms of future research, we suggest that research could benefit from a DSR perspective on method design and evaluation. As we accumulate design knowledge across multiple instances of a particular method, such as flow, we enable much stricter evidence-based design. In addition to accumulated knowledge about particular methods, we could also benefit from a DSR method that transcends various methods while remaining at least somewhat process-independent. For example, the design of an agile method may yield evidence that can benefit the design of flow, waterfall, or even in-house, commercially independent methods. However, in pursuing such evidence, the research community may need to rely on process-independent principles and metrics rather than method-specific metrics like flow's cycle and throughput.

Acknowledgements This work had financial support from the Science Foundation Ireland grant 13/RC/2094 and was co-funded under the European Regional Development Fund through the Southern & Eastern Regional Operational Programme to Lero, the Irish Software Research Centre (www.lero.ie).

References

Agerfalk, P. J., & Fitzgerald, B. (2005). Methods as action knowledge: Exploring the concept of method rationale in method construction, tailoring and use.

Akoka, J., Comyn-Wattiau, I., Prat, N., & Storey, V. C. (2017). Evaluating knowledge types in design science research: An integrated framework. In *International Conference on Design Science Research in Information Systems* (pp. 201–217). Cham: Springer.

Agerfalk, P. J., Fitzgerald, B., Holmstrom Olsson, H., Lings, B., Lundell, B., & Ó Conchúir, E. (2005). A framework for considering opportunities and threats in distributed software development.

Ahmad, M. O., Dennehy, D., Conboy, K., & Oivo, M. (2018). Kanban in software engineering: A systematic mapping study. *Journal of Systems and Software, 137*, 96–113.

Al-Baik, O., & Miller, J. (2015). The Kanban approach, between agility and leanness: A systematic review. *Empirical Software Engineering, 20*(6), 1861–1897.

Anderson D. (2013). *Lean software development*. Seattle, WA: Lean Kanban University (LKU).

Anderson, D., Concas, G., Lunesu, M. I., & Marchesi, M. (2011). Studying Lean-Kanban approach using software process simulation. In *International Conference on Agile Software Development* (pp. 12–26). Springer, Berlin, Heidelberg.

Anderson, D. J. (2010). *The Kanban Principles*. Blue Hole Press.

Anderson, D. J., & Roock, A. (2011). An agile evolution: Why Kanban is catching on in Germany and around the world. *Cutter IT Journal, 24*(3), 6.

Arthur, W. B. (1994). Inductive reasoning and bounded rationality. *The American Economic Review, 84*(2), 406–411.

Bell, S. C., & Orzen, M. A. (2016). *Lean IT: Enabling and sustaining your lean transformation*. CRC Press.

Csikszentmihalyi, M., & Csikszentmihalyi, I. (1975). *Beyond boredom and anxiety* (Vol. 721). San Francisco, California: Jossey-Bass.

Csikszentmihalyi, M., & Kleiber, D. A. (1991). Leisure and self-actualization. In O. L. Driver, P. J. Brown, & G. L. Peterson (Eds.), *Benefits of Leisure* (pp. 91–102). State College, PA: Venture Publishing.

Cocco, L., Mannaro, K., Concas, G. and Marchesi, M. (2011) Simulating Kanban and Scrum vs. Waterfall with system dynamics. In *International Conference on Agile Software Development*. 117–131. Springer, Berlin.

Conboy, K. (2009). Agility from first principles: Reconstructing the concept of agility in information systems development. *Information Systems Research, 20*(3), 329–354.

Dennehy, D., & Conboy, K. (2017). Going with the flow: An activity theory analysis of flow techniques in software development. *Journal of Systems and Software, 133*(2017), 160–173.

Dybå, T., & Dingsøyr, T. (2008). Empirical studies of Agile software development: A systematic review. *Information and Software Technology, 50*(9–10), 833–859.

Fan, W., & Gordon, M. D. (2014). The power of social media analytics. *Communications of ACM, 57*(6), 74–81.

Fitzgerald, B., & Stol, K-J. (2014). Continuous software engineering and beyond: trends and challenges. In *Proceedings of the 1st International Workshop on Rapid Continuous Software Engineering* (pp. 1–9). ACM.

Gigerenzer, G., & Goldstein, D. G. (1996). Reasoning the fast and frugal way: Models of bounded rationality. *Psychological Review, 103*(4), 650–669.

Gill, T. G., & Hevner, A. R. (2013). A fitness-utility model for design science research. *ACM Transactions on Management Information Systems (TMIS), 4,* 5.

Gleick, J. (1999). *The acceleration of just about everything.* New York: Pantheon.

Goldkuhl, G., Ågerfalk, P., & Sjöström J. (2017). A design science approach to information systems education. In *International Conference on Design Science Research in Information Systems* (pp. 383–397). Springer, Cham.

Gregor, S., & Jones, D. (2007). The anatomy of a design theory. In *Association for Information Systems.*

Gregor, S., & Hevner, A. R. (2013). Positioning and presenting design science research for maximum impact. *Management Information Systems Quarterly, 37,* 337–355.

Harb, Y., Noteboom, C., & Sarnikar, S. (2015). Evaluating project characteristics for selecting the best-fit agile software development methodology: A teaching case. *Journal of the Midwest Association for Information Systems, 1,* 33.

Birkeland, J. O. (2010). From a timebox tangle to a more flexible flow. In *International Conference on Agile Software Development* (pp. 325–334). Berlin, Heidelberg: Springer.

Helfert, M., & Donnellan, B. (2013). *Design Science: Perspectives from Europe: European Design Science Symposium, EDSS 2012, Leixlip, Ireland, December 6, 2012, Revised Selected Papers:* Imprint: Springer.

Helfert, M, Donnellan, B., & Kenneally J. (2014). Design Science: Perspectives from Europe: European Design Science Symposium EDSS 2013, Dublin, Ireland, November 21–22, 2013. Revised Selected Papers (Vol. 447). Springer.

Hevner, A. R. (2007). A three cycle view of design science research. *Scandinavian Journal of Information Systems, 19*(2), 4.

Hevner, A., & Chatterjee, S. (2010). *Design science research in information systems.* Boston, MA: Springer.

Kahneman, D. (2003). Maps of bounded rationality: Psychology for behavioral economics. *American Economic Review, 93*(5), 1449–1475.

Kamel, Boulos, M. N., Sanfilippo, A. P., Corley, C. D., & Wheeler, S. (2010). Social Web mining and exploitation for serious applications: Technosocial predictive analytics and related technologies for public health, environmental and national security surveillance. *Computer Methods and Programs in Biomedicine, 100*(1), 16–23.

Khurum, M., Petersen, K., & Gorschek, T. (2014). Extending value stream mapping through waste definition beyond customer perspective. *Journal of Software: Evolution and Process, 26*(12), 1074–1105.

Kniberg, H., & Skarin, M. (2010). *Kanban and Scrum-making the most of both.* Retrieved August 13, 2018, from https://www.infoq.com/minibooks/kanban-scrum-minibook.

Lee, G., & Xia, W. (2010). Toward agile: An integrated analysis of quantitative and qualitative field data on software development agility. *MIS Quarterly, 34*(1), 87–114.

Leffingwell, D. (2010). *Agile software requirements: Lean requirements practices for teams, programs, and the enterprise.* Addison-Wesley Professional.

Lindstrom, L., & Jeffries, R. (2004). Extreme programming and agile software development methodologies. *Information Systems Management, 21*(3), 41–52.

Lyytinen, K., & Rose, G. M. (2006). Information system development agility as organizational learning. *European Journal of Information Systems, 15,* 183–199.

Malone, T. W., Laubscher, R. J., & Johns, T. (2011). The age of hyper specialization. *Harvard Business Review, 89*(7–8), 56–65.

McKay, J., Marshall, P., & Hirschheim, R. (2012). The design construct in information systems design science. *Journal of Information Technology, 27*(2), 125–139.

Mujtaba, S., Feldt, R., & Petersen, K. (2010). Waste and lead time reduction in a software product customization process with value stream maps. In *2010 21st Australian Software Engineering Conference*, 139–148. IEEE.

Narayanan, S., Balasubramanian, S., & Swaminathan, J. M. (2009). A matter of balance: Specialization, task variety, and individual learning in a software maintenance environment. *Management Science, 55*(11), 1861–1876.

Nord, R. L., Ozkaya, I., & Sangwan, R. S. (2012). Making architecture visible to improve flow management in lean software development. *IEEE Software, 29*(5), 33–39.

Olerup, A. (1991). Design approaches: A comparative study of information system design and architectural design. *The Computer Journal, 34*, 215–224.

Orzen, M. A., & Bell, S. C. (2016). *Lean IT: Enabling and sustaining your lean transformation.* Florida: Productivity Press.

Petersen, K., Roos, P., Nyström, S., & Runeson, P. (2014). Early identification of bottlenecks in very large scale system of systems software development. *Journal of Software: Evolution and Process, 26*(12), 1150–1171.

Petersen, K., & Wohlin, C. (2011). Measuring the flow in lean software development. *Software: Practice and Experience, 41*, 975–996.

Poppendieck, M., & Poppendieck, T. (2003). *Lean Software Development: An Agile Toolkit: An Agile Toolkit*: Addison-Wesley.

Power, K. (2014). Definition of ready: An experience report from teams at cisco. In *Agile Processes in Software Engineering and Extreme Programming* (pp. 312–319). Springer.

Power, K., & Conboy, K. (2015). A metric-based approach to managing architecture-related impediments in product development flow: an industry case study from Cisco. In *Proceedings of the Second International Workshop on Software Architecture and Metrics* (pp. 15–21). IEEE Press.

Purao, S. (2002). Design research in the technology of information systems: Truth or dare [online], Pennsylvania State University. http://purao.ist.psu.edu/working-papers/dare-purao.pdf.

Rai, A. (2017). Editor's comments: Diversity of design science research. *MIS Quarterly, 41*(1), iii–xviii.

Reinertsen, D. G. (2009). *The principles of product development flow: second generation lean product development.* Canada: Celeritas Redondo Beach.

Robinson, H., Segal, J., & Sharp, H. (2007). Ethnographically-informed empirical studies of software practice. *Information and Software Technology, 49*(6), 540–551.

Rothenberger, & Kuechler, B. (Eds.). (2012). In *International Conference on Design Science Research in Information Systems* (pp. 381–397). Berlin, Heidelberg: Springer.

Shalloway, A. (2011). Demystifying Kanban. *Cutter IT Journal, 24*(3), 12.

Siegel, E., & Davenport, T. H. (2013). *Predictive analytics: The power to predict who will click, buy, lie, or die.* Wiley.

Simon, H. A. (1972). Theories of bounded rationality. *Decision and organization, 1*(1), 161–176.

Simon, H. A. (1982). Models of bounded rationality: Empirically grounded economic reason (Vol. 3). Cambridge: MIT press.

Simon, H. A. (1991). Bounded rationality and organizational learning. *Organization Science, 2*(1), 125–134.

Sonnenberg, C., & vom Brocke, J. (2012). Evaluations in the science of the artificial–reconsidering the build-evaluate pattern in design science research. In *International Conference on Design Science Research in Information Systems* (pp. 381–397). Berlin, Heidelberg: Springer.

Tremblay, M. C., Hevner, A. R., & Berndt, D. J. (2010). Focus groups for artifact refinement and evaluation in design research. *Communications of the Association for Information Systems, 26*, 27.

Venable, J., Pries-Heje, J., & Baskerville, R. (2016). FEDS: A framework for evaluation in design science research. *European Journal of Information Systems, 25*(1), 77–89.

Versionone. (2016). What is Kanban. https://www.versionone.com/what-is-kanban/.

Vidgen, R., & Wang, X. (2009). Coevolving systems and the organization of Agile software development. *Information Systems Research, 20*(3), 355–376.

Wastell, D., & Newman, M. (1993). The behavioral dynamics of information system development: A stress perspective. *Accounting, Management and Information Technologies, 3*(2), 121–148.

DSR in Process Management

Using Business Process Management for Effective and Efficient Quality Management

The Icebricks Approach

Jörg Becker, Nico Clever, Stefan Fleischer, Steffen Höhenberger, and Sebastian Rätzer

Abstract Business Process Management (BPM) and Quality Management (QM) are seldom seen as the perfect way to represent a company's trustworthiness to customers. Achieving a QM certification (e.g., with the ISO 9001:2015 certificate) can have great value for a company, especially in terms of reputation. However, although promoted by the latest version of the standard, applying BPM is not often considered a way to achieve such a certification, and the collection of necessary information is often costly and tedious. Therefore, we propose a conceptual BPM approach, along with a supporting tool, to be used for effective and efficient QM. We recapitulate the design and development of the icebricks BPM approach and tool and show by means of a concrete consulting project how BPM, especially process modeling, can support the ISO 9001 certification process. During the development and the consulting project, we learned that existing procedure models (possibly with some adaptions) are often not only useful for their described application but can even serve in related undertakings. Therefore, it is always useful to look for existing solutions that may be related to a project. We also learned that simplicity and flexibility of the procedure and the tools are the key factors in successfully applying BPM in an ISO 9001 project. In addition, the development of procedures and tools must be led by real practical assumptions, such as those proposed in DSR, instead of assumptions about a "perfect world," if they are to be applied in practice.

J. Becker (✉) · N. Clever · S. Fleischer · S. Höhenberger
European Research Center for Information Systems (ERCIS), University of Münster, Münster, Germany
e-mail: joerg.becker@ercis.uni-muenster.de

N. Clever
e-mail: nico.clever@ercis.uni-muenster.de

S. Fleischer
e-mail: stefan.fleischer@ercis.uni-muenster.de

S. Höhenberger
e-mail: steffen.hoehenberger@ercis.uni-muenster.de

S. Rätzer
Prof. Becker GmbH, Altenberge, Germany
e-mail: sebastian.raetzer@prof-becker.de

© Springer Nature Switzerland AG 2020
J. vom Brocke et al. (eds.), *Design Science Research. Cases*, Progress in IS,
https://doi.org/10.1007/978-3-030-46781-4_6

1 Introduction

Companies act under considerable strain caused by such conditions as globalization, hazardous competition, and technological changes, to name only a few. The bottom line is that entrepreneurial endeavors always come down to making decisions—ideally choosing the *best* option. Although a multitude of methods are available to support economical decisions, we argue that one cannot entirely eliminate the irrationality in human decision-making or fully eliminate the personal, subjective opinion and situational factors. One can only reduce the room for speculation by depicting the state of facts in a structured and comprehensible way using pragmatic and sophisticated approaches (Snowden & Boone 2007) that reduce uncertainty and irrationality and serve as a solid base for a company to achieve the best possible tangible and intangible value and the best possible use of their limited resources.

With respect to Quality Management (QM), companies should give their (potential) customers with a transparent and comprehensible representation of their products' and services' quality, especially in markets where it is customary or even obligatory, such as is the case for components suppliers in the automotive industry. One way to represent quality is by means of certifications that inform the customer about the firm's adherence to a well-known and accepted standard in support of the firm's independent evidence. The prevalent certification for QM is the 9000 series of the International Organization for Standardization (ISO). In 2016, ISO stated that it had certified 1.1 million companies globally (ISO, 2017). The standard DIN EN ISO 9000 provides the vocabulary and definitions, while the DIN EN ISO 9001 sets the requirements for QM Systems (QMS).[1] The 2015 version newly incorporates a strictly process-oriented approach (DIN 2015b) that facilitates a standards-compliant QM, as many companies have incorporated process-oriented thinking in recent years. Despite this opportunity, few companies have integrated the two fields during the certification process or afterwards; even though interest in certification in general is high, ISO certified only about 81,000 companies in the first year of the 2015 version worldwide (ISO, 2017).

We propose using a proven Business Process Management (BPM) approach to implement QM effectively and efficiently and according to the well-known ISO 9001 standard. With the help of a practical ISO 9001 certification case, we show that the icebricks BPM approach from Becker, Clever, Holler, Püster, and Shitkova (2013a) covers all that is demanded from a proper QMS within the ISO 9001.

The remainder of the article is structured as follows: Sect. 2 presents the context of this work is presented, while Sect. 3 depicts the design and development journey of the icebricks approach and tool along the Design Science Research Methodology (DSRM; Peffers, Tuunanen, Rothenberger, & Chatterjee, 2007). Section 4 presents

---

[1] The full denotation is DIN EN ISO 9000:2015–11, respectively DIN EN ISO 9001:2015, in which DIN stands for "Deutsches Institut für Normung," EN abbreviates "Europäische Norm," 9000 and 9001 distinguish the two standards, and 2015–11 refers to the year and month of adoption. For simplicity, we use the denotations ISO 9000 and ISO 9001 for the latest versions (2015). Where they are intended, other versions are explicitly mentioned in the text.

the final outcome and the application of the icebricks approach for effective and efficient QM. Section 5 summarizes and discusses the key lessons learned.

2   The Context

This work is positioned in the practice-oriented Design Science Research (DSR) stream, so theoretically well-founded insights eventually find their way into practice through case applications, transfer projects, and the like. Thus, research is conducted not only for its own sake but also creates a real benefit for all stakeholders, especially companies that seek to sustain proper QM, auditors who want a well-structured and integrated documentation approach, ultimately the customers who benefit from well-organized and certified companies.

Our case is that of an internationally operating manufacturing and trading company for industrial components and special tools. The family-owned company employs about 130 people in Germany and also has offices in several other countries. The headquarters in Germany is divided into five main departments: purchasing, production and warehouse, selling, management, and support. The company conducts an active QM process in production, repair, and other services.

To show the suitability of the icebricks BPM approach in effective and efficient QM and the ISO 9001 in particular, the two fields of BPM and QM have to be integrated. The ISO 9001 contains requirements that a company must fulfil to be certified. Broadly speaking, these requirements address the company's knowledge about its business processes, risks that can influence customer satisfaction, and the company's efforts toward continuous improvement. A proper QM requires adherence to seven principles: customer orientation, leadership, involvement of people, a process-oriented approach, improvement, fact-based decision-making, and relationship management (DIN 2015a).

The single requirements are divided into Chaps. 5–11 of the ISO 9001 standard[2]. The requirements detail, for example, the depiction of business processes, the assignment of responsibilities, and the planning for handling risks. The seven chapters are structured according to the Plan-Do-Check-Act (PDCA) cycle, where *Plan* comprises the setting of objectives and how they can be achieved, *Do* addresses implementation of the plan, *Check* is concerned with monitoring, and *Act* deals with (corrective) action based on the checks. Companies follow this cycle in pursuit of continuous improvement, so all of the individual requirements address part of the company's continuous improvement. The chapters can roughly be assigned to the PDCA phases, where Chaps. 5–7 belong to *Plan*, Chaps. 8 and 9 address *Do*, and Chaps. 10 and 11 cover *Check* and *Act*, respectively. What is new in the ISO 9001:2015 version lies in the strictly process-oriented approach and the risk-based thinking. However, even though its use is promoted by the standard, BPM is comparatively rarely used

---

[2]The chapters 0 through 3 cover introductory issues without stating actual requirements.

for ISO 9001 certifications, in part because of ignorance of the potential of BPM in general and of the ISO 9001 certification in particular.

Figure 1 shows two prominent procedural models for BPM, one by Weske (2012) and one by Becker, Kugeler, and Rosemann (2012). Becker et al.'s (2012) approach has a sequential component for reorganizing a company and a cyclic component for continuous maintenance. It starts with preparing the modeling project by setting, for example, the modeling language and then developing the organizational frame and the as-is process models in the second and third phases, respectively before analyzing and depicting the to-be processes. Finally, the organizational structure is changed according to the processes and the processes are rolled out. All phases are supported by project management. Once the company is reorganizes in this way, continuous maintenance begins.

While Becker et al.'s (2012) approach has two components, Weske's (2012) model has only a cyclic component with four phases. However, the basic procedure is similar: It starts with the design of business processes (as-is processes), which are then analyzed and improved. The configuration depicts the (pilot) roll-out, while the enactment addresses the continuous monitoring and controlling of the process execution. This is the basis for the evaluation. Figure 1 makes clear that the two approaches are similar. The colored ellipses in Fig. 1 highlight this similarity of both approaches.

The PDCA cycle fits well into the existing procedure models by connecting two adjacent phases. For example, the *Do* phase covers the support and operation within

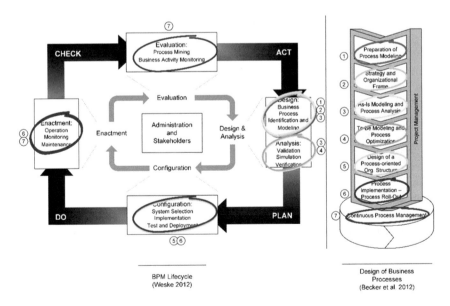

Fig. 1 Comparison of BPM procedure models and fitness for ISO 9001 Quality Management (based on Becker et al., 2012; Weske, 2012)

the ISO 9001 standard. Therefore, we argue that a proper BPM approach, along with a supporting tool, may fulfill the demands of the ISO 9001 for QM.

3 The Journey

The icebricks BPM tool, which facilitates effective and efficient QM, is an artifact in the context of DSR (Hevner, March, & Park, 2004). The tool was designed and implemented following the DSRM proposed by Peffers et al. (2007). This chapter presents the tool's objectives, design, and implementation. According to the DSRM, an artifact like the icebricks tool must be demonstrated in a real-world application case and must prove itself as well. Such a practical application is presented in Sect. 4.2. During the definition of objective(s) and the design and development of the approach, we focused on the requirements that emerged in BPM research, not on the concrete requirements of the ISO standard, so we could show that integrating BPM and QM works well.

3.1 Lap 1—Tool Objectives

We sought to combine existing requirements from the literature with our insights from several BPM consulting projects, so we searched the literature for requirements and incorporated them into our own objectives.

Understanding the Problem. In today's dynamic business environment, the process modeling tool must be easily accessible from anywhere at any time and must facilitate collaboration and conflict-free simultaneous access to the models' content for all project team members and stakeholders (Obj. 01). Depending on their role in the project, the project participants' access rights to the modeling tool functionality and content must differ (Obj. 02). For instance, modeling experts must be able to create, modify, and communicate models to the other project stakeholders, while model analysts and company managers have to be able to view, analyze, and create reports on the models. Keeping track of the changes made to the models (Obj. 03) is also a critical requirement, especially in distributed modeling project teams, to prevent hazardous modeling and loss of information (Clever, Holler, Püster, & Shitkova, 2013; Hadar & Soffer, 2006).

Depending on the purpose of the modeling project, the process models may contain a significant amount of information. In practice, collections of process models are created that consist of several hundred models, as in the repository of Dutch local governments council (Dijkman, Dumas, van Dongen, Käärik, & Mendling, 2011) or the SAP reference model (Mendling, Verbeek, van ongen, van der Aalst, & Neumann, 2008), or even several thousand models, as in the APROMORE collection of process models (Rosa & Reijers, 2011). Each model, in its turn, may consist of a few dozen up to hundreds of elements, such as process activities, events, IT and organizational elements, comments and annotations, and data objects. Such collections of process models become difficult to handle, understand, analyze and re-use, so effective and efficient management methods are needed for the process models that are created.

To facilitate (semi-) automated analysis, created models have to be comparable and understandable (Becker, Rosemann, & von Uthmann, 2000; Becker, Delfmann, Herwig, Lis, & Stein, 2009; Lindland, Sindre, & Solvberg, 1994). However, the freedom provided by existing modeling languages like Event-driven Process Chains (EPC) or Business Process Model and Notation (BPMN) represents a risk regarding inconsistencies in semantics and level of abstraction, so it endangers the models' comparability and understandability (Becker et al., 2013a; Mendling, Reijers, & van der Aalst, 2010a; Schütte & Rotthowe, 1998). Models' semantic and terminological standardization (Obj. 07) ensures their correctness (Becker et al. 2000), and element label structures have an effect on process models' understandability (Mendling, Reijers, & Recker, 2010b).

To reduce the chances of information overload and keep process models understandable, the models should have as few elements as possible and should minimize the occurrence of certain elements (Mendling, Reijers, & Cardoso, 2007). The same idea can be found in Becker et al. (2000), who also highlight the importance of standardizing the number of abstraction levels. At the same time, all necessary information must be reflected in the models to keep them relevant to the project goal (Becker et al., 2000). Therefore, a simple but powerful modeling notation (Obj. 04) with a standardized level of abstraction (Obj. 05) is needed that also allows the integration of enriched information in a way that prevents model overload (Obj. 06).

In addition to the standardization of modeling activities, facilitation techniques that allow easy creation of process models are needed. For example, the re-use of existing process knowledge (Obj. 08) helps save project resources (Becker et al., 2000; Becker & Schütte, 2006).

Finally, large collections of process models require specially designed analysis techniques that support process analysts and project stakeholders from the company's management in effective and efficient use of the process models' content. The full process information should be extractable in a human-readable form (Obj. 09), and the parts of the information that are of interest to the users should be easily identifiable (Obj. 10).

Understanding the Solution. We identified ten functional objectives on which the icebricks tool is based (Clever, 2016) and consolidated them into three groups (Table 1). The definition of objectives and their groups enabled us to guide the subsequent development activities.

Considering that process modeling tools are used not only by modeling experts but also by domain experts who have no specific IT knowledge, usability is a crucial requirement (Di Francescomarino & Tonella, 2009; Lohrmann & Reichert, 2012). Ensuring the usability of each of the artifact's functions during the design phase helps to reduce the tool's support costs (Bevan & Bogomolni, 2000). Therefore, a final,

Table 1 Tool objectives

Objective group	ID	Objective name
Collaboration	Obj. 01	Conflict-free multi-user access
	Obj. 02	Management of access rights
	Obj. 03	Version management
Complexity management and standardization	Obj. 04	Simple notation
	Obj. 05	Standardized level of abstraction
	Obj. 06	Integration of enriched process information
	Obj. 07	Semantic standardization
Model re-use and reporting	Obj. 08	Re-use of models
	Obj. 09	Full exportability of process documentation
	Obj. 10	Attribute-based reporting

non-functional objective for the artifact is a sufficient level of usability (Obj. 11) for all of the functional objectives.

3.2 Lap 2—Design and Development

When designing the tool, we deepened the objectives, assigned concrete design ideas to them, and related our development activities to the objective groups so we could coordinate duties between the developers and measure our progress.

Understanding the Problem. BPM projects usually required the involvement of many persons, so the artifact should be implemented in a *collaborative modeling* environment that enables the user to access the tool from basically everywhere by means of sophisticated user management. Version management and automatic conflict resolution support this multi-user approach.

Beyond these fundamentals, *model complexity* is the key factor in process models' acceptance, understandability and, hence, usage. While process models have to be as complex as necessary to serve the purpose of a modeling project, they must also be simple enough to be understandable. Only a few of the available elements of well-known modeling languages, such as the EPC and the BPMN, are actually used (zur Muehlen & Recker, 2008), but two fundamental constructs are shared by nearly all modeling languages: activities and flow. Hence, a newly developed approach should use these established constructs (Becker et al., 2013a, b).

Another central property of information models is abstraction (Stachowiak, 1973). A modeling project's level of detail depends on its purpose, and defining levels of abstraction is a common method by which to handle complexity. The models should also be enriched by organizational structures and IT architecture elements that are related to the processes, as these are important views of the models. Both can be modeled via a generic hierarchical construct in the tool and can be linked to the appropriate model elements. Using arbitrary phrase structures to label process elements in generic modeling tools leads to low-quality, non-comparable, unstandardized models (Delfmann, Herwig, & Lis, 2009; Indulska, Recker, Rosemann, & Green, 2009; zur Muehlen & Recker, 2008). A simple verb-object phrase structure, the most frequently applied technique, tends to lead to models of the highest quality (Delfmann et al., 2009; Mendling et al., 2010b).

The *model re-use* and *reporting* functionalities can provide value by reducing the effort in subsequent modeling projects. The use of reference models that can be adapted to changing circumstances in in similar enterprises increases the speed and the quality of modeling. The re-use of a model's parts can also speed up subsequent modeling processes and improve quality.

Understanding the Solution. The process-modeling method used in the tool presented here adheres to these principles based on certain rationales. For *collaboration*, the tool is implemented as a web application based on the Model-View-Controller (MVC) framework "Ruby on Rails," which is enriched with the JavaScript library jQuery in the front end. The tool features access rights and role management that allows for the separation of different permissions for different stakeholders, such as administrators, modelers, and managers.

To handle *complexity*, the tool uses a simple set of elements, a simple syntax, four predefined layers of abstraction, and attribution of process steps as a way to capture all of the process's relevant information, apart from the sequence of activities. The icebricks approach uses a simple verb-object phrase structure for labeling process elements. The artifact supports the incorporation of reference models and the *re-use of model parts* on every level of abstraction via a sophisticated interface. In addition, the ability to use references to existing elements in the modeling landscape that can be altered only in their original place reduces the effort involved in re-modeling similar processes and enhances the consistency and comparability of the models.

A basic *reporting functionality* is inherited in the tool as in BPM projects and in the later re-use of the resulting models, reporting to superiors is on the order of everyday business. Predefined standard reports, which can be configured if necessary, can be carried out for such purposes as the summation of throughput times in certain process variants. Moreover, the process model contents can be exported to Microsoft Word® and Excel® files, along with all attributed information. The tool also facilitates the communication of models besides the multi-user capabilities and reporting requirements. It is possible to export and import all of the environment's contents on any level of abstraction via a proprietary XML-based file format.

4 The Results

The objectives lead us to the current development status of the artifact, which is shown in detail in this section. The integration of the approach with the tool enabled us to apply the BPM tool in a consultancy project concerned with QM and to support the company during an ISO 9001 certification. Here we present the final tool, followed by a description of the application case and, finally, insights into the tool's perceived usability and our experiences in application cases.

4.1 Final Outcome

We developed a pure BPM tool to support companies with as much guidance as possible during modeling endeavors. We recognized that, since the 2015 revision of the ISO 9001 standard, our BPM tool can support companies well in earning the ISO certificate, which became possible based on the principles and constructs we used to achieve the objectives we set.

The icebricks approach predefines four levels of abstraction (Becker et al., 2013a, b). The first layer, the process framework, depicts the process landscape to be covered in a project and consists of main processes that can be positioned to represent any organizational circumstance, so no activity flow is needed on this level of abstraction. The main processes on the second layer consist of the steps carried out in a main process on a more detailed level. On the third level, the detail processes themselves consist of process building blocks (or process bricks), which represent atomic activities on the most detailed level. Finally, the control flow is introduced to depict temporal and logical predecessor-successor associations between the process steps.

Events were omitted if they added no value to the process model's semantics and expressiveness. The flow of activities is top-down and is automatically aligned by the modeling tool to enhance comparability and save time. No cyclic flows are allowed, and branching is possible only by design in its simplest form, so only single splits are allowed but with as many parallel elements as are needed.

Attributes, which are used on every level of abstraction, reduce the need for a complex control flow by encapsulating much of the detail in structured attributes. Standard attributes for each process step include elements like name and description, while structured attributes can be defined individually and can be of various types, such as simple textual or numerical attributes, hierarchy attributes, links to related process steps, and attachments. Unlike, for example, EPC and BPMN, where every additional bit of information is directly depicted in the model next to the process steps, the encapsulated form enhances the models' clarity by reducing the number of elements that are visible in the model.

A conceptual overview of the levels and elements and their relationships is shown in Fig. 2, while a detailed description of the underlying conceptual data model can be found in Becker et al. (2013a) and Clever (2016).

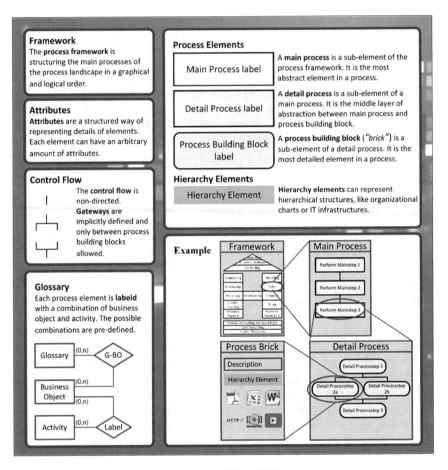

Fig. 2 Artifact elements and their relationships (Holler, 2015)

The web tool follows the conceptual overview shown in Fig. 2, while the actual implementation is depicted in Fig. 3. The so-called breadcrumbs navigation leads the user from the project (e.g., *Company*) to the subproject (e.g., *Processes@Company*) and from there through the process models. Figure 2 shows that the process brick *maintain stock type* is located in the detail process *maintain stock*, and the detail process is comprised in the main process *Warehouse*. All of them are shown in their standard variant. The variant concept enables the user to differentiate among variants of the same process, such as when the goods are issued to the customer or back to the supplier (in case of complaints). The process brick *maintain stock type* has three attributes: a description, a responsible person, and an IT support. While one can directly type in the description within the screen shown in Fig. 3 and let it appear by hovering the attribute, responsible persons and attributes have to be inserted in advance into the corresponding hierarches. (See Fig. 7 in Sect. 4.2 for an exemplary

Fig. 3 Web tool with process view

hierarchy.) The remaining attributes (e.g., *attachment*) can be assigned but do not have to be.

The icebricks tool has a strict naming convention. The label of the main processes consists of only one business object (e.g., *articles*), while the labels of detail processes and process bricks follow predefined combinations of business objects and procedures. For example, the business object *articles* and the procedure *check* form the process step *check articles*. This enforcement of a phrase structure, along with an underlying glossary of business objects and procedures, enables the modeling environment to be applied in any domain. In Fig. 4, the business object *articles* is shown along with its assigned procedures.

icebricks provides several reporting and export functionalities for analyzing and exchanging the process models. Predefined standard reports support the user in analyzing process models in such tasks as assigning responsibilities, process dependencies, or concrete values of attributes (e.g., processing times). For all reports, the layer to be analyzed can be selected based on the four-layer architecture. Figure 5 shows some basic reports of the icebricks tool. A full text search also enables the user to search all terms used in the process models, including all attributes, such as descriptions. At the press of a button, the export functionality to Microsoft Word generates a full documentation of the model's assigned attributes according to scientific formatting, and the Microsoft Excel export creates list of all process steps and their attributes for further processing. In addition, a process overview can be generated as a PDF file that contains all process steps on all levels (without attributes) to create an overview of the whole process model (see Fig. 6 in Sect. 4.2). The XML file export allows a user to pass models or parts of models to other users.

Fig. 4 Glossary with business objects

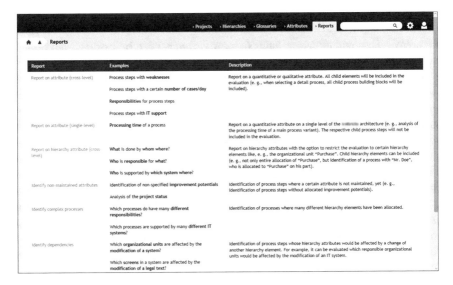

Fig. 5 Reports, including examples and descriptions

The aspects of BPM that we incorporated into our model enabled us to apply icebricks as means for structured process documentation in a consulting project with the goal of supporting an ISO 9001 certification.

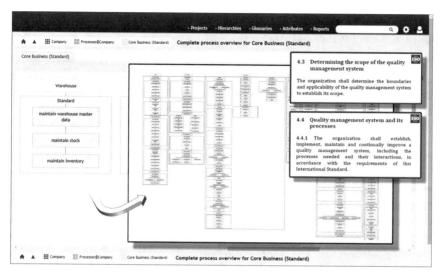

Fig. 6 Process overview for scope definition (including excerpts of ISO 9001 (DIN, 2015b)

4.2 Practical Application of ISO 9001

The application was carried out as a project, so the company established a quality manager and opted to pursue an ISO 9001 certification at the beginning of 2017 to implement and communicate the use of a QMS. The project to achieve this goal consisted of four phases:

1. Preparation of the process-modeling project
2. Identification and analysis of the current processes
3. Conception of the target processes
4. Implementation of the target processes and professional mentoring for the ISO 9001 certification.

The project took six months and ended with a successful ISO 9001 certification in late 2017. Process modeling and all supporting activities during the four phases were aligned with the quality manager at all times during the project. The CEO and management received a briefing at the beginning and the end of the project that focused on the final results and benefits, while the quality manager was given an individual introduction to the icebricks approach and the supporting tool during the course of the project.

QM, per the ISO 9001 definition, is structured according to the PDCA cycle (DIN, 2015b), which corresponds to the process orientation of the standard and enables a company to guarantee "that its processes are adequately resourced and managed, and that opportunities for improvement are determined and acted on" (DIN, 2015b, p. 9). In the following, the application of the icebricks approach and tool for an effective and efficient QM is described along the PDCA cycle, which is covered in Chaps. 5–11 of the ISO 9001 standard.

Plan. The description of the requirements of the PDCA cycle starts with Chap. 5 of the ISO 9001 standard, where the certification process starts with understanding the organization itself and its surroundings. Internal topics that are relevant to the certification comprise company-specific values, company culture, knowledge, and performance, while the external topics cover the company's legal, technological, competitive, market-related, cultural, social, and economic environment. Information about all of these topics must be collected, verified and monitored. In the next step, the needs and expectations of all stakeholders are identified and their requirements are documented. Then the scope of the QMS is defined, including all of its internal and external aspects, the interested parties and their requirements, and the company's products. Chapter 5 concludes by specifying all of the processes the QMS has to cover. As the QMS has various contact points on varying levels related to the company's business processes, the strict process-orientation of the 2015 version of the ISO 9001 standard is suitable for being applied at this point. Thus, the documentation of the business processes is carried out systematically with variable granularity to ensure the integrity, intelligibility, and traceability of QMS-related aspects of the processes, and a clear depiction of every process and its position in the whole process landscape is carried out. Figure 6 shows as an example the main process *Warehouse* and the company's complete process landscape using the icebricks tool, which is sufficient for the ISO 9001's scope definition and process inclusion.

In Chap. 4.4.1, the ISO 9001 requires documentation of all of the QMS's processes, including criteria and methods, resources and responsibilities, risks and opportunities (DIN, 2015b). These requirements are met via attribution of each main and detail process in icebricks, which makes meeting the requirement transparent and manageable.

This chapter of the ISO 9001 covers aspects of leadership and their commitment, quality policy, and responsibilities. The integration of those QMS requirements into the business processes is one of the most important tasks in the ISO 9001 standard and is covered by the icebricks approach. The person responsible is stated for every process and process step, and the person and all stakeholders are aware of this ownership. Figure 7 provides an example of such an implemented organigram of the case company.

A hierarchy element that represents a role in the company can be linked to any process element. The ISO 9001 demands this transparency, and with the icebricks approach, the company leadership can ensure and promote these process-based requirements of the standard. Furthermore, as indicated in Sect. 4.1, the definition and consequent use of a standardized notation with the help of a company-specific glossary with business objects and procedures prevents communication issues and ambiguities.

After the quality policy is defined, it is put to work. With the icebricks approach, all relevant information is available at any time to any involved stakeholder in the form of attributes, based on which stakeholders can execute reports or export all relevant

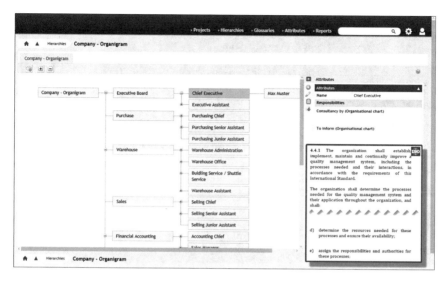

Fig. 7 Organigram depicting responsibilities (including excerpts of ISO 9001 (DIN, 2015b)

information and processes to external parties. icebricks proves export options to the Microsoft Word and Excel formats, where the process level, the attributes, and graphic process representations can be chosen freely. In addition, any stakeholder can directly access the latest information by consulting the process model in the web-based tool.

Chapter 7 of the ISO 9001 describes a main part of the ISO 9001 requirements: dealing with the risks and opportunities a company faces. Here, a systematic approach helps to identify risks and to develop and evaluate opportunities. By consistently recording the risks and opportunities, the company can reduce or enhance their effects. In icebricks, the use of attribute combinations facilitates the documentation of risks and opportunities, likewise, for every process at the right place. Figure 8 shows an example of an attribute combination that depicts a risk. The example shows a combination of several attributes and types, a textual description of risks and how they can be handled, and a drop-down list for the risk's likelihood. The tool also provides several other types of attributes, such as numerical attributes, file uploads, and dates.

Do. Chapter 8 of the ISO 9001 addresses all supporting aspects of the certification process, including resources, competencies, awareness, communications, and documented information. Resources belong to a specific process and can be internal or external, human or technological. In addition to the hierarchy of roles explained above, other hierarchical structures like IT infrastructures, applications, buildings, utilities, transportation resources, and ICT in general can be depicted and assigned using the icebricks approach in the same manner.

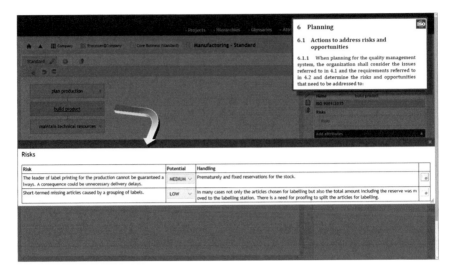

Fig. 8 Combination of attributes (including excerpts of the ISO 9001 (DIN, 2015b)

A central aim of the ISO 9001 is systematic knowledge management for a company's business processes. Central, well-structured digital storage for all relevant internal and external sources should be installed and kept current. The process building blocks of icebricks, as the most atomic type of activity, cover the whole knowledge and process structure of a company, facilitate all knowledge searches, and lead to full alignment with the company's overall process structure. The web-based tool ensures anytime-access for all relevant stakeholders.

Chapter 9 of the ISO 9001 covers tasks for the operation. Companies must meet the requirements for producing products and services, especially when external processes are involved, so another benefit of the icebricks approach is clear communication, whether internal or external. Both can be managed best when every company member uses the same wording, which can be ensured during process modeling. The icebricks approach's use of uniform business objects along with assignable procedures to prevent inconsistencies in the glossary and, in the end, the whole process landscape provides a sound basis for a clear communication. A common language improves all uses of internal and external communication channels and supports activities like the control of externally provided products or product releases.

Check. Chapter 10 of the ISO 9001 focuses on performance evaluation. Key figures and performance indicators should be used for measurement and analysis, which is done via attributes in the icebricks approach. A periodic evaluation of the quality and the QMS with a focus on key figures is required for optimization and improvements, so internal audits are to be carried out at defined intervals to check the complete QMS. Seamless documentation of all relevant information is crucial for these audits. The process documentation in icebricks supports arbitrary adjustments and simplifies internal and external audits, providing a central gateway for information. Reports can

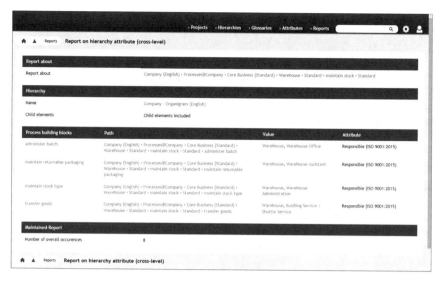

Fig. 9 Report on a hierarchy attribute showing process responsibilities

be used for management reviews, which Chap. 10 of the ISO 9001 also addresses. Several basic reports for the preparation and conduct of internal audits are available in icebricks, including reports on attributes (e.g., finding weak process steps), reports on hierarchy attributes (e.g., "Who is responsible for which process step?"), and reports that identify dependencies (e.g., "Which organizational units are affected by the modification of a system"). Figure 9 provides an example of a report that shows the responsibility for a process step—in this case, the most atomic process building blocks.

For a goal-driven comparison with previous reviews, which is achievable because of the clear, structured description of all processes and their attributes, the icebricks export depicts the status of all selected information at a defined moment. This documentation is part of evidence of the management reviews and the activities of the QMS, whose storage is recommended in Chap. 10 of the ISO 9001.

Act. The fourth and last step of the PDCA cycle of the ISO 9001 is concerned with improvements and is address in Chap. 11. Here, the results of the management review are transformed into possibilities for improvement, such as process changes for reorganization, resource optimization, and corrections. The aim of all improvements is the enhancement of customer satisfaction, but discrepancies like customer complaints demand actions that must be assessed, selected, and planned based on their feasibility. The icebricks approach supports this step by providing the necessary transparency and a structured documentation. Nonconformity, the actions taken, and their results must be documented per ISO 9001 as well. This measurement of the ongoing QMS improvement is done via a change report that depicts all modifications of business objects, procedures, and process elements.

4.3 Tool Evaluation

The goal of evaluation, an important step in DSRM, is to "observe and measure how well the artifact supports a solution to the problem" (Peffers et al., 2007, p. 56). The evaluation is performed in two ways: the functionality of the icebricks tool is compared to the functional objectives for the solution (Table 1) and its usability is measured via an experiment.

Table 2 presents the fulfillment status of each functional objective. Obj. 11 ("Usability") was evaluated separately by conducting an experiment (Clever, 2016; Neumann, 2016). The two latest versions of the icebricks tool were used in the evaluation. The newer version of the tool was improved by the introduction of a drag and drop functionality for process modeling, a better user interface design and a better navigation between the process model layers of abstraction. The goal of the experiment was to evaluate the effectiveness and efficiency of the implemented changes and the overall usability of the icebricks tool to demonstrate the tool's suitability for BPM.

Table 2 Fulfillment of the tool objectives

ID	Name	Tool functionality
Obj. 01	Conflict- free multi-user access	Login/Logout
		Access control
		User groups
Obj. 02	Access rights management	Access control
		User groups
Obj. 03	Version management	Conceptualized in Clever et al. (2013)
Obj. 04	Simple notation	icebricks notation (Becker et al., 2013a, b)
Obj. 05	Standardized level of abstraction	Four layers of abstraction (Becker et al., 2013b, c)
Obj. 06	Integration of enriched process information	Attributes and attribute values
		Modeling of hierarchies, use of hierarchies in the attribute values (Becker et al., 2013b, c)
Obj. 07	Semantic standardization	Glossary functionality
		Verb-noun phrase structures
		Shitkova, Clever, Holler, and Becker, (2015)
Obj. 08	Re-use of models	References
		Variants
		Import/export functionality
		Reference models
Obj. 09	Full process documentation export	Word export
Obj. 10	Attribute-based reporting	Reports

Table 3 Experiment participants

	Group 1 (older version)	Group 2 (newer version)
Number of participants	10 (9 m. + 1 f.)	11 (10 m. + 1 f.)
BPM experience (self-reported)	Low (2)	Low (3)
	Medium (1)	Medium (1)
	High (7)	High (7)
Icebricks experience (self-reported)	Low (7)	Low (8)
	Medium (1)	Medium (0)
	High (2)	High (3)

Twenty-one graduate and Ph.D. students of a faculty of Information Systems participated in the experiment. All participants were familiar with the topic of BPM from either university courses or practice-related projects. Some of the participants had already worked with the icebricks tool. The participants were divided into two groups of ten and eleven, with each group interacting with either the older or the newer version of the icebricks tool. The experiment's tasks were the same for both groups of participants. Table 3 shows statistics regarding the participants' experience with BPM and icebricks.

The experiment started with a brief explanation of the experimental procedure. The participants were also provided with a two-page description of the icebricks method and given time to familiarize themselves with it. Then the participants completed nine tasks using the icebricks tool: log into the system, navigate to a certain point in the model, create a new glossary object, create a process model according to the textual description provided using the glossary to name process elements, create an attribute, create a hierarchy element, assign attribute values to the process elements, create and interpret an attribute-based report, and log out from the system. All experimental runs were recorded using screen-recording software. At the end of the experiment, the participants filled in an after-task questionnaire that contained demographic questions (age, sex, experience level in BPM and icebricks), the System Usability Scale (SUS) questionnaire (Brooke, 1996), and fields in which to leave comments regarding the icebricks tool and the experiment.

Analysis of the experimental results was performed by experts who have experience in both BPM and usability. Two people analyzed each video to ensure the data collection was correct. The basic data that was collected for analysis answered five questions: Did the user try to perform the task? Did the user complete the task? Was the user's first action correct? How many actions (clicks) were incorrect? How long did it take to finish the task? This data was then used to calculate the usability metrics of effectiveness, efficiency, and learnability (Albert & Tullis, 2013).

The experimental results showed that the tool's overall usability could be significantly improved with the newer version (Clever, 2016; Neumann, 2016). The experimental results are condensed in Table 4.

Table 4 Experimental results

	Older version	Newer version
Average SUS value	48.19	58.33
Glossary use	81%	99%
Similarity of the labels, per Akkiraju and Ivan (2010)	0.77	0.95
Similarity of the labels, per Minor, Tartakovski, and Bergmann (2007)	0.61	0.85

Argumentative and experimental evaluations showed that the developed tool for the icebricks approach is suitable for application in BPM endeavors but that there is room for improvement, which is considered in the ongoing development of the tool.

We heard positive feedback from companies that have used icebricks in various cases, especially the company in the application case described in this project. The tool is easy to handle and used for process documentation purposes consistently throughout the company. The tool was also used during the certification audit; the auditors stated that it is a good approach with which to document all of the information that is necessary to earn the ISO 9001 certification, and they granted the certificate with no restrictions. The company adopted the tool for use in preparing other certifications, but some feedback suggested a change in versioning and authentication through the company's own single sign-on. The first requirement is currently in development, and we are evaluating the second requirement's feasibility.

4.4   Growth of Design Theory

The combination of scientific insights from deriving objectives, scientific development with a practical orientation, and practical application and evaluation of the tool often leads to good appropriability within the ISO certification case. The latest revision of the ISO 9001 standard to focus on process management accommodates our case since the main focus of the icebricks approach and tool is effective and efficient BPM. We showed in Sect. 2 that the QM and BPM disciplines fit well together from a theoretical point of view, and integrating both disciplines in practice as Davenport (1993) suggested is long overdue. QM incorporates parts of BPM, but their consistent integration is rarely lived in companies. This conceptual fit of BPM approaches in general, the approaches of Becker et al. (2012) and Weske (2012) in particular, and QM (per the ISO 9001 standard) constitute a starting point for further integration of the two approaches.

Our project shows through argumentative and experimental evaluation that the objectives that we collected based on the literature and practical experience serve as a valid foundation for a tool solution in the BPM context. Although the icebricks tool presented in this article fulfills these requirements, it is certainly not the only solution to the initially defined problem. Based on the objectives we gathered, other tool solutions can also provide a valid solution to the given problem.

5 Key Lessons

The aim of this work was to present a way to leverage BPM effectively and efficiently for proper QM. This paper shows that the well-known and widely accepted ISO 9001 standard, which is based on the PDCA cycle, does not differ significantly from prominent procedural BPM approaches like Becker et al. (2012) and Weske (2012); presents the design and development of icebricks, a sophisticated yet easily understandable process-modeling approach, along with its supporting web-based tool in the context of DSR; and offers a practical case that uses the icebricks approach and tool for the preparation of an ISO certification to show that they are appropriate means for such a QM endeavor.

However, even though all aspects of this research are grounded in a scientific basis, the concrete application is limited to one project presented here. Therefore, this work is only the starting point of research on and practical application of using the icebricks approach to facilitate QM undertakings, and we plan to refine and reassess our approach during currently running and upcoming projects. Furthermore, since not all of the ISO 9001 requirements could be met, we also seek to adjust our approach to cover all of ISO 9001's requirements and to determine which additional benefits BPM, especially process modeling, can provide for the ISO 9001 certification in particular and for QM in general.

During the practical application part of the project, we learned about the procedure to be used in BPM-based ISO 9001 projects and about the implications for the DSR-based development of our icebricks BPM tool. Regarding the procedure for creating an ISO 9001-compliant process model, we confirmed our theoretical assumption that established BPM procedure models can not only serve as a starting point but can even guide the modeler to create a process model that fulfills most of the ISO 9001 requirements. The four-phase procedure of *project and modeling preparation, process identification and analysis, conception of target processes,* and *implementation of target processes* builds a good basis for meeting the requirements, although we learned that the *conception of target processes* is not as important for ISO 9001 projects as the *performance evaluation* and the *continuous improvement* mentioned in Chaps. 9 and 10 of the ISO. These steps are often only implied in BPM procedure models, but they should be incorporated and discussed more prominently with respect to the ISO 9001 standard. We also learned that ISO 9001 auditors do not focus on process details as much as they do on the larger picture—that is, on the company's knowledge about its business processes in general. As a result, the framework construction we took from Becker et al.'s (2012) BPM procedure model was of great help during the certification process.

Regarding the development of our BPM tool, icebricks, we learned that simplicity and flexibility are central to success in creating process models for the ISO 9001. The auditors prefer process models that can be understood with one view over technical, complex process models. Even so, the ISO 9001 and the auditors require the representation of several aspects of the company and its activities. To incorporate these aspects in process models and obtain a single, consistent solution for the ISO 9001 documentation, the approach has to be flexible as well. We addressed this flexibility with our attribution concept, which ensures that the attributes are restricted during modeling but can also be freely chosen by authorized employees. This combination of simplicity and flexibility is the key to success for BPM projects, especially with respect to ISO 9001-compliant process models.

From what we learned three general recommendations that can applied to both ISO 9001 projects and the DSR development process emerged:

Use Established Models and Guidelines. The existing BPM procedure models and the modeling guidelines supported us in creating the ISO 9001-compliant process model, even thought they were not focused on the ISO 9001 when they were devised. We strongly recommend using existing (procedure) models and adapting them where necessary to save effort and gain benefits from the experience that led to their development.

Focus on Simplicity and Flexibility. Whether a procedure or tool will be used in practice depends heavily on its simplicity. If a company's employees do not understand a tool from the beginning, they will not put much effort into learning it but will use one that they do understand. Therefore, the first key to success in practical applications is simplicity. The second key is flexibility, which can be achieved by reducing the complexity (i.e., increasing simplicity). New functions should not just be incorporated into a procedure or tool one after another but should be integrated smoothly into the existing simple concept to prevent overloading a procedure or tool.

Consider the Practical Circumstances. Many tools and procedures work well as long as they are applied by the people who developed them. However, companies often reject the tools for practical application because research often assumes "perfect circumstances" instead of considering real practical circumstances, such as time and budget restrictions and lack of knowledge or motivation. One should always keep in mind that a tools and procedure models must address a company's real circumstances to be successful in practice.

Based on our experience in this project, we encourage future research to focus on pragmatism and practical usefulness in the development of such approaches and to share their findings to improve other approaches. We also encourage practitioners to align their businesses in a process-oriented way so they can benefit from the integration of the fields and theoretically well-backed approaches. We hope that our work will encourage more companies to approach QM and the ISO 9001 certification, supported by process modeling as an appropriate means for this endeavor.

References

Akkiraju, R., & Ivan, A. (2010). Discovering business process similarities: An empirical study with SAP best practice business processes. In *Service-Oriented Computing: 8th International Conference, ICSOC 2010* (pp. 515–526), Proceedings, San Francisco, CA, USA, 7–10 December 2010.

Albert, B., & Tullis, T. (2013). Measuring the user experience: Collecting, analyzing, and presenting usability metrics.

Becker, J., & Schütte, R. (2006). A reference model for retail enterprises. In P. Fettke, & P. Loos (Eds.), *Reference Modeling for business systems analysis* (pp. 182–205).

Becker, J., Kugeler, M., & Rosemann, M. (2012). *Prozessmanagement—Ein Leitfaden zur prozessorientierten Organisationsgestaltung.* Germany: Berlin/Heidelberg.

Becker, J., Rosemann, M., & von Uthmann, C. (2000). Guidelines of business process modeling. In: W. van der Aalst, J. Desel, & A. Overweis (Eds.), *Business process management. Lecture notes in computer science* (Vol. 1806). Berlin, Heidelberg: Springer.

Becker, J., Delfmann, P., Herwig, S., Lis, Ł., & Stein, A. (2009). Formalizing linguistic conventions for conceptual models. *Conceptual Modeling-ER, 2009,* 70–83.

Becker, J., Clever, N., Holler, J., Püster, J., & Shitkova, M. (2013a) Integrating process modeling methodology, language and tool—A design science approach. In *Proceedings of the 6th IFIP WG 8.1 Working Conference on the Practice of Enterprise Modeling (PoEM)* (pp. 221–235).

Becker, J., Clever, N., Holler, J., Püster, J., & Shitkova, M. (2013b). Semantically standardized and transparent process model collections via process building blocks. In *Proceedings of the the 5th International Conference on Information, Process, and Knowledge Management—eKNOW 2013* (pp. 172–177), Nice.

Becker, J., Clever, N., Holler, J., Püster, J., & Shitkova, M. (2013c). icebricks—Business process modeling on the basis of semantic standardization. In *Proceedings of the 12th International Conference on Design Science Research in Information Systems and Technologies (DESRIST)*, Helsinki.

Bevan, N., & Bogomolni, I. (2000). Incorporating user quality requirements in the software development process. In *Proceedings 4th International Software Quality Week Europe* (pp. 1192–1204), Brussels.

Brooke, J. (1996). SUS-A quick and dirty usability scale. *Usability Evaluation in Industry, 189,* 194.

Clever, N. (2016). *icebricks.* Berlin: Konstruktion und Anwendung eines Prozessmodellierungswerkzeugs.

Clever, N., Holler, J., Püster, J., & Shitkova, M. (2013). Growing trees—A versioning approach for business process models based on graph theory. In *ECIS 2013 Proceedings* (p. 157), Utrecht, Netherlands.

Davenport, T. H. (1993). Need radical innovation and continuous improvement? Integrate process reengineering and TQM. *Planning Review, 21,* 6–12.

Delfmann, P., Herwig, S., & Lis, Ł. (2009). Unified enterprise knowledge representation with conceptual models—Capturing corporate language in naming conventions. In *ICIS 2009 Proceedings*.

Di Francescomarino, C., & Tonella, P. (2009). Crosscutting concern documentation by visual query of business processes. In *Business process management workshops* (pp. 18–31).

Dijkman, R., Dumas, M., van Dongen, B., Käärik, R., & Mendling, J. (2011). Similarity of business process models: Metrics and evaluation. *Information Systems, 36,* 498–516.

DIN. (2015a). Quality management systems—Fundamentals and vocabulary (ISO 9000:2015).

DIN. (2015b). Quality management systems—Requirements (ISO 9001:2015).

Hadar, I., & Soffer, P. (2006). Variations in conceptual modeling: Classification and ontological analysis. *Journal of AIS, 7,* 568–592.

Hevner, A. R., March, S. T., & Park, J. (2004). Design science in information systems research. *MIS Quarterly, 28,* 75–105.

Holler, J. (2015). Tool support for consultants in business process modeling projects. Design and evaluation of the business process modeling tool icebricks.

Indulska, M., Recker, J., Rosemann, M., & Green, P.: Business process modeling: Current issues and future challenges. In: *Advanced Information Systems Engineering: Proceedings of the International Conference on Advanced Information Systems (CAiSE 2009)*.

ISO. (2017). *ISO Survey*. Retrieved from https://www.iso.org/the-iso-survey.html.

Lindland, O. I., Sindre, G., & Solvberg, A. (1994). Understanding quality in conceptual modeling. *IEEE Software, 11*, 42–49.

Lohrmann, M., & Reichert, M. (2012). Modeling business objectives for business process management. In: *S-BPM ONE–Scientific research* (pp. 106–126).

Mendling, J., Reijers, H. A., & Cardoso, J. (2007). What makes process models understandable? *Business Process Management, 4714*, 48–63.

Mendling, J., Reijers, H.A., & van der Aalst, W. M. P. (2010a). Seven process modeling guidelines (7PMG). *Information and Software Technology, 52*, 127–136.

Mendling, J., Reijers, H. A., & Recker, J. (2010b). Activity labeling in process modeling: Empirical insights and recommendations. *Information Systems, 35*, 467–482.

Mendling, J., Verbeek, H. M. W., van ongen, B. F., van der Aalst, W. M. P., & Neumann, G. (2008). Detection and prediction of errors in EPCs of the SAP reference model. *Data & Knowledge Engineering, 64*, 312–329.

Minor, M., Tartakovski, A., & Bergmann, R. (2007). Representation and structure-based similarity assessment for agile workflows. In: *Case-based reasoning research and development* (pp. 224–238).

Neumann, M. (2016). Application of usability methods to the development of a business process modeling tool. *The icebricks Case*.

Peffers, K., Tuunanen, T., Rothenberger, M., & Chatterjee, S. (2007). A design science research methodology for information systems research. *Journal of Management Information Systems, 24*, 45–77.

Rosa, M. La, & Reijers, H. (2011). APROMORE: An advanced process model repository. *Expert Systems with Applicat, 8*, 7029–7040.

Schütte, R., & Rotthowe, T. (1998). The guidelines of modeling—An approach to enhance the quality in information models. In T. W. Ling, S. Ram, & M.-L. Lee (Eds.), *Proceedings of the 17th International Conference on Conceptual Modeling* (pp. 240–254), Singapore.

Shitkova, M., Clever, N., Holler, J., & Becker, J. (2015). Towards increased comparability of business process models. Design, implementation and evaluation of semantic standardization functionality. In: *2015 IEEE 17th Conference on Business Informatics* (pp. 143–150).

Snowden, D. J., & Boone, M. E. (2007). A leader's framework for decision making. *Harvard Business Review, 85*, 1–8.

Stachowiak, H. (1973). *Allgemeine Modelltheorie*. Wien: Austria.

Weske, M. (2012). *Business process management—Concepts, languages, architectures*, Berlin/Heidelberg, Germany.

zur Muehlen, M., & Recker, J. (2008). How much language is enough? Theoretical and practical use of the business process modeling notation. In *Proceedings 20th International Conference on Advanced Information Systems Engineering*, Montpellier, France.

Usability Mining

Automated Analysis of Information System Usability Based on Process Mining

Sharam Dadashnia, Constantin Houy, and Peter Loos

Abstract The usability of information systems (IS) is a key characteristic in the context of software selection and IS design. IS are supposed to support various functions in business organizations in an effective and efficient way, to be *easy to use and easy to learn*, and to produce *satisfactory outcomes* for users. Research has sought to engineer IS based on automated usability checks, but while the concept of process mining offers considerable potential in this context, so far only little research has been done on the potential of process mining approaches for automating analyses of IS usability. We describe the journeys through and the results of several design research projects that have investigated the potential of combining process mining approaches and usability engineering (i.e., *usability mining*). The design artifacts presented in this study elucidate the potential of usability mining in the context of usability studies, focusing on mobile policing applications developed and used in several projects in Germany. We present a dedicated reference framework for the design of usability mining solutions and a software implementation that we use to illustrate the artifacts' applications in the mobile policing scenario. We present the results of several design projects in which we gathered experience concerning usability mining and its application in real-world scenarios. While the development of a usability mining solution can be managed according to certain design recommendations, data preparation and data cleansing present particular challenges in usability mining endeavors.

S. Dadashnia · C. Houy · P. Loos (✉)
Institute for Information Systems (IWi), German Research Center for Artificial Intelligence
(DFKI), Saarland University, Saarbrücken, Germany
e-mail: peter.loos@iwi.dfki.de

S. Dadashnia
e-mail: sharam.dadashnia@iwi.dfki.de

C. Houy
e-mail: constantin.houy@iwi.dfki.de

© Springer Nature Switzerland AG 2020
J. vom Brocke et al. (eds.), *Design Science Research. Cases*, Progress in IS,
https://doi.org/10.1007/978-3-030-46781-4_7

155

1   Introduction

Information systems (IS) are supposed to support many functions in business organizations effectively and efficiently, so they must be *easy to use, easy to learn*, and lead to a *satisfactory outcome* for users. In addition to these central aspects of *usability*, according to the common definition of *usability* provided by the International Organization for Standardization (ISO), other important usability characteristics include the *efficiency* of use ("quick task performance") and its *memorability* ("quick re-establishment of proficiency after a certain period of not using a product") (Nielsen, 1993). Usability is a key consideration in the selection of business application software and IS design (Thaler, 2014).

Against this background, the field of usability engineering has gained significance in the IS discipline, as it provides results that support the design and development of highly usable IS (Adams, 2015). Considerable research has gone into the usability of IS in general and in such environments as IS management (Batra & Srinivasan, 1992), visual programming (Green & Petre, 1996), websites and web-based business IS (Geng &Tian, 2015; Harms & Schweibenz, 2000a, b), and applications' user interfaces (Hilbert & Redmiles, 2000; Ivory & Hearst, 2001). In addition, several attempts have been made to develop automated approaches to usability analysis (Montero, González, & Lozano, 2005; Schuller, Althoff, McGlaun, Lang, & Rigoll, 2002), especially approaches that are based on established usability metrics (Hornbaeck, 2006; Seffah, Donyaee, Kline, & Padda, 2006), to support the design of IS. However, only a little research has been done on the potential of using process mining approaches to analyze the usability of IS with a dedicated reference to the business processes that an information system or application is supposed to support (Thaler, Maurer, De Angelis, Fettke, & Loos, 2015).

Process mining is a sub-area of data mining and a sub-area of business process management (BPM). The basis for process mining is log data that is produced by business applications or business IS, such as enterprise resource planning (ERP) systems or workflow management systems (WfMS), especially in the form of *event logs* that document the occurrence of particular events in a business process. Information can be extracted from this log data that can support the identification and description of business processes that have actually been executed (van der Aalst & Weijters, 2004). Process mining can serve several purposes, but three process mining approaches are distinguished with regard to their objectives: *discovery, conformance checking*, and *enhancement* (van der Aalst, 2012a, b):

Discovery refers to the procedure through which a process model is derived from an event log. Process discovery, which is used frequently, is an effective procedure with which companies can identify and document their actual business processes and working procedures.

Conformance checking supports the comparison of an existing process model (a to-be process model) to a model that is based on event logs (an as-is process model) or to the log data itself. Thus, conformance checking enables the identification of deviations between defined and actually executed business processes.

Enhancement supports the improvement of existing process models and process definitions by using new findings from the analysis of the actually executed processes that is documented in the event logs.

The authors took part in several research endeavors that investigated the potential of combining process mining approaches and usability engineering, focusing on a strong relationship between the use of application software or an information system and the underlying business process that is supported. The authors have also developed several artifacts and software components that demonstrate the potential of combining these approaches in several design science research (DSR) projects. Process mining can automate usability studies and usability engineering, which has been treated in scientific contributions under the umbrella term *usability mining* (Thaler, 2014; Thaler et al., 2015). Even real-time usability improvement is possible based on log data, which are detailed recordings of actual user behavior in a software application (Dadashnia, Niesen, Hake, Fettke, & Mehdiyev, 2016b). The artifacts presented in this study demonstrate the potential of usability mining in the context of mobile applications that support the German police in the acquisition of accident data and data concerning criminal complaints on the street.

The remainder of this study proceeds as follows: The next section describes the context of the design project, which brings together the worlds of process mining and usability engineering. Then we provide an overview of the research journey we undertook to develop and elaborate our idea of using process mining in usability studies. Several development phases or maturity levels of the resulting artifacts are described as we moved step-by-step toward a more automated analysis procedure while using process mining in our usability studies. We present the dedicated reference framework and software prototype that we developed to support automated process mining-based usability analysis in IS based on event logs. The next section presents the resulting artifact, its application, and its evaluation in a real-world context, as well as some considerations concerning the progression toward a dedicated design theory. Finally, we discuss the key lessons learned in this design journey.

2   The Context

This study explains and demonstrates the potential of process mining approaches in the context of usability engineering. Usability mining offers considerable potential for automated analyses of the usability of business IS. The design journey described in the following is related to several projects in the context of analyzing the use and usability of mobile applications that support the German police in the acquisition of accident data and data concerning criminal complaints. This topic is typically addressed in the literature using the term *mobile (digital) policing.*

The term *mobile policing* describes the use of mobile application systems, such as specialized software applications on mobile devices like smartphones or tablets, to support policework-related processes on the street or in the field with the goal of better information management independent of stationary information and communication systems, access networks, or specific locations (Houy, Gutermuth, Dadashnia, & Loos, 2019). Application software on mobile devices can support both the activities of the police in the field and their follow-up activities in the office, thus facilitating integrated information management and reducing the number of interfaces. Using a paper notebook and a pen to document relevant information related to a traffic accident is still common practice for police throughout the world. Then, after returning to the office, police officers have to enter the content of handwritten notes into the information system, which is not efficient and can result in faulty entries. Using mobile applications in an integrated information infrastructure can help them avoid errors and make the whole process more efficient. These positive effects are more likely if the underlying mobile applications have good usability.

Against this background, the following design journey describes several design phases and project iterations in the context of two usability engineering projects in which the authors participated:

(a) a *proof-of-concept* project that investigated the potential of mobile application software in the context of accident-data acquisition in Germany, using only a few mobile devices in a well-defined small application scenario, and

(b) a *pilot* project that investigated the economic aspects of using mobile application software in the context of accident-data acquisition and data concerning criminal complaints in Germany, using a larger number of mobile devices in a well-defined but broader application scenario.

The basis for the development of design ideas in these endeavors was the usability mining lifecycle proposed in Thaler (2014), which comprises six phases:

(1) *User monitoring*: In this phase the user behavior and interaction with an information system is monitored and documented by means of system log files.

(2) *Trace clustering*: In this phase, the log data is clustered according to criteria that are relevant to the following analyses (e.g., clustering the data concerning specific user groups).

(3) *Usage model derivation*: Based on the clustered log data, a usage model of the information system is automatically developed by means of process discovery approaches, resulting in an as-is process model of the information system usage. The log data allows the metrics that support the following analysis of the usage model to be computed.

(4) *Usage model analysis*: The usage model can be analyzed considering various potential metrics, including *model metrics* (e.g., concerning model size, model complexity, sequentiality), *process metrics* like execution time and error rate, and common *usability metrics* like irrelevant actions, undo actions, and use of the software's help function.

(5) *Recommendation derivation*: In this phase, the results of the analysis are interpreted to develop concrete design recommendations that will improve the usability of the system based on the users' needs.

(6) *Implementation of improvements*: Finally, the design recommendations derived from the analysis are implemented in the software system.

Although we developed our artifacts for usability mining in the context of police-work processes supported by mobile devices, the developed reference framework and the software prototype can be used in many other contexts because the basis for the resulting usability analyses are log files produced by application software, viz., business IS. Hence, the results of our design endeavor could easily be transferred to other application scenarios and application contexts.

3 The Journey

Like almost every design science endeavor, our design journey did not follow a linear process. Our understanding of the particular problems in the context of the *proof-of-concept* and the *pilot* project in the field of mobile policing, as well as possible solutions, improved throughout several design iterations. In the following, we describe our journey toward our prototype for automated usability mining in the case of analyzing mobile application software for the acquisition of accident data and data concerning criminal complaints used by the police in Germany.

3.1 Preliminary Studies

Several preliminary studies of usability mining were conducted at the authors' institution in various application contexts, most of which were relevant to business organizations (Thaler, 2014; Thaler et al., 2015; Dadashnia et al., 2016a, b; 2017). However, in the design science endeavor described here, the particular problems and possible solutions were heavily influenced by the specific conditions of the police context.

As mentioned, it is still common practice for police to use notebook and pen to document information related to a traffic accident and then to enter the content of the handwritten notes manually into the information system in the office. Therefore, at the beginning of the proof-of-concept project, we conducted interviews with police officers to model an "ideal" or at least a commonly accepted structure of this data-acquisition process on the street. We also observed the process of "manual" data acquisition in order to document several cases of actual data-acquisition processes, as well as the execution time of the process instances. Documenting the common process structure and some real-world process instances supported the design and customization of the data acquisition form provided by the mobile policing app on the mobile devices.

To support usability mining concerning the actual use of the mobile policing application, three design iterations were executed.

Table 1 Extract of an exemplary usage event log

Activity	Person	Time stamp
Start app usage	Officer 3	00:00:00
Create new accident case	Officer 3	00:00:20
Document time of accident	Officer 3	00:00:34
Document category of accident	Officer 3	00:00:48
…	…	…

3.2   Lap 1—Initial Usability Mining Solution

Understanding the Problem: When the proof-of-concept project began, the mobile policing app was not configured to produce event logs, as this feature could not be provided in the test setting. To be able to use process mining approaches in our usability mining solution, we had to capture event logs in another way. To avoid disturbing police officers in their work, the research team could not be present in most data-acquisition cases to observe and document the usage, so we had to find a workaround.

Understanding the Solution: In configuring our usability mining solution, we had to deal with the missing event log, so we used an additional screen-capturing software on the mobile devices and asked all proof-of-concept participants to record their interactions with the mobile policing app. Then we manually transcribed the resulting videos, thereby manually producing event logs that could be clustered and used for the derivation and analysis of the usage model by means of process mining techniques. Table 1 is an extract of an exemplary event log.

It was also possible to extract more coarse-grained usage data from the central SharePoint server, which received data from all mobile devices that participated in the mobile policing infrastructure. This usage data contained information about the use of various sub-areas of the app (form pages for persons involved (e.g., witnesses) or the cause of an accident) and could also support usability mining activities. Although no exact click-stream information could be obtained this way, this workaround helped us to gather further information, especially in cases that were not recorded by means of the screen-capturing software. This information served as an input for usability mining in the next phase.

The usage model partly shown in Fig. 1 was created using the filtering mechanisms of the process mining tool *Disco,*[1] which we used to analyze the usage and system interaction data. Based on this usage model, we could, for example, provide a recommendation concerning the identification of the nearest house number ("Nr.") on the street ("Straße") in which an accident had happened. Identifying a house number may quite time consuming if it is not directly recognizable, such as in the area of a large intersection or in streets with commercial buildings. While this problem has nothing to do with the application design but is due to the underlying technical process, such

---

[1] https://fluxicon.com/disco/.

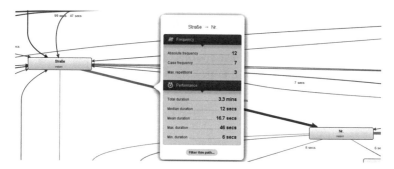

Fig. 1 Exemplary part of the usage model using the process mining tool Disco

cases often occur in real-life policing processes and are well suited to improvements in the work process and the supporting IT infrastructure. GPS-supported localization services were recommended based in this usage model to automate this step in the data acquisition.

Thus, the usability mining solution used in the proof-of-concept project consisted of a data-acquisition environment using a screen-capturing software on a mobile device and an existing process mining tool to enable usability mining. Figure 2 presents an overview of the usability mining solution that resulted from the first design iteration. An improvement on the approach that was realized in the following pilot project is demonstrated in the next section.

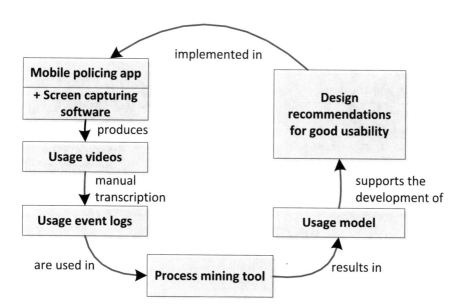

Fig. 2 Usability mining solution resulting from the first design iteration

3.3   Lap 2—Automation of Capturing the Usage Event Log

The second design iteration took place during the pilot project, which followed the proof-of-concept project. The pilot project used a larger number of mobile devices to investigate the economic aspects of using the mobile application software in the context of accident data acquisition and data concerning criminal complaints in Germany.

Understanding the Problem: The usability mining solution that was developed in the first design iteration relied on manual transcription procedures and would have caused too much effort in a scenario with a large number of mobile devices (about 100) over a period of several months. Hence, further automation steps concerning capturing the usage event log in the user-monitoring phase were needed.

Understanding the Solution: At the beginning of the pilot project, we developed a concept and a software implementation of a usage-logging script that allows usage event logs to be captured automatically in the mobile policing app. The software vendor then integrated this logging script into the mobile policing app used in the pilot project. Thus, the user monitoring phase could be automated, and the usability mining procedure was much more efficient and could also deal with the higher amount of data acquired during the pilot project. We used two tools to analyze the usage event logs: Disco for process mining and Microsoft Power BI for further data analysis procedures that were useful in the usability mining context. Figure 3 illustrates the usability mining solution that resulted from the second design iteration.

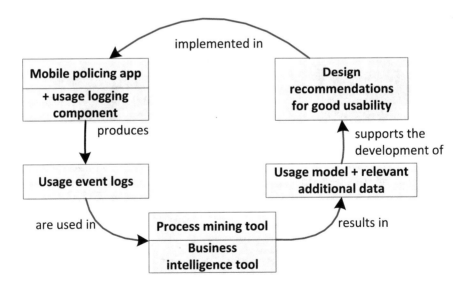

Fig. 3   Usability mining solution resulting from the second design iteration

The next section demonstrates an improvement of our second approach that was also realized in the pilot project.

3.4 Lap 3—Automatic Calculation of Usability Metrics

Understanding the Problem: While the usability mining solution developed in the second design iteration provided the usage models and helpful data analyses like common process key performance indicators (KPI), we still lacked precise information related to peculiarities of the system usage that could be measured with metrics commonly used in the field of usability engineering. Usability metrics and related information generated based on process mining methods can be helpful in detecting usability problems concerning IS quickly.

Understanding the Solution: To improve the functionality of our solution for analyses, we developed a concept and a software implementation for the automated calculation of usability metrics from the automatically captured usage event logs. This development step resulted in a concrete usability mining solution and a more general reference framework for automated usability mining, which is presented in the following section in more detail. Figure 4 illustrates the usability mining solution that resulted from the third design iteration.

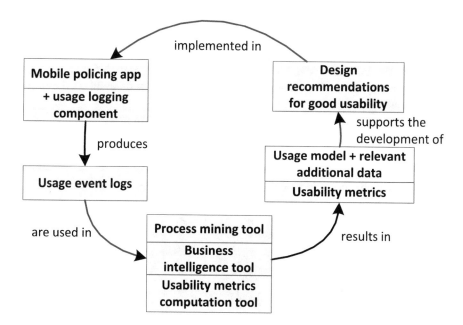

Fig. 4 Usability mining solution that resulted from the third design iteration

4   The Results

4.1   Presentation of Artifact(s)

4.1.1   Reference Framework for Automated Usability Mining

This section introduces a new reference framework for automated usability mining. In contrast to the lifecycle concept presented in Thaler (2014), the automation of all possible steps of the usability mining process is a central aspect of our reference framework.

We focus on a detailed presentation of the automated calculation of usability metrics and the related components in the reference framework. The reference framework can serve as a design recommendation for individual automated usability mining solutions. An instantiation of this reference framework was used in the pilot project. The term *artifact* in the following discussion refers to either the reference framework or its instantiation in the context of the pilot project. The major purpose of the artifact is to support both software developers and usability experts with its usability engineering knowledge. The reference framework consists of three major components, visualized in the Fig. 5 and explained in more detail in the following.

The advantage of the framework is its focus on business IS and the underlying business processes, which allows the conformance of the actual user behavior with the defined business processes to be measured.

1. **Data collection**: The first component offers experts and system developers the possibility to generate usage event logs while using business IS, to store them appropriately, and to ensure they are in a suitable form for later analysis. This component should offer the use of multiple data sources and should also be easily extendable.

2. **Automated metric calculation**: The second component supports the automated calculation of usability metrics based on the data collected by the first component. Usability metrics and methods from the field of process mining are used to exploit the potential for automation. The artifact provides calculation rules for the metrics in the form of, for example, pseudocode and the use of process mining algorithms

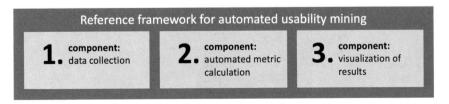

Fig. 5   Three components of the reference framework for automated usability mining

or their extensions or a combination of approaches. Conceptual interfaces for extending metrics by adding additional data sources are also part of the artifact.

3. **Visualization of results**: The third component of the artifact manages the visualization of the generated results in a process-aware way. Here, the calculated usability metrics are added in order of the process based on the usage model created by means of process discovery approaches. Hence, the usage model is a fine-grained process model in which individual click activities can be assigned to a function in the business process model, ensuring that technically incorrect sequences or paths in the system can be detected visually. The goal is to highlight individual click activities in the same color if they belong to the same business process function, which is essential in applications that depict large business processes. (For example, efficiency improvements can easily be visualized through color gradients.) Here, exploration in the usage model can directly support the detection of rebounds or poorly arranged functionalities, as such patterns that occur frequently can indicate inefficiently arranged elements of the user interface. Frequent rebounds can also indicate an outdated process. The color highlighting, in combination with calculated and annotated metrics, is an innovation in the context of existing applications for analyzing application systems' operational usability.

4.1.2 Instantiation of the Reference Framework for Automated Usability Mining in the Context of the Pilot Project

Here we provide a detailed review of the artifact using a running example of an automated calculation of usability metrics. We focus on the second component, *automated metric calculation*. While we explain the basic concepts for all components, we also describe the technical concept and the implementation of the second component and illustrate the component's application by means of an example. Figure 6 illustrates the focus in the following explanations of our instantiation of the reference framework.

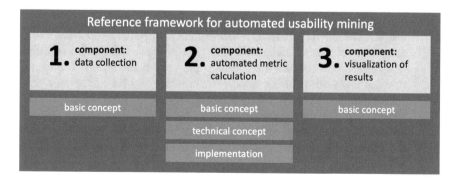

Fig. 6 Focus of the explanations of the reference framework

Literature has provided about fifty usability metrics with automation potential, which we classified in terms of their automation potential in literature review (the publication of the literatur review including with the respective classification is forthcoming). Certain metrics were already automatable, but some metrics can be raised to a new level of granularity in the information provided using process mining methods. In the following, we present the automated calculation of one metric, *usage effectiveness*, to demonstrate the artifact's development process. The automated calculation of this metric is based on the approach presented in Saleh, Ismail, and Fabil (2017), which supports analyses of software systems' effectiveness. To provide meaningful results, certain manual steps, such as task definition and measurement of duration times, must be executed at the beginning. The ISO definition of usage effectiveness is important for the software systems that support a firm's essential core business processes if the processes are to be effective and have low duration times (ISO:9241, 1998). Effectiveness refers to how well the system supports the user in achieving high-quality results. Saleh et al. (2017) refer to the *number of touches* with the software as indicating effectiveness by showing how many interactions are required to achieve a goal. The metric provides insights into *successfully executed tasks*, so it indicates the software's effectiveness in a usability-aware way. For example, in the context of our pilot project, the *usage effectiveness* metric indicates how many interactions are necessary for a police officer to acquire all of the accident data when using the mobile policing application.

Next, we present the basic concepts concerning the artifact in relation to our running example.

1. **Data collection**

   Usage event logs play an important role as an input variable to the metric calculation. In the context of our pilot project, the usage event log records the actual use of the accident-data acquisition forms and the police officers' interactions with the mobile device. Here we provide requirements specifications to ensure that all necessary data is collected by a corresponding software component. We describe the necessary data attributes for log entries to calculate the *usage effectiveness* metric in the context of the pilot project:

   1. **caseID**: The individual caseID is automatically generated by the system when an officer records an incident. In the pilot project scenario, the caseID is generated by a control system from a previous process step. The caseID remains unchanged during the entire recording and the subsequent post-processing.

   2. **timeStamp**: The time stamp, which saves the exact time of every interaction with the system, consists of a customer-specific time specification for when the action is executed so the sequence of activities and the time between them are recorded.

   3. **divElementID**: The div-element ID is a unique ID for each separate part of the form document (div-element) used during the action, such as the Textbox, the Dropdown Menu, or the Checkbox. This ID enables a clear mapping

of a log entry and a corresponding screen element. For two identical div-elements on different views, different labels are used, so the div-elements can be distinguished in later analyses.

4. **versionNumber**: The version number, which refers to the application's version, highlights the differences in the versions and documents the process of the application development.

Besides the user's interaction data, a process model designed for the common workflow must be used in the analysis. The common workflow can be imported to the system via a sequence of click events, which must be enriched with the corresponding activity from a business process perspective to ensure conformance with the process. In our pilot project, we defined a best-practice process model for the accident-data acquisition in mobile policing, which was the basis for the conformance checks in the project.

2. **Automated metric calculation**

The described component measures how many of the activities specified in a task are actually executed by the user. For this purpose, the *longest common subsequence* (LCS) of process steps executed and corresponding activities in the model is gauged. The length of the LCS is compared to the number of required activities, relaying the cases in which only certain activities were completed and which activities are the most frequent. Hence, weak points can be uncovered and badly functioning task sections can be improved. The metric used is based on Tullis and Albert (2008), who introduced the binary or ordinal evaluation of tasks under the term *task success*. A clear start and end state must be defined at the beginning of any study, and success must be defined. In our case, we already knew the start and end events as well as the process's goal (e.g., successfully saved accident data). Saleh et al. (2017) propose an automatic measurement of the number of successfully completed tasks in relation to the number of tasks begun, but the extant research describes no evaluation algorithm. Therefore, we describe the technical concept considering the available process knowledge.

Technical Concept: The usage behavior we consider here normally deals with the completion of a task like acquisition of accident data. Otherwise, the log must be examined for the task's activities and its start and end states, and relevant data must be determined. Therefore, the LCS is used, and the information that can be deduced from the defined process (in our case, the best-practice process for acquisition of accident data). We use the task to be analyzed and the given log as input variables. In this context, we describe the task as a sequence of single activities. For each case, we calculate the LCS to get an overview of the executed process instances' conformance. These subsequences are stored in a result set, which is the input parameter for the metric calculated later regarding the effectiveness ("correctly executed instances of a corresponding task") (Fig. 7).

The score is calculated as follows: The sum of the frequency of the single LCS and the length of the single sequences is divided by the related cases and the length of the given task. (We ensure that we calculate with only the subsequences of a given

Fig. 7 Pseudocode for the
calculation of the LCS result
set

```
Input: task, log
C ← set of all cases in log
result ← Ø
with rᵢ ∈ result: (lcs, caselist)
foreach case in C do
   clcs ← LCS(task, case)
   if (clcs, _ ) exists in result then
   |   update(results, results.lcs = clcs, (caselist.add(case)))
   else
   |   result.add((clcs, list(case)))
   end
end
return(result)
```

task; otherwise, the result set would be empty.) The result is a metric that gives the relative frequency of the task to be executed and the actual executed sequences. If the result is 1, the software system and the corresponding business process (e.g. the actual mobile policing data acquisition process) are effective, as they conform to the best-practice process in terms of time and order of activities. If the result is <1, there are problems with the process, and critical tasks should be investigated. The metric is calculated according to Eq. (1):

$$E_p = \frac{\sum_{i=0}^{n} length(lcs_i) * |caselist_i|}{|cases| * |task|} \quad using \quad i = |result| \tag{1}$$

The Eq. (1) Automated metric calculation for *usage effectiveness*.

3. **Visualization of results**

   The visualization component presents the calculated metrics and other information in an appropriate dashboard. Other information displayed in this dashboard includes information about the conformance of as-is processes presented in the form of (sub-)sequences, and all variants of the process documented in the usage event logs.

4.1.3   Technical Aspects of the Artifact's Instantiation

To ensure proper use of the artifact, a software prototype was developed based the findings of our design journey. In the first step, we designed an appropriate system architecture. The prototype is a software artifact that primarily illustrates the concept and is the basis for the further development of the artifact. The software prototype was developed as a web application.

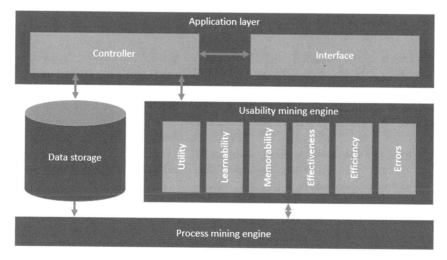

Fig. 8 Usability mining solution architecture from the third design iteration

For the implementation, we needed a suitable process mining engine. We used an R-based solution called *bupaR*[2] in the third design iteration. The developed application is a "classic" web application with a client server architecture. During the implementation, we set a high value on the possibility of integrating additional components into the artifact in the future. The individual components were developed using *ShinyR* and *Shiny Dashboard*,[3] which are extensive packages for setting up a web app and supporting quick creation of interactive interfaces. We used a file-based data model to guarantee a high level of autonomy and quick operational use of the prototype. In addition to the *bupaR* package, the *QualV* package was used for the sequence analysis. To create interactive diagrams, we use the JavaScript-based libraries *plotly* and *ggplot2* in combination. We also modified the *bupaR*-generated process models with the library *svg-pan-zoom* to ensure ease of navigation through the graphs.

The technical overview of the software prototype is shown in Fig. 8. The application layer describes the interface for developers and usability experts.

Besides the user interface of the dashboard, we developed the usability mining engine that retrieves the relevant data from a controller component, which itself retrieves the data from the local storage. We also use a process mining algorithm for the automated calculation of every usability metric.

---

[2]https://www.bupar.net/.

[3]https://shiny.rstudio.com/.

4.2   Application of Artifact(s)

In addition to the technical implementation, we present the concrete application of the implemented concept for the use case "data acquisition concerning criminal complaints." The usage event logs of the mobile policing application in the pilot project were also captured using the logging script that we introduced in the journey section. We used the import screen shown in Fig. 9 to import the appropriate user interaction data, which was collected over a six-month period for this use case (24 data sets), into the usability mining solution.

The import view consists of three sections. Section 1 provides an overview of currently uploaded datasets. We need four datasets for the calculation: the log ("Usage event log"), a sequence of the defined usage process ("Tasks"), the assignment of the tasks and the click events ("Assignments"), and a list with all possible actions in the system ("Overall actions"). Section 2 provides selection fields based on the various parameters for the process mining algorithm. The user can choose which activities should be shown in the process model based on their occurrence. Section 3 allows the analysis of the implemented usability metrics to be started. For data management, the user should be able to import documents in XES or CSV format, save them, delete them if necessary, and obtain an overview of all available documents. The XES file contains the usage log to be examined, and the CSV files contain the activity grouping, the task, and the number of elements in the system. The input data for analyses should be stored separately from each other so they are reusable for further analyses.

The system generates a process model based on the event log provided and enriches it with classic process mining information like duration times, frequencies, and an appropriate visualization. For each of the developed usability dimensions, a separate site provides the results and the visualization of the metrics. In addition, a key measure can be determined and displayed for each dimension. In the *usage effectiveness case* presented later, we find an *effectiveness* value of 0.33 (Fig. 10). Under the assumption that the analysis of real data can lead to unforeseen deviations

Fig. 9   Usability mining tool: data import screen

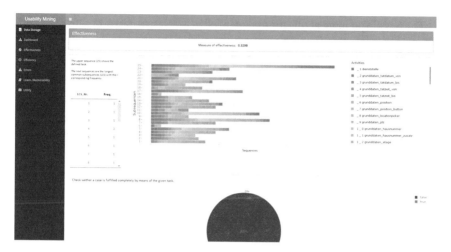

Fig. 10 Usability mining tool: screen for the measurement of effectiveness

from the theoretical concept and that there is no one correct result but a multitude of correct results, the presentation of the analysis' results should be interactive and explorable (Günther & van der Aalst 2007).

Figure 10 presents the measured *effectiveness* and the task-execution sequences. One sequence effectiveness screen shows all activities of the complete process ("Task"), while others present the LCS of all twenty-four recorded usage process instances. The screen also shows the frequencies of each calculated LCS, and users can access an overview of detailed information by hovering the pointer over the screen's elements, such as the corresponding cases. The screen also provides a pie chart that shows how often a task was successfully executed. In this particular use case, no cases were completely performed in the intended way; every sequence and subsequence was either not completed or not performed in the intended way.

4.3 Evaluation of Artifact(s)

We applied the developed artifacts to the real-world scenario of the pilot project to validate and evaluate them. This section presents the results of using the prototype and demonstrates the artifact's feasibility and the value added (Gregor & Hevner 2013). In our case, the functional feasibility of an innovative solution for a previously unsolved problem is shown, along with additional insights into existing design problems. For this purpose, the usage data on the mobile policing application we captured was analyzed with the help of the prototype. The automatically generated usability metrics should also be compared with the findings of manual in-depth analyses of the developed usage models to determine the explanatory power and the informative value of the automatically computed metrics.

The mobile policing application is intended to accelerate the recording of relevant data in the field and, thus, to improve the administrative process and reduce its costs. We investigated the case of capturing and analyzing data concerning criminal complaints using a data set with twenty-four user-interaction logs.

First, the data available in CSV format was prepared. Then incorrectly formatted entries were corrected, and the labels, especially the activity labels, were normalized to ensure the resulting process models are easy to understand. The entries were then converted to the XES format using Disco and saved in application-specific event logs. Each event has the following attributes: caseID, timestamp, activity, location, form type, and data origin. We analyzed the data under the assumption that the group of users is stable and that the individual users have approximately the same level of experience after their introduction to the mobile policing app at the beginning of the project. To create the data entries, we assigned an interface element to each activity in the log. The target model, which describes the recording of the criminal complaint using the app, was defined as a task made up of individual interactions and the sequence of using the interface elements.

The automatically calculated value of *effectiveness* and the visualization of the sequence diagrams in Fig. 10 already indicate that the execution quality of the task in our example case can be significantly improved. The score indicates that an average of 33% of the defined activities were executed in the intended order in the use case example and that none of the twenty-four cases fulfills the task completely; even the "best" LCS reaches less than two-thirds of the target. None of the process instances contains all of the defined steps. This result can be traced back to activities that never occur in the target model, as they are seldom used in real-life cases. Thus, there is a considerable discrepancy between the target model and the actual executions, indicating potential for improvement in the application's usability. Next, we made several improvement recommendations and suggestions for further customizing of the mobile policing app based on the results provided by our prototype. One example was already illustrated in the journey section of this chapter. (see Fig. 1 and the related explanations.)

We concluded that the artifact, especially its software implementation, provides a feasible and valuable solution to the problem of automating the usability metric calculation based on process mining techniques.

4.4 Growth of Design Theory

The design of our usability mining solution was developed in the context of real-world projects with the German police. This project context had considerable influence on design decisions and the resulting artifact, especially the earlier design iterations. However, we believe that the current state of our usability mining artifact has considerable potential for many classes of business and governmental IS. The results of our design journey can also contribute to the growth and development of design theory of usability mining.

While there is no widely accepted definition of the term *design theory* and no consensus on what the constituent parts or components of a design theory should be—the discussion can be traced in, for example, Baskerville and Pries-Heje (2010), Fischer, Winter, and Wortmann (2010), Gregor (2006), Gregor and Jones (2007), Mandviwalla (2015), Suh (1998), and Walls, Widmeyer, and El Sawy (1992, 2004), and —there is consensus that design theory "says how a design can be carried out in a way which is both effective and feasible" (Walls et al. 1992, p. 37). We believe that the reference framework we developed is useful in many contexts of IS usage. Against this background, we are currently developing a more detailed presentation of the reference framework that takes the information presented here to a more generalized level. However, we can present some essential *design prescriptions* (DP) concerning how to develop a usability mining tool that is both effective and feasible and how to use it.

DP₁: The development of a scalable usability mining tool requires that the developer use adequate interfaces to acquire event log data automatically from the IS that is to be analyzed.

DP₂: The development of a versatile usability mining tool with all the functionality needed to go through the common usability mining lifecycle requires that the developer integrate automated analysis functionalities concerning the discovery of the usage model, the analysis of process execution metrics (etc.), and the computation of usability metrics.

DP₃: To provide useful application design recommendations based on the results of using a developed usability mining tool, the developer and system administrator should ensure that the users' system usage interactions are always documented in relation to the underlying tasks in a business process.

DP₄: To provide proper conformance checking results with a developed usability mining tool, those responsible for business process modeling should annotate additional business process-related information, such as the duration of the process or task, to the business process model.

DP₅: To provide useful design recommendations with a usability mining tool, the user should use all available information from the usage model, the process metrics, and the usability metrics.

The next section presents key findings and lessons learned from our design journey in the process of developing the usability mining reference framework and its instantiation in the proof-of-concept and the pilot project.

5 Key Lessons

As in many data science projects, data cleansing and preparation were a major issue in our design endeavor. Unusable data sets, target-oriented clustering, and obvious outliers must be addressed before meaningful usage models can be created and can serve as a basis for additional improvements of the business IS being analyzed.

Therefore, we had to ensure we included enough time in our schedule to deal with these issues.

Information about business processes and the information from the user interaction logs must be included if new usability information is to be generated, along with consideration of the underlying business process, which probably provides the most important benefits from using usability mining in organizations.

A particularly important success factor in using our usability mining solution in the various project phases was the granularity of the data. In our case, we first manually collected data in an "old fashioned" but also business-process-function-aware way (*Lap 1*). This data was useful in such analyses as overall duration time and other metrics in the context of business process analysis. (However, this data is not appropriate for detailed analyses regarding interaction problems.) Later, using the logging script, we had more fine-grained data, which could support our usability analyses.

Besides the granularity of the user-interaction data, the addition of relevant metadata can be useful, although such data were not part of the projects described here for reasons of privacy. User data like age and department could serve in additional investigations. The collection of other information can also be helpful in classifying process instances and the surrounding circumstances of the process instance execution. For example, when a user collects data in a noisy environment like a highway, the noise could cause certain parts of the process to take a longer time to complete, as noise can affect concentration and communication.

Another important success factor was the use of a tailored process mining solution in later iterations. In the first lap, we used an out-of-the-box process discovery solution. The detection of potential usability problems that resulted from using this tool was promising. However, the necessary detailed analysis could be done only using significant manual effort, so there was a demand for the automated detection of usability problems based on established usability engineering methods, especially the metrics. Therefore, we provided a framework and used adaptable process mining functionalities in our instantiation, which can be extended further. The goal is to enable users of the framework to build on its existing components to develop new approaches regarding new data sources or new usability metrics. There is also a demand to use standards like XES for the log generation and to provide concepts and methods to extend such standards.

Clearly, every solution can be developed further, which is also the case with the artifact presented here and certain details concerning the automated calculation of usability metrics. We are working on a more detailed presentation, definition, and implementation of the most common usability metrics, which can serve for automated usability analyses.

Acknowledgments The research described in this chapter was supported in part by a grant from the German Federal Ministry of Education and Research (*Bundesministerium für Bildung und Forschung, BMBF*), project name: "RUMTIMe: Real-Time Usability Improvement based on Process Mining," supported by the Software Campus Initiative. The research was also supported in part by a grant from the German Federal Ministry of Education and Research, project name: "Pro-PlanE—Echtzeit-Process-Mining in der Produktionsplanung mit Kundenbezug," support code FKZ

S01IS16040A. The authors of this chapter thank Matthias Adams for supporting the development and furthermore all project partners for their cooperation. Our special thanks go to all involved ministries and police authorities in Saarland and Rhineland-Palatinate, Accenture Deutschland GmbH, Avanade Deutschland GmbH, icomedias GmbH and Microsoft Deutschland GmbH.

References

Adams, K. M. (2015). *Understandability, usability, robustness and survivability. Nonfunctional requirements in systems analysis and design* (pp. 201–220), Heidelberg.

Baskerville, R., & Pries-Heje, J. (2010). Explanatory design theory. *Business and Information Systems Engineering, 2*(5), 271–282.

Batra, D., & Srinivasan, A. (1992). A review and analysis of the usability of data management environments. *International Journal of Man-Machine Studies, 36*(3), 395–417.

Dadashnia, S., Niesen, T., Fettke, P., & Loos, P. (2016a). Towards a real-time usability improvement framework based on process mining and big data for business information systems. *Tagungsband Multikonferenz Wirtschaftsinformatik (MKWI-16)*, Ilmenau, Germany.

Dadashnia, S., Niesen, T., Hake, P., Fettke, P., Mehdiyev, N., & Evermann, J. (2016b). Identification of distinct usage patterns and prediction of customer behavior. In *Sixth International Business Process Intelligence Challenge (BPIC'16) located at BPI Workshop/BPM* 2016, Rio de Janeiro, Brazil.

Dadashnia, S., Houy, C., & Loos, P. (2017). Mobile Verkehrsunfallerfassung bei der Polizei im Saarland—Zur wissenschaftlichen Begleitforschung des Projektes VU-App. *Veröffentlichungen des Instituts für Wirtschaftsinformatik (IWi) im Deutschen Forschungszentrum für Künstliche Intelligenz (DFKI)—IWi-Heft 204*. Saarbrücken, Germany.

Fischer, C., Winter, R., & Wortmann, F. (2010). Design theory. *Business and Information Systems Engineering, 2*(6), 387–390.

Geng, R., & Tian, J. (2015). Improving web navigation usability by comparing actual and anticipated usage. *IEEE Transactions on Human-Machine Systems, 45*(1), 84–94.

Green, T. R. G., & Petre, M. (1996). Usability analysis of visual programming environments: A cognitive dimensions framework. *Journal of Visual Languages and Computing, 7*(2), 131–174.

Gregor, S. (2006). The nature of theory in information systems. *MIS Quarterly, 30*(3), 611–642.

Gregor, S., & Hevner, A. R. (2013). Positioning and presenting design science research for maximum impact. *MIS Quarterly, 37*(2), 337–355.

Gregor, S., & Jones, D. (2007). The anatomy of a design theory. *Journal of the AIS, 8*(5), 312–335.

Günther, C. W., & van der Aalst, W. M. P. (2007). Fuzzy mining—Adaptive process simplification based on multi-perspective metrics. In G. Alonso, P. Dadam, & M. Rosemann (Eds.), *Business Process Management (BPM)* (pp. 328–343), Berlin.

Harms, I., & Schweibenz, W. (2000a). Testing web usability. *Information Management & Consulting, 15*(3), 61–66.

Harms, I., & Schweibenz, W. (2000b). Usability engineering methods for the web. Results from a usability study. In G. Knorz, & R. Kuhlen (Eds.), *Informationskompetenz—Basiskompetenz in der Informationsgesellschaft. Proceedings des 7. Internationalen Symposiums für Informationswissenschaft* (ISI 2000) (pp. 17–30), Dieburg, Germany.

Hilbert, D. M., & Redmiles, D. F. (2000). Extracting usability information from user interface events. *ACM Computing Surveys, 32*(4), 384–421.

Hornbaeck, K. (2006). Current practice in measuring usability: Challenges to usability studies and research. *International Journal of Human-Computer Studies, 64*(2), 79–102.

Houy, C., Gutermuth, O., Dadashnia, S., & Loos, P. (2019). Digitale Polizeiarbeit. In T. Klenk, F. Nullmeier, & G. Wewer (Eds.), *Digitalisierung in Staat und Verwaltung,* Wiesbaden.

ISO:9241. (1998). Ergonomic requirements for office work with visual display terminals. Part 11: Guidance on usability.

Ivory, M. Y., & Hearst, M. A. (2001). The state of the art in automating usability evaluation of user interfaces. *ACM Computing Surveys, 33*(4), 470–516.

Mandviwalla, M. (2015). Generating and justifying design theory. *Journal of the AIS, 16*(5), 314–344.

Montero, F., González, P., Lozano, M., & Vanderdonckt, J. (2005). Quality models for automated evaluation of web sites usability and accessibility. In J. Vanderdonckt (Ed.), *International COST294 workshop on user interface quality models* (pp. 37–43). Rome: Italy.

Nielsen, J. (1993). *Usability engineering,* Boston.

Saleh, A., Ismail, R., & Fabil, N. (2017). Evaluating usability for mobile application: A MAUEM approach. In *Proceedings of the 2017 International Conference on Software and e-Business* (pp. 71–77), New York, NY, USA.

Schuller, B., Althoff, F., McGlaun, G., Lang, M., & Rigoll, G. (2002). Towards automation of usability studies. In A. El Kamel, K. Melloui, & P. Borne (Eds.), *2002 IEEE International Conference on Systems, Man and Cybernetics.*

Seffah, A., Donyaee, M., Kline, R. B., & Padda, H. K. (2006). Usability measurement and metrics: A consolidated model. *Software Quality Journal, 14*(2), 159–178.

Suh, N. P. (1998). Axiomatic design theory for systems. *Research in Engineering Design, 10*(4), 189–209.

Thaler, T. (2014). Towards usability mining. In E. Plödereder, L. Grunske, E. Schneider, & D. Ull (Eds.), *Informatik 2014* (pp. 2269–2280), Innsbruck, Austria.

Thaler, T., Maurer, D., De Angelis, V., Fettke, P., & Loos, P. (2015). Mining the usability of business process modeling tools: Concept and case study. In J. Mendling, & J. vom Brocke (Eds.), In *Proceedings of the Industry Track at the 13th International Conference on Business Process Management 2015 (BPM 2015)* (pp. 152–166), Innsbruck, Austria.

Tullis, T., & Albert, B. (2008). *Measuring the user experience: Collecting, analyzing, and presenting usability metrics,* Amsterdam.

van der Aalst, W. (2012a). Process mining. *Communication of the ACM, 55*(8), 76–83.

van der Aalst, W. M. P. (2012b). Process mining: Overview and opportunities. *ACM Transactions on Management Information Systems, 3*(2), 7:1–7:17.

van der Aalst, W. M. P., & Weijters, A. J. M. M. (2004). Process mining: A research agenda. *Computers in Industry, 53*(3), 231–244.

Walls, J. G., Widmeyer, G. R., & El Sawy, O. A. (1992). Building an information system design theory for vigilant EIS. *Information Systems Research, 3*(1), 36–59.

Walls, J. G., Widmeyer, G. R., & El Sawy, O. A. (2004). Assessing information system design theory in perspective: How useful was our 1992 initial rendition? *Journal of Information Technology Theory and Application, 6*(2), 43–58.

Designing Process Guidance Systems the Case of IT Service Management

Stefan Morana and Alexander Maedche

Abstract Organizations specify the processes that need to be followed in order to standardize employees' work and improve their process execution. One important challenge in this context is the users' lack of process knowledge. Employees' process knowledge is a necessary prerequisite for proper process execution and a critical factor for achieving successful process standardization, improvement, and ultimately process performance. Therefore, it is key for organizations to support their employees with the proper process knowledge. In order to address this challenge, we propose the concept of process guidance and design process guidance systems to increase users' process knowledge and their process execution performance. We argue that users require (1) general information on the process, such as an overview of all the steps and their sequence, (2) specific information on how to execute the steps to navigate through the process, and (3) the possibility to identify their current position within the process. When reflecting our DSR project, we identified three major key learnings. First, it was important to have identified multiple literature streams for the grounding of our design. Second, involving in a real-world case and engaging with our case company helped us to improve the relevance as well as the contribution of our research. Third, another important lesson learned is that researchers applying the DSR approach should be engaged with the DSR community, in particular the International Conference on Design Science Research in Information Systems and Technology (DESRIST) conference.

S. Morana (✉)
Junior Professorship for Digital Transformation and Information Systems, Saarland University, Saarbruecken, Germany
e-mail: stefan.morana@uni-saarland.de

A. Maedche
Karlsruhe Institute of Technology (KIT), Institute of Information Systems and Marketing (IISM), Karlsruhe, Germany
e-mail: alexander.maedche@kit.edu

© Springer Nature Switzerland AG 2020
J. vom Brocke et al. (eds.), *Design Science Research. Cases*, Progress in IS,
https://doi.org/10.1007/978-3-030-46781-4_8

1 Introduction

Organizations specify the processes that need to be followed in order to standardize employees' work and improve their process execution (Davenport & Short, 1990; Rosemann & vom Brocke, 2015). Employees need to conform with predefined process specifications in order to enable organizations to profit from the benefits of such a process standardization (Schaefer, Fettke, & Loos, 2013). Employees' process knowledge is a necessary prerequisite for proper process execution and a critical factor for achieving successful process standardization, improvement, and ultimately process performance (Amaravadi & Lee, 2005; Münstermann, Eckhardt, & Weitzel, 2010; Seethamraju & Marjanovic, 2009). Particularly novice users require support in their process execution because their process knowledge is often limited. Because of their insufficient process knowledge, these users are likely to choose less effort-expensive strategies, like workarounds (Alter, 2014), to carry out their daily work and execute processes without considering the specifications, which may lead to a loss of accuracy (Singh, 1998). More importantly, deviating from or even violating organizational defined process specifications can lead to serious consequences: For example, a critical accident that occurred at a nuclear fuel processing facility in Japan in 1999 can be traced back to a change in the operating process that had neither been approved nor communicated (Bhanot, 2000). Deviations from the process can also result in lower organizational performance and decreased satisfaction of the organizations' customers (Frei, Kalakota, Leone, & Marx, 1999). Thus, proper process execution is critical to organizations' success, and it is therefore important for organizations to support their employees by providing them with the required process knowledge (Amaravadi & Lee, 2005; Münstermann et al., 2010).

Traditional organizational support structures, such as handbooks or training, are known to be less successful at supporting users' process performances (Sykes, 2015), whereas embedded support concepts have proved to be successful at increasing users' knowledge and helping them to make proper decisions (Limayem & DeSanctis, 2000). In the context of processes, guidance promises to be a valuable concept to address users' lack of process knowledge. In particular, novice users with a limited understanding of existing process specifications are expected to benefit from guidance (Dhaliwal & Benbasat, 1996; Gregor & Benbasat, 1999).

Process guidance is comparable to car navigation, which provides car drivers with the required spatial information. When moving from location A to B, individuals require information on the upcoming route and how to follow this route to reach the desired destination. Since processes can be very complex and highly branched, users require support when trying to find their way during their process execution. Especially novice users can use systems providing process guidance "*prospectively, as a guide to what actions ought to be taken*" (Feldman & Pentland, 2003, p. 105). The concept of guiding users in process execution has been investigated in the information systems (IS) context for approximately two decades, and the first evaluation results provide evidence for the usefulness of process guidance (Burkhart, Krumeich,

Werth, & Loos, 2012; Dorn, Burkhart, Werth, & Dustdar, 2010; Reimer, Marge-lisch, Novotny, & Vetterli, 1998). However, existing research primarily focuses on the concept's evaluation by implementing prototypes or systems. Their underlying design and its theoretical justification are under-reported. We address this gap in our research project by providing design knowledge for process guidance systems (PGSs). We ground our design on two research streams, namely research on spatial knowledge and navigation, as well as research on decisional guidance and explanations, and propose three design principles for PGS. Instantiating the proposed design, the resulting PGS artifact guides or navigates users through their process execution by providing the required process information (Pentland & Feldman, 2005) and enabling them to build the required process knowledge (Amaravadi & Lee, 2005). We argue that users require (1) general information on the process, such as an overview of all the steps and their sequence, (2) specific information on how to execute the steps to navigate through the process, and (3) the possibility to identify their current position within the process. In our research project we follow the design science research (DSR) approach (Hevner, March, Park, & Ram, 2004) and address the following research question:

How can a process guidance system be designed to increase users' process knowledge and improve process execution performance?

2 The Context

The context of this DSR project is the execution of organizational-defined (business) processes from an individual perspective (Rosemann & vom Brocke, 2015). As introduced above, one important challenge in this context is the users' lack of process knowledge and the (potentially) resulting low process execution performance. In order to address this challenge, we propose the concept of process guidance and design process guidance systems (PGS) to increase users' process knowledge and their process execution performance. Our DSR project targets at understanding the concept of process guidance, deriving meta-requirements for the design of PGS, and formulating according design principles grounded in existing design knowledge and theories. Based on the design principles, we instantiated artifacts and subsequently, evaluated these PGS artifacts to validate the proposed design and to investigate the effects of PGS.

We cooperate with an industry partner that is also the research project's case company. As formulated by Hevner (2007) "*good design science research often begins by identifying and representing opportunities and problems in an actual application environment*" (Hevner, 2007, p. 89). The industry partner is highly aware of its employees' challenges related to process knowledge and process execution. Thus, a joint research project was started in the year 2012. The case company is a global supplier, developer, and service partner for customers in various sectors, including automotive, civil aviation, and mechanical engineering. At the end of 2015, the case company employed 15,146 employees at over 45 sites worldwide and had sales of more than €2.27 billion. Within the joint research project, several departments of the case company's IT organization were included. More specifically, the industry partner supported our research project in the following three areas. First, it supported us in the grounding of the identified research problem in a real-world scenario. Second, the real-world case and the conducted interviews with employees of the case company helped us with the requirements elicitation for the PGS design. Third, cooperating with the case company enabled us to demonstrate the effects of a PGS that delivers the proper process information at the right time to users in a real-world scenario.

The IT governance team of the case company is responsible for the creation, management, and monitoring of the IT related services. They defined an IT service management (ITSM) concept which follows the IT infrastructure library (ITIL) framework (Tan, Cater-Steel, & Toleman, 2009) to structure their offered IT services. In total, there are four different types of tickets defined by the IT governance team: service requests, incidents, non-standard demands, and requests for change. These ticket types are used to classify and handle requests from the business and IT departments regarding the offered IT services. A service request ticket, for example, is created when a user needs a new account. If there are issues with an application, the employee has to create an incident ticket. For all the ticket types, there are distinct, specified processes defining how such tickets have to be processed. The company uses an IT tool to support the execution of these ticketing processes. This tool, in the following referred to as ticketing system, implements the four ticketing processes of the case company and the employees are required to use the tool as well as to comply with the defined processes. There are two different clients available for the ticketing tool, a rich client and a web client. The rich client is primarily used in the European sites of the case company and the web client is used in the US sites of the case company. In the beginning of 2015, the existing IT ticketing processes were updated and rolled out to the US sites, which had previously no specified ticketing processes. Basically, all employees of the case company are affected by these ticketing processes in order to request and/or fulfill IT related services. Employees from the business side are primarily requesting services, being the starting point of the ticketing processes. In contrast, employees of the IT departments are executing the ticketing processes to fulfill the requested services. Although the ticketing processes are completely specified by the IT governance team and there exists a tool to support their execution, there were challenges. The IT governance team reports, among other challenges, a lack of users' knowledge of the ticketing processes and difficulties in the execution of these processes. Overall we argue that the ITSM context is suitable for the evaluation of the process guidance concept in a field environment.

3 The Journey

The overall project is conducted as a DSR project following the suggestions by Kuechler and Vaishnavi (2008) and is divided into three subsequent design cycles as depicted in Fig. 1.

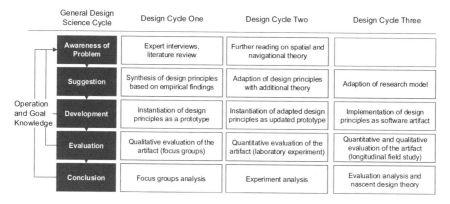

Fig. 1 Design cycles for DSR project (Kuechler & Vaishnavi, 2008)

DSR projects should target at both, a high rigor and a high relevance of the research (Hevner, 2007). Increasing the relevance of the research, we selected an appropriate industry partner serving as the case company of the research project. The case company provides the context for the conducted research. Accordingly, the case company serves for identifying real-world problems and research opportunities in a first step. These requirements influence the overall research project. In addition to providing the research context and delivering requirements, the case company also serves for the evaluation of the resulting design. Increasing the rigor of the research, Hevner (2007) suggested to include existing knowledge bases for grounding the design. Although, the design, or more specifically the design principles, addresses some (real-world) problems, they should be based on existing research. Moreover, the resulting design knowledge of the DSR project should be returned to the knowledge base. Rigor in DSR is influenced by the researchers selection and application of appropriated theories, design knowledge, and methods for the creation and evaluation of the resulting design artifacts (Hevner, 2007). The central design cycle(s) *"iterate[s] between the core activities of building and evaluating the design artifacts and processes of the research"* (Hevner, 2007, p. 88). In our research project, this iteration between relevance and rigor is done in the various activities within the three consecutive design cycles. Both, the activities for ensuring a high rigor and high relevance as well as the actual design activities are considered in the three cycle view on DSR by Hevner (2007) as depicted in Fig. 2.

In the following, we outline the main research activities in the three consecutive design cycles.

3.1 Design Cycle 1

The first design cycles served for the derivation of the theory-grounded design principles and a first evaluation of a prototypical instantiation of the PGS design. As

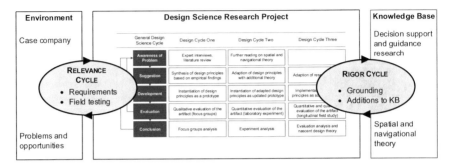

Fig. 2 DSR project with relevance and rigor cycles (Hevner, 2007)

suggested by Hevner (2007), the research project started with a series of expert interviews with employees of the case company to investigate current challenges in the execution of processes. The conducted expert interviews revealed that the employees had difficulties in executing processes according to their definitions as well as suffer from a lack of understanding the process specifications. In particular, one of the interviewees requested some *"…guidance, claiming the system which needs to be used in a particular business process step"* (Morana, Schacht, Scherp, & Maedche, 2013, p. 497). Thus, we reasoned that there is a need for guidance that support users in their process execution.

Subsequently we conducted a systematic literature review on the guidance concept and guidance design features in IS research (Morana, Schacht, Scherp, & Maedche, 2017). Guidance design features support individuals in decision-making, problem solving, and task execution. Various IS instantiate guidance design features, which have specifically been researched in the field of decision support systems for decades. However, because of the lack of a common conceptualization, it is difficult to compare the research findings on guidance design features from different literature streams. In our literature review, we analyze the work of the research streams of decisional guidance (Silver, 1991), explanations (Gregor & Benbasat, 1999), and decision aids (Todd & Benbasat, 1991) conducted in the last 25 years. Building on and grounded by the analyzed literature, we theorize an integrated taxonomy on guidance design features. This taxonomy allows us to describe the design of PGS using a set of predefined dimensions and characteristics. Moreover, the identified decision support research was used to ground the PGS design.

Building on the results of both research activities, we derived a set of meta-requirements for PGS and three design principles were formulated. These meta-requirements describe the goals of the artifact (Gregor & Hevner, 2013; Walls, Widmeyer, & El Sawy, 1992), for example, one meta-requirement describes the need to provide process guidance while executing a particular process (Morana, Schacht, Scherp, & Maedche, 2014). We matched the identified meta-requirements against the developed guidance design feature taxonomy in order have a (nearly) complete set. The design principles are grounded in the identified guidance research. We considered the concepts of decisional guidance (Silver, 1991) and explanations

(Gregor & Benbasat, 1999) in particular because they form the foundation of the body of knowledge on guidance. By reflecting and incorporating existing research from the knowledge base, the rigor of the research is ensured. The design principles were then instantiated in the form of a PGS prototype, fitting to the context of the case company. Subsequently, the artifact and the design principles were evaluated qualitatively in a series of explorative focus group workshops (Tremblay, Hevner, & Berndt, 2010) with employees of the case company, ensuring the relevance of the research. Based on the feedback from the participants, the third design principle was refined in order to adapt the guidance content to the user. A detailed description of the first design cycle including the applied methodology and the research results are described in Morana et al. (2013), Morana et al. (2014).

3.2   Design Cycle 2

We started the second design cycle with further reading on spatial and navigational theory (Goldin & Thorndyke, 1982; Thorndyke & Hayes-Roth, 1982) to enrich our design's theoretical basis. Although the existing design is theoretically grounded in decision support research (see Morana et al., 2014), an additional theoretical lens enriches the design. Therefore, we updated the existing design principles to the new theoretical lens taken from spatial navigation and knowledge research. In so doing, we aimed to increase the validity of our design.

We evaluated the adapted design principles for PGS in a laboratory setting. The laboratory setting and the applied approach of the experiment ensures a high internal validity. Nevertheless, in order to have an adequate external validity, the experiment context was adapted from the case company's ITSM team. The case company's IT ticketing process is simplified and adapted for the experiment. Therefore, the required application systems (an email client, a ticket system, and a service catalog) were implemented for the experiment. The experiment investigated the effects of the proposed PGS design on users' process knowledge and process execution performance. The validity of the design principles was assessed by testing various instantiations of the PGS artifact that implemented the functionality either described in a design principle or explicitly did not implement the described functionality. Overall, we implemented three PGS artifacts for the laboratory experiment. As process guidance primarily aims to support users having limited knowledge and experiences in process execution, the experiment was performed with 118 undergraduate (Management Information Systems) and graduate (Management Information Systems and Business Administration) students from a public university in Germany. Students can be perceived as an adequate sample for novice users and as process guidance primarily serves for supporting novice users, the selection of students as experiment sample is reasonable. Overall, we could confirm the proposed effects of process guidance in the laboratory experiment and could show that the PGS artifact had a significant effect on the users' process knowledge and process execution performance.

A detailed description of the second design cycle is given in Morana, Kroenung, Maedche, and Schacht (2019).

3.3 Design Cycle 3

In the third design cycle, we replicated our results of the second design cycle in a real-world context balancing the rigor and relevance of our research. Responding to the call by Peffers, Rothenberger, Tuunanen, and Vaezi (2012) and the suggestions by Venable, Pries-Heje, and Baskerville (2016) for more real-world evaluations of DSR artifacts, we evaluated the functionality of all three design principles by instantiating them in a fully functioning PGS artifact for the IT ticketing process of the case company.

In a first workshop, we presented the process guidance concept, the three theory-grounded design principles, and the existing PGS prototypes realized in design cycle one and two to the IT governance team. The IT governance team presented their ticketing processes and the existing ticketing tool. The case company specified the four ticketing processes in detail including all mandatory and optional process steps. We instantiated the design in the form of a fully functioning software system named ITSM ProcessGuide (Morana, Gerards, & Maedche, 2015) and integrated it into the IT ticketing application of the case company. All users of the case company are required to comply with the IT ticketing processes for requesting IT related services. The IT departments of the case company use the ticketing system for keeping track of the requested services and executing the ticketing processes. As the ITSM Process-Guide is integrated into the ticketing system, all users of the IT departments are potential users of the PGS. Moreover, all IT department users are potential participants for the evaluation of the PGS design. The evaluation was conducted as a mixed-methods longitudinal study. First, three months after the go-live, we evaluated the effects of the PGS quantitatively with a survey based on the measurements used in the laboratory experiment. We identified a set of constructs and items forming the basis of the questionnaire. This questionnaire was distributed among all potential users of the ITSM ProcessGuide. In addition to the quantitative evaluation, a qualitative approach was performed to evaluate the ITSM ProcessGuide. Therefore, a series of confirmatory focus group workshops was conducted with European IT employees of the case company. As the focus group approach was not feasible for US IT employees, the evaluation of these users was performed as expert interviews. In both forms of qualitative evaluation, the participants were asked to assess the artifact on its usefulness and the strengths, weaknesses, opportunities and threats (SWOT-analysis) of the design principles and the ITSM ProcessGuide. Summed up, the evaluation at the case company ensures the high relevance of the research project and the resulting design knowledge. Overall, we could confirm the proposed effects of process guidance on the employees' process knowledge and their process execution performance. Moreover, we received valuable qualitative feedback on the process guidance concept and the implemented ITSM ProcessGuide. The qualitative evaluation of the third design cycle is presented in Morana, Schacht, and Maedche (2016) and the qualitative evaluation is presented in Morana et al. (2019).

4 The Results

4.1 Presentation of Artifact(S)

This research project aimed to design a solution for the challenge of users' lack of process knowledge and the related low process execution performance. We argue that the provision of the required process information in the proper format at the right time in the form of a PGS artifact can address these challenges related to the users' process execution. Thus, we designed a PGS artifact that provides (1) general information on the process, such as an overview of all the steps and their sequence, (2) specific information on how to execute the steps to navigate through the process, and (3) the possibility to identify users' current position within the process. Process knowledge is important for users to execute their daily work (Amaravadi & Lee, 2005; Münstermann et al., 2010) and we propose that three different forms of process knowledge are required to navigate and support users in their process execution (Morana et al., 2019). We argue that an assistance systems (Maedche, Morana, Schacht, Werth, & Krumeich, 2016) in the form of a PGS can support the users' process execution performance by providing process information that the user translates into process knowledge. We propose three types of process information that a PGS can provide to the user, namely process orientation information, process overview information, and procedural process information. Ideally, all three types are provided to the user and we refer to this superset as process information.

In the following, we present the three design principles and their grounding in decision support as well as spatial knowledge and navigation theories (a detailed discussion of the design principles derivation in the course of the three design cycles can be found in Morana et al. (2014) and Morana et al. (2019).

Orientation knowledge enables users to locate themselves with respect to their existing survey and procedural knowledge. Combining survey and procedural knowledge enables the user to navigate from one location to another by using an alternate route and circumventing an obstacle on the original route (Klatzky, Loomis, Beall, Chance, & Golledge, 1998) (see Fig. 3A). Thus, orientation knowledge is a prerequisite for users to navigate and move in an environment. Similarly, a PGS should enable users to locate themselves within the process by providing process orientation information as a prerequisite to executing a process. In so doing, users will be aware of the current process step in which they find themselves, the activities required next, and the activities within the process that have already been carried out, as illustrated in Fig. 3A1. In general, providing process guidance should be done only when users request it, since automatically providing it *"might irritate more than it guides"* (Silver, 2006, p. 110). In addition, providing the required process information during

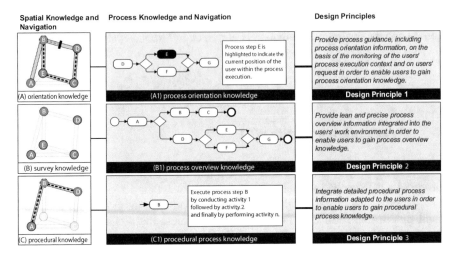

Fig. 3 Spatial knowledge theories for process knowledge and three design principles for process guidance systems

the process execution to the users will "*reduce [their] cognitive strain as the information that is primed in memory during task performance*" (Dhaliwal & Benbasat, 1996, p. 349). Moreover, we argue that a PGS needs to monitor user behavior and context in the current process execution to provide the appropriate process orientation information and process guidance in general (Gregor & Benbasat, 1999). Summed up, we propose our first design principle as follows:

Design Principle 1: *Provide process guidance, including process orientation information, on the basis of the monitoring of the users' process execution context and on users' request in order to enable users to gain process orientation knowledge.*

Spatial knowledge theory states that users require an overview of the map (survey knowledge) to be aware of the location and the orientation of specific points on a map (Thorndyke & Hayes-Roth, 1982) (see Fig. 3B). In the process context, users similarly require an overview of the various process steps and their sequence within the process. We refer to such knowledge as "process overview knowledge." To support users in process navigation, a PGS should visualize the various process steps and their relationship, as illustrated in Fig. 3B1. Similarly to survey knowledge in spatial navigation (Goldin & Thorndyke, 1982), we argue that by providing such process overview knowledge users can form mental maps of processes. Moreover, researchers show that it can be useful to externalize (process) information for cognitive tasks (van Nimwegen, Burgos, van Oostendorp, & Schijf, 2006), ease problem solving (Zhang & Norman, 1994), and support users to learn through task experience (Glover, Prawitt, & Spilker, 1997). In addition, process overview knowledge is required during users' current process execution and in their work environment to prevent media disruptions (Heinrich & Paech, 2010). Thus, a PGS needs to visualize processes to foster process overview knowledge. Consequently, we propose the need for process overview knowledge to arrive at our second design principle:

Design Principle 2: *Provide lean and precise process overview information integrated into the users' work environment in order to enable users to gain process overview knowledge.*

In addition to survey knowledge, users also require procedural knowledge (Goldin & Thorndyke, 1982) for spatial navigation (see Fig. 3C). Adapted to the process context, we propose that users require procedural process knowledge to execute specific process steps within the entire process. Thus, the PGS should offer procedural process information on how to execute a particular process step in addition to process orientation and process overview knowledge. As illustrated in Fig. 3C1, procedural process knowledge addresses information on what to do in the current process step. Such "how to do it" instructions assist users in their task execution (Carroll & Aaronson, 1988). Novice users in particular benefit from "what to do next" instructions when they are uncertain or afraid to make mistakes (Good, Whiteside, Wixon, & Jones, 1984). By contrast, more experienced users or experts require more specific information to solve a specific problem or exception within the process (Gönül, Önkal, & Lawrence, 2006). It is important to consider the expertise of the user when providing the adequate form of guidance (Gregor & Benbasat, 1999; Ye & Johnson, 1995). Thus, we argue that the provided procedural process information should be adapted to the user and his/her expertise. We address this with procedural process knowledge in our third design principle for PGSs:

Design Principle 3: *Integrate detailed procedural process information adapted to the users in order to enable users to gain procedural process knowledge.*

In summary, the theory on spatial knowledge and navigation in combination with research on decision support serves as a valuable theoretic foundation for the three design principles. In Fig. 3, we map the proposed three types of process knowledge to the three design principles for PGS.

To assess the completeness of the proposed design, we used the taxonomy of guidance design features that we derived from our systematic literature review (Morana et al., 2017) in the first design cycle. The taxonomy is derived from research and theories on decisional guidance (Silver, 1991, 2006), explanations (Dhaliwal & Benbasat, 1996; Gregor & Benbasat, 1999), and decision aids (Todd & Benbasat, 1991, 1999) and consist out of ten dimensions characterizing the provided guidance systems. Following Fig. 4 depicts the classification of process guidance according to the guidance design features taxonomy.

By assigning the appropriate characteristic from each of the ten dimensions, we can demonstrate that the proposed design for process guidance systems is complete with respect to the guidance design features taxonomy.

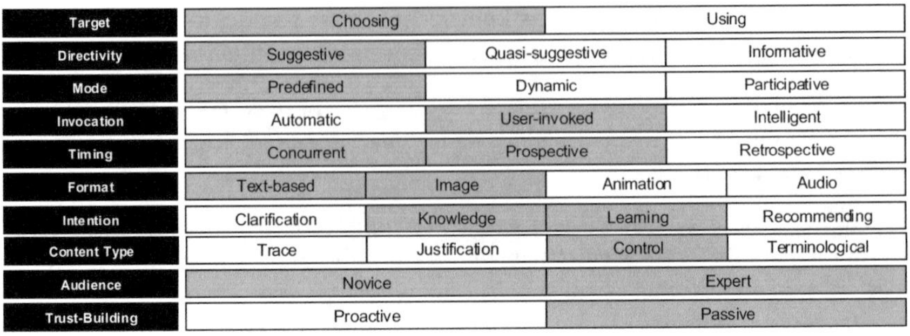

Target	Choosing		Using	
Directivity	Suggestive	Quasi-suggestive	Informative	
Mode	Predefined	Dynamic	Participative	
Invocation	Automatic	User-invoked	Intelligent	
Timing	Concurrent	Prospective	Retrospective	
Format	Text-based	Image	Animation	Audio
Intention	Clarification	Knowledge	Learning	Recommending
Content Type	Trace	Justification	Control	Terminological
Audience	Novice		Expert	
Trust-Building	Proactive		Passive	

Fig. 4 Design of PGS mapped to the taxonomy of guidance design features

4.2 Application of Artifact(S)

During the course of the research project, we developed a PGS artifact for each evaluation episode within the three design cycles. In the following, we present the third, fully functioning PGS deployed at our case company. A description of the PGS artifacts instantiated in the first and second design cycle can be found in Morana et al. (2014) and Morana et al. (2019).

Before the actual implementation, we discussed each design principle with the IT governance team to specify their instantiation. The PGS should support the case company's users in executing the IT ticketing process and should be integrated into the existing IT ticketing tool. Thereby, the PGS should provide the required process information during the actual process execution.

In order to implement the first design principle (**DP1**), a button is added into the ticketing system, which opens the ITSM ProcessGuide and provides the current users' process context. The current process context is determined by the type of ticket, the current state of the ticket, and if the user is using the web or rich client. These information are then used to visualize the process guidance to the user (**DP2**). In order to keep the process guidance lean and precise for the given ticketing processes, the PGS provides only the process steps for the current process state to the user. Each process state includes various mandatory and optional steps, which the user must or can execute for the current ticket state. For all the steps, the PGS provides detailed information in the form of explanations on how to execute the particular process step (**DP3**). The explanations can be expanded and collapsed in order to prevent information overload of the users. Within the explanations, the ITSM team can describe how to execute the specific process activities and also provide links to other applications or websites. Considering the two different client versions, the PGS is implemented as a web-based application. Thus, the PGS can be opened in both versions of the client in the form of a browser window which is included in the users' work environment (**DP2**).

The first version of the PGS implementation for the ITSM context was discussed with the IT governance team. Based on the discussion within the workshop, a simplified and aggregated process model diagram was added to the PGS. Furthermore, the layout and look and feel of the developed PGS was improved. The resulting PGS was named ITSM ProcessGuide. Figure 5 depicts a screenshot of the resulting PGS (foreground) with the rich client of the ticketing system (background) and highlights the instantiation of the design principles.

Figure 6 depicts the high-level architecture illustrating the basic functionalities and the interaction of the PGS components. The overall architecture follows the Model-View-Controller (MVC) pattern and is divided into three components: (1) the view, the actual visualization of the ITSM ProcessGuide (see Fig. 5), (2) the frontend and backend controller, and (3) the data storage. Both, frontend and backend are implemented using Microsoft Visual C# as a web application. The frontend and backend controller run on a Microsoft Windows Internet Information Server. For storing the process guidance information, a Microsoft SQL database is used.

Once the user requests process guidance in the ticketing system by clicking on the plugin button, the request is passed to the frontend controller. In the frontend controller, the process context is analyzed and the required information are queried from the database. The information are processed and then passed to ITSM ProcessGuide view, which displays the process guidance.

For the maintenance of ITSM ProcessGuide, a web-based backend for the PGS was developed. In this backend, the IT governance team can maintain the process states, steps, and explanations. Another use case of ITSM ProcessGuide is the easy and quick possibility to communicate changes of the ticketing processes. The ITSM team can easily change the explanations of the process steps in the backend and announce the changes to the employees. Then the users can see the changes when using the ITSM ProcessGuide.

4.3 Evaluation of Artifact(S)

We structured the evaluations of our PGS design based on the FEDS—a framework for evaluating DSR artifacts (Venable et al., 2016). Within the three consecutive design cycles, we performed four evaluation episodes to assess the proposed PGS design. Thereby, we followed the FEDS strategy, which suggests planning out an evaluation in four steps (Venable et al., 2016). The purpose of our evaluation was to provide evidence that the proposed design could be instantiated in the form of an artifact that addresses the outlined problems and achieves the expected environmental utility, e.g. the increase in users' process knowledge and process execution performance. For the evaluation strategy, we decided to follow the technical risk & efficacy strategy, which should be adapted "*if it is prohibitively expensive to evaluate with real users and real systems in the real setting*" and "*if a critical goal of the evaluation is to rigorously establish that the utility/benefit is due to the artefact, not*

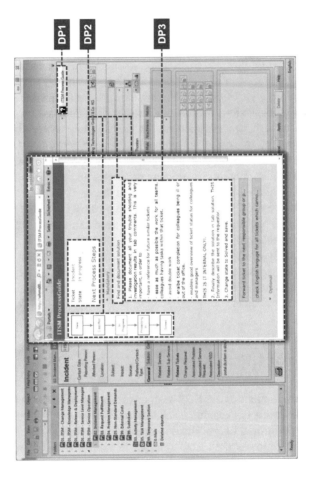

Fig. 5 ITSM ProcessGuide with highlighted design principles

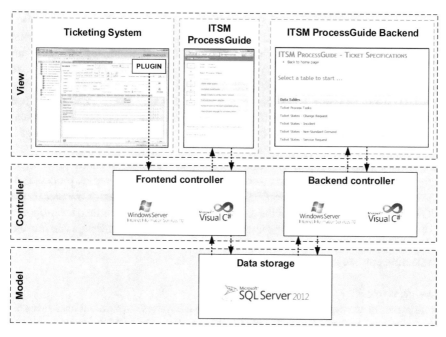

Fig. 6 High-level architecture

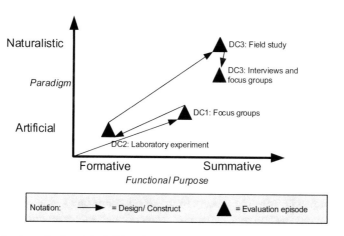

Fig. 7 Evaluation episodes of the PGS project

something else" (Venable et al., 2016, p. 82). Figure 7 depicts the four complementary evaluations episodes following the suggestions by Venable et al. (2016).

Design Cycle 1

When following the technical risk & efficacy strategy, Venable et al. (2016) recommend "*start[ing] with a laboratory experiment to clarify the boundaries of the technology*" (p. 83). However, before the laboratory experiment, we decided to perform two exploratory focus group workshops at the end of the **first design cycle** to receive qualitative feedback on the proposed design (Tremblay et al., 2010). The focus group workshops enabled us to receive feedback on the PGS design and we received valuable ideas for the further improvement of the design. Among other findings, we identify the need to adjust the provided process guidance to the user and therefore adapted design principle 3. One participant stated that with such a PGS "*help is just one click away*" and highlighted the possibility to directly access the "*help without postponing the current work*". Furthermore, we were able to identify several strengths of using process guidance, such as enabling users to understand the entire process chain and the description of the current process in real-time. In addition, we identified several opportunities, such as the visualization of even complex processes of the entire organization in one tool and the relatively lean knowledge transfer by the PGS. Summed up, the results of the explorative focus groups confirmed the proposed process guidance concept and the intended effects of process knowledge and process execution performance. The methodology and a detailed discussion of this qualitative evaluation episode is given in Morana et al. (2014).

Design Cycle 2

Subsequently, we evaluated the PGS design in a laboratory experiment in the **second design cycle**. An experimental research design also ensures high internal validity and moderate external validity (Bhattacherjee, 2012) and therefore enables us to demonstrate that the observed effects are because of the PGS artifact rather than other factors that cannot be influenced. The laboratory experiment assesses the functionality described in the design principles and the effects of their instantiation in isolation from each other and thus can be categorized as a formative evaluation episode (Venable et al., 2016).

We implemented three variants of a PGS by explicitly instantiating the functionality described in a design principle or not. In this laboratory experiment, we focused on the evaluation of the second and third design principle and postponed the evaluation of the first design principle to the third design cycle. Thus, we instantiated in total three PGS artifacts, the extended process guidance (EPG) artifact (implementing DP2 and DP3), the basic process guidance (BPG) artifact (implementing DP2 only), and the no process guidance (NPG) artifact (implementing no design principle) serving as the control group. In the experiment, the participants had to process eight instances of the simplified IT ticketing process from our case company and we measured their process execution performance. Thereby, the participants were randomly assigned to one of the PGS artifacts during the experiment. We tested their process knowledge before and after the experiment with a multiple-choice test to check for an increase in their knowledge because of the provided process guidance. For the analysis, we compared the mean values of the three groups' process execution performance and process knowledge against each other. Following Table 1 contains the descriptive results from the experiment.

Overall, we found that providing process guidance had a significant, positive, and small to medium-sized effect on the users' process execution performance and process knowledge in comparison with the experiment results of the control group

Table 1 Descriptive results of the laboratory experiment

Group	n	Process knowledge[a]			Process execution effectiveness[b]	Process execution time[c]
		Pre	Post	Delta		
All	118	9.780 (2.578)	10.356 (2.061)	0.576 (1.968)	4.814 (2.620)	11.954 (4.442)
EPG	39	10.205 (2.114)	10.949 (1.679)	0.744 (1.644)	5.641 (2.259)	11.932 (4.748)
BPG	38	9.711 (2.910)	10.447 (2.086)	0.737 (1.983)	4.500 (2.770)	12.557 (5.122)
NPG	41	9.439 (2.595)	9.707 (2.178)	0.268 (2.187)	4.317 (2.608)	11.416 (3.223)

NPG: No process guidance| BPG: Basic process guidance| EPG: Extended process guidance
[a]measured on a scale from 1 to 13
[b]measured on a scale from 0 to 8
[c]measured in minutes

receiving no process guidance. A detailed description of the laboratory experiment (including the tested hypotheses, experiment design, detailed analysis, and discussion of the results) can be found in Morana et al. (2019).

Design Cycle 3

Armed with a more detailed understanding of the effects of process guidance, we then decided to evaluate the PGS design and the effects of its instantiation (all three design principles together in an artifact) in a field study to increase the generalizability (Bhattacherjee, 2012) in the **third design cycle**. This naturalistic evaluation episode in the form of a survey-based field study and a series of confirmatory focus group workshops is conducted in our case company with real users who have real problems (Venable et al., 2016). With respect to the evaluation properties, we focused on the validity of our overall design and the effects of its instantiation on users' process knowledge and process execution performance. For the survey-based field study, we adapted the propositions and research model from the laboratory experiment (Morana et al., 2019) to create a survey using established items from literature. The survey included items addressing the constructs perceived usage of the ITSM ProcessGuide (Bajaj & Nidumolu, 1998), perceived process knowledge (Bera, Burton-Jones, & Wand, 2011), perceived process execution efficiency (Bhattacherjee & Premkumar, 2004; Compeau, Higgins, & Huff, 1999), and process execution effectiveness (Bhattacherjee & Premkumar, 2004; Compeau et al., 1999). We distributed the survey three months of the go-live of the ITSM ProcessGuide and 78 employees (response rate 29.8%) provided valid responses. We used SmartPLS (Hair, Hult, Ringle, & Sarstedt, 2014) to analyze the survey data and found weak effects with respect to the explanatory power of the three dependent variables (Urbach & Ahlemann, 2010). In addition, we applied a one-tailed t-test and found all three paths to be significant (p-values < 0.001) as well as that all paths have a medium effect size (Urbach & Ahlemann, 2010). Figure 8 depicts the research model with the t-statistics and effect size.

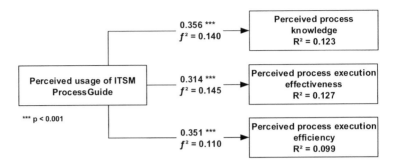

Fig. 8 Results of survey-based field study

Summed up, the quantitative survey-based field study confirmed the proposed effects of the PGS design and the detailed description of this evaluation episode can be found in Morana et al. (2019).

In addition to the quantitative evaluation episode, we conducted a qualitative evaluation episode to get an in-depth understanding on when employees' use the ITSM ProcessGuide and under which conditions they perceive the process guidance as supportive. We used two different methods, since some of the users are located in US sites and others in European sites of the case company. Due to the spatial proximity, we conducted a series of confirmatory focus group workshops (Tremblay et al., 2010) with employees of the European sites and an interview series with employees of the American sites. Although, we conducted different forms of qualitative data collections, both activities followed the same procedure. In both activities, the participants had to assess the strengths, weaknesses, opportunities, and threats (SWOT-analysis) of the ITSM ProcessGuide and the particular instantiations of the DPs. Thereby, the SWOT analysis purely served as a guideline enabling a structured discussion in the workshops and interviews. Overall 34 employees of the case company's IT departments participated in both activities resulting in seven focus group workshops and five interviews. We audio-recorded all sessions, transcribed the recordings, and applied an inductive coding approach to analyze the transcriptions. In total, we identified 66 quotes addressing the PGS design and the effects of using the PGS. The positive feedback dominated with 22 quotes on the strengths and 16 quotes on the opportunities related to the DPs and the PGS. We grouped the quotes into four code clusters addressing the PGS design and five clusters addressing the effects of using the PGS as summarized in Table 2.

Overall, we the found that the PGS provides a "useful overview on the process and states what to do" and, therefore, the "next steps are visible." Moreover, the participants acknowledged that this form of process visualization is especially useful for users to get an "overview of the process and the optimal process execution" without overloading them mentally. In addition, we found evidence that the PGS enables the users to identify their current position within the process. One participant highlights this feature of the PGS as it shows: "where am I, and what needs to be

Table 2 Code clusters, codes and exemplary quotes addressing the PGS design and effects of using the PGS

Code cluster		Exemplary codes	Exemplary quote
PGS Design	Process overview	• Depiction of processes • Increased process knowledge • Process context • Need for proper process specifications	I do like that it is minimal and small on the screen. […] That is good that you have something side-by-side, where you can look at what the instruction is, or what the guide is and also look at what you question is. That's a real good strength, I would say
	Process information	• Content of process guidance • Access to process resources • Availability of process information	The strength of the first [DP] is that it is easy to use and easy to get information on the process. Usually, these [information] are bulky PDFs and long—if there is something at all
	Guidance format	• Audio output of guidance content • Information overload • Combined visual and textual format	I think, it would be an opportunity to add sound to the process guidance. So, in addition to the text, a spoken text would enable the user that he does not have to read the entire descriptions
	Invocation	• Automatic invocation needed	User must click by himself. I think it would be good if it [process guidance] would be implemented as mouse-over for every field. For our CRM system, it is the same. No one clicks on the help. The people need to be encountered more intensively on the support

(continued)

Table 2 (continued)

Code cluster		Exemplary codes	Exemplary quote
Effects of using the PGS	Administration	• Effort of changing the process in PGS • Actuality of process content • User involvement and feedback • Process specifications • Process change management	If the tool is not maintained, it does not provide an added value and thus, will not be accepted. The tool lives due to its content. Thus, the documentation needs to be complete
	Performance	• Increased effectiveness and efficiency • Ease of use of PGS • Usability of PGS	The PGS saves time and provides some certainty to the end user. In addition it improves the work load of the ITSM team
	Process knowledge	• No learning due to PGS • Learning and process compliance due to PGS • Process awareness/visibility	The usefulness of the system decreases the more a user uses the system, because the user builds up knowledge over time. The process guide is rather used to build up process knowledge
	Training	• Supports missing or bad training • Does not replace training • Training of novices • Replaces training and reduces training effort	One opportunity of the tool is that it promotes the process understanding. I have used the tool to explain the American colleagues some fundamental things, to explain the processes and to create a rudimentary understanding. It is difficult to understand the process by only using the tool, but in order to explain the process,, the tool is very helpful

(continued)

Table 2 (continued)

Code cluster		Exemplary codes	Exemplary quote
	Process Acceptance	• Increased acceptance • Decreased acceptance due to wrong content • Ignorance of PGS	A threat, I guess, would be that few of people are aware of it. Even if they are aware of it, it is easy to find, it is easy to use; people just don't want to use it. I guess this could be

done." A detailed description of the qualitative evaluation of the third design cycle is given in Morana et al. (2016).

4.4 *Growth of Design Theory*

To date, research on PGS in the business process management domain (Burkhart et al., 2012; Krumeich, Werth, & Loos, 2012; Maus, Schwarz, Haas, & Dengel, 2011; Tekinerdoğan, Bozbey, Mester, Turançiftci, & Alkışlar, 2011) and software development (Becker-Kornstaedt et al., 1999; Grambow, Oberhauser, & Reichert, 2011; Holz, Maus, Bernardi, & Rostanin, 2005) has focused on the development of artifacts for a specific context and their evaluation but offered few insights into the underlying design of their PGS. We addressed this shortcoming in our research project by systematically deriving three theoretically grounded design principles and proposing a nascent design theory for PGS.

We instantiate the functionality described in the three design principles in three related PGS artifacts (Morana et al., 2019; Morana et al., 2014; Morana et al., 2015). Our design extends the existing body of process guidance research (Becker-Kornstaedt et al., 1999; Burkhart et al., 2012), which predominantly provides process guidance within one distinct application system. With respect to existing research, the combination of a visual and a textual format for providing process guidance, the monitoring and extraction of the users' process context, and the potential to provide process guidance for multiple application systems are all new. We decided to develop the PGS as a standalone application because of the resulting flexibility and in most cases, it is not possible to modify the application systems required to perform the processes. One approach to guide a user in the execution of a process could be to restrict the systems and their user interface. System restrictiveness refers to a system's ability to "*limit the users' decision-making processes to a subset of all possible processes*" (Silver, 1990, p. 52). Despite the positive effects of applying system restrictiveness for certain use cases to enforce consistency and completeness (Mălăescu & Sutton, 2015), it requires strictly specified processes and the resulting implementation in the application system. Especially for commercial application systems or information systems, it is not possible to modify and restrict the user interface explicitly for the execution of one process step. Moreover, as we intend to propose a PGS design that supports various types of processes and multiple application system at the time, we consider system restrictiveness as outside the scope of our process guidance context.

In summary, by presenting a situated instantiation (Level 1) in the form of two PGS artifacts and by formulating "*more general artifacts (Level 2) in the form of constructs, methods, models, and design principles*" (Gregor & Hevner, 2013, p. 346), our research contributes to improving current solutions. Table 3 summarizes our findings in the form of a nascent design theory (Gregor & Hevner, 2013; Gregor & Jones, 2007).

5   Key Learnings

When reflecting our DSR project, we identified three major key learnings. First, it was important to have identified multiple literature streams for the grounding of our design. We ground our design on two different research streams, namely decision support research as well as theories on spatial knowledge and navigation. Although both streams are different and at first sight do not seem to have anything in common, combining them for our design made a lot of sense. The existing findings and design knowledge in both streams helped us to address our (design) challenges with respect to the lack of users' process knowledge and low process execution performance. We therefore, recommend conducting both systematic as well as exploratory literature reviews to address both, getting a detailed overview on a specific problem domain as well as identifying potentially related research streams in other domains. Often related research streams in other domains (e.g. computer science, psychology, economics, etc.) addressed similar (design) problems and provide valuable (design) knowledge that can be leveraged. Thereby the DSR project can prevent re-inventing the wheel and should consider lessons learned the related research.

Second, involving in a real-world case and engaging with our case company helped us to improve the relevance as well as the contribution of our research. Having access to real-world problems enabled us to get new insights on the identified research problem, asides from the sole scientific point of view. The discussion with the employees of the case company showed us different facets of the problem and revealed furthermore suggestions for its solution. The on-site evaluation episodes in design cycle one and three provided us with valuable feedback addressing the PGS design and the usage of the PGS. Overall, we conclude that the evaluation in a real-world scenario enabled us to get results that are more interesting and increase the contribution of our DSR project.

Third, another important lesson learned is that researchers applying the DSR approach should be engaged with the DSR community, in particular the International Conference on Design Science Research in Information Systems and Technology (DESRIST) conference. The participation in the DESRIST doctoral consortium and

Table 3 A nascent design theory for process guidance systems

Component	Description
Purpose and scope	Process guidance increases users' process knowledge and process execution performance. We propose three theoretically grounded design principles for process guidance systems
Constructs	We defined the following constructs below: process knowledge in general, three distinct types of process knowledge grounded in spatial knowledge and navigation, and process execution effectiveness and efficiency **Process knowledge** (in general): information about a process, including how it is configured, how it is coordinated, how it is executed, what outputs are desirable, and what impacts it has on the organization (Amaravadi & Lee, 2005) **Process orientation knowledge**: information enabling users to locate themselves within the entire process **Process overview knowledge**: information about the various process steps and their sequence within the entire process **Procedural process knowledge**: information on how to execute a specific process step within the entire process **Process execution effectiveness**: the number of times the user correctly executes a process instance (i.e., the process was executed, and the intended outcome/quality was achieved) (Dennis, Haley, & Vandenberg, 1996) **Process execution efficiency**: the ratio between the correctly executed process instances and the time spent to execute the process instances (Dennis et al., 1996)
Principle of form and function	On the basis of existing literature, we derived three theoretically grounded design principles for process guidance systems and evaluated the proposed design quantitatively in a laboratory experiment and through a field study **Design Principle 1**: Provide process guidance, including process orientation information, on the basis of the monitoring of the users' process execution context and on users' request in order to enable users to gain process orientation knowledge **Design Principle 2**: Provide lean and precise process overview information integrated into the users' work environment in order to enable users to gain process overview knowledge **Design Principle 3**: Integrate detailed procedural process information adapted to the users in order to enable users to gain procedural process knowledge
Justificatory knowledge	The PGS design is grounded in research on decision support, as well as research on spatial knowledge and navigation

(continued)

Table 3 (continued)

Component	Description
Testable propositions	We derived three testable propositions to evaluate the PGS design **Proposition 1**: Process information in a process guidance system leads to users having increased process knowledge **Proposition 2**: Process information in a process guidance system leads to users having increased process execution effectiveness **Proposition 3**: Process information in a process guidance system leads to users having increased process execution efficiency
Artifact mutability	We discuss the mutability of the provided process guidance information, as well as the actual instantiation of the design in two different artifacts in this paper
Principles of implementation	We provide examples of how to instantiate the proposed design in the form of the two artifacts. Especially, the ITSM ProcessGuide can serve as a baseline for further process guidance systems
Expository instantiation	We develop a distinct process guidance system for each evaluation episode. One of the artifacts, the ITSM ProcessGuide, is used productively in the case company

the ongoing exchanging with other DSR scholars helped us a lot to gain a better and more holistic understanding on how to conduct DSR projects and improve the outcome of our DSR projects.

References

Alter, S. (2014). Theory of Workarounds. *Communications of the Association for Information Systems, 34*, 1041–1066.

Amaravadi, C. S., & Lee, I. (2005). The dimensions of process knowledge. *Knowledge and Process Management, 12*(1), 65–76.

Bajaj, A., & Nidumolu, S. R. (1998). A feedback model to understand information system usage. *Information & Management, 33*, 213–224.

Becker-Kornstaedt, U., Hamann, D., Kempkens, R., Rö, P., Verlage, M., Webby, R., & Zettel, J. (1999). Support for the process engineer: The spearmint approach to software process definition and process guidance. In M. Jarke & A. Oberweis (Eds.), *Lecture Notes in Computer Science. Advanced Information Systems Engineering* (Vol. 1626, pp. 119–133). Berlin, Heidelberg: Springer Berlin Heidelberg.

Bera, P., Burton-Jones, A., & Wand, Y. (2011). Guidelines for designing visual ontologies to support knowledge identification. *MIS Quarterly, 35*(4), 883–908.

Bhanot, K. (2000). Preliminary fact finding mission following the accident at the nuclear fuel processing facility in Tokaimura, Japan (Vienna: IAEA). *Journal of Radiological Protection, 20*(1), 73–77.

Bhattacherjee, A. (2012). Social science research: principles, methods, and practices. Textbooks Collection. Book 3. Retrieved from http://scholarcommons.usf.edu/oa_textbooks/.

Bhattacherjee, A., & Premkumar, G. (2004). Understanding changes in belief and attitude toward information technology usage: A theoretical model and longitudinal test. *MIS Quarterly, 28*(2), 229–254.

Burkhart, T., Krumeich, J., Werth, D., & Loos, P. (2012). Flexible support system for email-based processes: An empirical evaluation. *International Journal of E-Business Development, 2*(3), 77–85.

Carroll, J., & Aaronson, A. (1988). Learning by doing with simulated intelligent help. *Communications of the ACM, 31*(9), 1064–1079.

Compeau, D., Higgins, C. A., & Huff, S. (1999). Social cognitive theory and individual reactions to computing technology: A longitudinal study. *MIS Quarterly, 23*(2), 145–158.

Davenport, T. H., & Short, J. E. (1990). The new industrial engineering: information technology and business process redesign. *Sloan Management Review, 31*(4), 1–31.

Dennis, A. R., Haley, B., & Vandenberg, R. (1996). A meta-analysis of effectiveness, efficiency, and participant satisfaction in group support systems research. In ICIS *1996 Proceedings*.

Dhaliwal, J. S., & Benbasat, I. (1996). The use and effects of knowledge-based system explanations: Theoretical foundations and a framework for empirical evaluation. *Information Systems Research, 7*(3), 342–362.

Dorn, C., Burkhart, T., Werth, D., & Dustdar, S. (2010). Self-adjusting recommendations for people-driven Ad-hoc processes. In *Proceedings of the 8th international conference on Business process*.

Feldman, M. S., & Pentland, B. T. (2003). Reconceptualizing organizational routines as a source of flexibility and change. *Administrative Science Quarterly, 48*(1), 94.

Frei, F. X., Kalakota, R., Leone, A. J., & Marx, L. M. (1999). Process variation as a determinant of bank performance: Evidence from the retail banking study. *Management Science, 45*(9), 1210–1220.

Glover, S. M., Prawitt, D. F., & Spilker, B. C. (1997). The Influence of decision aids on user behavior: Implications for knowledge acquisition and inappropriate reliance. *Organizational Behavior and Human Decision Processes, 72*(2), 232–255.

Goldin, S. E., & Thorndyke, P. W. (1982). Simulating navigation for spatial knowledge acquisition. *Human Factors, 24*(4), 457–471.

Gönül, M. S., Önkal, D., & Lawrence, M. (2006). The effects of structural characteristics of explanations on use of a DSS. *Decision Support Systems, 42*(3), 1481–1493.

Good, M. D., Whiteside, J. A., Wixon, D. R., & Jones, S. J. (1984). Building a user-derived interface. *Communications of the ACM, 27*(10), 1032–1043.

Grambow, G., Oberhauser, R., & Reichert, M. (2011). Contextual generation of declarative work-flows and their application to software engineering processes. *International Journal On Advances in Intelligent Systems, 4*(4&3), 158–179.

Gregor, S., & Benbasat, I. (1999). Explanations from intelligent systems: Theoretical foundations and implications for practice. *MIS Quarterly, 23*(4), 497–530.

Gregor, S., & Hevner, A. (2013). Positioning and presenting design science research for maximum impact. *MIS Quarterly, 37*(2), 337–355.

Gregor, S., & Jones, D. (2007). The Anatomy of a design theory. *Journal of the Association for Information Systems, 8*(5), 312–335.

Hair, J. F., Hult, T., Ringle, C., & Sarstedt, M. (2014). A primer on partial least squares structural equation modeling (PLS-SEM). Los Angeles, CA [etc.]: SAGE.

Heinrich, R., & Paech, B. (2010). Defining the Quality of Business Processes. In G. Engels (Ed.), *GI-Edition/Proceedings* (Vol. 161, pp. 133–148)., Modellierung 2010. 24.–26. März 2010, Klagenfurt, Österreich Bonn: GI.

Hevner, A. R. (2007). A three cycle view of design science research. *Scandinavian Journal of Information Systems, 19*(2), 87–92.

Hevner, A. R., March, S. T., Park, J., & Ram, S. (2004). Design science in information systems research. *MIS Quarterly, 28*(1), 75–105.

Holz, H., Maus, H., Bernardi, A., & Rostanin, O. (2005). From lightweight, proactive information delivery to business process-oriented knowledge management. *Journal of Universal Knowledge Management, 0*(2), 101–127.

Klatzky, R. L., Loomis, J. M., Beall, A. C., Chance, S. S., & Golledge, R. G. (1998). Spatial updating of self-position and orientation during real, imagined, and virtual locomotion. *Psychological Science, 9,* 293–298.

Krumeich, J., Werth, D., & Loos, P. (2012). Business process learning on the job: A design science oriented approach and its empirical evaluation. *Knowledge Management & E-Learning: An International Journal, 4*(4), 395–414.

Kuechler, B., & Vaishnavi, V. (2008). Theory Development in Design Science Research: Anatomy of a Research Project. *European Journal of Information Systems, 17*(5), 489–504.

Limayem, M., & DeSanctis, G. (2000). Providing decisional guidance for Multicriteria decision making in groups. *Information Systems Research, 11*(4), 386–401.

Maedche, A., Morana, S., Schacht, S., Werth, D., & Krumeich, J. (2016). Advanced user assistance systems. *Business & Information Systems Engineering, 58*(5), 367–370.

Mălăescu, I., & Sutton, S. G. (2015). The effects of decision aid structural restrictiveness on cognitive load, perceived usefulness, and reuse intentions. *International Journal of Accounting Information Systems, 17,* 16–36.

Maus, H., Schwarz, S., Haas, J., & Dengel, A. (2011). CONTASK: Context-sensitive task assistance in the semantic desktop. In W. van der Aalst, J. Mylopoulos, N. M. Sadeh, M. J. Shaw, C. Szyperski, J. Filipe, & J. Cordeiro (Eds.), *Lecture Notes in Business Information Processing.* Enterprise Information Systems (Vol. 73, pp. 177–192). Berlin, Heidelberg: Springer Berlin, Heidelberg.

Morana, S., Gerards, T., & Maedche, A. (2015). ITSM ProcessGuide—a process guidance system for IT service management. In B. Donnellan, M. Helfert, J. Kenneally, D. VanderMeer, M. Rothenberger, & R. Winter (Eds.), *Lecture Notes in Computer Science.* New Horizons in Design Science: Broadening the Research Agenda (Vol. 9073, pp. 406–410). Cham: Springer International Publishing.

Morana, S., Kroenung, J., Maedche, A., & Schacht, S. (2019). Designing process guidance systems. *Journal of the Association for Information Systems, 20*(5), 6.

Morana, S., Schacht, S., & Maedche, A. (2016). Exploring the design, use, and outcomes of process guidance systems—A qualitative field study. In J. Parsons (Ed.), *Lecture Notes in Computer Science.* Tackling society's grand challenges with design science (Vol. 9661, pp. 81–96). Springer International Publishing.

Morana, S., Schacht, S., Scherp, A., & Maedche, A. (2013). User guidance for document-driven processes in enterprise systems. In D. Hutchison, T. Kanade, J. Kittler, J. M. Kleinberg, F. Mattern, J. C. Mitchell, … M. Rossi (Eds.), *Lecture Notes in Computer Science.* Design Science at the Intersection of Physical and Virtual Design (Vol. 7939, pp. 494–501). Berlin, Heidelberg: Springer Berlin Heidelberg.

Morana, S., Schacht, S., Scherp, A., & Maedche, A. (2014). Designing a process guidance system to support user's business process compliance. In *ICIS 2014 Proceedings.*

Morana, S., Schacht, S., Scherp, A., & Maedche, A. (2017). A review of the nature and effects of guidance design features. *Decision Support Systems, 97,* 31–42.

Münstermann, B., Eckhardt, A., & Weitzel, T. (2010). The performance impact of business process standardization. *Business Process Management Journal, 16*(1), 29–56.

Peffers, K., Rothenberger, M., Tuunanen, T., & Vaezi, R. (2012). Design Science Research Evaluation. In D. Hutchison, T. Kanade, J. Kittler, J. M. Kleinberg, F. Mattern, J. C. Mitchell,… B. Kuechler (Eds.), Lecture Notes in Computer Science. Design Science Research in Information Systems. Advances in Theory and Practice (Vol. 7286, pp. 398–410). Berlin, Heidelberg: Springer Berlin Heidelberg.

Pentland, B. T., & Feldman, M. (2005). Organizational routines as a unit of analysis. *Industrial and Corporate Change, 14*(5), 793–815.

Reimer, U., Margelisch, A., Novotny, B., & Vetterli, T. (1998). EULE2. *ACM SIGGROUP Bulletin, 19*(1), 56–61.

Rosemann, M., & vom Brocke, J. (2015). The Six Core Elements of Business Process Management. In J. vom Brocke & M. Rosemann (Eds.), *Handbook on business process management 1* (pp. 105–122). Berlin, Heidelberg: Springer.

Schaefer, T., Fettke, P., & Loos, P. (2013). Control patterns—bridging the gap between is controls and BPM. In *ECIS 2013 Proceedings*.

Seethamraju, R., & Marjanovic, O. (2009). Role of process knowledge in business process improvement methodology: A case study. *Business Process Management Journal, 15*(6), 920–936.

Silver, M. (1990). Decision support systems: directed and nondirected change. *Information Systems Research, 1*(1), 47–70.

Silver, M. (1991). Decisional guidance for computer-based decision support. *MIS Quarterly, 15*(1), 105–122.

Silver, M. (2006). Decisional guidance: Broadening the scope. *Advances in Management Information Systems, 6*, 90–119.

Singh, D. T. (1998). Incorporating cognitive aids into decision support systems: The case of the strategy execution process. *Decision Support Systems, 24*(2), 145–163.

Sykes, T. A. (2015). Support structures and their impacts on employee outcomes: A longitudinal field study of an enterprise system implementation. *MIS Quarterly, 39*(2), 437–495.

Tan, W.-G., Cater-Steel, A., & Toleman, M. (2009). Implementing IT service management: A case study focussing on critical success factors. *Journal of Computer Information Systems, 50*(2), 1–12.

Tekinerdoğan, B., Bozbey, S., Mester, Y., Turançiftci, E., & Alkışlar, L. (2011). An aspect-oriented tool framework for developing process-sensitive embedded user assistance systems. In D. Hutchison, T. Kanade, J. Kittler, J. M. Kleinberg, F. Mattern, J. C. Mitchell, … W. Joosen (Eds.), *Lecture Notes in Computer Science*. Transactions on Aspect-Oriented Software Development VIII (Vol. 6580, pp. 196–220). Berlin, Heidelberg: Springer Berlin Heidelberg.

Thorndyke, P. W., & Hayes-Roth, B. (1982). Differences in spatial knowledge acquired from maps and navigation. *Cognitive Psychology, 14*(4), 560–589.

Todd, P., & Benbasat, I. (1991). An experimental investigation of the impact of computer based decision aids on decision making strategies. *Information Systems Research, 2*(2), 87–115.

Todd, P., & Benbasat, I. (1999). Evaluating the impact of DSS, cognitive effort, and incentives on strategy selection. *Information Systems Research, 10*(4), 356–374.

Tremblay, M. C., Hevner, A., & Berndt, D. J. (2010). Focus groups for artifact refinement and evaluation in design research. *Communications of the Association for Information Systems, 26*(27), 599–618.

Urbach, N., & Ahlemann, F. (2010). Structural equation modeling in information systems research using partial least squares. *Journal of Information Technology Theory and Application, 11*(2), 5–40.

van Nimwegen, C. C., Burgos, D. D., van Oostendorp, H. H., & Schijf, H. H. J. M. (2006). The paradox of the assisted user: guidance can be counterproductive. In *The SIGCHI Conference* (pp. 917–926).

Venable, J., Pries-Heje, J., & Baskerville, R. (2016). FEDS: a framework for evaluation in design science research. *European Journal of Information Systems, 25*, 77–89.

Walls, J. G., Widmeyer, G. R., & El Sawy, O. A. (1992). Building an information system design theory for vigilant EIS. *Information Systems Research, 3*(1), 36–59.

Ye, L. R., & Johnson, P. E. (1995). The impact of explanation facilities on user acceptance of expert systems advice. *MIS Quarterly, 19*(2), 157–172.

Zhang, J., & Norman, D. A. (1994). Representations in distributed cognitive tasks. *Cognitive Science, 18*(1), 87–122.

DSR in Knowledge Management
and Education

Designing Platforms to Support Knowledge-Intensive Organizational Work

Sandeep Purao and Arvind Karunakaran

Abstract This is a story of a design science research project that started in one domain, petrochemical refineries, before extending into another, technology consulting. Across the two domains, the problem was scoped, defined and refined as one of supporting knowledge-intensive work that takes place over time and across locations with teams of specialists. Significant empirical work and design efforts in fields like knowledge management, collaborative work, and business process design have yet to provide clear paths to successful intervention in this problem. We relied on design science research (DSR) and action design research (ADR) methods as we worked to develop two context-specific solutions. One solution, SPA, used semantic analysis of operator procedures for organizations in petrochemical refining to generate meaningful instruction sets in support of collaborative work on the refinery floor. The other solution, ReKon, decomposed consulting templates into meaningful sections for technology consulting so knowledge workers could access these templates across project phases in response to new consulting assignments. Together, the two artifacts exemplify a key design principle: anchoring knowledge units, not task sequences, in concrete artifacts may improve knowledge workers' ability to respond to emergent complexities in knowledge-intensive work. The research project revealed three primary lessons. First, the time-consuming tasks of stakeholder interaction and development of seemingly simple artifacts allowed us to surface the complexities of organizational knowledge work in these domains. Second, ongoing and intense reflection away from the project activities was necessary to appreciate the theoretical depth. Third, the messy nature of design continued to grate against the systematic approach suggested by research methods.

S. Purao (✉)
Bentley University, Waltham, MA, USA
e-mail: spurao@bentley.edu

A. Karunakaran
McGill University, Montreal, Canada
e-mail: arvind.karunakaran@mcgill.ca

© Springer Nature Switzerland AG 2020
J. vom Brocke et al. (eds.), *Design Science Research. Cases*, Progress in IS,
https://doi.org/10.1007/978-3-030-46781-4_9

1   Introduction

The research project on which we reflect in this paper followed the tenets of design science research (DSR) (Hevner et al. 2004) and the action design research (ADR) (Sein et al. 2011) methodology in designing and developing tools to manage and make accessible knowledge hidden in operating procedures and practice templates in two domains (He, 2014; Karunakaran & Purao, 2012). The work was carried out over four years with partners in the petrochemical and consulting industries. The first project received funding from a consortium of petrochemical companies, and the second was carried out as part of a project supported by funding from the National Science Foundation.

We designed two artifacts. The first was the Semantic Procedure Analyzer (SPA), which performed semi-automated semantic analysis of operator procedures. Here, operator procedures (e.g., hydrocracker shutdown, an emergency procedure for acidic cooling towers and hundreds of other emergencies) refer to the action knowledge that operators in the petrochemical refineries rely on to orchestrate complex patterns of work on the refinery floor, over time, and across locations. The continuing interactions with the stakeholders and efforts to develop an artifact increased our appreciation of the nuances of complex, knowledge-intensive work in an industrial setting. This artifact was developed over three years using a combination of technologies and was subjected to several rounds of formative evaluation. As we learned more about the nature of work in this industry and how knowledge-intensive it remains, we realized that the problem we addressed was similar to one faced in other industries, such as technology consulting. This realization led us to extend the frame we were developing to another domain, technology consulting.

The second artifact we developed was ReKon: Recombining Template Chunks for Consulting Projects. This artifact generated and presented chunks of practice templates, codified wisdom about what works in what settings, to consultants and project managers. The templates (e.g., requirements gathering, code review, and several others) were guides for the project participants in carrying out important tasks. The ReKon artifact was developed over two and a half years (partially overlapping with the three-year period for the first artifact) in collaboration with mul-tiple consulting firms that contributed the practice templates and was subjected to multiple rounds of formative evaluation during the process.

The two artifacts, one developed in an industrial setting and the other in a post-industrial setting, provided the research team several opportunities for reflection. It was often difficult to extricate ourselves from the demands of the project work to reflect on the underlying theoretical framing. However, the opportunities for reflection revealed a rich set of possibilities, the most promising of which had to do with viewing and supporting knowledge-intensive work processes that take place over time and across locations with teams of specialists in complex organizational settings. This theme has been the focus of much empirical and design work in several fields, including knowledge management, collaborative work, and business process design, but designing and deploying artifacts to support such work in organizational settings remains difficult.

The artifacts we designed also provided opportunities to engage in theorizing and theory-testing across multiple settings. Some of the lessons we learned were the importance of appreciating the context, which can be a rich source for theorizing and theory extension; the importance of reflection, which, in spite of the demands of technology development and stakeholder interaction, allows the research team to engage with the deeper theoretical questions; and an acknowledgement of the messy nature of design, which remains despite efforts to outline systematic accounts of DSR projects.

This case report first describes the project's context(s), followed by the journey we undertook, including iterations, before moving to the results and outcomes, such as the artifacts and efforts to generate theory. We conclude with key lessons learned.

2 The Context

The research project was initiated in an industrial setting, petrochemical refining, where much of the work is characterized by field and console operators who coordinate tasks in a complex plant that is spread across several acres. As the work progressed, a second domain was added from a post-industrial setting, technology consulting, where much of the work is characterized by projects that teams of specialists work on in several phrases that are based on each project's unique needs.

In both contexts, stakeholders described the work as knowledge-intensive. This section describes both projects, with a slightly greater emphasis on the petrochemical refineries project because the conceptual distance to work in this domain is greater for the IS audience and because the project was initiated in this domain. As we describe this context, we point out key similarities between this domain and the technology consulting domain (particularly, software integration). The petrochemical refining industry, an industrial setting, consists of about 150 refineries in the US. A typical petrochemical refinery is modularized into many plant sub-units that are interconnected via numerous upstream and downstream material flows that can be highly time-sensitive. A disruption in one of the sub-units can disrupt operations in the entire plant, jeopardizing the functioning of the refinery. The disruption can also cause accidents that damage industrial assets or lead to loss of life in surrounding communities. However, such accidents are less likely today than was once the case (Nivolianitou, Konstandinidou, & Michalis, 2006) because of significant ef-fort over several decades on the part of the refineries and the operators. Therefore, expert operators in the field and in the console room are critical for the refinery to function effectively (Fig. 1). These operators acquire and cultivate significant expertise, often as tacit knowledge about running the plant, which may include hidden dependencies between sub-units, tactics for mitigation of flow delays, di-agnosis of instrument failures, the ability to read signs of impending emergencies, and the like. The initial

Fig. 1 Work in the petrochemical refineries

impetus for this research was a prospective wave of re-tirements among expert operators, creating the potential for a train-wreck scenario. The problem statement for the industry was simple: *with the impending wave of retirements, how can the refineries leverage available knowledge to sustain and manage the complex nature of their work?*

The other domain, consulting for software integration (a post-industrial setting), is also ridden with complexities. Software integration work requires domain knowledge, knowledge of the processes followed at the client site, and system-specific knowledge, including details like native data formats, file structures, da-tabase schemas, APIs, interoperability standards, data-porting rules, and the like. Such knowledge is often tacit, acquired and internalized over the years by system architects and senior integration engineers (Karunakaran, Purao, & He, 2009, 2012; Umapathy, Purao, & Barton, 2008). Software integration work requires assembling not systems, but systems of systems (Brownsword et al., 2006), which cannot be treated as monoliths, as they emerge and evolve without complete visibility to or control by any single individual or team engaged in the integration effort (Lam, 2005). As a result, the track record for such integration projects tends to be sub-par (Charette, 2005). In addition, a high turnover rate in the software industry makes it difficult for software-integration organizations to leverage the experiential knowledge that their individual architects and engineers acquire over the years. Based on these concerns, the problem statement for the industry asks: *how can knowledge about these complex organizational efforts be captured and made available to successive generations of systems integration professionals?*

In both industries, a set of artifacts–operator procedures in the petrochemical industry, and practice templates in the technology consulting industry–are critical to supporting complex organizational work. Both provide important scaffolds that organizational actors use to carry out knowledge-intensive tasks. One set of artifacts, operator procedures, describes a sequence of tasks while maintaining significant agency for the operators, while the other, practice templates, outlines what must be done while leaving the consultants with considerable freedom in determining how these tasks may be done. Next, we describe in more detail these artifacts in one domain (operator procedures in the petrochemical refinery), acknowledging that similar observations can be made about practice templates in the technology consulting domain.

A typical petrochemical refinery maintains hundreds of operator procedures that operators can access to support production work. Some procedures are carried out at regular intervals (e.g., daily or weekly), while others guide such infrequent work as start-up and shutdown of certain kinds of equipment. The procedures help operators coordinate upstream and downstream activities and implement complex "recipes" across interdependent staging stations that must maintain physical constraints like volume, temperature, and pressure. The scale of operations, the size of the specialized units, and physical distances across units mean that several operators (in the field and in a console room) must coordinate their actions using different parts of the operator procedures in an intricate manner. These operator proce-dures are not workflows

Fig. 2 Operator procedures in petrochemical refineries

but describe tasks that skilled operators enact relying on tacit and explicit knowledge (Nonaka, Toyama, & Konno, 2000). Thus, the operator procedures provide a foundation that skilled operators can use to enact organizational routines. Most refineries maintain the operator procedures simply as a set of files stored in folders and shared—sometimes in printed form in large binders and sometimes in electronic form on the refinery's intranet (Anon 2013)—with the operators (Fig. 2).

An operator procedure represents months or years of work by expert operators to codify the complex tasks and steps. A typical operator procedure for the organizations with which we worked can be anywhere between a short page and thirty pages in length, and may cover activities that take just a few hours to more than a week, interspersed with periods of inaction so physical processes can be completed. These procedures often describe actions that require coordination from several operators and that are not easily automated. Consider this example of an instruction in a procedure: examine and tighten valve on the line from V2 to the next unit. Executing this task requires an operator to interpret the weather conditions, examine various gauges, and consider any planned actions, including planned dis-charges from upstream equipment, before deciding how much to tighten the valve. Therefore, we characterize operator procedures as descriptions of knowledge-intensive work, where the procedures provide starting points that the operators must interpret and enact in the current context.

Practice templates in the technology consulting industry can be characterized in a similar manner. These templates, which can also be in the hundreds, contain outlines for actions like gathering requirements and reviewing code. They may be specified as Word documents or Excel spreadsheets, with several slots defined that themselves serve as guides that consultants can use to plan and coordinate their work on various projects. These practice templates also describe knowledge-intensive work, where the templates provide starting points that the operators must interpret and enact in the current context. Considerable effort was made in understanding these contexts and defining these problems before the research project began.

3 The Journey

The research project we describe in this case had a tumultuous journey that led to the development of two unique research artifacts, SPA and ReKon, and included multiple empirical inquiries about organizational routines and operators' behav-iors. The work was carried out with the help of a small research team that included graduate students and undergraduate students, who helped develop the artifacts, gather primary data, and analyze data. Partners from both domains provided an important set of inputs into the research focus and continued guidance. This case study describes the design science elements of the overall research project, focus-ing on the design, refinement, and ongoing evaluation of the two artifacts and contributions to kernel theories that contributed to the design of the artifacts. We first return to the core problem that was the impetus of the work to identify the multiple perspectives that we considered as we initiated the project. During the larger project, the research team followed up on some of these directions (Fig. 3).

The research focus was not a foregone conclusion when the research project started. In fact, the other perspectives outlined in Fig. 3 were pursued as part of the larger research project, allowing the research team to deepen their appreciation of the phenomenon under consideration. We identified a number of pivotal events that, in retrospect, punctuated the project's trajectory and shaped the project. Each is described below as an iteration, or "lap," that was initiated by a key event.

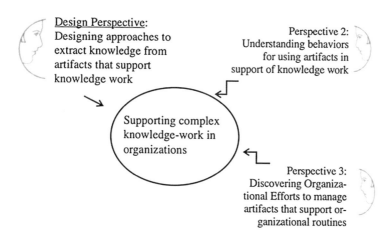

Fig. 3 Choosing the design perspective

3.1 Lap 1—Problem Awareness and Framing

This lap started with the first key event, an informational interaction and meeting with the group of industry stakeholders in the petrochemical refineries domain, where the lead researcher described current research on knowledge management and cautioned the group against excessively high expectations. The industry partners emphasized the impending wave of retirements of expert operators and explained why it was a critical issue for the industry to determine how to support complex, knowledge-intensive work. (This framing was suggested by the research team.) As the project took off (with tempered expectations), the emphasis was on designing a situated implementation of an IT artifact that would analyze poorly structured operator procedures, stated in natural language with a view to extracting clusters of instructions for the operators.

This lap, which we label the Problem Awareness lap, included ongoing participation in consortium meetings, visiting petrochemical plants operated by member organizations to define the problem scope, and developing accurate scenarios that illustrated the use of operator procedures. The understanding and appreciation of the context and scale the project team gained during this lap shaped several activities throughout the project, including the project's scope, consideration of design alternatives, and choice of kernel theories.

Understanding the problem: A number of perspectives were considered during this phase, driven primarily by practice-driven considerations. For example, the problems that surfaced during discussions with the stakeholders were related to internal champions of the work. Candidates included operations, human resources, safety, and the information technology groups. The operations group became the focus because its issues were the primary motivation for the industry group. With this focus, the problem was narrowed down, although multiple perspectives remained (Fig. 3). As the discussion moved forward and the research team visited some of the refineries, specific design goals were articulated that could then drive the design work.

Characterizing possible solutions: During this problem awareness lap, the research team generated and developed buy-in to the idea of focusing on actionable outcomes like extracting knowledge from the operator procedures. The emphasis re-mained on supporting complex, knowledge-intensive work. As the research team moved to a crisper definition of the project over a period of about six months, a solution emerged in terms of a tool that could analyze the hundreds of procedures, which could have overlaps and varied writing styles, with a view to streamlining them and extracting information that could then be delivered to operators when they needed to perform actions.

3.2   Lap 2—Stakeholder Meetings and Weighing Alternatives

The first reporting meeting, which took place about six months into the project, set the tone for this lap. As the researcher described what had been learned from visits to several refineries, the discussion moved to new paths for design and intervention, including training for novice operators, developing organizational poli-cies for knowledge management, and building a tool for extracting procedural knowledge (the original intent). The emphasis shifted during this meeting to exploring possible research streams and theoretical foundations that could provide ways to address these problems.

Understanding the problem: During this phase, our understanding of the problem became more nuanced and focused as the research team came to appreciate the scale of the problem and worked with several authentic examples of operator procedures. A decision was made to prepare a number of critical scenarios that would allow the research team to scope the problem and develop alternative strategies in response.

Characterizing possible solutions: The research team also identified a number of possibilities for designing solutions, such as techniques for text analysis, expert-driven procedure analysis, and empirical inquiries into operators' use of procedures. Input from the stakeholders that described how organizations in the group maintained their procedures helped the team to weigh and select from these possibilities.

3.3   Lap 3—Artifact Development in Domain 1

After several additional meetings and multiple rounds of design and evaluation, a first prototype that would analyze operator procedures was designed and built. During this lap, a good deal of the work focused on choosing and working with technology platforms, programming and debugging, and working with examples to ensure that the program worked as intended. The discovery of new problems like how to convert the procedures into simple text representations, how to embed pictures into procedures, and how to develop a lightweight ontology of terminol-ogy used in the procedures kept the research team working on this lap. About eighteen months into the project, the team shared a first version of the prototype with the stakeholders, and the modifications continued. After that, the emphasis shifted to adding technological precision and ongoing formative evaluation.

Understanding the problem: During this phase, our understanding of the problem became more entrenched in the need to analyze unstructured text, learn with continued expert input, and develop terminologies that would assist in parsing the unstructured text. The discussion also surfaced several categories of users that could use the solution we designed.

Characterizing the solution: The design work was carried out with external packages that required considerable customization, envisioning, and development of user interactions with the research prototype. Several learning mechanisms were considered, along with parameters for improving the artifact's effectiveness, and a lightweight ontology of terms and abbreviations was constructed by extracting them from the procedures. This phase also served as the first opportunity to understand the solution we were building in terms of a framework or a platform that could be conceptualized beyond the specific instance we were implementing.

3.4 Lap 4—Expanding Research Efforts to Domain 2

The research team realized that examining the interplay between operator procedures and work practices presented a key opportunity. A second domain, consult-ing services, was added, and another IT artifact was constructed. Although this additional work is described here as Lap 4, the lap had several "sub-phases," as the research team worked with a new set of stakeholders (consulting organizations), obtained a number of practice templates from them, and created components from the templates based on expert decisions. These sub-phases loosely mirrored the first three laps undertaken in the first domain and led to the design and construction of another artifact.

Understanding the problem: With the two domains and two artifacts under consideration, the research team was able to focus on reflection and theorizing based on choices made among kernel theories. The emphasis shifted to developing a more nuanced understanding of the nature of the knowledge we were trying to extract using these artifacts, and how organizational actors could use it in support of complex tasks.

Understanding the solution: A second artifact, ReKon, was constructed and populated with chunks of templates generated from several hundred practice templates contributed by partners in the technology consulting industry. With the two artifacts and a shift in emphasis to reflection and theorizing, the research team could develop the contours of a framework that could describe the artifacts like those we were designing across the two domains. The research team used the empirical work that had accompanied the design science efforts to outline several frameworks, one of which was intended to outline the class of solutions, while another was developed to explicate how organizational work could be supported by such solutions.

3.5 Lap 5—Ongoing Formative Evaluation

Continued formative evaluation is better described as concurrent refinement of the artifact than as a separate lap in the journey. The formative evaluation also served to ensure that "relevance" remained an important consideration. For example, a set of operator procedures obtained from one of the refineries served as the basis for the initial design of the artifact, but the research team moved to obtain second and third sets from other organizations to ensure that the research focus remained on developing a solution and that any artifact would be appropriate for a corpus that included varied procedures. Without the ongoing formative evaluation, the re-search team would have been tempted to pursue rigor (increasingly accurate pars-ing) at the expense of relevance.

Understanding the problem: The trade-off between rigor and relevance added further nuanced understanding of the problem space. For example, discussion of formative evaluation results with the stakeholders improved the research team's understanding of the importance of the "human-in-the-loop" nature of knowledge extraction from operator procedures, as confidence in the outcomes of the knowledge extraction process was more important than concerns like accurate parsing. Another aspect of the problem that became apparent during this lap was the importance of local, organization-specific terminologies, which led to new decisions in the solution space.

Understanding the solution: The importance of "human-in-the-loop" and other local terminologies led to another set of key decisions about the artifacts, so ideas related to learning from past instances and developing a lightweight ontology became infused with these considerations. At this time, work across the two domains was also influential in the next iterations of the artifacts. For example, the natural interaction styles across the two domains differed in terms of how the artifacts were designed, yet they appeared to adhere to the same principle of allowing key organizational actors visibility into the process and control over any algorithmic or heuristic decisions that the prototype would make.

3.6 Lap N—Continued Refinement and Reflection

The research team continued their refinement and evaluation of both artifacts. Although it is tempting to move on and leave a design science project behind, it is often difficult for the research team to do so simply because of the wicked nature of design. SPA, the artifact designed for the petrochemical companies, was released to the care of the companies, which continued to work on possibilities for commer-cialization. ReKon, the artifact designed for the technology consulting organizations, remained a research prototype and continued to support teaching efforts. Therefore, both artifacts continue to be the subjects of ongoing work by the research team, including additional levels of theorizing, extensions of the ideas to new domains and, in some cases, discovering new avenues for evaluation.

4   The Results

The project's output consisted of two technology-based prototypes, SPA and ReKon, that were designed and implemented, and two frameworks that elaborated what the research team learned about the problem space and the design space. Ad-ditional reflection about these artifacts also allowed the research team to outline possible contributions to theory.

4.1   Presentation of Artifact(S)

4.1.1   The SPA Artifact

The first artifact we designed was SPA, the Semantic Procedure Analyzer (Fig. 4). Its implementation followed a modular architecture with the Java platform at the core and connections to other modules for tagging parts of speech and supervised learning.

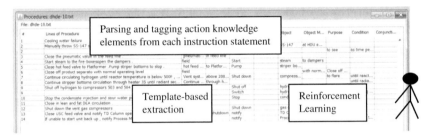

Extraction of Action Knowledge Elements from Each Statement

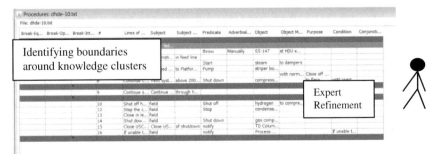

Definition of Knowledge Clusters by Identifying Boundaries

Fig. 4 The SPA artifact

4.1.2   The ReKon Artifact

The second artifact we designed and implemented was ReKon, which was populated with chunks of ~ 1,200 templates acquired from our industry partners, with each chunk placed in a matrix of Phases and Tasks (Purao et al. 2012). Figure 5 shows a screenshot of the ReKon artifact built to contain these template chunks.

The software implementations were accompanied by frameworks that described the problem and the solution class (not described here). A brief recap of these implementations is provided in the "Growth of Design Theory" section.

4.2   Application of the Artifact(S)

Building scenarios, a simple technique, was used to communicate with the stakeholders and demonstrate the use and usefulness of the artifacts we designed. This section provides examples of two scenarios, the first of which is a broad scenario that describes how the SPA artifact may be used in a refinery and the second of which follows a more traditional scenario structure with hypothetical actors to demonstrate the need for the ReKon artifact in a consulting organization.

Scenario 1: Using the SPA artifact in a refinery. Consider, for example, a chemical plant or refinery (or an organization in another process industry). The plant/refinery may have several hundred procedures that have been developed over a long period of time. Although a general structure of these procedures may have been established, they may have been written by different individuals or groups, follow different writing conventions, and use different terminology, including acronyms and descriptive terms that may have changed over the years. Although these procedures provide an essential component of the organizational work that the field and console operators perform

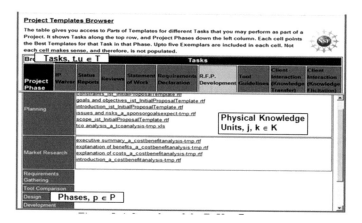

Fig. 5 The ReKon artifact

in the plant, they can be managed only as a set of files. Without an artifact like SPA, the knowledge contained in the procedures remains isolated, but with SPA the set of operator procedures can be converted into knowledge clusters with multiple potential uses, such as designing training programs.

Scenario 2: Using ReKon in a consulting company. Imagine that John, Mary, and Sam are deciding how they should approach a new integration effort for a client, Painters R Us. The effort involves constructing services from a legacy scheduling application that contractors and customers can use and outlining processes that connect other legacy applications in a similar manner. The three designers are concerned about scalability and security but are also unclear about how to align current business processes. Project templates that codify lessons learned from previous projects do not permit direct mapping against all of their concerns. In these coarse-grained templates are detailed instructions and worksheets for structuring tasks like working with clients to uncover requirements, designing, and testing. John, Mary, and Sam realize that their project with Painters R Us will require several components from these templates, as they cannot be found in a single template. Without an artifact like ReKon, the team spends weeks trying to understand and select templates to guide their efforts or creates an ad hoc approach, relying on their experience instead of leveraging the knowledge contained in the templates. With ReKon, they are able to explore different components, and select the components that are relevant to their specific project with Painters R Us.

4.3 Evaluation of Artifact(S)

4.3.1 Evaluation of the SPA Artifact

Evaluation efforts targeted to the SPA artifact included evaluation by a panel of experts, evaluation of each phase implemented in the artifact, and evaluation of the learning mechanisms. We highlight two of these. The first is an evaluation experiment that focused on performance of the knowledge-extraction component's parsing and tagging of knowledge statements and learning mechanisms that improve the parsing and tagging performance. Figure 6 shows the outcomes.

The second evaluation effort was carried out with a panel of experts (similar to Purao and Storey 1997), who were invited to use SPA prototype to analyze a procedure of his or her choice. The expert selected a procedure, shepherded it through its phases, and produced knowledge clusters from the procedure. The recording capability in the SPA prototype allowed the research team to capture the process and the outcomes. The outcomes were compared against the expert solution (see Table 1).

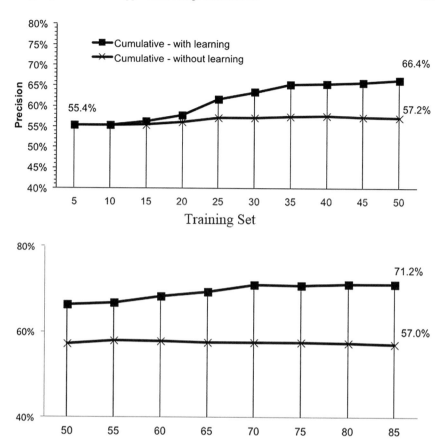

Fig. 6 Cumulative precision rates for action knowledge extraction

Table 1 Evaluating performance of the SPA artifact with experts

Correctness (%)	A	B	C	D	E	Avg
Detect instruction statements	100	100	100	100	100	100
Extract action knowledge	54.2	58.7	48.9	58.7	58.7	55.8
Identify knowledge clusters	33.3	−0.1	66.7	60.0	66.7	56.7

4.3.2 Evaluation of the ReKon Artifact

The ReKon research artifact was subjected to several regimes of evaluation. Subjects were novice users who had been recruited from a course on systems integra-tion and were working on real-world projects to implement integration solutions. In the course of individual interviews, the users were asked to reflect on the com-parative

Table 2 Coarse-Grained templates versus hypothetical availability of chunks of templates

Selected prompts	Representative comments
Although I may not have used all of the sections, it is useful to have the complete template	(Positive) [it is] useful to have the template because most of the information we have to come up with ourselves so to have a guide line to fill in is very helpful to the success of this project (Negative) [it] is difficult to determine if a section is relevant or not. Figuring out what needs to be included is work in itself
It is better to have each section available separately, so we can create the document we need by combining the sections that are relevant to our project	(Positive) Most groups will not use all sections and it may be easier to make your own document (Negative) … I'd rather error on the side of caution when it comes to including all possible sub-sections. Having the sections available separately poses the risk of missing something

usefulness of a coarse-grained template versus a hypothetical scenario in which sections from the template would be available separately. Table 2 shows selected comments from this part of the formative assessment.

The responses suggested ambivalence among the users in rating the relevance of individual sections of a template. Although they found some sections useful, others were not (97% found scope definition to be relevant, but only 33% found the related projects section to be relevant). After the subjects had a few weeks to explore the ReKon platform populated with template chunks, they assessed the granularity, size, appropriateness of classification, and relevance of the knowledge units, as well as its usefulness in projects Table 3 shows the results.

The results were encouraging because it is often difficult to operationalize "rules of thumb" like how large a template chunk should be. A more direct assessment was provided when subjects answered whether the template chunks satisfied and were relevant to the needs of a project based on a knowledge unit that the participants chose. Comments from the respondents provided additional suggestions for improvement: One suggested the need for additional meta-data, as "further explanation may be needed in the templates. … to have a better understanding." Another suggested a "quick-view feature that opens it up in a tiny thumbnail to view" to locate and retrieve

Table 3 Assessment of appropriateness of template chunks

Criteria	Outcome (N = 29)
Size of template chunks (1: too small; 5: too long)	2.65 (SD = 0.93)
Satisfies project needs (1: all; 5: very little)	2.71 (SD = 1.01)
Relevance of template chunks (1: all relevant; 5: none relevant)	2.82 (SD = 1.02)

appropriate chunks quickly. One commented that "some of the chunks ... should possibly be re-worked to make them easier to understand." Together, the responses helped the research team to build and refine the underlying design principles.

4.4 Growth of Design Theory

The designs and evaluations of SPA and ReKon pointed to the potential useful-ness of the two artifacts. In the case of ReKon, the evaluation was done with users who were working on complex real-world process-intensive projects for imple-menting integration solutions. In the case of SPA, the evaluation was conducted using example procedures from multiple organizations and an expert panel to as-sess the appropri-ateness of outcomes. The outcomes suggested that the artifact was able to parse and chunk the operator procedures into smaller knowledge units. By building these two artifacts and based on the evaluation results, we were able to refine the design prin-ciples. Here, we describe how we reflected on the results and the emerging design principles to develop three key foundational principles for designing artifacts like SPA and ReKon (Table 4).

First, the design science research effort, along with the empirical inquiry that accompanied it, showed how organizational actors might use existing artifacts during the day-to-day performance of their work. Although the knowledge needed to navi-gate the complexities of work is often tacit, it is also materially anchored in these artifacts, which play a dual role in that they can be used as maps when an actor embarks on a new complex task and as devices to trigger action when an actor encoun-ters a contingency while performing a task. Therefore, the design science outcomes provided a more feasible alternative for managing the complexity of organizational work than the higher abstraction and coarse-granularity offered by business process modeling approaches.

Table 4 Foundational principles for supporting complex knowledge work with artifacts like SPA and ReKon

	Foundational Principles
1	The knowledge needed to navigate the complexities of work is often tacit, but it can be materially anchored in concrete artifacts that are starting points for actors in performing their work
2	Chunking and digitizing these artifacts in the form of knowledge units and making them available to organizational actors can provide them the agency needed to handle the ongoing contingencies of work in real time
3	Artifacts that capture and present these knowledge units must be open, incomplete, and underspecified so the artifact can generate digital options in real time that organizational actors can recombine and reuse over time

Second, because the artifacts were digitized, they allowed a certain agility beyond modularization and hierarchical decomposition. The chunking could be accomplished in a variety of ways (e.g., time-based, event-based, actor-based), allowing the chunks to have layered modularization (Yoo Boland, Lyytinen, & Majchrzak, 2012) and ensuring that relationships and rules across chunks were not necessarily fixed and pre-specified (Baldwin & Clark, 2000). In the context of complex organizational work, this lack of specificity (Garud, Kumaraswamy, & Langlois, 2009) ensures that rigidities do not become performance traps (Garud & Kumaraswamy, 2005; Repenning & Sterman, 2002). For instance, actors might not be able to apply their past experiential learning to handle contingencies in real time (Weick & Sutcliffe, 2001). The layered modularization and the incompleteness that is inherent in it affords the possibility to recombine digitized chunks, thus putting residual control in the hands of actors on the ground for handling emergent contingencies with workarounds (Strauss, 1988; Suchman, 2007).

Third, we learned that the artifacts we designed could support self-referential (Yoo et al., 2012) and emergent (Garud, Kumaraswamy, & Sambamurthy, 2006) aspects of layered modularization. For example, one could derive new templates and procedures by recombining existing templates and procedures, and the results could still be kept open for additional contributions from users. These continual contributions could then strengthen organizational memory and generate digital options (Sambamurthy, Bharadwaj, & Grover, 2003) in real time.

5 Key Lessons

The project provided several opportunities to learn about the domain in which we conducted the research, the process of building design science artifacts, the use of design science methods, and the nuances related to applying design science meth-ods in particular contexts. Several of these are outlined below as reflections.

The time-consuming tasks of stakeholder interaction and seemingly simple artifact development were essential entry points that allowed us to surface the complexi-ties of organizational knowledge work in these domains. We realized that knowledge to support organizational work in both settings was more difficult to conceptualize as a sequence of steps than to represent as modular knowledge units (chunks). This insight shaped later design iterations, guided the search for new theoretical foundations, and allowed our understanding of the design artifact(s) to evolve. These efforts helped the research team to develop and refine the three foundational principles articulated above iteratively (Table 4). These design principles were not only used to build the SPA and ReKon, they also allowed the research team to appreciate the nature of complex knowledge work and how IT artifacts may be designed to support such work.

Ongoing and intense reflection away from the project activities was difficult but necessary to appreciate the theoretical depth. When we were embedded in the research context and involved in the design process, it was difficult to step back and think about how we can derive principles or build theoretical implications. The re-search team traced this tension primarily to the conflict between context-driven realism and generalized outcomes that is inherent in the DSR process. The conflict became acute as the research team added a second domain for investigation, but the additional issues that came up for consideration also provided the team a natural avenue for generalization. In retrospect, it was clear that understanding and managing these demands better would have helped the research project. One approach to doing so could be to monitor and appreciate the notion of a research trajectory, where these demands are not necessarily seen as "conflicting demands" but as demands from the various stakeholders on the research team (researchers, partner practitioners) that could be emphasized at different phases during the project (McGrath, 1981). Such a shift in emphasis across the phases may allow a more proactive stance to managing and meeting these demands to emerge.

Third, the way the research team worked to identify and articulate the foundational principles and the more specific design principles to distill the outcomes was some-what open and was subject to considerable uncertainty and iteration. The research team learned that the problems (significant as they were) were less about the form of these principles than they were about the process one may follow to identify and refine them and the sources one may rely on to make the articulation defensible. In retrospect, the process we followed was largely ad hoc and relied heavily on the researchers' expertise to gauge the depth we achieved in each iteration, how we engaged in connecting these to our work, prior theoretical positions, and the evaluation data we collected.

Fourth, the messy nature of design continued to go against the systematic approach that a research methodology required, prompting us to focus on the design science work and to relegate the presentation of work in a research manuscript to a secondary concern. This conflict surfaced several times as the research team moved from understanding the context, to using the right computational and representational techniques, and back to demonstrating the artifact under construction for the industry partners. The choice of moves across these perspectives was not driven by methodological mandates but by the need to respond to various stakeholders.

Although the key lessons learned may be seen as just pointers, we believe that each of them can help readers think about new directions. As a relatively recent entrant to the spectrum of methodological offerings, DSR continues to surprise its practitioners because it continues to point to new and interesting challenges. Some of these challenges are related to the tension between a focus on the research and the need to respond to different stakeholders. Others are related to expectations of outcomes' generalizability and how attention to the context can take the research team away from it. Yet others are related to the inherently future-oriented nature of DSR and the theories related to human behavior that must build on past observations. Many of the challenges we encountered can be traced to these tensions. We hope that the design science project we outlined here will give the reader a sense of how these tensions can manifest in design science projects.

References

Anon. (2013). *Personal communication with a senior plant manager in a petro-chemical refinery.*

Baldwin, C. Y., & Clark, K. B. (2000). *Design rules: The power of modularity* (Vol. 1). MIT press.

Brownsword, L. (2006). *System-of-systems navigator: An approach for managing system-of-systems interoperability.* Software Engineering Institute, Carnegie Mellon University, Pittsburgh, PA.

Charette, R. (2005). Why software fails. *IEEE Spectrum, 42*(9), 36.

Garud, R., & Kumaraswamy, A. (2005). Vicious and virtuous circles in the management of knowledge: The case of Infosys technologies. *MIS Quarterly, 29*(1), 9–33.

Garud, R., Kumaraswamy, A., & Sambamurthy, V. (2006). Emergent by design: Performance and transformation at infosys technologies. *Organization Science, 17*(2), 277.

Garud, R., Kumaraswamy, A., & Langlois, R. eds. (2009). *Managing in the modular age: Architectures, networks, and organizations.* Wiley.

He, J. (2014). *Managing and leveraging action knowledge: the case of front-line operators in the petrochemical industry.* Doctoral Dissertation. College of IST, Penn State University.

Hevner, A., March. S. T., Park, J., & Ram, S. (2004). Design science in information systems research. *MIS Quarterly, 28*(1), 75–105.

Karunakaran, A., & Purao, S. (2012). Designing for recombination: process design through template combination. Design Science in Information Systems and Technologies Conference (DESRIST), Las Vegas, NV: LNCS Press, May.

Karunakaran, A., Purao, S., & He, J. (2009). From 'Method Fragments' to 'Knowledge Units': A fine-granular approach. *International Conference on Information Systems*, Phoenix, AZ.

Karunakaran, A., Purao, S., & Cameron, B. (2012). Designing to support complex organizational work: a pragmatic approach. *Proceedings of the IT Artefact Design Workshop (in conjunction with European Conference on Information Systems (ECIS).* Barcelona, Spain. June.

Lam, W. (2005). Investigating success factors in enterprise application integration: A case-driven analysis. *European Journal of Information Systems, 14*(2), 175–187.

McGrath, J. E. (1981). Dilemmatics: The study of research choices and dilemmas. *American Behavioral Scientist, 25*(2), 179–210.

Nivolianitou, Z., Konstandinidou, M., & Michalis, C. (2006). Statistical analysis of major accidents in petrochemical industry notified to the major accident reporting system (MARS). *Journal of Hazardous Materials, 137*(1), 1–7.

Nonaka, I., Toyama, R., & Konno, N. (2000). SECI, Ba and leadership: A unified model of dynamic knowledge creation. *Long Range Planning, 33*(1), 5–34.

Purao, S., & Storey, V. C. (1997). Intelligent support for retrieval and synthesis of patterns for object-oriented design. In International Conference on Conceptual Modeling (pp. 30–42). Berlin, Heidelberg: Springer.

Purao, S., Karunakaran, A., & Cameron, B. (2012). A platform for recombining process knowledge chunks. In *Enterprise, Business-Process and Information Systems Modeling* (pp. 31–45). Springer, Berlin, Heidelberg.

Repenning, N. P., & Sterman, J. D. (2002). Capability traps and self-confirming attribution errors in the dynamics of process improvement. *Administrative Science Quarterly, 47*(2), 265–295.

Sambamurthy, V., Bharadwaj, A., & Grover, V. (2003). Shaping agility through digital options: Reconceptualizing the role of information technology in contemporary firms. *MIS Quarterly,* 237–263.

Sein, M., Henfridsson, O., Purao, S., Rossi, M., & Lindgren, R. (2011). Action design research. *MIS Quarterly, 35*(1), 37–56.

Strauss, A. (1988). The articulation of project work: An organizational process. *The Sociological Quarterly, 29*(2), 163–178.

Suchman, L. (2007). *Human-machine reconfigurations: Plans and situated actions.* Cambridge University Press.

Umapathy, K., Purao, S., & Barton, R. R. (2008). Designing enterprise integration solutions: Effectively. *European Journal of Information Systems, 17*(5), 518–527.

Weick, K., & Sutcliffe, K. (2001). Managing the unexpected: Assuring high performance in an age of uncertainty. *San Francisco: Wiley, 1*(3), 5.

Yoo, Y., Boland, R. J., Jr., Lyytinen, K., & Majchrzak, A. (2012). Organizing for innovation in the digitized world. *Organization Science, 23*(5), 1398–1408.

Chunking Big Journeys into Smaller Trips: Combining Peer Creation and Gamification to Design a Continuing Education Concept for Energy Consultants

Sarah Oeste-Reiß, Sofia Schöbel, Matthias Söllner, and Jan Marco Leimeister

Abstract Designing socio-technical systems like IT-supported teaching-learning systems that motivate learners while at the same time stimulating knowledge transfer has become challenging. Teaching-learning techniques that consist of a social context that interacts with and is supported by information technologies are often bundled in a holistic design artifact. To explore a socio-technical design artifact, one must recognize that it consists of several sub-artifacts, each of which must have its own design approach. We introduce the research approach of designing and piloting the IT-supported teaching-learning concept, sensitized to the demand of distinguishing among several socio-technical sub-artifacts. We present the purpose of our design science research (DSR) journey and differentiate among several design artifacts, each of which make prescriptive knowledge contributions and, thus, represent diverse types of theory in information systems. The first artifact is a *Peer Creation Process for enhancing knowledge transfer and documentation*, which contributes to a nascent design theory. The second artifact is a U*ser-Centered Process to gamify LMSs*, which contributes to a theory of design and action. We describe the DSR journey that was part of the project StaySmart, the purpose of which was to design and evaluate a teaching-learning concept for knowledge workers. Teaching-learning artifacts usually have one purpose: to design and evaluate the learning experience. However, designing such artifacts requires identifying their sub-purposes, which

S. Oeste-Reiß · S. Schöbel · M. Söllner · J. M. Leimeister (✉)
University of Kassel, Kassel, Germany
e-mail: janmarco.leimeister@unisg.ch

S. Oeste-Reiß
e-mail: oeste-reiss@uni-kassel.de

S. Schöbel
e-mail: sofia.schoebel@uni-kassel.de

M. Söllner
e-mail: soellner@uni-kassel.de

M. Söllner · J. M. Leimeister
University of St. Gallen, St. Gallen, Switzerland

© Springer Nature Switzerland AG 2020
J. vom Brocke et al. (eds.), *Design Science Research. Cases*, Progress in IS,
https://doi.org/10.1007/978-3-030-46781-4_10

leads to designing and evaluating several design artifacts, which we call teaching-learning techniques, so a holistic design artifact usually has several design artifacts. Therefore, the project makes distinct prescriptive knowledge contributions and has the potential to create distinct types of theory in information systems. Our case provides guidance in developing artifacts for a holistic design artifact and in understanding how such artifacts can be separated into sub-artifacts that have their own design science approaches.

1   Introduction

One must learn by doing the thing, for though you think you know it, you have no certainty until you try it.

Sophocles, 496-406 B.C.

The demographic shift comes with a range of concerns regarding how essential knowledge can be retained in the organization to ensure its ability to compete in the future. Current forecasts claim that the number of employees in Germany will fall from 29.6 million in 2020 to 22.04 million in 2050 (Textor, 2016), a decline that presents a major challenge for economic sectors like the energy sector. Already, 45% of all employees that work in energy supply companies or in companies that focus on energy consulting are older than age fifty, and a third of these will retire in 2025 (Textor, 2016). In parallel, other developments, such as digitization and globalization, are changing society and the nature of work. Skills like cooperation can help companies cope with competing demands (Bolden & Gosling, 2006), but they must find better ways to save the experiential knowledge that employees they have gained during their working lives (Wegge, Roth, Neubach, Schmidt, & Kanfer, 2008) so the companies can transfer it to new and inexperienced employees (Wegge et al., 2008).

Besides posing new challenges, digitization also provides new possibilities for ways to save and transfer such knowledge. For example, effective IT support can help to structure pedagogic approaches from peer learning in a way that their potential can be leveraged easily by domain experts who lack pedagogical knowledge and collaboration expertise (Oeste-Reiß et, Söllner, & Leimeister, 2016). Research has shown that especially complex knowledge related to work processes can hardly be learned from theory, so learners should be involved in the learning process such that they can apply their newly acquired knowledge right away, such as in peer learning settings (Tynjälä, 2008). Approaches like gamification can help to motivate employee to use IT-based solutions for knowledge transfer and documentation, but t designing an effective IT-based approach for overcoming the challenge outlined here is a complex endeavor.

This paper presents a design science research (DSR) journey toward developing an IT-based solution for knowledge transfer and documentation in the energy sector, implemented using a learning management system (LMS). We focus on two parts of our integrated solution: a *Peer Creation Process for enhancing knowledge transfer and documentation* by developing learning nuggets that are then provided in a LMS, and a *User-Centered Process to gamify LMS* and enhance learners' motivation. In focuses on these two parts of the solution, we answer two research questions (RQs), each of which focuses on the development of one of the design artifacts:

RQ1: What are characteristics of a Peer Creation Process for transfer and documentation of knowledge that can be used regardless of tool support and that helps learners to expand their knowledge base?

RQ2: How should a user-centered process to gamify LMSs be designed to motivate the system's users?

To answer these RQs, we started two smaller DSR studies (Alan, March, Park, & Ram, 2004; Gregor & Hevner, 2013). In so doing, we seek to contribution to a nascent design theory and a theory of a design and action of the improvement type (Gregor & Hevner, 2013). However, the theoretical knowledge needed to design an effective solution differed between the two design artifacts. In answering RQ1, we could rely on a broad foundation of insights from the literature, allowing us to engage comparatively quickly in the iterative design and evaluation of the Peer Creation Process. In answering RQ2, we had to rely on previous research's user-centered gamification process for LMS, which required conducting an empirical study on user preferences regarding game design elements before we could explain the meaning and relevance of game design elements to learning and its relationship to users' needs. Consequently, we contribute to gamification theory by investigating the preferred game design elements and bundles in the content of LMS. We also provide insights into how DSR journeys can be adapted based on the degree to which the knowledge base is ready to inform artifact design.

The remainder of the paper is structured as follows. After motivating our research, we describe our context and the journey. Then we outline our two design artifacts and close with key findings.

2   The Context

The challenges that have arisen from digitization and demographic shifts has required adjusting teaching-learning concepts (Neij, Heiskanen, & Strupeit, 2017). The energy sector and university courses in particular are faced with problems that are due to inadequate learning and teaching concepts for sharing and making knowledge available to others. Innovative teaching-learning techniques are required that support individuals in obtaining, building and exchanging their professional skills and experiential knowledge (Malcolm, Hodkinson, & Colley, 2003). Because of increasing digitization, individuals must improve their competencies and knowledge about using information technologies, especially since energy consultants' work routines and processes involve on-site consultations that require using mobile devices.

Furthermore, the demographic shift and the increasing tendency toward employee churn require employees to ensure their knowledge is current through informal learning, which follows constructivist learning theories and is not organized (Edvinsson & Sullivan, 1996). In other words, informal learning is learning by experience, so knowledge develops over a long period of time and differs from individual to individual (Malcolm et al., 2003). Knowledge that is based on informal competencies is increasingly relevant to companies that want to make it available for all employees, especially new ones. Since no one teaching-learning technique can cope with all those demands, new teaching-learning concepts that bundle several teaching-learning techniques are required to help knowledge workers in their everyday work and to offer them the possibility of learning independent of location and time.

We consider three bodies of literature ing designing innovative teaching-learning techniques: the literatures of peer learning, collaboration engineering, and gamification. We use peer learning and collaboration engineering to enhance knowledge exchange between individuals, to train their social competencies, and to process experienced employees' knowledge. Often, employees must be motivated to improve their IT skills and competencies and to share their knowledge with others, for which we use the motivation concept of gamification. We outline these three bodies of literature in the next sections.

Peer Learning

Self-regulated learning and collaborating and interacting with other system users have become important components of managing competencies. To meet the needs and challenges they face, companies must offer LMSs that allow their employees to regulate their own learning process, perhaps by joining in a collaborative learning experience with other users or peers. Such peer learning, is an effective way to increase the interactions between individuals (Topping, 2005). A characteristic of peer learning is a change in behavior based on each individual's experiences (Gagne, 1984) with conversations and discussions (Wegener & Leimeister, 2012). Peer learning involves a group of people who learn together through ad hoc social interactions (Dillenbourg, 1999), which can foster reflection and cognitive processes (Arbaugh, 2010). Positive effects for learners include improved communication skills and a strengthened sense of responsible for their activities. We use peer learning to save and share experienced workers' knowledge so it is available to others and to improve individuals' social competencies through working and sharing experiences with others.

Collaboration Engineering

Collaborative engineering can be used as a design methodology in designing and deploying collaborative work practices like innovative teaching-learning techniques that use collaboration (Mathieu, Heffner, Goodwin, Salas, & Cannon-Bowers, 2000). Collaboration refers to working with others and making joint efforts, so it involves multiple individuals who combine their efforts to achieve a pre-defined goal (Briggs, Kolfschoten, Gert-Jan, & Douglas, 2006; Vreede & Briggs, 2005). The aim of collaboration engineering is to develop predictable and reusable designs that support participants in recurring collaborative work (Bittner & Leimeister, 2013). More precisely, collaboration engineering can increase the shared understanding of concepts and the words and phrases that are used to express them (Briggs et al., 2006).

The heart of the collaboration engineering design methodology is Briggs et al.'s (2014) Six-Layer Model of Collaboration, which considers the design of collaboration processes at six levels of abstraction. At each layer are different phenomena-of-interest and so different design concerns, metrics, theories, modeling conventions, design patterns, best practices, and worst practices. The patterns of collaboration that organize collaborative activities in the procedure layer consist of generate, reduce, clarify, organize, evaluate, and build consensus (Briggs et al., 2006). The generate pattern is used to produce new ideas, while the reduce pattern focuses on a specific concept, clarify develops a shared understanding about the topic, organize explains the relationships among the concepts, evaluate determines the relative value of the concepts, and build consensus generates commitment to a proposal (Briggs et al., 2006). Over time, techniques for evoking variations on these patterns have emerged. ThinkLets are named and scripted techniques that create predictable, repeatable, and useful variations of the six patterns for people who are working toward a goal (Briggs et al., 2014). Based on these ThinkLets, collaboration engineers can use collaboration tools like the facilitation process model (FPM) (Winkler et al., 2019) and the internal agenda to model and communicate their collaborative work practice (Vreede et al. 2009).

Our research uses collaboration engineering and the Six-Layer-Model in particular, to structure peer learning activities to help learners acquire new knowledge and increase shared understanding.

Gamification

Motivation mechanisms must be considered when designing IT-supported teaching-learning concepts that address these issues. Several possibilities can motivate individuals to use a system regularly, one of which is gamification. The two best-known definitions of gamification are provided by Deterding et al. (2011) and Hamari, Koivisto, and Sarsa (2014). Deterding et al. (2011, p. 2) defined gamification as *"the use of game design elements in non-game contexts"*. Hamari et al. (2014, p. 2) defined gamification as *"a process of enhancing services with (motivational) affordances to invoke gameful experiences and provoke behavioral outcomes such as continuous use"* and suggested that gamification includes three parts: the directly induced psychological outcomes, the implemented motivational affordances, and the consecutive behavioral outcomes. Other definitions include that from Thiebes, Lins and Basten (2014, p. 3), who defined gamification as *"the application of game principles to existing organizational real-world problems, situations, or processes."* Using these definitions, we define gamification as the use and combination of game design elements in non-entertainment-based contexts (Deterding, 2011) to induce positive psychological outcomes (Hamari et al., 2014) and, by addressing users' needs and interests, to provoke desired behavioral outcomes. One sub-artifact of our holistic artifact focuses on the development of user-centered gamification processes that consider users' needs and preferences to make the concept more meaningful to them.

The next section outlines our design journey.

3   The Journey

Our journey focuses on two design artifacts–a peer-creation process to enhance knowledge transfer and documentation and a user-centered process to gamify LMSs–that are part of a larger DSR initiative to develop an IT-based solution for knowledge documentation and transfer in the energy sector in an LMS, a Continuing Education Concept for Energy Consultants. Figure 1 illustrates the hierarchical order of the design artifacts and the respective design goals.

This paper focuses on two design goals for our two design artifacts:

A Peer Creation Process—Design Goal I: Leverage the power of collaborative knowledge transfer to enhance knowledge among learners and ad hoc documentation of this knowledge.

A User-Centered Process to Gamify LMSs—Design Goal II: Consider user preferences in the selection and number of game design elements to motivate learners.

Since each design artifact must be developed against the background of its own theoretical requirements, both are designed in parallel DSR endeavors. Following this way of thinking allows us to make several contributions to the literature. To inform our design choices with insights from practice and the literature, our DSR initiatives follow the Three Cycle View (Hevner, 2007). Figure 2 illustrates the DSR initiative for each design artifact and outlines the subsequent in-depth presentation of each artifact' design.

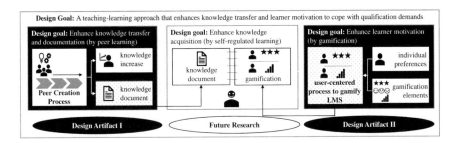

Fig. 1 Design artifacts and their design goals

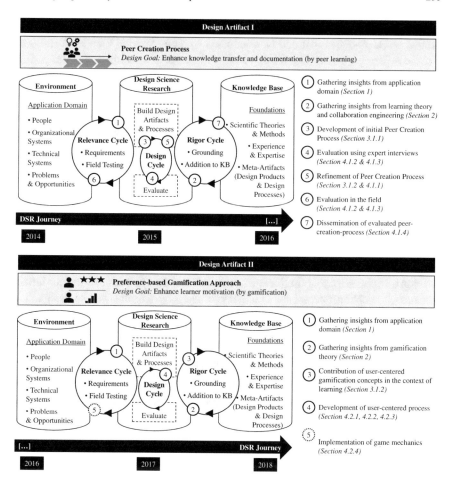

Fig. 2 The DSR journey and its design artifacts

3.1 The Peer Creation Process—Lap 1

Understanding the problem: Knowledge transfer and documentation remain common challenges in practice. Peer learning, a learning technique that is based on constructivist learning theories, might be a way to empower learners to collaborate with other learners to transfer, reflect and discuss knowledge and acquire a sophisticated understanding of it (Jones & Brader-Araje, 2002). However, peer learning requires that learners not be restricted in their learning experience and that they can execute ad hoc collaboration (Webb, 2010), which requires collaboration expertise and comes with distractions, so peer learning tends not to be reusable and demands an experienced lecturer. In contrast, collaboration engineering provides a design methodology with which to bundle collaboration expertise to create reusable collaborative work practices that can be conducted by non-experts (Vreede et al. 2009; Vreede & Briggs, 2018). Combining insights from peer learning and collaboration engineering in the form of a reusable Peer Creation Process might provide an answer to one of our RQs (Oeste, Söllner, & Leimeister, 2014):

- *RQ*: What are characteristics of a Peer Creation Process for transfer and documentation of knowledge that can be used regardless of tool support and that helps learners to expand their knowledge base?
- *Design goal*: Leverage the power of collaborative knowledge transfer to increase learners' knowledge and improve its documentation.
- *Design artifact*: A reusable collaborative work practice in the form of the Peer Creation Process.

Our study focuses on collaborative knowledge documentation. Knowledge documentations (e.g., textual explanations, visualization, video) demand a sophisticated understanding of knowledge concepts and their connections. IT tools are needed to develop transferable collaborative work practices that are applicable to various infrastructures, so one must determine whether peer learning activities can be designed in a reusable way to evoke predictable results in learner satisfaction and outcomes and whether they can be transferrable to other contexts and situations. Against that background, a first proof of concept and proof of value[1] (Nunamaker, Briggs, Derrick, & Schwabe, 2015) were needed to gain insights into the question.

Understanding the solution: We call our findings in the form of a reusable collaborative work practice the Peer Creation Process, that bundles collaboration and pedagogical expertise and makes prescriptive knowledge contributions to a nascent design theory (Gregor & Hevner, 2013). The Peer Creation Process As a reusable collaborative work practice, the Peer Creation Process describes the design and sequence of peer learning activities, including instructions, tool support, and work products (i.e., the collaborative outcome of several activities) (Oeste-Reiß et al., 2016). Making that kind of contribution to knowledge requires completing several design/evaluate cycles, including field testing of the Peer Creation Process with all involved stakeholders (e.g., lecturers and learners). We based the validation of the Peer Creation Process on a mixed-method approach that consists of qualitative and quantitative data, which helped us to iteratively refine our design artifact. Since we need to ensure that the Peer Creation Process leverages knowledge transfer in a reusable manner and that it is applicable to various infrastructures in practice, we started in our DSR initiative in 2014 and can now report our insights from two major laps.

---

[1] *Proof of concept* research demonstrates the functional feasibility of a solution, while *proof of value* research investigates whether a solution can create value in a variety of conditions.

3.1.1 Identifying Stumbling Blocks Using Expert Interviews—Lap 1.1

For the initial design of the Peer Creation Process we completed a rigor and a relevance cycle. This initial design was informed by insights from the application domain and the peer learning and collaboration engineering literature (Oeste et al., 2014; Oeste-Reiß et al., 2016). We tested this initial design with experts from practice—lecturers and collaboration experts—to make a proof of concept, identify whether the design copes with peer learning and collaboration engineering demands, and identify any stumbling blocks existent. A walkthrough using expert interviews characterizes the validation and its collection of qualitative data. A qualitative content analyses and a category system helped us to get first insights toward our design goal. The gathered insights (e.g., reduce the granularity of activities, clarify the instructions formed in the Peer Creation Process, reduce the number of changes in the group formation) constitute the starting point for refining the Peer Creation Process and, thus, the starting point for the next lap (Oeste et al., 2014; Oeste-Reiß et al., 2016).

3.1.2 Identifying Knowledge Transfer by Field Tests—Lap 1.2

In the next step we started a second design/evaluate cycle, so the refined design of the Peer Creation Process informed primarily by insights from lap 1.1. Then we started a relevance cycle, taking the Peer Creation Process back to the field and testing the refined design with learners during field tests. The purpose of the field tests was to gain insights into the process's potential to enhance knowledge transfer and to be applicable to various kinds of tool support to ensure its transferability. Thus, this validation was conducted as a proof of value. During several field tests that executed the Peer Creation Process with paper-based tools vs. IT-supported tools, we gathered quantitative and qualitative data (Oeste-Reiß et al., 2016). The learners also completed pre and post knowledge tests and a satisfaction survey. The results from the knowledge tests helped us to determine whether the learners acquired knowledge, while the satisfaction measures (SP—Satisfaction with process, SO—satisfaction with outcome, TOOLDIF—tool difficulty, PROCDIF—process difficulty) helped us to determine whether the learners were able to execute the process (Briggs, Kolfschoten, Vreede, Lukosch, & Albrecht, 2013). The results from the field tests gave us insights into applying the Peer Creation Process with various tools and, thus, its transferability in practice (Oeste-Reiß et al., 2016).

3.2 Gamification Approach—Lap 2

Understanding the problem: Here we describe the purpose and scope of the user-centered process of gamifying an LMS and refer to the class of unsolved problems, RQs, and the design goal. In referring to development of user-centered gamification approaches in learning, previous research has not specified the meaning of individual game design elements, which makes it more difficult to adapt gamification concepts to users' needs (Schöbel & Söllner, 2016). Since several research studies' understanding of the meaning of game design elements differ, it is difficult to develop a user-centered gamification concept (Schöbel & Janson, 2018), and it is difficult to combine game design elements because a combination could change their meaning and relevance to the intended target group (Hanus & Fox, 2015). Seaborn & Fels (2015), who summarized identified research gaps, explained that how game design elements should be designed to influence users' motivation is unclear. They contended that there are no useful procedures with which to design reward structures in gamification but that it is useful to focus on a user-centered design by considering users' needs and interests so gamification concepts are more meaningful. Considering these problems, we suggest the following problem solution:

- *RQ*: How should a user-centered process with which to gamify LMSs be designed to motivate the system's users?
- *Design goal*: Identify a process to develop a user-centered gamification concept for LMSs.
- *Design artifact*: A process with which to gamify LMSs.

It is useful to get insights into the structure and meaning of game design elements by evaluating which elements users prefer (Schöbel & Janson, 2018). Such knowledge allows us to identify what is necessary to gamify LMSs that appeal to users and motivate them to use the system regularly. More precisely, although many research studies have focused on gamifying LMSs, additional research should concentrate on identifying the most and least preferred game design elements for specific contexts and specific target groups (Seaborn & Fels, 2015). Therefore, user preferences should be a part of a user-centered process for gamifying LMSs.

Understanding the solution: Three process steps are necessary to gamify an LMS with consideration given to what users need and like.

Information system designers are required to initiate early and continuous interactions with a target group to determine what they need (Baek, Cagiltay, Boling, & Frick, 2008). Actually, system designers need to better understand how to adapt gamification concepts to the needs and interests of users (Reed, 2014). Hence, when gamifying information systems, designers should integrate users' needs into the selection and combination of design elements (Schöbel & Söllner, 2016). Thus, a first step in developing a user-centered process with which to gamify LMS was to determine the kind of game design elements users prefer, and a second step was to determine how many game design elements users prefer to avoid straining users and demotivating them. We used the findings from these two steps to implement the gamification concept.

4 The Results

This section describes our two design artifacts and their development. We begin by presenting the design artifact of the Peer Creation Process, followed by the results of our user-centered process to gamify LMSs.

4.1 Peer Creation Process

4.1.1 Understanding the Design Artifact and Its Scope

The outcome of the design study is a collaborative work practice for enhancing knowledge transfer and documentation, embodied in the Peer Creation Process's components (Oeste-Reiß et al., 2016). This artifact contributes prescriptive knowledge to a nascent design theory, so we communicate our solution in terms of its purpose and scope, generalizable requirements and principles of form and function, and principles of implementation (Gregor & Jones, 2007).

The *purpose* of the Peer Creation Process is to enhance knowledge transfer and documentation among learners. The literature differentiates among factual knowledge, conceptual knowledge, procedural knowledge, and metacognitive knowledge (Krathwohl, 2002). While factual knowledge comprises the basic elements of solving a problem, conceptual knowledge refers to the interrelationships among knowledge concepts (Krathwohl, 2002), and procedural knowledge refers to knowledge on how to do something, such as how to use methods (Krathwohl, 2002). Factual knowledge is easily accessed, but procedural knowledge is often tacit. Procedural knowledge is often more valuable than factual knowledge since it is often only indirectly visible (Nonaka, 2000). Typically, this kind of knowledge demands a more sophisticated understanding of the knowledge concepts and their relationships.

Against that background, *the scope* of the Peer Creation Process goes beyond factual knowledge. Collaborative knowledge transfer helps to achieve the learning effects that commonly emerge in social interactions between at least two people (Oeste et al., 2014), which can facilitate the reflection on and the exchange, application, evaluation, and creation of knowledge (Moll, 2013; Oeste-Reiß et al., 2016; Oeste-Reiß, Bittner, & Söllner, 2017). Therefore, a learning task with a defined outcome is needed that will trigger that kind of collaboration.

Visualization of complex knowledge concepts demands a sophisticated understanding of the domain knowledge. Explanation videos and even storyboards for explanation videos can explain a solution for a complex problem in easily understandable language, enriched with visual animation (Chen & Wu, 2015). A storyboard contains all relevant knowledge and documents the explanation of knowledge in the form of text and visualizations.

Referring to our Peer Creation Process, the collaborative outcome that the learners produce is a knowledge document in the form of a storyboard. Consequently, knowledge transfer has two benefits: direct knowledge transfer in the form of knowledge gained and indirect knowledge transfer in the form of documentation of knowledge (Oeste et al., 2014). In addition to the purpose and scope, we derived *generalizable requirements (GR)* to guide our design choices and ground them in the body of peer learning literature. Table 1 shows the GR that should be considered when creating a Peer Creation Process.

Another result was our *principles of form and function* of the Peer Creation Process. We used insights from the collaboration engineering literature to design and communicate the Peer Creation Process, our collaborative work practice for enhancing knowledge transfer and documentation. We used Briggs et al.'s (2014) six-layer model to bundle collaboration expertise and documented the solution in the form of the FPM (Vreede et al. 2009; Winkler et al., 2019), which provides an abstract overview of the process and an internal agenda that provides guidance. Figure 3 shows the FPM and the internal agenda for the Peer Creation Process (Oeste-Reiß et al., 2016). The group goal that the learners had to achieve was to *increase the individual knowledge base by collaboratively developing one storyboard for an explanation video that describes complex domain knowledge in the form of abstract visualizations and brief text explanations within the next six hours.* To achieve this group goal, the learners completed a sequence of collaborative activities. The FPM shows the sequence of collaborative activities (Fig. 3).

In Fig. 3, each square represents one activity. The number of each activity can be seen in the left corner of each square. Activities 1 and 2 (first and second square in Fig. 3) trigger learners to reflect on knowledge in general so they can determine what knowledge is relevant, create a shared understanding, and trigger cognitive processes among less knowledgeable learners. Activities 3, 4, and 5 (Third, fourth, and fifth square in Fig. 3) trigger a collaborative creation of a rough concept of the storyboard, clarify the storyboard's focus, and organize the group's initial ideas. To structure the ideas, a storyline with key scenes is developed during activity 6 (Sixth square in Fig. 3) as the participants join in a plenary discussion and derive key scenes for the storyboard. The refined concept of the storyboard is developed during activities 7, 8 and 9 (Seventh, eight, and ninth square in Fig. 3), and several evaluations ensure that the documented knowledge is correct. Activity 10 (last square in Fig. 3) provides insights into whether the collaboration comes to an end or refinement is needed (Oeste-Reiß et al., 2016).

To build an exemplary instance of the Peer Creation Process and apply it in the classroom, *principles of implementation* are needed. In our case, the principles of implementation refer to constraints and preparation activities. The facilitator who conducted and moderated the Peer Creation Process had to consider:

- *Plenary group size*: The Peer Creation Process can be used for plenary groups with sized between ten and thirty participants.
- *Subgroup size*: The Peer Creation Process can be used for subgroups with sized between two and six participants.

Table 1 Generalizable requirements for enhancing knowledge transfer (based on Oeste-Reiß et al., 2016)

Interac. Type	Generalizable requirements (GR) from peer learning	
Learner-Learner Interaction (Dillenbourg, 1999; Gagne, 1984; Hall and Stegila, 2003; Harris, 1998; Krathwohl, 2002; Pearce et al., 2009; Topping, 2005)	GR 1	*Group formation*: Put together a group of learners and reconcile them on the same knowledge
	GR 2	*Reciprocity*: Foster social interactions between learners by providing learning tasks that demand discussion and creating a collaborative outcome and tools that support interactions
	GR 3	*Interdependence*: Ensure positive interdependence between learners through tools and learning tasks
	GR 4	*Accountability*: Use social pressure to make learners accountable for their activities
	GR 5	*Group atmosphere*: Constitute a positive group atmosphere by empowering learners to add value to their activities
	GR 6	*Objectives*: Ensure focused learner activities by providing learning objectives.
Learner-Lecturer Interaction (Harris, 1998; Jones, 2014; Pearce et al., 2009)	GR 7	*Lecturer*: Provide a lecturer to guide the learners though their peer learning activities
	GR 8	*Expectations*: Communicate expectations (e.g., instructions on how to solve learning task; quality indicators) to learners to ensure focused peer learning activities
	GR 9	*Feedback*: Give learners direct feedback about their progress
	GR 10	*Constructive Feedback*: Provide feedback criteria to ensure constructive feedback
	GR 11	*Reflection*: Enhance discussions about the solution among learners to ensure knowledge reflection
Learner-Content Interaction (Hall and Stegila, 2003; Jones, 2014; Leacock and Nesbit, 2007)	GR 12	*Type of assignment*: Provide a learning task that requires learners to brainstorm solutions on their own before discussing the task in the group
	GR 13	*Learning task structure*: Divide learning tasks into subtasks
	GR 14	*Learning task wording*: Define the learning task in an understandable manner (e.g., question, nature of outcome, time)
	GR 15	*Structure of outcome*: Provide templates to ensure a logical and consistent approach to documentation

(continued)

Table 1 (continued)

Interac. Type	Generalizable requirements (GR) from peer learning	
	GR 16	*Complexity of outcome*: Demand abstract visualizations and descriptions of complex knowledge concepts to ensure understandable language in the collaborative outcomes
	GR 17	*Correctness of outcome*: Integrate proofreading and peer-review mechanisms to ensure collaborative outcomes are correct

- *Number of subgroups*: The number of subgroups depends on the number of subtasks (= knowledge topics/categories) that the facilitator prepares (e.g., five subtasks = five subgroups).
- *Learning task and subtasks*: The facilitator must create a learning task that can be divided into independent subtasks that refer to knowledge topics and categories. Activities 1 and 3 require independent subtasks.
- *Duration*: Based on the maximum number of five subgroups, the Peer Creation Process will have duration of six hours.
- *Scenes*: A number of scenes will occur during the Peer Creation Process, so the facilitator must divide the number of identified scenes equally among the subgroups.

4.1.2 Applying the Peer Creation Process in the Field

The application and validation of the Peer Creation Process consists of several laps with two kinds of stakeholders who participated in the validation: *Facilitators*, independent experts with pedagogical and collaboration backgrounds who examined the Peer Creation Process during a walkthrough, and *Learners*, who were students in a master's course on collaboration procedures at a German and a Swiss university.

Expert interviews with *walkthroughs* characterized the first application of the Peer Creation Process in the field. In the walkthroughs, the facilitators examined two documents, the FPM and the internal agenda, and marked what they saw as potential stumbling blocks. Then a structured discussion between the facilitators and us, the designers, followed to address the identified stumbling blocks in the process design. Field tests with learners followed the walkthroughs using a quasi-experimental procedure by which only the tool support was manipulated while all other design concerns were the same. This approach allowed us to conduct the Peer Creation Process with paper-based tools and IT-supported tools using ThinkTank, a group support system (GSS. After two field tests with learners, we gathered data from a satisfaction survey (adapted from Briggs et al., 2013), a pre-/post knowledge test containing true/false questions, and a participating observation (Table 2).

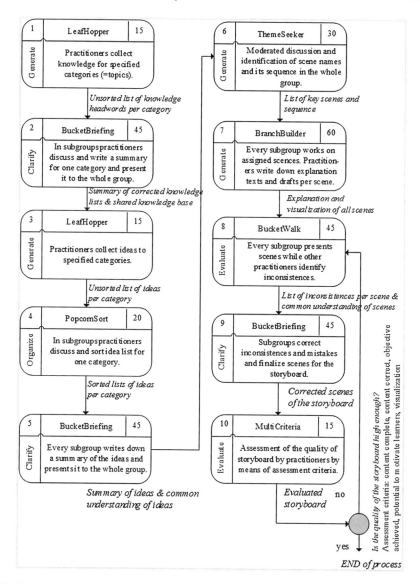

Fig. 3 Sequence of collaborative activities of the peer creation process (based on Oeste-Reiß et al., 2016)

4.1.3 Evaluation of the Artifact

To determine whether the Peer Creation Process has the potential to enhance collaborative knowledge transfer, we compared the results from the knowledge test to the self-reported knowledge measures, and we used satisfaction measures adapted from Briggs et al. (2013) to investigate whether the Peer Creation Process can be used

	Pre-evaluation measures	Post-evaluation measures
Table 2 Pre- and Post-measures of the field test of the peer creation process	*5-item knowledge test* [true/false]	*5-item knowledge test* [true/false]
	Self-reported level of knowledge [5-point Likert scale] – Type of documenting knowledge (storyboard) – Procedural knowledge	*Self-reported level of knowledge* [5-point Likert scale] – Type of documenting knowledge (storyboard) – Procedural knowledge *Satisfaction measures* (SO, SP, PROCDIF, TOOLDIF) [5-point Likert scale]

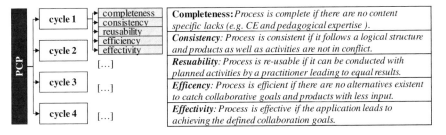

Fig. 4 Category system of the content analysis (based on Oeste-Reiß et al., 2016)

with both paper-based and IT-supported tools. Before doing so, however, we used a qualitative content analysis (Mayring, 2004) and derived a theory-informed category system to identify stumbling blocks in the process's design (Leimeister, 2014) (Fig. 4).

Insights from lap 1.1 "identifying stumbling blocks"—qualitative data analysis (Oeste-Reiß et al., 2016): In the first lap of our DSR initiative we designed peer learning activities using collaboration engineering as a design methodology for the first time. The granularity of activities in this version was high because peer learning activities were designed using existing facilitation techniques called ThinkLets. Based on our category system (Fig. 5), the walkthrough disclosed questions about the consistency of the Peer Creation Process. For example, a facilitator asked *"When do the learners work in groups? […] What should the learners do to solve an assignment?"* Therefore, for this initial design we refined the comprehensiveness of the wording and the structure of the learning tasks and reduced the number of changes in group formations. These refinements led to insights into how to tighten the granularity of collaborative activities and, thus, how to design the whole Peer Creation Process using existing thinkLets. The facilitators concluded that the Peer Creation Process would be effective, noting, *"it will work and the participants will be excited!"*

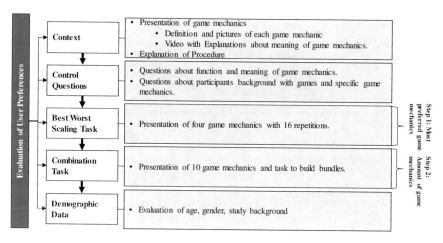

Fig. 5 Structure of analysis

Insights from lap 1.2 "identifying knowledge transfer"—quantitative data analysis: In the second lap of our DSR initiative, we refined the Peer Creation Process and used a field test in which we executed the Peer Creation Process with paper-based and IT-supported tools. Table 3 depicts the results of the descriptive data analysis, which compared satisfaction with the field tests based on the type of tool support they used. The results provided insights into how learners experienced participating in the Peer Creation Process and into the differences that occur when the tool support changes. These results have a high mean on a 5-point Likert scale in both field test samples, although they were better in the group that used paper-based tools than they are in the group that used IT-supported tools.

Table 4 compares the results for both groups (the one that used a paper-based tool and the other one that worked with an IT-supported tool) regarding learners' performance in the pre- and post-evaluation knowledge tests with their self-reported level of knowledge. No significant differences between the two groups were found,

Table 3 Learner satisfaction with the peer creation process (based on Oeste-Reiß et al., 2016)		Paper-based tools N = 8/Mean (SD)	IT-supported tools N = 11/Mean (SD)
	SP—Satisfaction with Process	4.33 (0.44)	2.76 (0.87)
	SO—Satisfaction with Outcome	4.35 (0.45)	2.73 (1.23)
	TOOLDIF—Tool Difficulty	4.43 (0.47)	3.73 (0.45)
	PROCDIF—Process Difficulty	3.78 (0.61)	3.38 (0.49)

5-point Likert scale (1 = negative; 5 = positive)

Table 4 Learner's knowledge increases with the peer creation process (based on Oeste-Reiß et al., 2016)

	Paper-based tools N = 8			IT-supported tools N = 11		
	Pre-test	Post-test	Spread	Pre-test	Post-test	Spread
	Mean (SD)	Mean (SD)		Mean (SD)	Mean (SD)	
Knowledge test	67%	71%	↑4%	72%	76%	↑ 4%
	(0.52)	(0.64)		(0.52)	(0.63)	
Self-reported level of knowledge						
About kind of documenting knowledge (storyboard development)	2.75 (1.28)	3.88 (0.64)	↑1.13	2.10 (0.57)	3.40 (0.84)	↑ 1.30
About procedural knowledge	3.13 (0.35)	3.63 (0.52)	↑0.50	3.40 (0.52)	3.70 (0.48)	↑ 0.30

5-point Likert scale (1 = very low; 5 = very high)

which indicates that the participants started with comparable levels of knowledge. Comparing the pre- and post-test performance in each sample showed that the level of knowledge increased in both groups (Oeste-Reiß et al., 2016), which indicates that the Peer Creation Process has the potential to enable a knowledge transfer among participants using either paper-based or IT-supported tools.

4.1.4 Growth of Design Theory

In this DSR study we presented the development and validation of the Peer Creation Process as a generalizable solution for enhancing collaborative knowledge transfer. The aim of the study was to gain first insights into whether structured peer learning activities enhance collaborative knowledge transfer. Against that background, the validation in our first lap served as a proof of concept (Nunamaker et al. 2015). In the second lap, we used field tests to investigate proof of value. Since our solution is a new solution for solving the problem of knowledge transfer, this mixed-methods approach seemed to be appropriate for designing and evaluating our artifact.

To discuss the Peer Creation Process in terms of its growth toward becoming a design theory, we start with a brief discussion of our results from the field test. The design goal of this study was to *leverage the power of collaborative knowledge transfer to increase and enhance knowledge and documentations thereof among learners.* The results from the field test (Table 2) indicate that the Peer Creation Process is a feasible solution to this design goal. Comparing the pre- and the post-tests of the paper-based group indicate an increase in the knowledge test results from 67 to 71% and an increase from in the IT-supported group from 72 to 76%.

We also asked the learners to self-report on their level of knowledge. Like the results of the knowledge test, the results for the self-reported level of knowledge increased as well. The increases in terms of knowledge test performance and the self-reported level of knowledge in both the paper-based and the IT-based groups indicate that there is a knowledge increase and that the learners experience this increase correctly. In addition, we investigated whether the Peer Creation Process is transferable and reusable for other infrastructures in practice. The satisfaction measures (adapted from Briggs et al., 2013) and our qualitative data from simulations and walkthroughs showed that an IT-supported collaboration leads to approximately the same results in terms of knowledge transfer as a paper-based collaboration (Table 3), but the learners who used paper-based tools were more satisfied with the process and the outcome and were more comfortable with the tools and the process's level of difficulty.

During the execution with paper-based and IT-supported tools, the group dynamics differed, perhaps because of differences in the relationships between facilitators and learners in the two groups (Oeste-Reiß et al., 2016), as the relationship in the paper-based group appeared to closer than it was in the IT-supported group. The paper-based tool required more frequent interactions between the facilitator and the learners because of the use of place cards and flip charts, activities that the GSS took over in the IT-supported group and consequently, decreasing the frequency of direct interactions between the facilitator and the learners in that group by replacing some of the moderator's instructions and activities so learners worked more independently. Clearly, the facilitator must find entry points to interact directly with the learners to generate a positive group atmosphere (Oeste-Reiß et al., 2016), but knowledge transfer increased in both groups, indicating that the design of the Peer Creation Process is effective with either kind of tool support.

We reported findings on the design of a collaborative work practice, the Peer Creation Process, and its potential to leverage knowledge transfer. We justified peer learning as an effective basis for knowledge-transfer activities. We identified generalizable requirements from the peer learning literature and used collaboration engineering as a design methodology to design and communicate our Peer Creation Process. For the evaluation and refinement of the Peer Creation Process, we completed several design/evaluate cycles using walkthroughs and field tests and showed that the Peer Creation Process meets pedagogical demands, can be used with different kinds of tool support, and can leverage collaborative knowledge transfer.

Our results contribute to theory and practice, as we provide generalizable requirements for designing collaborative work practices for knowledge transfer and provide principles of form and function that are inherent in the description of Peer Creation as a generalizable solution for a collaborative work practice. Thus, our evaluation showed that peer learning activities can be designed in a reusable way by structuring learners' activities and tasks. Against that background, our Peer Creation Process provides prescriptive knowledge that can be classified as a contribution of the "improvement" type (Gregor & Hevner, 2013) and that resembles components of a nascent design theory (Gregor & Hevner, 2013). It is a new solution since it uses process restrictions and established collaboration techniques to enhance peer learning activities that enable knowledge transfer.

4.2   Gamification Approach

4.2.1   Challenges in Gamification Design

Little is known about how to develop user-centered gamification concepts (Schöbel & Söllner, 2016), and no processes have been developed that can be used to gamify information systems. This issue can be observed in the many combinations and results of previous gamification studies. Most research studies have used competitive game mechanics to reward their users (Alcivar & Abad, 2016; Attali & Arieli-Attali, 2015; Christy & Fox, 2014; Davis & Singh, 2015; Denny, 2013; Domínguez et al., 2013), but none has considered whether users are interested in competition (Hanus & Fox, 2015). Other researchers have used collaborative reward structures to gamify their information systems (Boticki, Baksa, Seow, & Looi, 2015; Jurado, Collazos, & Paredez, 2014; Knutas, Ikonen, Nikula, & Porras, 2014; McDaniel, Lindgren, &Friskics, 2012; Melero, Hernández-Leo, & Manatunga, 2015), but, again, they have not considered their users' needs and preferences. Therefore, we sought to clarify the elements of game design. One of the best-known frameworks was developed by Hunicke, LeBlanc, and Zubek (2004), who defined the so-called MDA framework (mechanics, dynamics, and aesthetics). Game mechanics like leaderboards (Hamari, 2013) and levels (Hiltbrand & Burke, 2011) are functioning components that allow a designer to control the levers of a gamified application, while dynamics like challenges and competition refer to the user's interaction with mechanics (Zichermann & Cunningham, 2011). Dynamics can correspond to a variety of motives (Blohm & Leimeister, 2013).

Table 5 presents the existing game mechanics, dynamics, and motives that can be used to develop a user-centered gamified LMS. By evaluating which of these mechanics LMS users prefer, we can explain which dynamics and motives are most useful in learning settings and which motives can have a positive impact on users' motivation and behavior (Schöbel, Söllner, & Leimeister, 2016). Considering the meaning of each game mechanic before it is implemented in an information system is a central issue in designing user-centered information systems

Research still has to evaluate the role of users by considering their individual differences (Hamari et al., 2016). Before we could to gamify our LMS, we focused on analyzing the literature and,, in line with Seaborn and Fels (2015), we observed that most research has not used user-centered concepts to gamify LMS. Game design elements are usually randomly selected and integrated into LMS without considering the effects certain game mechanics can have on a user's motivation. Therefore, a second step is necessary for a user-centered process to gamify LMS: identifying the number of game mechanics that are implemented in an LMS.

After identifying the relevant game mechanics and the number of game mechanics, we were able to implement the game mechanics in an LMS.

Table 5 *Game Design Elements* (based on Blohm & Leimeister, 2013)

Mechanic	Definition	Dynamic	Motive
Level	Visualizes a user's experiences over time and challenges him or her to reach higher stages	Acquisition of status	Status
Status bar	Informs a user about his or her progress on tasks or activities	Collection	Achievement
Points	Rewards users for successful activities or actions		
Badges (Icons)	Given to users for successfully completing tasks and activities		
Leaderboard	Offers the opportunity to compare one's results with those of others	Competition	Social recognition
Virtual goods	Intangible objects that can be earned and traded	Cooperation	Social exchange
Virtual character	Represents a user during his or her system activities and actions	Organization	Self-determination
Loss aversion	Influences a user's action by avoiding punishment	Challenge	Cognitive stimulation
Time pressure	Creates pressure on completing tasks or activities		
Goals	Can be reached by successfully completing a task or activity		

4.2.2 Identifying User Preferences in Gamification

To evaluate which game mechanics LMS users prefer, we used "best worst scaling" (BWS) and conducted a discrete choice task. Developed by Louviere et al. (2013), this method is an extension of Thurstone's (1927) MaxDiff scaling. BWS describes a cognitive process by which respondents repeatedly choose the two objects in varying sets of three or more objects that they feel have the largest perceptual difference on a described continuum of interests (Finn & Louviere, 1992). Among BWS's advantages is that it provides a high level of ranking information because each decision for a pair of attributes provides implications for the unchosen attribute (Marley & Louviere, 2005; Thiebes et al., 2014). It is also scale-free, which prevents response styles (such as selecting only the first option again and again), so it does not affect the mean value or the variance obtained (Lee, Ceyhan, Jordan-Cooley, Sung, 2013; Thiebes et al., 2014). Finally, BWS avoids other response biases (Lee, Soutar, & Louviere, 2007). Overall, comparisons with other rating methods show that BWS provides better results for discriminating between attributes (Matzner, Hoffen, Heide, Plenter, Chasin, 2015). Before using BWS with our participants, we explained the function and meaning of game mechanics and then evaluated their knowledge about and understanding of them.

Next, we identified which combination of game mechanics LMS users prefer. We presented a list of game mechanics to our LMS users and asked them to construct their own bundles, adding other game mechanics to the list we provided if they wished. Besides identifying and analyzing which combinations they preferred, we were able to validate our BWS by showing that the game mechanics that the users preferred most frequently were those that we identified in our BWS. Our analysis finished with an analysis of the participants demographic data and background information. Figure 5 illustrates the structure of our analyses.

We collected 287 completed surveys for our analysis of LMS users, of which 145 (50.52%) were female, and 142 (46.98%) were male. The youngest participant was 17 years old and the oldest 51 years old, and the participants' average age was 26 years. In analyzing our results, we used the statistical software program R, which provides several packages for analyzing BWS results: We performed ed a counting analysis and two kinds of conditional logistic regressions to help us rank the game design elements. We evaluated the combinations of game design elements using relative and absolute means.

The next section presents the results of our BWS, which are in line with the results of our regression analyses.

4.2.3 Identification of the Most Preferred Game Mechanics

To identify which game mechanics LMS users prefer, we first analyzed the results of our BWS using a counting analysis and two regression analyses. Then we analyzed which game mechanics our participants combined, and compared the results with those of our BWS. The results can be seen in Table 6.

The counting analysis was used to calculate a score for each game mechanic for each of the 287 respondents. First, we calculated the difference between the number of times each game mechanic was chosen as most preferred (best) and the number of times each was chosen as least preferred (worst). We divided the difference by the number of times each game mechanic was shown (six times) multiplied by the total number of responses (Finn & Louviere, 1992; Flynn, Louviere, Peters, & Coast, 2007; Louviere, Lings, Islam, Gudergan, & Flynn, 2013; Severin, Schmidtke, Mühlbacher, & Rogowski, 2013). A higher score indicates a greater preference.

As for our two conditional logistic regressions, Marley & Louviere (2005) and Orme (2005) outlined that a conditional logistic regression should deliver the same results as the counting approach. Since regression analysis requires a dependent variable, we followed Flynn et al. (2007) and Hair (2010) in using used a binary coded dummy variable, creating one observation for each possible best-worst pair per choice set per respondent and used the game design elements as independent variables. To avoid the dummy variable trap, we chose one independent variable as a reference category and excluded it from our data sets (Hair, 2010). Both regression analyses delivered the same ranking positions based on their calculated coefficients.

Table 6 Results of counting analysis (based on Schöbel & Söllner, 2016)

Counting analysis					
Element	B	W	Mean	STD	Rank
Level	826	82	0.432	0.367	1
Points	746	60	0.398	0.386	2
Goals	752	99	0.379	0.453	3
Status bar	550	209	0.198	0.198	4
Badges	312	450	−0.080	0.521	5
Leaderboard	396	538	−0.082	0.613	6
Virtual goods	319	495	−0.102	0.564	7
Avatar	158	604	−0.259	0.482	8
Time pressure	189	646	−0.265	0.517	9
Loss aversion	49	1114	−0.618	0.387	10

B = Best; W = Worst; STD = Standard Deviation

To determine whether any of the game design elements are closely related to the overall levels of preference for game design elements, we calculated Kendall's tau correlations between the most and least scores from the counting analysis and the ten game design elements (Finn & Louviere, 1992). The strongest positive correlation was identified for the element *level* (.080), and the strongest negative correlation was for *loss aversion* (-.11), confirming the results of our counting analysis. Overall, the four gamification elements *level*, *points*, *goals*, and *status* were positively correlated, while all other game design elements were negatively correlated. *Loss aversion* had the strongest negative correlation.

The first step of our process in gamifying LMS was to identify the game mechanics LMS users most prefer (which were levels, points, status bar, and goals). In the second step, we used our survey to determine the best number of game mechanics for an LMS.

Identification of Bundles of Game Mechanics

Referring to our user-centered process of gamifying LMSs, we evaluated how many game mechanics LMS users prefer in a bundle by having respondents construct their own bundles. We calculated the frequency of the number of game mechanics the respondents included in a combination; most participants combined four game mechanics (mean = 4.163), but the participants created bundles of as few as one and as many as eight game mechanics. We identified 167 combinations, with most consisting of four (48 combinations) or three (37 combinations) game mechanics. Twenty-four combinations had five game mechanics, and twenty-seven combinations had six. Ten and five combinations had seven and eight game mechanics, respectively. In the next step, we evaluated the frequency of the game mechanics in the constructed bundles by counting each game mechanic in the combinations in relation to the total number of participants and found that the frequency of game mechanics in the combinations

Table 7 Frequency of game design elements in combinations (Based on Schöbel et al., 2016)

Game design elements	Frequency (in %)	Rank BWS
Points	75.61	2
Goals	66.55	3
Level	63.41	1
Status bar	54.01	4
Leaderboard	41.46	6
Virtual goods	27.87	7
Badges	26.83	5
Avatar	26.48	8
Time pressure	26.48	9
Loss aversion	7.67	10

was similar to the results of the BWS, although the order of the frequency differed from that of the BWS. The results are shown in Table 7.

The results of the BWS and the combination analyses delivered insights into which game mechanics LMS users prefer. Each game mechanic has its own structure and meaning that can be used to develop a more user-centered process with which to gamify LMSs.

4.2.4   Implementation of Game Mechanics

The goal of our study was to identify process steps for a user-centered concept to gamify LMSs. Based on the negative correlations of badges, leaderboards, virtual goods, avatars, time pressure, and loss aversion, we conclude that LMS users are less interested in these mechanics than they are in others.

Having identified the most preferred game mechanics and the number of game mechanics LMS users prefer, we designed the gamification concept for our LMS as including the motivators of points, goals, levels, and a status bars. Figure 6 provides an overview of how the most preferred game mechanics were designed for an LMS that is used by energy consultants.

To make our game mechanics more meaningful for our target group of energy consultants, we used an energy label that visualizes a house's energy consumption, thereby informing the user about its eco-friendliness. After logging into the LMS, energy consultants can complete various leaning modules, each of which has the same structure—beginning with goals and continuing with self-assessment scales, learning material, test questions, another self-assessment evaluation, and a learning module evaluation. We embedded our game mechanics in the goal sections as well as in the individual test section and group test section so each user can see the goals he or she can meet and collect points for correct answers in both test sections. The label was used as status bar to visualize a user's individual progress in working on tasks and activities in the LMS. The label itself has stages from A + to H that represent

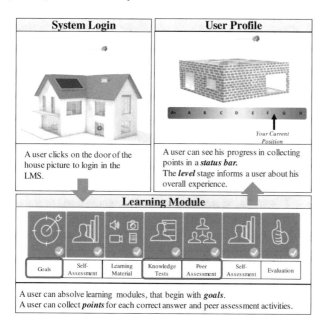

Fig. 6 Implementation of game elements in a LMS

the levels and serve as challenges for users, such that the higher the level, the more experienced the user.

Our next step is to evaluate how each game mechanic addresses the users' motivation.

Summarizing our results, a user-centered process to gamify LMS should consist of three steps. The first step is to evaluate which game mechanics users prefer to guide them in their individual learning progress. We noted that LMS users prefer competing against themselves instead of other users, so using game design elements like *levels* instead of *leaderboards* is likely to be more suitable to challenge users of LMSs to achieve learning outcomes than, say, *leaderboards*. Therefore, game mechanics that are used in a learning context should refer to task completion by rewarding the users' individual success (Schöbel et al. 2017a). Referring to learning outcomes, our results indicate the importance of experiences that are intrinsically motivating, so such experiences could serve as predictors.

The second step in gamifying a user-centered LMS is to identify the number and combination of game mechanics to be used (Schöbel et al. 2017b), as implementing a large number of game mechanics might have contrary effects on a user's motivation and learning outcomes (Hanus and Fox, 2015).

In the third step, the game mechanics are adapted to the context in which the LMS is used. Although the first and second steps delivered a combination of game mechanics, additional refinements of the game mechanics should adapt them to the needs of the target group.

In our suggested process, a fourth step could be included that evaluates the game mechanics after they are implemented in an LMS.

5 Key Lessons

During our journey, we learn what can improve the effectiveness and efficiency of forthcoming DSR journeys. We also believe that these lessons can help other researchers in designing and running successful DSR endeavors.

The *first lesson* is related to the value of breaking a complex DSR challenge like designing an IT-supported teaching-learning concept into several related design artifacts–in our case, the *Peer Creation Process* and the *User-Centered Process to Gamify LMSs*. This decision proved valuable for us for several reasons. First, it allowed us to apply related but still individualized research approaches to designing each design artifact, so the literature's being incomplete when it comes to a user-centered gamification concept did not stop our whole endeavor but just postponed this part while the design and evaluation of the other design artifacts continued as planned. We realized that gamifying a user-centered LMS involves more than just selecting game mechanics and implementing them in an LMS, as each game mechanic has its own constitution and its own effects on learners' motivation. Each process step in gamifying LMS delivers new insights into learners' needs and motivational structures and helps us to explain the meaning and relevance of motivation in learning that is supported by game mechanics.

The second advantage of breaking our DSR challenge into related design artifacts is that it allowed us to tailor our evaluations to the needs of each design artifact and to conduct more focused and rigorous evaluations than an evaluation of the overarching design challenge would have been. As a result, the evaluations yielded precise insights into how to improve each design artifact.

Third, we were able to focus on addressing the specific challenges of each design artifact. For the Peer Creation Process, we could focus on designing a process that ensures knowledge transfer and knowledge documentation with reasonable effort from the participants. For the process to gamify LMS, we could focus on addressing the issues of user motivation and continuous use. If we were to account for all challenges on the level of the overarching design challenge, our design decisions might have been affected by mixing the challenges for these distinct parts.

A *second lesson* is related to the need to find gaps in the knowledge base before the DSR journey begins. Whereas our journey went smoothly for the Peer Creation Process, such was not the case for the user-centered process to gamify LMSs. Even though we had gathered literature on gamification design before starting the journey, we did not invest enough effort in investigating this literature's inconsistencies and the "designability" of the insights presented. These journeys should begin with a thorough assessment of the knowledge base. On the upside, we believe that the insight that the available literature cannot be used yet to design effective gamification approaches for specific situations or system is useful, as DSR studies have the potential to highlight gaps in the knowledge base and, thus, areas for future behavioral research. Furthermore, by focusing on a step-wise development of a peer creation and gamification process, we can improve our understanding of each of the process steps we analyzed and enlarge our overall DSR studies.

A *third lesson* is that, even though a gap in the knowledge base is a challenge for a DSR endeavor, DSR researchers can resolve this issue by conducting an empirical study, thus addressing the problems in the rigor cycle. In our case, after observing the gap, we designed and conducted an empirical study to tease out LMS users' preferences regarding single game mechanics and their combinations. This additional effort came with two advantages: It allowed us to generate an additional theoretical contribution (e.g., Schöbel et al., 2016), and by conducting new primary research instead of relying on insights published in other studies, we were assured that we covered the preferences of the later users of our artifact. By conducting this empirical study, we demonstrated the value of involving users from the first step of a development process to the last. Most gamified LMSs are based on a random selection and combination of game mechanics, whereas our empirical studies indicated that specific game mechanics are not particularly effective in facilitating learning. Conducting an empirical study for a theory of design and action can deliver important insights that can improve the contribute to the theory to be developed.

We are thinking of being more critical in assessing the value of the available knowledge base and to weigh the advantages and disadvantages more regularly, such as by doing primary research related to the knowledge base prior to starting the DSR journey. By conducting this additional effort, we believe that we were able to close the gap in the knowledge base and to develop a user-centered process to gamify LMSs that fit better with the boundary conditions of our DSR challenge than an approach that was based on the extant literature.

Our experiences in this DSR journey will help us to design and run better DSR journeys in the future, and we hope that some or all of what we learned will help other DSR researchers ensure that their journeys will help them reach their goals.

References

von Alan, R. H., March, S. T., Park, J., & Ram, S. (2004). Design science in information systems research. *MIS Quarterly, 28*(1), 75–105.

Alcivar, I., & Abad, A. G. (2016). Design and evaluation of a gamified system for ERP training. *Computers in Human Behavior, 58,* 109–118.

Arbaugh, J. B. (2010). *Online and blended business education for the 21st Century: Current research and future directions.* Burlington: Elsevier Science.

Attali, Y., & Arieli-Attali, M. (2015). Gamification in assessment: Do points affect test performance? *Computers & Education, 83,* 57–63.

Baek, E.-O., Cagiltay, K., Boling, E., & Frick, T. (2008). User-centered design and development. *Handbook of research on educational communications and technology, 1,* 660–668.

Bittner, E. A. C., & Leimeister, J. M. (2013). "Why shared understanding matters–engineering a collaboration process for shared Understanding to improve collaboration effectiveness in heterogeneous teams, *Hawaii International Conference on IEEE*, pp. 106–114.

Blohm, I., & Leimeister, J. M. (2013). Design of IT-Based enhancing services for motivational support and behavioral change. *Business & Information Systems Engineering (BISE), 5*(4), 275–278.

Bolden, R., & Gosling, J. (2006). Leadership competencies: Time to change the tune? *Leadership, 2*(2), 147–163.

Boticki, I., Baksa, J., Seow, P., & Looi, C.-K. (2015). Usage of a mobile social learning platform with virtual badges in a primary school. *Computers & Education, 86,* 120–136.

Briggs, R., Kolfschoten, G., Gert-Jan, V., & Douglas, D. (2006). Defining key concepts for collaboration engineering, *AMCIS 2006 Proceedings*, p. 17.

Briggs, R. O., Kolfschoten, G. L., Vreede, G.-J. de, Albrecht, C., Lukosch, S., & Dean, D. L. (2014). A six-layer model of collaboration. *Collaboration Systems*, pp. 221–228.

Briggs, R. O., Kolfschoten, G. L., de Vreede, G.-J., Lukosch, S., & Albrecht, C. C. (2013). Facilitator-in-a-box: Process support applications to help practitioners realize the potential of collaboration technology. *Journal of Management Information Systems, 29*(4), 159–194.

Chen, C.-M., & Wu, C.-H. (2015). Effects of different video lecture types on sustained attention, emotion, cognitive load, and learning performance. *Computers & Education, 80,* 108–121.

Christy, K. R., & Fox, J. (2014). Leaderboards in a virtual classroom: A test of stereotype threat and social comparison explanations for women's math performance. *Computers & Education, 78,* 66–77.

Davis, K., & Singh, S. (2015). Digital badges in afterschool learning: Documenting the perspectives and experiences of students and educators. *Computers & Education, 88,* 72–83.

Denny, P. (ed.). (2013). The effect of virtual achievements on student engagement. *Proceedings of SIGCHI Conference on Human Factors in Computing Systems*, pp. 763–772.

Deterding, S., Dixon, D., Khaled, R., & Nacke, L. (2011). "rom game design elements to gamefulness: Defining gamification, *Proceedings of the 15th International academic MindTrek Conference*, pp. 9–15.

Dillenbourg, P. (1999). *What do you mean by collaborative learning?*. Oxford: Elsevier.

Domínguez, A., Saenz-De-Navarrete, J., De-Marcos, L., Fernández-Sanz, L., Páges, C., & Martínez-Herráiz, J.-J. (2013). Gamifying learning experiences: Practical implications and outcomes. *Computers & Education, 63,* 380–392.

Edvinsson, L., & Sullivan, P. (1996). Developing a model for managing intellectual capital. *European Management Journal, 14*(4), 356–364.

Finn, A., & Louviere, J. J. (1992). Determining the appropriate response to evidence of public concern: The case of food safety. *Journal of Public Policy & Marketing*, pp. 12–25.

Flynn, T. N., Louviere, J. J., Peters, T. J., & Coast, J. (2007). Best-worst scaling: What it can do for health care research and how to do it. *Journal of Health Economics, 26*(1), 171–189.

Gagne, R. M. (1984). Learning outcomes and their effects: Useful categories of human performance. *American psychologist 39*(4), 377.

Gregor, S., & Hevner, A. R. (2013). Positioning and presenting design science research for maximum impact. *MIS Quarterly, 37*(2), 337–355.

Gregor, S., & Jones, D. (2007). The anatomy of a design theory. *Journal of the Association for Information systems, 8*(5), 312–335.

Hair, J. F. (ed.). (2010). *Multivariate data analysis:* Pearson College Division.

Hall, T., & Stegila, A. (2003). Peer mediated instruction and intervention. *Wakefield, MA: National Center on Accessing the General Curriculum. Retrieved February* (8), p. 2007.

Hamari, J. (2013). Transforming homo economicus into homo ludens: A field experiment on gamification in a utilitarian peer-to-peer trading service. *Electronic Commerce Research and Applications, 12*(4), 236–245.

Hamari, J., Koivisto, J., & Sarsa, H. (2014). Does gamification work?–a literature review of empirical studies on gamification. *Hawaii International Conference on System Science*, pp. 3025–3034.

Hamari, J., Shernoff, D. J., Rowe, E., Coller, B., Asbell-Clarke, J., & Edwards, T. (2016). Challenging games help students learn: An empirical study on engagement, flow and immersion in game-based learning. *Computers in Human Behavior, 54,* 170–179.

Hanus, M. D., & Fox, J. (2015). Assessing the effects of gamification in the classroom: A longitudinal study on intrinsic motivation, social comparison, satisfaction, effort, and academic performance. *Computers & Education, 80,* 152–161.

Harris, A. (1998). Effective teaching: A review of the literature. *School Leadership & Management, 18*(2), 169–183.

Hevner, A. R. (2007). A three cycle view of design science research. *Scandinavian journal of information systems* (19:2), p. 4.

Hiltbrand, T., & Burke, M. (2011). How gamification will change business intelligence. *Business Intelligence Journal* (16:INL/JOU-11-21248).

Hunicke, R., LeBlanc, M., & Zubek, R. (2004). MDA: A formal approach to game design and game research. In *Proceedings of the AAAI Workshop on Challenges in Game AI.*

Jones, J. M. (2014). Discussion group effectiveness is related to critical thinking through interest and engagement. *Psychology Learning & Teaching, 13*(1), 12–24.

Jones, M. G., & Brader-Araje, L. (2002). The impact of constructivism on education: Language, discourse, and meaning. *American Communication Journal, 5*(3), 1–10.

Jurado, J. L., Collazos, C. A., & Paredez, L. M. (2014). Collaborative framework for the management of knowledge, an approach from gamification techniques. *Proceedings of the XV International Conference on Human Computer Interaction,* p. 70.

Knutas, A., Ikonen, J., Nikula, U., & Porras, J. (2014). Increasing collaborative communications in a programming course with gamification: A case study. *International Conference on Computer Systems and Technologies,* pp. 370–377.

Krathwohl, D. R. (2002). A revision of Bloom's taxonomy: An overview. *Theory into Practice, 41*(4), 212–218.

Leacock, T. L., & Nesbit, J. C. (2007). A framework for evaluating the quality of multimedia learning resources. *Journal of Educational Technology & Society, 10*(2), 44–59.

Lee, J. A., Soutar, G. N., & Louviere, J. (2007). Measuring values using best-worst scaling: The LOV example. *Psychology & Marketing, 24*(12), 1043–1058.

Lee, J. J., Ceyhan, P., Jordan-Cooley, W., & Sung, W. (2013). GREENIFY: A real-world action game for climate change education. *Simulation & Gaming, 44*(2–3), 349–365.

Leimeister, J. M. (2014). *Collaboration Engineering: IT-gestützte Zusammenarbeitsprozesse systematisch entwickeln und durchführen:* Springer.

Louviere, J., Lings, I., Islam, T., Gudergan, S., & Flynn, T. (2013). An introduction to the application of (case 1) best-worst scaling in marketing research. *International Journal of Research in Marketing, 30*(3), 292–303.

Malcolm, J., Hodkinson, P., & Colley, H. (2003). The interrelationships between informal and formal learning. *Journal of Workplace Learning, 15*(7/8), 313–318.

Marley, A. A. J., & Louviere, J. J. (2005). Some probabilistic models of best, worst, and best-worst choices. *Journal of Mathematical Psychology, 49*(6), 464–480.

Mathieu, J. E., Heffner, T. S., Goodwin, G. F., Salas, E., & Cannon-Bowers, J. A. (2000). "The influence of shared mental models on team process and performance. *Journal of Applied Psychology* (85:2), p. 273.

Matzner, M., Hoffen, M. von, Heide, T., Plenter, F., & Chasin, F. (2015). A method for measuring user preferences in information systems design choices. *European Conference on Information Systems.*

Mayring, P. (2004). Qualitative content analysis.

McDaniel, R., Lindgren, R., & Friskics, J. (2012). Using badges for shaping interactions in online learning environments. *International Professional Communication Conference,* pp. 1–4.

Melero, J., Hernández-Leo, D., & Manatunga, K. (2015). Group-based mobile learning: Do group size and sharing mobile devices matter? *Computers in Human Behavior, 44,* 377–385.

Moll, L. C. 2013. *LS Vygotsky and education:* Routledge.

Neij, L., Heiskanen, E., & Strupeit, L. (2017). The deployment of new energy technologies and the need for local learning. *Energy Policy, 101,* 274–283.

Nonaka, I. (2000). A dynamic theory of organizational knowledge creation. *Knowledge, groupware and the internet*: Elsevier, pp. 3–42.

Nunamaker, J. F., Jr., Briggs, R. O., Derrick, D. C., & Schwabe, G. (2015). The last research mile: Achieving both rigor and relevance in information systems research. *Journal of Management Information Systems, 32*(3), 10–47.

Oeste, S., Söllner, M., & Leimeister, J. M. (2014). Engineering peer-to-peer learning processes for generating high quality learning materials. *International Conference on Collaboration and Technology*, pp. 263–270.

Oeste-Reiß, S., Bittner, E., & Söllner, M. (2017). Yes You Can—empowering lecturers to simulate collaboration among learners in the disciplines of problem-solving and critical thinking regardless of class size. *International Conference on Wirtschaftsinformatik*, pp. 761–775.

Oeste-Reiß, S., Söllner, M., & Leimeister, J. M. (2016). Development of a peer-creation-process to leverage the power of collaborative knowledge transfer. *Hawaii International Conference on System Science*, pp. 797–806.

Orme, B. (2005). Accuracy of HB estimation in MaxDiff experiments," *Sawtooth Software Research Paper,* http://www.awtoothsoftware.com/download/techpap/maxdacc.pdf.

Pearce, J., Mulder, R., & Baik, C. (2009). Involving students in peer review. *Case studies and practical strategies for university teaching.*

Reed, W. A. (2014). User-centered design: A guide to ROI with ISO 9241-210. *Texology Sci Google Scholar.*

Schöbel, S., Söllner, M., & Leimeister, J. M. (2016). The agony of choice analyzing user preferences regarding Gamification elements in learning management systems. *International Conference on Information Systems.*

Schöbel, S., & Söllner, M. (2016). How to Gamify information systems—adapting gamification to individual user preferences. *European Conference on Information Systems (ECIS). Istanbul, Turkey.*

Schöbel, S., Söllner, M., & Mishra, A. N. (2017). Does the Winner Take it All? Towards an Understanding of why there might be no One-Size-Fits-All Gamification Design. *European Conference on Information Systems (ECIS). Guimarães, Portugal.*

Schöbel, S.; Janson, A.; Ernst, S. -J. & Leimeister, J. M. 2017b. "How to Gamify a Mobile Learning Application—A Modularization Approach," *International Conference on Information Systems (ICIS). Seoul, South Korea.*

Schöbel, S., & Janson, A. (2018). Is it all about Having Fun?—developing a taxonomy to Gamify information systems. *European Conference on Information Systems (ECIS). Portsmouth, UK.*

Seaborn, K., & Fels, D. I. (2015). Gamification in theory and action: A survey. *International Journal of Human-Computer Studies, 74,* 14–31.

Severin, F., Schmidtke, J., Mühlbacher, A., & Rogowski, W. H. (2013). Eliciting preferences for priority setting in genetic testing: A pilot study comparing best-worst scaling and discrete-choice experiments. *European Journal of Human Genetics, 21*(11), 1202–1208.

Textor, M. (2016). *Bevölkerung und Gesellschaft.* http://www.zukunftsentwicklungen.de/gesellsch aft.html.

Thiebes, S., Lins, S., & Basten, D. (2014). Gamifying information systems-a synthesis of gamification mechanics and dynamics. European Conference on Information Systems.

Thurstone, L. L. (1927). A law of comparative judgment. *Psychological Review* (34:4), p. 273.

Topping, K. J. (2005). Trends in peer learning. *Educational Psychology, 25*(6), 631–645.

Tynjälä, P. (2008). Perspectives into learning at the workplace. *Educational Research Review, 3*(2), 130–154.

Vreede, G. J. de, & Briggs, R. (2018). Collaboration engineering: Reflections on 15 Years of research & practice. *Hawaii International Conference on System Science*, pp. 410–419.

Vreede, G. J. de, & Briggs, R. O. (2005). Collaboration engineering: Designing repeatable processes for high-value collaborative tasks. *Hawaii International Conference on System Science*, pp. 1–10.

de Vreede, G.-J., Briggs, R. O., & Massey, A. P. (2009). Collaboration engineering: Foundations and opportunities: Editorial to the special issue on the journal of the association of information systems. *Journal of the Association for Information systems, 10*(3), 121–137.

Webb, N. M. (2010). Peer Learning in the Classroom. In P. Peterson, E. Baker, & B. McGraw (Eds.), *International encyclopedia of education* (pp. 636–642). Oxford: Elsevier.

Wegener, R., & Leimeister, J. (2012). Peer creation of e-learning materials to enhance learning success and satisfaction in an Information Systems Course. *European Conference on Information Systems.*

Wegge, J., Roth, C., Neubach, B., Schmidt, K.-H., & Kanfer, R. (2008). Age and gender diversity as determinants of performance and health in a public organization: The role of task complexity and group size. *Journal of Applied Psychology, 93*(6), 1301.

Winkler, R., Briggs, R., O.; Vreede, G.-J. de; Leimeister, J.M., Oeste-Reiß, S., & Söllner, M. (2019): "Towards a Technique for Modeling New Forms of Collaborative Work Practices—The Facilitation Process Model 2.0." *Hawaii International Conference on System Sciences.*

Zichermann, G., & Cunningham, C. (2011). Gamification by design: Implementing game mechanics in web and mobile apps: " O'Reilly Media, Inc.".

A Situational Knowledge Network Nexus: Exploring Kernel Theory Extensions Using Design Science Research

Magnus Rotvit Perlt Hansen and Jan Pries-Heje

Abstract When organizations realize that they need to innovate, they often have their knowledge workers participate in inter-organizational "knowledge networks" that have the purpose of developing their participants' skills and competencies through facilitated meetings. The main problem of knowledge networks is that it can be difficult to evaluate whether the network group is "healthy" and follows its purpose and whether its participants gain any value as a result, so the design problem faced in this study was "How to design a tool to assist network coordinators with the continuous development of network groups." The problem was broken into three sub-problems: identifying the types of knowledge networks, identifying a tool for gauging a knowledge network's "health," and identifying a process through which knowledge networks can be effectively established, maintained, and ended. The problem was complicated by the need to identify common interests among the knowledge networks' main stakeholders, for whom the solution had to provide value. The stakeholder groups were identified as network sponsors, network facilitators, and network participants. Three artifacts were designed to solve the problems identified. Artifact 1 was a visualization of the process of how to establish, maintain, operate, and evaluate and/or end a knowledge network. To support this process, two additional interactive artifacts were designed. The second artifact was a document called a "network charter" to be used by the facilitator and network participants at the beginning of and during the knowledge network process. The third artifact was an assessment tool for assessing seven key parameters of the selected knowledge network using a radar chart. Three main lessons were learned in the DSR project. First, we found that the DSR approach can be beneficial in creating new kernel theories, not just design theory. The concept of knowledge network archetypes was extracted through a combination of a literature review on knowledge networks and through the empirical activities involved in uncovering participant value and network facilitators' evaluation of the artifacts. Second, we learned that designing artifacts

M. R. P. Hansen · J. Pries-Heje (✉)
Department of People and Technology, Roskilde University, Roskilde, Denmark
e-mail: janph@ruc.dk

M. R. P. Hansen
e-mail: magnuha@ruc.dk

© Springer Nature Switzerland AG 2020
J. vom Brocke et al. (eds.), *Design Science Research. Cases*, Progress in IS,
https://doi.org/10.1007/978-3-030-46781-4_11

that provide value to various stakeholders with asymmetric power relationship on multiple levels should be pursued by DSR researchers. Third, DSR can be used to provide situational solutions, not just normative ones.

1 Introduction

Imagine that you own a successful small business, even a consultancy start-up. You have reached the point of maturity at which your customer base is growing and you can no longer rely on your ability to be involved in every company decision. You are well aware that you need to expand, which involves increasing your staff, formalizing business processes, using more advanced technology to handle customer relationships, and so on. You are especially worried about increasing your staff because you need to hire middle managers who can take care of everyday operations and staff while you focus more on strategic management. Where can you turn to gain information about how to handle all this?

The past ten years have seen the rapid rise of inter-organizational knowledge networks, where businesses engage their employees in formalized network groups with other related businesses (Dolińska, 2015). In these network groups participants can share and gain knowledge and competencies with their peers (Batonda & Perry, 2003). While you may wonder why you would engage in collaboration with some of your competitors, studies have shown that doing so is actually mutually beneficial (Möller, Rajala, & Svahn, 2005). However, despite positive results, for several reasons, knowledge networks can still be difficult to establish, maintain, and end. For example, the participants of such a group have to meet around busy schedules and prioritized work tasks, so meetings can be difficult to coordinate, and rarely can every participant attend, so a meeting frequency of only four to six times a year is common. In addition, participants have to build rapport and trust with one another if they are to share knowledge and grow competences (Busquets, 2010), which takes time and can be difficult if not facilitated properly. Finally, there must be some kind of purpose or value pursuit that is common for the participants on both the individual and organizational levels (Batonda & Perry, 2003) to keep group members from abandoning the group.

One of the attempts to address these three challenges has been to establish an external "sponsor" organization to coordinate knowledge meetings. These sponsor organizations can be groups of businesses or groups of support organizations of businesses divided into the types of support they provide (e.g., consultancies, production), geographical areas, whole industries (e.g., farming, fishing), or combinations thereof. Sponsors take charge of coordinating the knowledge networks and providing external facilitators who are in charge of facilitating the network meetings, thereby "greasing the wheels" to keep the network group on track and moving forward.

However, even with a sponsor organization to assist with coordination, hosting, and facilitation of network meetings, it can be difficult to assess how well a network group is working. A knowledge network creates its value through human relationships, interactions, and personal growth, not necessarily in terms of any production-oriented parameters. One cannot assess how much knowledge is "produced" by a knowledge network, as the knowledge created and shared is highly tacit and seldom comes to fruition in a short timeframe. For example, how to ride a bicycle is tacit knowledge that cannot easily be transferred into or learned from articulated knowledge—that is, you cannot simply tell someone how to ride a bike (Hedlund, 1994; Nonaka, Takeuchi, & Umemoto, 1996). One can argue that the knowledge gained from networks will eventually be "embedded in routines and processes which enable action" (Baskerville & Dulipovici, 2006, p. 83).

The success of a knowledge network is determined by the satisfaction and participation of its participants, so it is usually impossible to extract key performance indicators based on generic performance standards. This feature presents a conundrum concerning how to gain funding for a knowledge network when there is likely to be an expectation to report the results, that is, to show that the money put into these networks has been spent in the interests of the funder.

In addition, the essential component of a knowledge network is its participants. Since they are human actors, their interactions during meetings cannot (and probably should not) be directed by tools like rules, procedures and structures, as relationships are inherently social in nature and are based on communication and real-life interaction. For technology to work with human interactions, technologies that are designed to afford specific tasks, solutions, and workflows are diametrically opposed to the open nature of how humans communicate and relate to each other. The spectrum of technology design runs between designs that are "closed" (focusing how to perform tasks) to designs that are "open" (focusing on addressing multiple tasks and supporting dialogue and discussion).

Organizing, facilitating, and evaluating network groups can, then, be considered a *wicked* problem. Wicked problems are characterized as those that do not have a *best* solution and for which any well-fitting solution must fit within contexts that are impossible to exhaust because of the emergent nature of learning about the problem while solving it (Rittel & Webber, 1973). Many recipes and tools can be used, but predicting the results based on the tools can be incredibly difficult because the solution tools themselves change the problem. Hence, tools that are designed to support network groups should not be normatively pushed down on their participants but should allow room for actions and responses. Nevertheless, there is a need for tools that facilitators of networks can use to become better facilitators and participants can use to participate in the (re)negotiation of the knowledge network to steer it on the right course.

Enter Design Science Research (DSR). DSR can be used as a learning process, as the DSR cycle of analyzing, designing, constructing and evaluating is a rigorous and iterative approach to improving and learning about a domain. The input and output of DSR processes draw on an existing body of knowledge to solve a problem (Hevner et al., 2004), and design theories can be extrapolated by generalizing the solution artifact and the problem (Lee & Baskerville, 2003).

In this chapter, we investigate how a DSR process that leads to the evaluation of a product can not only solve the conundrum of assessing a network group's performance but can also provide insights into knowledge networks. The design journey is a learning process through the domain of knowledge networks, where participants from various organizations participate in establishing new, innovative products or processes or simply want to learn about new best practices.

Through a qualitative case of a DSR project to design multiple artifacts guided by multiple design principles to improve knowledge networks' facilitation, participation, and sponsorship, we identify three learning points in the process of designing for knowledge network groups. The problem was a wicked design problem, as no best solutions could be identified, and a solution would have to depend heavily on the situational context of each knowledge network. We show how selected fragments from prior theories on knowledge networks (also known as *kernel theories*) are used as components in the design of principles and resulting artifacts.

2 The Context

The problem of managing network groups is a real one that the authors have encountered. We were contacted by a sponsor organization called Company Forum Thy (CF Thy) in Denmark's Northern Jutland. Thy is located in Northern Denmark and has a strong industry in fishing, agriculture, tourism, and transportation and many opportunities for start-ups. For many years, CF Thy had been creating possibilities and growth for small to medium-sized companies and entrepreneurs by coaching entrepreneurs and helping them find new customer bases and grow competencies through courses, and gathering the various companies in clusters of network groups. The knowledge networks that had been established encompassed businesses from agriculture, the maritime industry, transportation, telecommunications, independent accounting firms, and elsewhere. Membership in CF Thy provided significant opportunities to engage in activities that support growth. When CF Thy contacted us, it had more than 265 companies as members, and it was growing so fast that establishing, maintaining, and evaluating the network groups had become increasingly difficult. The team behind CF Thy consisted of a promotion officer, who was responsible for the organization's strategy, two or three industry consultants, a project coordinator, an administrative coordinator, and a marketing consultant. All other employees, such as facilitators, teachers, and coaches, were hired on a freelance basis depending on the funds that were available through local, national, or European Union funding. The primary concern of CF Thy as a network sponsor and administrator was that, when the networks were established, it was difficult to identify what kind of value would be provided either directly to participants or indirectly back to the geographical area of Thy.

The motivation for a technological tool to help assess the health of knowledge network groups came partially from market demand and partially from demands from the external actors who supplied the funding for CF Thy's activities. The results of a survey of businesses in the geographical area of Thy indicated that the businesses that had already participated in one or more network groups wanted to increase the fulfilment of needs from their existing participation or by engaging in new and better knowledge networks. Participants noted that only a few of the businesses had an explicit strategy and purpose for their networking, as they engaged in many networks at once and subjectively determined which ones to stick with.

Instead of this haphazard approach, CF Thy wanted a rigorous tool that (a) could help potential participants identify the value, purpose, and strategy of their network groups; (b) could assist their freelance facilitators with creating purpose, value, and strategy and help them grow their facilitation competences; and (c) could help assist the management of CF Thy to provide assessments of their existing knowledge networks to determine on which ones to focus, which ones needed help to reinvigorate, and which ones to terminate because they had run their course.

3   The Journey

The case of CF Thy was a wicked design problem, so we used a nexus approach, which has been shown to be able to solve wicked design problems. In DSR, a *kernel theory* is a theory that informs the designed artifact, and "creation relies on existing kernel theories that are applied, tested, modified, and extended through the experience, creativity, intuition, and problem-solving capabilities of the researcher" (Hevner et al., 2004, p. 76). In other words, kernel theories (in this case, analytical, explanatory, and design theories on knowledge network groups) should be sought out to inform the DSR project about its domain, as should theories on its solution approach (in this case, theory on the nexus approach). The nexus approach is based on the premise that some contexts and situations can be so complex that, for a tool to provide information about the context or to help in making decisions, one must probe and assess the context domain thoroughly. Then the results should be viewed as suggestions to be reflected on, rather than to be applied blindly. A nexus theory approach provides five steps to create a nexus (Pries-Heje & Baskerville, 2008):

1. Identify the problem area and create an overview of existing literature and solutions to the problem. The specific case domain of the present study is the literature on network groups, knowledge sharing in the business domain, entrepreneurship, human interaction in groups, and how to support said groups with technology.
2. Analyze the identified solution approaches with a focus on the conditions under which each approach has worked by finding actions that can be taken and techniques that can be used in network groups, analyzing the elements of which a network group consists, determining how a network group progresses over time (from inception to termination), and identifying the conditions that make network groups successful.
3. Design and construct an artifact–a product or process—taking into account the conditions identified in the analysis. An artifact here can be some sort of prototype

tool that captures central data points that are based on the previous conditions and elements. A product-based artifact could reveal the assessment of the network group, while a process-based artifact would help identify the sequential actions and events of a network group.

4. Design a decision-making process based on the conditions and the evaluation, mapping the suggestions for action to the result of the evaluation and evaluating, for example, "if A is high, do X and Y but not Z."
5. Integrate the results–alternative solution approaches, the artifact, and the decision process–into an artifact, the tool to solve this wicked problem. The proposals for actions to solve the problems identified should be designed into the existing artifact so the users can navigate and decide which approaches to try more easily.

While the nexus design theory approach guided the actions, these actions were not taken sequentially, as knowledge about the context (the situation and problem with the knowledge networks), the domain (taking place with multiple representatives from small and medium-sized enterprises in Thy), and the possible design solutions was gradually revealed. The design journey took place over three central laps of design. Not all laps included explicit artifacts, although all laps included changes to existing artifacts.

3.1 Lap 1—Desire for a Design Solution from Network Sponsor

The first lap focused on understanding the network sponsor's practical problem statement given and identifying the phenomenon of "knowledge network groups" empirically.

For example, nexus steps 1 and 2 were performed simultaneously by examining the survey results and creating an interview guide based on what the network sponsor mentioned and knew. We did not focus on solution approaches here but on the conditions of the network group, defined as dimensions.

We used the dimensions as input for the focus group interviews that helped us to find solution approaches based on the participants' experiences and backgrounds. Two focus group interviews were held, one with six participants and one with four, all of whom were members of various knowledge networks in the region of Thy. The interview sessions were open-ended and focused on dimensions like expectations, knowledge-sharing, the facilitator's role, value, activities, relationships, professional interests, sustainability, and business background. Participants took turns in answering questions and providing input on how their own networks created value and motivation to keep participating.

Participants in the focus group interviews were chosen based on a pre-assessment of their professional experience and their experience with knowledge networks. The first focus group session had participants with considerable experience while the second focus group's participants had less experience.

The initial desire was to design an artifact that could be used to visualize and assist project sponsors and facilitators in assessing how successful the specific knowledge networks were. The problem was divided into multiple sub-problems, each of which was solved by identifying a kernel theory that enlightened the area or domain of the particular sub-problem and also give input as to how to measure any possible dimensions.

The nexus approach's steps 3, 4, and 5 were followed by designing an initial prototype of a radar visualization chart, which Avison and Pries-Heje (2008) originally used in a project management context. One of the network sponsor representatives wanted this design from the beginning and also wanted the tool to include survey questions for assessments, a visualization, and proposals for actions related to how to respond to the knowledge network's assessed status. The structure of the prototype followed nexus steps 4 and 5 because the dimensions and solution approaches were embedded into a process of assessing the dimensions with proposals for solutions.

The radar visualization chart was not sufficient as the only artifact, as input from the focus groups revealed additional needs were uncovered, so two other artifacts were designed. For example, while assessing the status of a knowledge network seemed important, the assessment was done on a momentary cross-section that was inherently static, so the results could not reflect the fact that a knowledge network is initialized, maintained, and at some point terminated. Instead, the data from nexus steps 1 and 2 indicated that additional solutions were performed by facilitators (initiating and terminating a network), with several proposals for how to do them or how they could be done better. The focus groups indicated that one solution for "unsticking" a network was to use collective reflection and feedback between the participants and the facilitator so the network participants could assess whether the network's purpose was still relevant. Specifically, the dimensions on which the network participants had given feedback were changed and aligned with their interests and experiences. For example, we investigated the importance of having an external, stable facilitator for a network in the literature on how to design inter-organizational business networks, and approaches that had worked well were integrated into the dimensions based on where the participants had noted issues with their networks. For example, one participant noted that an approach called "the hot seat" had worked well when the group was small as a way to liven up their usual activities, an approach that directly related to the "size" and "activities" dimensions. The dimensions and approaches were then integrated through the nexus approach's steps 3, 4, and 5: designing a tool, designing a decision-making process, and integrating the dimensions into the solutions. (The decision-making process of step 4 where suggestions for actions are provided has been covered relatively well in the literature.) Using this knowledge, we reiterated the nexus approach's steps 3, 4, and 5 and produced three working prototypes:

– A list of parameters for measuring a knowledge network: seven dimensions with up to three questions to score the dimensions and visualize them on a radar chart. The questions were derived from the network sponsors' and network participants' comments on when a knowledge network worked well and when they were confused and returned with little value after a network meeting. We called this artifact the Structural Assessment Survey (SAS).

- A model of a knowledge network's life cycle, divided into five states: This model came from the participants' confusion about where the knowledge network currently was. We called this artifact the Network State Model (NSM).
- A network charter document: a document for making explicit the beginning steps of establishing a network. This artifact arose from confusion about the purpose and scope of the knowledge network when it had been running for a long time since the participants changed what they wanted from the network as they grew in experience. We called this artifact the Knowledge Network Charter (KNC).

3.2 Lap 2—From Normative to Situational

The second lap focused on establishing working products that could be used as artifacts in a pilot test with five facilitators who worked for CF Thy. We went through the nexus approach's steps once again, this time with the literature and supporting kernel theory to support the approach's steps 1 and 2. Five facilitators were interviewed using questions that assessed one of their own knowledge networks, and the radar chart visualization was used to visualize the knowledge network's dimensions. The interviews sought information about practical actions that the facilitator could take to make the knowledge network flow better based on the dimensions, thus ensuring that all steps in the nexus approach were covered and evaluated. One facilitator expressed special interest in the project and was interviewed twice. Each facilitator was asked to use one knowledge network as an example and to provide comments based on one or two dimensions to ensure that all dimensions were evaluated.

The most interesting part of the process was the designers' ideas for how to solve the design problem. Based on the network sponsor's and the participants' interviews, the authors assumed that certain values in a knowledge network's dimensions could indicate problems, while other values could indicate health. This assumption harkened back to the project management's initial inspiration from the radar chart visualization, which had a much more normative context. A dimension could be difficult to cope with or it could be easy. For example, we assumed that no communication in a project was always a bad sign, but this assumption was proven to be wrong when it was applied to knowledge networks. In addition, facilitators came from different *types* of knowledge networks, which meant that, for some networks, a large number of network participants was actually desirable, while for other networks a small size was much more preferable, ruining the idea that all networks could be treated equally. As a result, questions, dimensions, and actions had to be completely reworked.

3.3   Lap 3—Summative and General Evaluation

While a knowledge network group and a project may seem to share similarities, they are very different entities altogether, as the purpose and motivation to progress in network groups are determined by the participants themselves, while projects often have external purposes and less intrinsic control of the goal. Therefore, it was difficult to use a "one size fits all" approach to the measurements, and the measurements had to be reinterpreted in light of each individual network's context and relational structure. The necessity for this reinterpretation was disheartening, as the design problem was then reset once again. After all, if all relevant information must be disseminated and retrieved on the level of the network itself, gauging the network's health would be similar to visiting each network, something that the network sponsor did not have time to do. Furthermore, how would possible actions be generated or applied if all networks differed from one another? A design solution had to be placed somewhere between measurement and completely immersing oneself with the networks. Therefore, the nexus approach's steps 4 to 5 were reviewed so the decision-making process and the integration of approaches and conditions were rethought. The interviews with the participants and the facilitators were recoded for clues for how to solve the new problem, resulting in the identification of six archetypical types of knowledge networks. The six archetypes made it possible to more easily determine specific assessment values that would show whether a knowledge network was doing well. We did this by introducing specific tolerance levels for each dimension so the knowledge network group would distinguish itself as belonging to a type. Then the algorithm based on the assessment would provide a gross list of actions that facilitators and participants could sort through. Rather than providing normative actions to do, facilitators and participants could themselves determine which to use.

With a revised artifact and decision-making process, two facilitators unrelated to CF Thy evaluated the tool by using it from start to finish and then reflecting on its merits and usefulness. The final evaluation pointed to the need for further clarification of a knowledge network. (During the third lap a knowledge network was called "innovation network," which did not work well, as certain networks were not innovative but focused on sharing, reusing, and applying knowledge.) From the evaluation both facilitators gained new ideas for how to handle their networks though the list of six types. We also found that the list of six types could easily be expanded. As a result, the third lap of the design showed that the design theory and the artifacts provided were nascent and should be designed to evolve continually. See Fig. 1 for a full overview of the process approach.

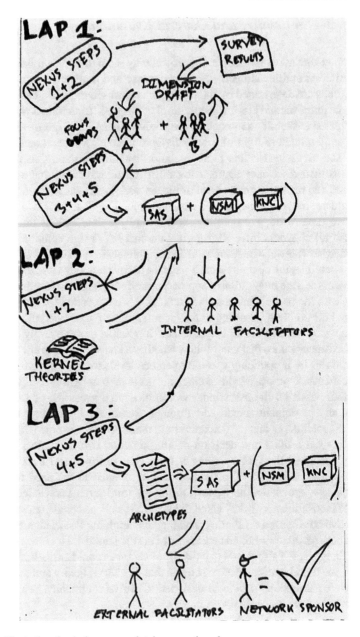

Fig. 1 Illustrating the design approach taken over three laps

4 The Results

4.1 Presentation of Artifact(S)

Each of the three laps of the design journey ended with artifacts, each supporting a unique part of the knowledge network facilitation process. The initial problem of assessing knowledge networks was both a process and structural problem, and these artifacts had to account for both of these conditions, so the artifacts were situational in nature and designed to help the sponsor, facilitator, and participants navigate through the journey of establishing, maintaining, and evaluating a knowledge network group. There was no single best way to steer or navigate, yet it was still necessary to design instruments that could help set a course through the sometimes-troubled waters of engaging network participants in activities and providing value. As a result, the artifacts had to be combined to provide a full picture of a knowledge network— its established purpose, its current status, and its current location. The combination of the three artifacts solved two main problems: discovering the situational and contextual aspect of knowledge networks and establishing common interests between asymmetrical stakeholders.

The first artifact, the NSM, was a visual artifact representing the flow of a knowledge network from its initiation to its termination. Prior literature supports the notion that group-based collaborations should be designed as life cycles to ensure compatibility with other organizational activities (Smart et al., 2007). Others have found that phase/stage models should be combined with state models instead because network groups tend to be unpredictable and volatile (Batonda & Perry, 2003). The NSM artifact was an attempt to convey a general linear movement of knowledge networks while also acknowledging that, based on the current conditions, the state of the network could change. For example, a knowledge network group usually forms in the "initiation" stage, after which the network moves on to the "definition" stage by having participants interact, negotiate, and create relationships, often by means of an external facilitator's mediation. When a knowledge network has been defined, it moves on to more steady operations, where actions are taken according to what has been established implicitly or explicitly as its purpose through planning, meeting, and evaluating. When some end condition is met (e.g., by fulfilling the purpose, lacking funding or participants), the knowledge network group is terminated. See Fig. 2 for how the NSM was visualized. The purpose of the NSM was educational: informing the sponsor, facilitator, and participants where the network group is located and what would typically be the next logical state. For example, a knowledge network had multiple interested participants with no clear purpose or formal structure would indicate that the knowledge network needed more formal backing to move to the "definition" stage. Likewise, an older network that had been meeting many times but still had had no formal evaluation performed would indicate that it was in the "action-taking" stage with a strong need for an evaluation of its purpose and health. A knowledge network with little explicit evaluation will eventually risk moving involuntarily to the "terminating" phase, as participants would drop out or simply not

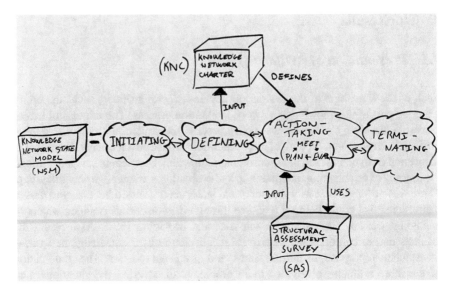

Fig. 2 Showing the Network State Model (NSM) and how it relates to the other two artifacts

show up because of dissatisfaction or because they feel that no more value could be gained.

The second artifact, the KNC, was developed to support the early states of the knowledge network. A large amount of a knowledge network is socially constructed such that, the more explicit knowledge, rules, and structures can be made, the easier it is for participants and facilitators to navigate the network and take action. For example, if it is not explicitly agreed that critiquing each other and providing helpful advice is allowed in a network, participants may feel intimidated. Another example is that, if no explicit purpose of the network has been stated (e.g., learn how to program robots to take over production), then network participants may hold widely different ideas of what they want and need to learn, making it difficult for a facilitator to focus on activities that live up to this purpose. The KNC was inspired by a template from Project Management International (PMI) since many networks resemble what can be deemed a "project": a temporary organization of people to fulfill a predefined purpose. The main elements of the KNC was to help the network sponsor, facilitators, and/or participants to fill out the following information:

– **Network description**: Describe the purpose of the network in one sentence
– **Network scope**: What needs will the network fulfill? What problems will the network solve? Which opportunities are taken advantage of?
– **Expected returns**: What are some of the benefits that the network will bring?
– **Critical success factors**: What are critical success factors for the network? How is success to be measured?

- **Assumptions and prerequisites**: What assumptions should be made for the network to succeed? What prerequisites are necessary for the network to begin and be maintained?
- **Budget and funding**: What is the annual budget? What are the sources of income?
- **Roles and responsibilities**: Who is the network sponsor and facilitator, and who are the central participants? What are the stakes and responsibilities, and what actions should be taken when certain conditions are met?

The third artifact was designed to assess the network groups and was the main interaction tool to be used by all the stakeholder groups. The artifact, called the SAS, consisted of three main elements as part of the decision-making process: questions related to seven dimensions of knowledge networks (Fig. 3), a visual radar chart that plotted the results of the questions and compared them to six archetypical types of knowledge networks (Fig. 4), a set of proposals for actions that a facilitator or participants can take to increase or decrease the values of the dimensions. Questions were rated on a scale from 1 to 5, with the being the less problematic rating.

The dimensions and questions indicating dimensional values

The seven dimensions of knowledge network groups were identified from the initial participant interviews and later revised and verified through a literature search. When a stronger theoretical understanding was needed, further domain-independent literature was included to support the dimensions (Table 1).

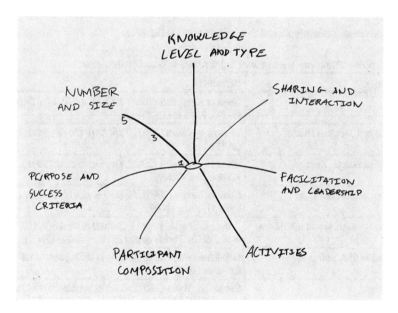

Fig. 3 Visual representation of the dimensions of the SAS

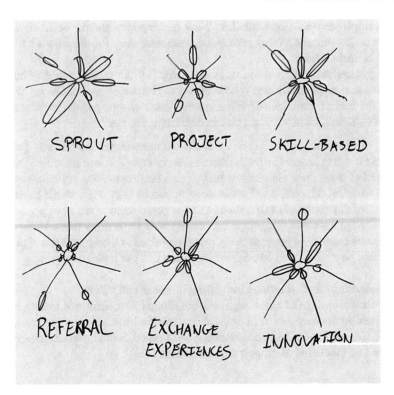

Fig. 4 All network archetypes and their tolerance levels (bubbles)

Table 1 Table of the dimension of knowledge networks based on the literature

Dimension	References
Size	Ghisi & Martinelli (2006), Jack et al. (2010), Mitchell (1974), Zhao et al. (2010)
Purpose and success criteria	Hannah & Walsh (2002), Jack et al. (2010), Möller et al. (2005)
Participant composition	Ghisi & Martinelli (2006), Gruenfeld et al. (1996), Klerkx et al. (2009)
Knowledge level and type	Cook & Brown (1999), Nonaka et al. (1996) Orey (2010), Polanyi & Sen (2009)
Knowledge-sharing and interaction	Brown & Duguid (1991), Connell & Voola (2007), Jack et al. (2010), Porras et al. (2004), Tsoukas (2009)
Facilitation and leadership	Hannah & Walsh (2002), Kirkels & Duysters (2010), Schwarz (2002)
Activities	Connell & Voola (2007), Cook & Brown (1999), Jack et al. (2010), Möller et al. (2005), Schwarz (2002)

Dimension "Size"

The size of knowledge is the single most important variable for the network's health (Zhao et al., 2010). However, one must also assume that, since regular network meetings are necessary (Mitchell, 1974), cancellations must be rare, and the same participants should show up from meeting to meeting until a critical mass has been attained (Jack et al., 2010).

Dimension "Purpose and success criteria"

Knowledge networks operate on a certain level of formality (Ghisi & Martinelli, 2006) because they often are formed as part of an organizational strategy (Möller et al., 2005). As a result, network participants must, to a large extent, refer to their management, so some kind of explicit purpose must be written down to align business strategy with the network's strategy (Hanna & Walsh, 2002).

Dimension "Participant composition"

Competencies and experience are just two aspects of the participants' composition (Ghisi & Martinelli, 2006); the types of the participants' organizations and lines of business are also central components (Klerkx et al., 2009). If the variety in the network's composition is too wide, a lack of innovation may result (Klerkx et al., 2009) and tasks may take too long or be difficult to complete (Gruenfeld et al., 1996).

Dimension "Knowledge level and type"

The main purpose of knowledge networks can vary among generating, sharing, and rethinking various types and levels of knowledge. Types of knowledge have been placed into two main categories: explicit, measurable knowledge (Nonaka et al., 1996) and tacit knowledge (Polanyi & Sen, 2009). Other ways to distinguish knowledge include individual-, group-, and collective-level knowledge, with various levels of contextualization possible (Cook & Brown, 1999). Knowledge in terms of learning has also been divided into multiple levels, ranging from pure summarizing to the design and innovation of completely new knowledge (Orey, 2010).

Dimension "Knowledge-sharing and interaction"

When knowledge needs to be applied, used, or shared, the dynamics of participant interaction come into play. A high level of trust is needed to make the knowledge network work as a strategic alliance. Trust is defined as the belief in reciprocal actions (Connell & Voola, 2007; Jack et al., 2010), despite a contradiction between identities in the network and in the original organization (Brown & Duguid, 1991). Dialogue and reflection can help network participants develop trust and feel comfortable with each other (Tsoukas, 2009).

Dimension "Facilitation and leadership"

Facilitators in a knowledge network can ensure that a group moves symmetrically toward its purpose or at least in some desired direction (Schwarz, 2002). Facilitators can be neutral (Hanna & Walsh, 2002) or professionally obliged to keep up to date, depending on the knowledge network (Kirkels & Duysters, 2010).

Dimension "Activities"

During meetings, common activities have to be performed to enable sensemaking and to facilitate some kind of affection for the network's purpose and trust between participants (Connell & Voola, 2007; Jack et al., 2010). Having a formalized agenda is often preferred, but whether one is needed depends very much on the network (Möller et al., 2005). The network's activities range from problem-solving to decision-making and experimenting (Kolb & Kolb, 2005; Schwarz, 2002), each of which handles and disseminates knowledge in its own way (Cook & Brown, 1999). As such, conforming to a specific type of activity can work well in some networks and be a hindrance in others.

The value of each dimension is meant to be used in conjunction with comparisons to archetypical types of knowledge networks. Each type is denoted with a tolerance level that indicates that values within the tolerance levels are normal and desired for that type of knowledge network. Values outside the tolerance levels indicate challenges and should result in a set of specific actions to address them. Tolerance levels for the networks should be seen only as propositions, as they have only been evaluated on face value (and are a ripe subject for further research).

Type 1: The "sprout" network is the beginning of creating new networks. The sprout typically aims at attracting as many participants as possible by exploring common interests through social activities or themes. The critical mass usually exceeds twenty participants to ensure sufficient subcategories of interests that can be used to create more focused knowledge networks. As a result, purpose and success criteria are often vague and limited to learning about something in order to whet the participants' appetites. Facilitators of the sprout type of network often change from meeting to meeting and take on many roles and activities to attract a broad target audience. Several interviewees pointed out that they had initially met during these types of network meetings and then stopped attending when they found more suitable networks to join.

Type 2: The "project" network is structured with few participants and serves a narrow purpose with outcomes and performance indicators that can be measured. The project network is often composed of specialists with specific knowledge and focuses on finding solutions to a known problem. A business consultant with a high level of knowledge often drives the network and is responsible for assembling specific competencies so the network can work as a team. A project network operates over a far shorter time than other networks, and when and how it will be terminated is typically clear from the outset. One example that emerged from the interviews concerned a project network that was constituted to design and develop for small accounting firms an inexpensive IT system that could help them compete with larger accounting firms.

Type 3: The "skill-based network" has the purpose of sharing tools, methods, and other types of action-oriented knowledge among participants. Progress can be measured by the advancement of participants' skills as they grow and use them in their work. For a skill-based network to be successful, the composition of participants in terms of their organizations and business lines should be relatively streamlined. A facilitator typically needs access to information and knowledge and is expected to have a certain level of knowledge of the subject area and to keep up to date with related events and knowledge. One of the facilitators gave the example of a 3D printing network in which the participants relied on the facilitator to inform them about any new areas of knowledge that had been discovered since the last meeting.

Type 4: The "referral network" is a more mechanical and rigid type of interaction with the purpose of exchanging information, such as providing other participants with the names of new customers or products. Thus, value is directly measured through participation. Smaller businesses often rely on these networks to explore new business opportunities. Referral networks are often heterogeneous in their composition to avoid saturate the network with multiple businesses that compete for customers. One interviewee noted that his referral network took turns hosting and facilitating, and the host always had a strict set of guidelines and an agenda to follow.

Type 5: The "exchange of experience network" is a network whose participants have high levels of trust and knowledge-sharing. Participants are encouraged to share their experiences and give each other advice. Participants determine themselves what they want to do or focus on, so the purpose often changes over time. The facilitator must be trustworthy and listen to the participants while also reinvigorating the activities and themes from time to time to keep the discussion fresh. Some of the interviewees mentioned a strategic network that had been going on for years, and the participants had a high social stake between them. However, because the group's facilitators changed often, the participants felt that very few new ideas were introduced to the group and as though the purpose should be revised or the network terminated.

Type 6: The "innovation network" is similar to a project network, although the project network often has a known solution that has to be designed, applied, and implemented, and the innovation network does not. As such, the innovation network can be seen as the precursor to a project network, which makes a set timeframe and measurable success criteria difficult because innovation means finding something new. In the interviews, we heard about a minor network group of three farmers and one biologist that had been established to explore new ways to irrigate. This network illustrates the need for heterogeneous composition, as varied knowledge of an area is often needed to create innovative ideas.

4.2 Application of Artifact(S)

The three artifacts provide a way to gain knowledge about a knowledge network at a moment in time and to relate that status to the network's overall process. The next section draws on three use scenarios from three stakeholder groups.

Use by network sponsor
Network sponsors are primarily interested in establishing an overview of the knowledge network groups for which they are responsible. As such, these stakeholders

Fig. 5 Comparison between measured values (dotted lines) and the tolerance levels (bubbles on the dimension spectrum) of an archetypical innovation network

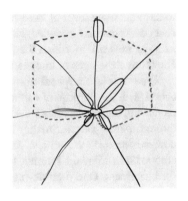

resemble typical managers, as it is in their interest that their groups are doing well. Because they typically have multiple groups, network sponsors need some way to simplify and reduce the vast amount of information about each network into key performance indicators. The artifact allows them to open a report on each knowledge network through the SAS for a quick visual overview of where the network may be experiencing problems. Since all of the artifacts are designed to create a foundation for dialogue, the network sponsor can also use the visual overview in future status meetings with facilitators to gain more qualitative information about what the measured dimensions could mean and how to mitigate potential risks. For example, for a sprout network a "medium" value for "size" could indicate a need to work on the network's content, purpose, or public relations to gain more participants or to shut it down, as a sprout network requires a large number of members, preferably with heterogeneous composition of backgrounds. See Fig. 5 for an example of such a visualization.

Another example of using the artifacts is when the network sponsor is interested in establishing a knowledge network, such as when external funding is acquired that is strategically marked for establishing and creating innovation in certain topics. In this case, the network sponsor would use the NSM to draft the main purpose of the new knowledge network and then use existing sprout networks to find potential participants for the network.

Use by network facilitators

Facilitators have an interest in ensuring that their networks thrive, but since they are much closer to the networks than the network sponsor is, the simplified measurement dimensions are likely to be limited. Instead, the facilitator may send the network's participants a questionnaire at regular intervals (e.g., three months) and then adjust the values of the SAS based on the type of network and suggestions from the questionnaire of actions that can be taken to increase or decrease the network's values. The network facilitator can use the aggregated, anonymous responses to identify areas where he or she may have misunderstood the general consensus of the participants or even overlooked some perceptions that can be difficult to share in the group's discussions, such as perceptions related to the facilitator or the activities being planned and performed during network meetings.

Another possibility for the facilitator's use of the SAS artifact is to engage other facilitators in the same organization in an experience-sharing knowledge network group and use the SAS results to get feedback from other facilitators on how their practices can be improved. The facilitators can also use the KNC and the NSM with their participants to discuss in which state of the NSM the knowledge network currently resides and how to move to another desired state. For example, a learning network usually requires a moderate number of participants with relatively uniform composition of backgrounds in terms of experience and type of organization to limit the content of each network meeting. If a facilitator realizes that there are issues with the composition of the participants, he or she can divide the network into smaller networks with more homogeneous participant backgrounds (if the network is large enough). Another possibility provided by the SAS is to divide the participants into smaller groups based on their interests and backgrounds to ensure that a collective idea of how to solve problems is used. The SAS and KNC may even be used to evaluate or terminate the knowledge network group if its purpose has been attained or is no longer relevant or if the participants no longer want to pursue its purpose (Fig. 6).

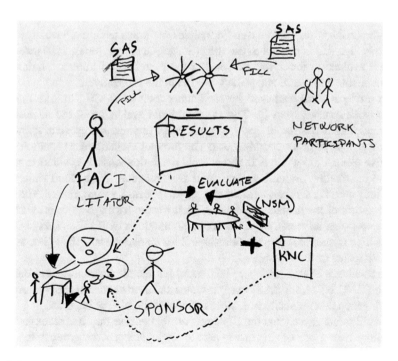

Fig. 6 Use case(s) for the main stakeholders using the three artifacts

As such, the results of the SAS encourage human interactions and dialogue regarding the groups' values in the dimensions, and can be used for continuous improvement.

Use by network participants

The network participants can use the artifacts in multiple ways. For an existing knowledge network group, continuous use of the SAS can provide a structure for reflection on whether the participants gain value from participating in the group. The SAS can also create a focus on the network participants as active agents of the network, as through its assessments they can impact the shape of the network. In short, the SAS can increase participation and involvement from the participants, rather than letting them lie back and let the facilitator do the work. A central area for a knowledge network is the power that social relationships hold in terms of willingness to participate. If social relationships are strong, which the sharing dimension can be used to indicate, then there are also strong opportunities for creating multiple new knowledge networks with the original participants based, for example, on their common interest in new topics.

4.3   Evaluation of Artifact(S)

The three artifacts rely heavily on "principles of implementation," which refer to the knowledge that is needed to use the artifacts (Gregor & Jones, 2007). As such, a central evaluation focus was on whether the principles of implementation were understandable and useful and provided value to the stakeholders.

The artifacts were evaluated by facilitators internal to CF Thy and the original network sponsor from CF Thy. An additional evaluation of the artifacts was performed with two external facilitators who were facilitators of several knowledge network groups in other organizations. The internal facilitators' evaluation was a formative evaluation, while both the internal network sponsor's evaluation and the external facilitators' evaluations were held as summative "think aloud" interviews, where they used the artifacts and commented on them as they progressed. The longitudinal nature of the artifacts made it difficult for the participants to provide evaluations, as doing so would have required naturalistic ex post strategies outside the initial scope of the DSR project. See Table 2 for an overview of the types, lengths, and participants of the evaluations.

The facilitator evaluations were held as "think aloud" interviews, and the three artifacts (KNC, NSM, and SAS) were presented and used on an exemplary knowledge network group that the facilitators were actively facilitating at the time.

All facilitators agreed that the KNC was useful because they had all experienced frustrations over a lack of structure in how to establish a network group in the initiation phases. All facilitators agreed that the NSM correctly represented how network groups evolved, but since they were already aware of this, it held little value for them. However, the network sponsor found the NSM, combined with the KNC, very

Table 2 Participant data in evaluation laps 2 and 3. "FAC'' is short for ''facilitator''

Evaluation participant	Role	Years of experience	Type of evaluation	Length in minutes	Current work with networks	Main result
Facilitator (FAC) 1	Internal facilitator (CF Thy)	2+	Formative	2 × 65	Exchange-of-experience networks	The importance of reinvigorating a network using the KNC
FAC 2	Internal facilitator (CF Thy)	17+	Formative	1 × 74	Skill-based network	The importance of keeping up to date and livening up activities
FAC 3	Internal facilitator (CF Thy)	4+	Formative	1 × 76	Innovation network	Innovation networks and their composition
FAC 4	Internal facilitator (CF Thy)	4+	Formative	1 × 71	Project network	Notion of network sprouts and the difficulties of coordination and "no-shows"
FAC 5	Internal facilitator (CF Thy)	10+	Formative	1 × 58	Network sprouts	Clusters of networks and network sprouts
Steen	External facilitator (Learning-Driven Innovation)	15+	Summative	1 × 96	Network sprouts and exchange-of-experience networks	The various types of networks were useful and caused reflection on how to handle them with the network sponsor
Jonas	External facilitator (Danish IT)	5+	Summative	1 × 112	Skill-based networks	Reflections on actions to take as a facilitator to improve the network were useful
John	Internal sponsor (CF Thy)	N/A	Summative	1 × 20	N/A	The immediate value from the KNC was high

useful. The facilitators differed in experience, competencies, and personality and had currently active network groups that they were facilitating. As a result, they each found useful application of the artifacts on various levels. One of the facilitators (FAC 2), who had considerable experience, did not see the usefulness of the proposals of facilitator actions at the end of the SAS, as they were too simple and she already knew how to handle the issues that arose through tools and activities. However, she found the assessment with visualization itself very useful. The idea of using the SAS with other facilitators (perhaps in a facilitator knowledge network group) and sharing knowledge, learning, and reflecting on the problems she faced was of much more value. She also pointed out that she had sorely missed a tool like the KNC as a standard form for every knowledge network with which she engaged. Some of the less experienced facilitators found the KNC highly useful as well for initiating their network groups with the participants, and they felt that it could be used as a list of guidelines list for contacting members who rarely showed up or seemed uninterested. This would then be an objective way to weed out participants who should be removed. The SAS was also useful to the less experienced facilitators, as a couple of them had network groups that were languishing in their pursuit of their purpose. This particular finding actually echoed from the network participants' focus group interviews, where several participants noted that their network group really should be changed or "rebooted" with the use of a new KNC since the network had fulfilled its original purpose (exploring and learning about strategic management). The participants continued meeting only because they enjoyed each other's company, not for any particular professional reason.

The most important insights from the summative external facilitator evaluation included the notion that more types of knowledge networks could exist or that certain networks were "hybrid" networks. Another insight was that, by simply answering the questions, the facilitators reflected on their answers. One of the facilitators noted that scoring his own networks made him aware of many issues of which he had been unaware regarding his own practice as a facilitator. Another facilitator mentioned issues with the purpose and scope of one of his network groups based on the multiple network sponsors who were attached. His own activities and facilitation were directly related to the purpose he had been told from the network sponsors, yet the differences between them meant that the network sponsors had to agree on a single focus for the network if it was to progress.

The final summative evaluation came from the network sponsor, who primarily focused on the KNC and implemented it as a standard practice for establishing networks. He proudly proclaimed that this was a part of his organization's marketing on its website and that the organization had applied the KNC to the initiation of new networks. The usefulness and implementation of the SAS and NSM were not discussed because of their longitudinal nature.

4.4 Growth of Design Theory

The main kernel theory for the design method was the wicked design problem solution approach called the "Design Theory Nexus" (Pries-Heje & Baskerville, 2008). This approach was used and incorporated into two conference papers and a journal paper. While we deviated from the approach (e.g., literature on solution approaches was scarce, and empirical methods were used to initiate the process), the process of writing papers and dissecting the DSR into multiple elements resulted in the emergence of an increasingly strong design theory.

The first conference paper, Hansen and Pries-Heje (2016), was an exploration of design principles for designing tools to be used between people in inter-organizational collaboration settings. This paper explored the three artifacts from a design process perspective that was closely focused on the classical DSR approach.

The second conference paper, Pries-Heje and Hansen (2016), focused on the relationships among the participants to determine how to design for value-creation in socially constructed settings. The paper focused on the domain and the archetypes of knowledge networks and the important relationships among elements, participants, and facilitators.

Finally, the journal paper, Hansen and Pries-Heje (2017), extended and elaborated on our analysis of the design principles and presented five principles as part of a design theory for building tools to support networks of people:

Principle 1 (P1)   The principle of enabling continuous process improvement
Principle 2 (P2)   The principle of creating participatory value
Principle 3 (P3)   The principle of visualizing dimensional status
Principle 4 (P4)   The principle of comparing network types to contextual ideals
Principle 5 (P5)   The principle of visualizing potential actions.

5 Key Lessons

The DSR had multiple key success factors. That all stakeholders were broadly engaged in the process as it progressed was a large part of its success. Specifically, the evaluation with facilitators was central to our understanding the complexity of the problem space and the design. We also experienced a constant need to balance thinking about possible solutions in a "systems thinking" approach, where all the variables must at some point be represented by a number value so the design researcher could discuss and evaluate internally while also exploring the domain of CF Thy and the context of the knowledge network groups.

The project ended with three key lessons learned: (1) DSR can be used to increase knowledge about a domain by *extending kernel theory*; (2) information technology tools used in groups must be designed to support facilitated knowledge creation; and (3) conflicting stakeholder interests can be overcome by designing artifacts that support the assessment of both process and structure.

5.1   DSR Can Be Used to Increase Knowledge About a Domain by Extending Kernel Theory

In practice, DSR projects tend to reveal knowledge and central concepts regarding the domain in which it is applied. Sometimes the domains are largely unexplored, and a pragmatic approach to uncovering kernel theories from similar domains must be taken. Once a DSR project is applied by constructing an artifact, the artifact itself can be seen as an intervention in the existing work practice, much like an action research project. When the artifacts were tested, the tests revealed additional aspects of the domain of knowledge networks, so we found that there are invisible walls in learning about the domain that cannot be passed or seen until something tangible has been designed and tested. While this finding is not new, evaluation of the artifacts led to several insights into the context of knowledge networks, where the difference between domain and context is essential. While the domain was focused on small and medium-sized start-up entrepreneurial firms in the Thy region, the context was much more general, revolving around the phenomena of interorganizational knowledge networks. Exploring, designing, and evaluating the specific empirical domain, combined with the literature, produced new insights to be used as *kernel theory extensions*. Kernel theory extensions revealed the concepts of the phenomena of knowledge network groups as:

- situational: The purpose and needs of knowledge networks are influenced by their participants, available resources, and other variables that make it impossible to determine a best path or situation in a given situation.
- facilitative: The motivation of a knowledge network and its participants are strongly influenced by who is facilitating its meetings and how the meetings are facilitated.
- stakeholder-dependent: The interests of knowledge networks in general depend heavily on the networks' stakeholders—the network sponsors, facilitators, and participants.
- structurally dependent: The budget, administration, and formal rules of a network can be considered its structural foundation within which procedural change can occur, but rarely will the changes to a network exceed these structures.
- containing central dimensions: A knowledge network can be defined by seven or more dimensions.
- instances of archetypical types: A knowledge network is typically an instance of an archetype, of which we defined six.
- containing tolerance levels that are socially constructed: The values of a knowledge network's dimensions are not absolute but are indicators of its participants' coherence. For each knowledge network, certain tolerance levels exist within which the network can be considered functional, even if certain levels are exceeded.
- founded on a state model: The process of a knowledge network, from initiation to termination, occurs in multiple stages and can be renegotiated, as these stages

typically follow a flow but can abruptly return to other states by, for example, re-initiating or terminating because of a lack of interest.

The kernel theory and its extension provided here are not prescriptive, so the kernel theory is not a design theory (Gregor & Jones, 2007). Instead, it can be seen as containing analytical and explanatory elements in terms of being able to understand, analyze, and disseminate knowledge network groups in general and as encompassing more than a specific instance of a knowledge network. As such, its concepts can be used to analyze how well a knowledge network is doing and explain why it has problems, if it does.

5.2 Information Technology Tools Used in Groups Must Be Designed to Support Facilitated Knowledge Creation

The second major lesson learned relates to the ontological and epistemological connotations of the previous extension of the kernel theory. When people are connected through artifacts, measuring parameters as dimensions should be done situationally, not normatively. Previous attempts in other domains (Avison & Pries-Heje, 2008) have shown that best practices can be found, but they are highly context-dependent and will work well only as long as the human participants who are using the tools choose to play along. The idea that the context for which the design was made was evolutionary and constantly changing made it difficult to apply a static tool. A normative, dynamic process tool failed as well because it did not adhere to the needs of two of the central stakeholders: knowledge network participants and facilitator. Instead, the new design problem became that of designing a tool that could be used less as an absolute truth than as a facilitative tool for engaging constructive dialogue that may change the desired path.

5.3 Conflicting Stakeholder Interests Can Be Overcome by Designing Artifacts that Support the Assessment of Both Process and Structure

Finally, the third lesson learned was that it is possible to design one or more artifacts that together can encompass all stakeholders' needs. From a critical point of view, stakeholder conflict is inherent in any organization, which may never change. The theme of stakeholder conflict is a classical theme known from information systems and change management (Keen, 1981). The archetypical network sponsor could be considered "top management" or "a project owner" who owns the means of production and resources and is interested in key performance indicators to monitor the overall work systems in progress. Facilitators could be considered "middle managers" or "project managers" who are responsible for ensuring that results are delivered

while communicating and delivering status reports to top management. The participants of a network group could be considered "employees" with their own agendas,
as well as project participants who are given extrinsic incentives to make progress
with the project. Thus, motivations and interests among the stakeholders differ since
a network sponsor primarily has extrinsic interests (living up to some kind of performance and net worth), a facilitator has both intrinsic and extrinsic interests (wanting
to improve his or her own facilitation competencies while also being paid to perform
well), and network participants have purely intrinsic interests (e.g., "what's in it
for me?"). With these classical archetypes in play, it becomes clear that conflicts
and interests may arise in terms of how tools should look and work and even what
information should be required, assessed, analyzed, and revealed—and for whom.
However, we found that enough common interests were present so they could be
collected and handled by combining cross-sections of existing measurements with a
process approach used over time.

5.4   Limitations and Further Research

The size and scope of the project overwhelmed us, which leads to the question
concerning what should have been done differently. With three stakeholder groups
to handle and three artifacts, the final design suffered in terms of both the depth and
the level of the technology.

Regarding the depth of the artifacts, the proposed design theory remained nascent,
providing several central answers regarding the specificity of the elements, such as
the number of measurements, the phrasing of questions, and the tolerance levels
presented in the archetypical knowledge networks. As DSR projects become increasingly complex, the minor artifacts and elements tend to be downplayed in favor of
overall problem-solving. While we found that the artifacts lived up to their purpose
in the sense that the case organization and external facilitators were satisfied, the artifacts and the specific values, wording, and phrases should be further researched and
evaluated. Questions' metrics, tolerance levels, and so on are all aspects of the design
theory that should be explored further. The minor elements of the artifact could need
more rigid and systematic evaluation, although the results were the consequence of
finding a balance between relevance and rigor. The process did suffer from the issues
that knowledge network groups have: evaluating the proposed artifacts to evaluate
in terms of immediate usefulness may be straightforward, although the artifacts'
longitudinal purpose can make it more difficult because network groups work well
only after six to twelve months. Therefore, exploring the use of the artifacts further
is central to the network's ongoing learning and evolution.

Another important point was that identifying a problem and finding solutions
required many resources that were spent on the initial artifacts and the principles
of implementation, with little time left to develop and improve the artifacts in the
technical realm. While a more technical and automatic method would have been
beneficial, having to balance design with technical construction was not feasible

because of a lack of resources. Nevertheless, the importance of making plans for construction and organizational implementation of low-tech artifacts should not be understated.

References

Avison, D., & Pries-Heje, J. (2008). Flexible information systems development: Designing an appropriate methodology for different situations. In *Proceedings of the International Conference on Enterprise Information Systems 2007* (pp. 212–224).

Baskerville, R., & Dulipovici, A. (2006). The theoretical foundations of knowledge management. *Knowledge Management Research & Practice, 4*(2), 83–105.

Batonda, G., & Perry, C. (2003). Approaches to relationship development processes in inter-firm networks. *European Journal of Marketing, 37*(10), 1457–1484.

Brown, J., & Duguid, P. (1991). Organizational learning and communities-of-practice: Toward a unified view of working, learning, and innovation. *Organization Science, 2*(1), 40–57.

Busquets, J. (2010). Orchestrating smart business network dynamics for innovation. *European Journal of Information Systems, 19*(4), 481–493.

Connell, J., & Voola, R. (2007). Strategic alliances and knowledge sharing: Synergies or silos? *Journal of Knowledge Management, 11*(3), 52–66. https://doi.org/10.1108/13673270710752108.

Cook, S. D. N., & Brown, J. S. (1999). Bridging epistemologies: The generative dance between organizational knowledge and organizational knowing. *Organization Science, 10*(4), 381–400.

Dolińska, M. (2015). Knowledge based development of innovative companies within the framework of innovation networks. *Innovation: Organization & Management, 17*(3), 323–340.

Ghisi, F. A., & Martinelli, D. P. (2006). Systemic view of interorganisational relationships: An analysis of business networks. *Systemic Practice and Action Research, 19*(5), 461–473.

Gregor, S., & Jones, D. (2007). The anatomy of a design theory. *Journal of the Association for Information Systems, 8*(5), 312–335.

Gruenfeld, D. H., Mannix, E. A., Williams, K. Y., & Neale, M. A. (1996). Group composition and decision making: How member familiarity and information distribution affect process and performance. *Organizational Behavior and Human Decision Processes, 67*(1), 1–15.

Hanna, V., & Walsh, K. (2002). Small firm networks: A successful approach to innovation? *R&D Management, 32*(3), 201–207.

Hansen, M. R. P., & Pries-Heje, J. (2016). Out of the bottle: Design principles for GENIE tools (Group-Focused Engagement and Network Innovation Environment). In *Proceedings of the 4th International Conference on Design Science Research in Information Systems and Technology* (pp. 131–146). Springer, Cham. https://doi.org/10.1007/978-3-319-39294-3_9.

Hansen, M. R. P., & Pries-Heje, J. (2017). Value creation in knowledge networks. Five design principles. *Scandinavian Journal of Information Systems, 29*(2), 26.

Hedlund, G. (1994). A model of knowledge management and the N-Form corporation. *Strategic Management Journal, 15*(S2), 73–90.

Hevner, A. R., March, S. T., Park, J., & Ram, S. (2004). Design science in information systems research. *MIS Quarterly, 28*(1), 75–105.

Jack, S., Moult, S., Anderson, A. R., & Dodd, S. (2010). An entrepreneurial network evolving: Patterns of change. *International Small Business Journal, 28*(4), 315–337. https://doi.org/10.1177/0266242610363525.

Keen, P. G. W. (1981). Information Systems and Organizational Change. *Communications of the ACM, 24*(1), 10.

Kirkels, Y., & Duysters, G. (2010). Brokerage in SME networks. *Research Policy, 39*(3), 375–385. https://doi.org/10.1016/j.respol.2010.01.005.

Klerkx, L., Hall, A., & Leeuwis, C. (2009). Strengthening agricultural innovation capacity: Are innovation brokers the answer? *International Journal of Agricultural Resources and Ecology, 8*(5/6), 409. https://doi.org/10.1504/ijarge.2009.032643.

Kolb, A. Y., & Kolb, D. A. (2005). Learning styles and learning spaces: Enhancing experiential learning in higher education. *Academy of Management Learning & Education, 4*(2), 193–212.

Lee, A. S., & Baskerville, R. L. (2003). Generalizing generalizability in information systems research. *Information Systems Research, 14*(3), 221–243. https://doi.org/10.1287/isre.14.3.221. 16560.

Mitchell, J. C. (1974). Social networks. *Annual Review of Anthropology, 3*(1), 279–299.

Möller, K., Rajala, A., & Svahn, S. (2005). Strategic business nets – Their type and management. *Journal of Business Research, 58*(9), 1274–1284. https://doi.org/10.1016/j.jbusres.2003.05.002.

Nonaka, I., Takeuchi, H., & Umemoto, K. (1996). A theory of organizational knowledge creation. *International Journal of Technology Management, 11*(7–8), 833–845.

Orey, M. (Ed.). (2010). Bloom's taxonomy. In *Emerging perspectives on learning, teaching, and technology* (pp. 41–48). Global Text.

Polanyi, M., & Sen, A. (2009). *The tacit dimension*. Chicago and London: University of Chicago press.

Porras, S. T., Clegg, S., & Crawford, J. T. (2004). Trust as networking knowledge: Precedents from Australia. *Asia Pacific Journal of Management, 21*(3), 345–363.

Pries-Heje, J., & Baskerville, R. (2008). The design theory Nexus. *MIS Quarterly, 32*(4), 731–755.

Pries-Heje, J., & Hansen, M. R. P. (2016). Net up your innovation value. In U. Lundh Snis (Ed.), *Nordic contributions in IS research* (pp. 70–85). Springer.

Rittel, H. W. J., & Webber, M. M. (1973). Dilemmas in a general theory of planning. *Policy Sciences, 4*(2), 155–169.

Schwarz, R. (2002). *The skilled facilitator: A comprehensive resource for consultants, facilitators, managers, trainers, and coaches*. San Fransisco: Wiley.

Smart, P., Bessant, J., & Gupta, A. (2007). Towards technological rules for designing innovation networks: A dynamic capabilities view. *International Journal of Operations & Production Management, 27*(10), 1069–1092. https://doi.org/10.1108/01443570710820639.

Tsoukas, H. (2009). A dialogical approach to the creation of new knowledge in organizations. *Organization Science, 20*(6), 941–957.

Zhao, X., Frese, M., & Giardini, A. (2010). Business owners network size and business growth in China: The role of comprehensive social competency. *Entrepreneurship & Regional Development, 22*(7–8), 675–705. https://doi.org/10.1080/08985620903171376.

DSR in Application Domains

Setting Sail for Data-Driven Decision-Making an Action Design Research Case from the Maritime Industry

Tiemo Thiess and Oliver Müller

Abstract To react to new market dynamics, OEM, one of the largest marine equipment manufacturers in the world, was facing the task of transforming its aftersales business from key-account-manager-driven sales processes to more proactive and customer-centric processes. The company had recently implemented an organization-wide customer relationship management (CRM) system to facilitate this transformation. However, the system was not fully used because of a lack of proactive work practices that the system could support. Based on this diagnosis, we developed and applied a method for data-driven lead-generation that uses advanced analytics and automation to leverage internal and external data sources to identify and assess sales leads. To guide the design process, we ingrained the artifact with theory about data-driven decision-making (DDD) and value creation in the form of initial design principles. After several iterations of building the artifact, examining the organizational context, and evaluating the changes that those interventions introduced, we formalized a set of design principles and abstracted them to the broader class of DDD artifacts, highlighting decision quality but also the importance of model comprehensibility, domain knowledge, and actionability of results.

1 Introduction

Marine equipment manufacturers have traditionally focused their efforts on the product development phase in the product lifecycle and the market for newly built main engines and their designs. However, shipbuilders and marine equipment manufacturers have recently suffered from a major drop in demand for newly built vessels and engines because of an over-supply of certain types of vessels in the market. As a result, equipment manufacturers have challenged their traditional business

T. Thiess · O. Müller (✉)
IT University of Copenhagen, Copenhagen, Denmark
e-mail: olmy@itu.dk

T. Thiess
e-mail: tith@itu.dk

© Springer Nature Switzerland AG 2020
J. vom Brocke et al. (eds.), *Design Science Research. Cases*, Progress in IS,
https://doi.org/10.1007/978-3-030-46781-4_12

291

models and shifted their focus from a traditional product-centric approach to a holistic customer-centric approach. In a customer-centric approach, the aftersales phase in the product lifecycle offers considerable potential for innovation. In the approximately twenty years of marine engines' lives, manufacturers generate most of their earnings from sales of spare parts and services like maintenance, repair, and overhaul. As a result, the market for aftersales products and services is much more competitive than the market for newly built engines, in part because the barriers to entry are much lower, as marine engines usually do not require original spare parts or service from only the engine producers.

Against this background, we started an action design research (ADR; Sein, Purao, & Lindgren, 2011) project at OEM (an alias is used for pseudonymization), one of the biggest marine equipment manufacturers in the world. OEM had recently implemented a company-wide customer relationship management (CRM) system to facilitate the transformation from a product-centric to a customer-centric approach in their aftersales business. The CRM system is a promising and necessary tool for this endeavor, but OEM's sales processes had been predominantly key-account-driven and were based on pull mechanisms. Therefore, the existing sales processes were not well aligned with the CRM system's functionalities, which are intended to afford proactive (rather than reactive) sales practices based on a concept of lead and opportunity management. This assessment led us to formulate our first problem diagnosis:

- Under-use of CRM system because of a lack of proactive business processes

We recognized this problem diagnosis as a knowledge-creation opportunity for generating design theory about information systems, particularly about data-driven decision-making (DDD) artifacts. DDD describes organizational decision-making practices that emphasize the use of data and statistical analysis instead of relying only on human judgment (Brynjolfsson, Hitt, & Kim, 2011). Existing research strongly suggests that DDD improves the quality of individual decision-making and generates business value at the organization level (Brynjolfsson et al., 2011; vom Brocke, Debortoli, Müller, & Reuter, 2014; Müller, Fay, & vom Brocke, 2018). However, the current body of knowledge on DDD lacks prescriptive knowledge on how to design and implement it in complex organizational settings. According to Sharma, Mithas, and Kankanhalli (2014), DDD artifacts do not create value simply by being applied; their output must be further processed into actionable judgments. The conversion from insights to decisions to actions and business value appears to be especially challenging (Sharma et al., 2014) in part because the implementation of DDD, unlike large enterprise systems, is often not accompanied by change-management activities (Hollander, Vroom, & Yetton, 1973; Kayande, De Bruyn, Lilien, Rangaswamy, & van Bruggen, 2009; SAS 2012; Ransbotham, Kiron, & Prentice, 2015), perhaps because of an over-emphasis on the extraction process of insights from data in scientific and industry publications. Therefore, there is a need for research that investigates the role of decision-making processes, human judgment, and change management in generating the outcome of DDD implementations (Sharma et al., 2014).

Another diagnosis that resulted from the initial problem evaluation was that, among the aftersales organization's portfolio of analytical apps, the apps with the most use were those that support and improve an existing business process. In contrast, more explorative apps, which are not embedded in a current or new business process, had the least use, even though, in the long run, they might be much more promising than others. This observation supports Wu, Hitt, and Lou's (2017) finding that the value generated from DDD is mostly exploitative. There is a need to develop business processes around DDD solutions, thus shifting the focus in DDD away from the data-to-insight process alone to the holistic data-to-insight-to-decision-to-value process (Sharma et al., 2014) to increase user adoption and value creation of DDD artifacts. This observation led us to formulate our second problem diagnosis:

- No business process embeddedness in low-use DDD applications.

Based on those diagnostics, we formulated the following research question:

- How can proactive CRM processes be enabled via DDD?

Against this background, this chapter reports the results of a multi-year ADR project in which IT artifacts for DDD were designed and implemented at one of the world's largest ship engine manufacturers.[1]

2 The Context

OEM is the power engineering arm of Engineering AG (an alias is used for pseudonymization). OEM is primarily a manufacturer of large bore 2- and 4-stroke diesel engines that can be used in marine vessels and power plants, but it also produces gas engines, dual fuel engines, and turbomachinery. OEM also provides power-generating 4-stroke engines, propulsion solutions, and turbochargers for marine vessels.

OEM has a global aftersales organization that offers original spare parts and ad hoc and contract-based operation and maintenance service via a worldwide network of local sales companies. The ADR case presented here is situated in the marine engine aftersales-service part of OEM. The marine engine aftersales market is a complex and dynamic market that depends heavily on the number of newly built high-sea ships. Overcapacity in the supply of ships currently pressures the market, causing OEM's aftersales-service business to grow in importance, as ship owners prefer exploiting and upgrading their existing fleets to ordering new ships, so customers become more interested in long-term service agreements, which are more like subscription-based business models.

---

[1]Earlier stages and iterations of the artifact of this ADR study have been reported in an unpublished master's thesis and, with a focus on developed design theory, in the proceedings of the European Conference on Information Systems (Thiess & Müller, 2018).

The growing importance of the aftersales service business forced the company to undergo significant changes in their sales processes, which have been built on long and close customer relationships with a strong focus on key-account-management practices. To leverage the potential of the aftersales market, OEM wants to enhance its traditional sales approach, for instance, via a digitization initiative. A cornerstone of this initiative is to create more proactive sales processes and services that are built on in-depth knowledge of their customers' needs.

The market for newly built ships is highly transparent. Most major yards are known, as are the main competitors in this market. Moreover, new ships have to be registered with the International Maritime Organization (IMO), which requires detailed information on the type of ship, the ownership structure, and the type of engine. In this market, OEM's large licensee partners are valuable business partners that produce most of OEM's engines, for which OEM grants them access to its state-of-the-art and continually improved designs. In contrast, in the aftersales business, it is often unclear who the competitors are, as marine engines can be serviced by many, often small, companies that do not necessarily have to use original spare parts for repairs. In addition, the licensee partners that are producing engines for OEM are themselves among OEM's strongest competitors in the aftersales market, as they can use OEM's regional network and customer relationships. What's more, as most engines are sold without long-term service agreements, the aftersales market is characterized by high uncertainty, especially with regards to CRM and customer life-cycle management. For instance, it is difficult to define when an aftersales customer relationship starts, when it ends, and what sales volume it will generate.

Current sales practices in the aftersales market are often based on recommendations regarding how many spare parts an engine should use for a certain number of running hours to guarantee high performance. However, information about an engine's running hours are not always easy to obtain, as the engines are owned by the ship owners, and information on running hours is retrievable only from particular customers during periodic on-board service visits. Another problem is that service visits are documented in text form, so from a data perspective, they are not in an easily analyzable format. Consequently, the information from these reports is not stored in the organization's data warehouse, creating situations in which sales and engineering professionals lack a coherent overview of customers because they have to deal with several unconnected lists and reports in varying formats. Because of the challenges in obtaining an engine's running hours, the ship's age, together with an expert estimation, is typically used as a proxy for running hours. This approach is intuitive and comfortable but not always accurate, as it does not incorporate information about, for example, downtime, breakdowns, or dry-dockings. Therefore, in the context of OEM's digitization initiative, projects were initiated to improve the quality of data for engines' running hours, thereby facilitating more accurate product-lifecycle management. One of these projects uses satellite data on ships' positions to estimate running hours, while another builds an Internet-of-Things (IoT) infrastructure that facilitates the collection and transmission of running hours and other performance data via sensor networks. The goal is to monitor running hours and other performance indicators of connected equipment centrally so OEM's technical experts can optimize engine operations and maintenance.

For the large 2-stroke main engines, another driver of the aftersales business is the dry-dockings of ships that occur approximately every five years because they are required by international shipping societies before certifications can be granted or renewed (International Maritime Organization, 2015). Dry-docking may also be done for cleaning, hull maintenance, damage repair, and other unplanned events. As most systems and engines on board are turned off during dry-docking, it is a perfect occasion to perform minor and major overhauls on the engines. However, as with the running hours, when such a dry-docking is taking place is not always easy to know. External databases contain data about the approximate date of the next dry-docking that the registration societies require, but where the dry-docking is taking place and the date on which it actually takes place is difficult to determine.

These problems are just two examples of challenges that companies in non-contractual market settings face. These settings are usually characterized by a high degree of uncertainty regarding customer behavior and life-cycle management (Fader & Hardie, 2009), and when a customer makes its next purchase is usually unclear. Therefore, OEM is focusing on improving its long-term-service-agreement business in a gradual transformation from a mostly non-contractual to a mostly contractual setting. These developments go along with transforming the overall aftersales business model from a product-focused to a service- and customer-oriented model. As a result, increasingly fine-grained and high-quality customer data will become available to facilitate the delivery of smarter services (Beverungen et al., 2017), which is an opportunity to improve products and CRM.

CRM systems and proactive sales processes are today broadly applied in business-to-consumer (B2C) industries like private banking, but they are not used extensively by companies that operate in complex business-to-business (B2B) industries. Among the first implications of OEM's new customer-centric digitization initiative is the recent introduction of a company-wide CRM system, a unified platform that will help to align sales processes with improved product and customer lifecycle management, more customer centricity, and proactivity. The system gives OEM the opportunity to improve how it addresses its mostly non-contractual customer base and supports improvement in the company's understanding and identification of customers with a high potential need for long-term service contracts. Thus, it supports turning non-contractual customers into contractual customers. Relationships with contractual customers also benefit when OEM's abilities to prevent churn and generate up- and cross-selling effects improve. However, the platform is still in its implementation phase, so its full potential has not yet unfolded. Many existing business processes still need to be adapted to the new sales tool, and in many cases, entirely new proactive processes are required if the platform's capabilities are to be used fully.

Finally, it is necessary to define OEM's aftersales customers clearly. OEM's customer can be a shipowner or, more often, a technical manager of a ship who is authorized to order spare parts and other aftersales services (also called a motor manager). However, when OEM implements more advanced CRM practices, it can be helpful to define the customer as a particular ship or even as an engine on a ship, especially when sales activities need to be closely aligned with the product's lifecycle. The purchase of a certain combination of spare parts could indicate, for instance, a particular event in an engine's lifecycle. Such insights are much harder to gain when the broader definition of a customer as the technical manager of a ship is used because a technical manager is often responsible for not just one but a whole fleet of ships.

3 The Journey

3.1 The Action Design Research Process

To generate prescriptive design knowledge in the form of design principles, we employed ADR as a research method. ADR is "a research method for generating prescriptive design knowledge through building and evaluating ensemble IT artifacts in an organizational setting" (Sein et al., 2011, p. 40). ADR combines aspects of action research and design science research (Purao, Rossi, & Sein, 2010). In particular, the action-research-related concepts of diagnosing field problems, planning action, taking action, and evaluating the effects of the actions taken to specify general learnings (Susman & Evered, 1978) are reflected in the ADR method that Sein et al. (2011) propose. Moreover, and in contrast to traditional action research, ADR emphasizes the intervention into an organizational context via designing IT artifacts through an iterative building, intervention, and evaluation stage that adopt, for instance, the concepts of design cycles and rigor cycles from design science research (Hevner, 2007).

The ADR method has four main stages (Fig. 1). The first stage, the problem-formulation stage, is based on the principles of practice-inspired research and theory-ingrained artifacts and encourages researchers to identify or diagnose field problems and define them as knowledge-creation opportunities and, in particular, as opportunities to develop design theory in, for instance, the form of design principles. Sein et al. (2011) propose three ways of using prior theory in ADR: to structure the problem, to identify solutions, and to guide the actual design using design theories. The concept of ingraining IT artifacts with theory in ADR stems from the idea that IT artifacts are socio-technical assemblages and that researchers can manifest theory by embedding it in an artifact so it can be recognized in a social form (Orlikowski & Iacono, 2001).

The second stage, the building, intervention, and evaluation stage, with its principle of reciprocal shaping, acknowledges that IT artifacts shape and are shaped by the context in which they are applied. Another principle is mutual influence and learning among the roles involved in the design process, including researchers, practitioners, and end-users. The third principle of the building, intervention, and evaluation stage is authentic and concurrent evaluation of the artifact throughout the design process (Sein et al., 2011). In this regard, the design evaluation process proposed by ADR may differ from design science research, as in the latter, the relevance, design, and

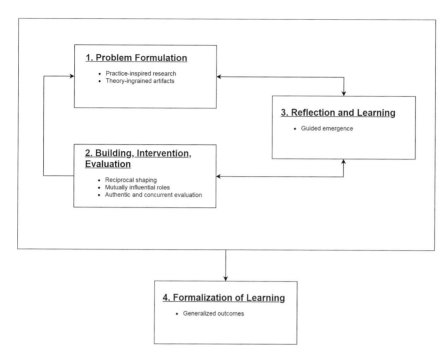

Fig. 1 The action design research (ADR) method (Sein et al., 2011)

rigor cycles are more separated and often follow a traditional stage-gate approach (Hevner, 2007). As a result, ADR focuses on keeping the artifact construction process as authentic and coherent with the design context as possible: "Consequently, authenticity is a more important ingredient for ADR than controlled settings" (Sein et al., 2011, p. 44). The third stage, the reflection and learning stage, is based on the principle of guided emergence and consists of reflecting on refinements of the problem and solution that are visible in the shape and state of the artifact. This stage enables the researchers to adapt and change initial design principles and to recognize newly emerging design principles (Sein et al., 2011).

Finally, in the fourth stage, what has been learned is formalized as generalizable outcomes. This can be difficult due to ADR´s situated nature. Sein et al. (2011) suggest three ways to generalize outcomes in ADR: the generalization of the problem instance, generalization of the solution instance, and derivation of design principles from the design research outcomes (Sein et al., 2011). In our case, we related the emerging design principles to existing theory, thus generalizing our ADR outcomes by means of abduction.

3.2 Our Journey

The ADR team consisted of the authors and a group of practitioners from OEM's aftersales analytics department. One of us, who had been working in the department for around eighteen months when the ADR project started, was employed as an industrial Ph.D. fellow at OEM. The practitioners included the application manager of the CRM system, the department manager, a senior data warehouse architect, and other data and business analysts from the department, who we occasionally involved. Besides the core ADR team, the end-users were valuable contributors of knowledge during the design process. Following the ADR methodology, we, as the researchers, were involved during all iterations and stages of the ADR process, from defining the problem to building and evaluating the artifact to developing and formalizing the design principles. The practitioners were involved primarily in building and evaluating the "alpha versions" of the artifact but also in supporting design decisions with their domain knowledge (Fig. 2).

We started our journey by analyzing the current situation at OEM to gain an understanding of the field problem. During the project, we were situated in OEM's aftersales business intelligence processes and analytics department, which is built around a mature data warehouse that builds the basis for a broad portfolio of analytical applications. The department is responsible for extracting, loading, and transforming transactional data from the company's enterprise resource planning (ERP) systems into ready-to-analyze multi-dimensional data models. Moreover, it is developing and frequently updating analytical reports for a broader audience of business users.

A diagnosis that guided our initial understanding of the problem was that, in the department's portfolio of analytical applications, applications that directly enhanced a business process or led to creating and implementing an entirely new business

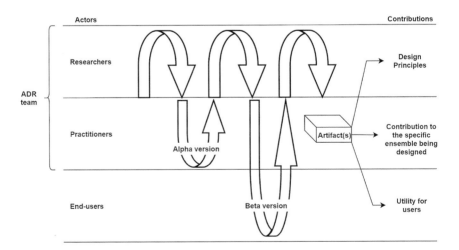

Fig. 2 ADR team, journey, and contributions (Sein et al., 2011)

process were the most frequently used and most successful ones. In contrast, more innovative applications, which often showed great potential but neither supported existing processes nor straightforwardly showed how a new process could be created around them, were less frequently used and less often successful. This observation is in line with Wu and Hitt's (2016) findings that the value created from analytics is primarily exploitative and only to a lesser degree exploratory. Therefore, we concluded that in order to generate sustainable business value from DDD applications, new business processes have to be developed alongside the actual DDD applications.

Moreover, we found that the new CRM platform had considerable potential for transforming sales processes to proactivity and customer-centricity. However, many of the existing sales processes were key-account-manager-driven, so they did not align well with the platform's capabilities. This observation led us to our second problem diagnosis: Even though the platform was ready to use from a technical perspective, it still lacked users, content, and proactive sales processes.

Based on our understanding of the problem, we evaluated several theories that could support our design process. We selected the cross-industry standard process for data mining (Shearer et al., 2000) to guide the design of the DDD artifacts and the information-decision-insights-supervision framework (IDA-S; Dearden, 2001) because of the principle of partial automation that we intended to incorporate into the artifact. We also chose Sharma et al.'s (2014) data-to-insight-insight-to-decision-decision-to-value conceptualization as a structural framework for integrating theory regarding the challenges of implementing DDD in the solution.

Our general understanding of the solution was informed by the initial design principles of proactivity, embeddedness, partial automation, and being data-driven that were derived from the diagnosed field problems and the selected theory. The main design objective was to design a DDD artifact that creates a new data-driven and proactive lead generation-process within the CRM system.

In the first iteration, the alpha version, we intended to generate data-driven leads through detecting and predicting significant events in the life cycle of an engine by relating a customer's spare parts transaction history for a particular engine to the recommended amount of spare parts consumption according to OEM's engine manuals. We received positive feedback when we presented this approach to senior managers at OEM. However, the project was complicated and required expertise from many stakeholders. Because of the complexity of the predictive models that were based on black-boxed machine-learning algorithms, it was difficult to explain the model's inner workings. As a result, and because of the project's overall complexity, we chose to look for a more generic and versatile approach for generating data-driven leads while keeping the already developed alpha version (Fig. 3) of the artifact in our back pockets for future iterations of the project.

In the second iteration, we revised the initial artifact and developed an operational pipeline for data-driven lead generation that is not limited to a specific type of lead (Thiess & Müller, 2018). Specifically, we wanted to use a wide variety of data sources that can be connected to the existing data warehouse so we can train and automatically deploy data models on it to generate sales leads. However, to avoid too many leads

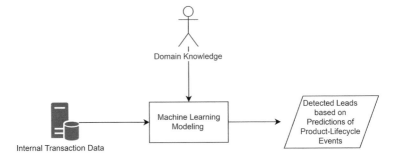

Fig. 3 Data-driven lead-generation artifact after the first iteration

being created automatically, we looked into the marketing literature to find ways to segment and prioritize customers and leads. We chose to train so-called buy-till-you-die models (BTYD) on customer data to calculate customers' future lifetime values (CLV). Such models enable segmenting and scoring of generated leads based on the predicted CLVs of the concerned customer base, so that, for instance, one can prioritize the top ten leads of customers with the highest future CLV. At this point, the focus of the artifact was on the lead-generation process and did not specify how the leads would be transferred to the CRM system and assigned to a responsible salesperson (Fig. 4).

In the development of the third iteration, the beta version (Fig. 5), we reached out to potential end-users of our artifact. In particular, we scheduled meetings with OEM's local sales companies to get feedback on the current version of the data-driven lead-generation artifact. In particular, we gathered information on the types of lead events

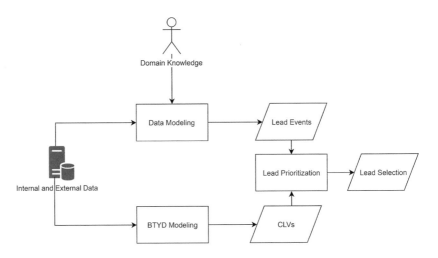

Fig. 4 Data-driven lead-generation artifact after the second iteration

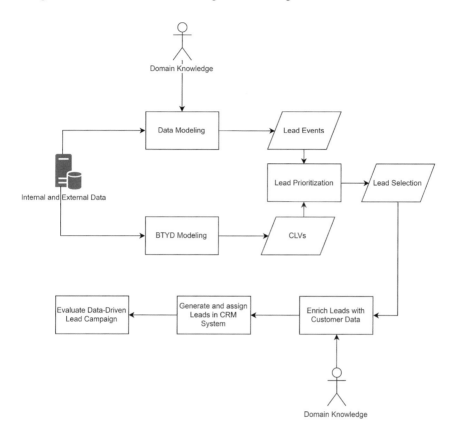

Fig. 5 Data-driven lead-generation artifact after the third iteration

that could be extracted from data. As a first lead campaign, changes in the ownership of vessels were identified as lead events that have a high potential to be converted into aftersales business for OEM. In addition, OEM's main aftersales customers are the technical managers of ships. The engines on those ships determine OEM's aftersales market; thus, when a ship's technical manager changes, the customer's relationship with OEM may change too. After a change in ownership, OEM might want to contact the new technical manager of a ship to ensure that the existing service relationship with the affected ship will continue. Changes in technical management are also good opportunities to re-evaluate the customer relationship and seek cross- and up-selling business.

To detect technical management changes automatically, we used an external database of worldwide high-sea ship registrations that is maintained by the international ship registration societies. To that point, OEM's sales professionals could get information regarding changes in the management of ships only via occasional talks with customers or updates of OEM's master data in the standard ERP systems. However, it can take months for this master data to be updated, and even if it is updated, a sales professional must still actively search for the information. To make this process more proactive and faster, we proposed keeping a change log of the technical management registrations in the database. This way, every change in the technical management of ships can be detected automatically via business rules and similarity-matching algorithms. Meetings with sales professionals uncovered an additional need for customer data to enable immediate decision-making and action-taking. In particular, the sales professionals did not want to open multiple IT systems to look for information that they require in order to follow up on leads. In reaction to this, we created two additional reports and attached them to the leads. The first report showed the quote and order history of a particular ship, and the second report contained metadata about the ship and its installed engines.

Another important design question was how to present the leads so they are usable in the CRM system. Because of its potential for automation, we chose an approach based on XML templates that are filled with data about the generated leads. The leads are then automatically assigned to a sales team and uploaded in bulk directly into the system.

In the fourth iteration, we abstracted the instantiation of a data-driven lead-generation pipeline to a method for generating data-driven leads in many contexts. This design iteration was informed by the experience that we gained from the design journey and from the conceptualization of a data-driven decision-making process by Sharma et al. (2014). The fourth iteration, the final solution artifact, is described in detail in the next section.

4 The Results—Data-Driven Lead Generation

4.1 Presentation of the Artifact: The Data-Driven Lead-Generation Artifact

This section introduces the final artifact and explains all of its parts in detail. The key result of the design journey is manifested in the data-driven lead-generation artifact depicted in Fig. 6. It is a method to generate data-driven lead pipelines that can flexibly accommodate various kinds of lead events and business contexts. The final artifact contains eight steps for creating business value via operational data-driven lead pipelines. The artifact is constructed as an iterative method that allows the user to fall back to prior steps when necessary. Steps 1 through 7 are the core of a data-driven lead-generation pipeline and account for a full data-driven decision-making process. Step 8 primarily evaluates whether a data-driven lead-generation pipeline should move from a beta state to a fully operational one. However, even after a pipeline is fully operational, it is advisable to apply Step 8 periodically to re-consolidate and evaluate the success of the pipeline.

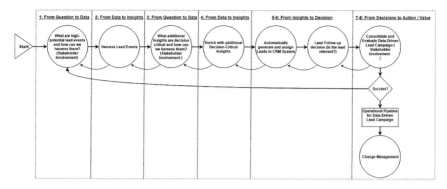

Fig. 6 The final data-driven lead generation artifact

The design of the artifact was informed by a generic DDD process that we built based on the terminology Sharma et al. (2014) introduced. The process consists of four main elements:

1. **From Question to Data**: This element defines an initial analysis question, which also entails planning and selecting an algorithmic analytics approach. Then data on which the planned analytics (algorithms) can be applied are made accessible (see Shearer et al., 2000; Leek & Peng, 2015, for a broader description of this element).
2. **From Data to Insight**: This element refers to the application and technical execution of the planned analytics instance (Sharma et al., 2014; Thiess & Müller, 2018).
3. **From Insight to Decision**: This element refers to the human-cognition-based decision-making process (Sharma et al., 2014; Thiess & Müller, 2018).
4. **From Decision to Action/Value**: This element establishes measures to implement decisions from which to create continuously positive effects (Sharma et al., 2014).

Overall, the final artifact has eight steps that are explained in the following sections.

Step 1: What are high-potential lead events? (Stakeholder involvement)
In Step 1 of the data-driven lead-generation artifact, stakeholders are involved in determining high-potential lead events for a given business context. An important stakeholder group to involve in this step is the potential users of a data-driven lead pipeline—likely those responsible for sales. When the capabilities regarding data-driven lead generation are already established, involvement can also be triggered by stakeholders, but sufficient change management (Kotter, 1995) is necessary to reach that point. In Step 1, high-potential lead events are identified by defining an initial analysis question, planning and selecting an initial analytics approach, and thinking about data sources that may be accessible to the analytics team. From an organization's perspective, data sources are internal and external. Internal data

are usually accessible via ERP systems and data warehouses but can also be, for example, SharePoint lists and text documents. External data can be accessed from public application programming interfaces (API). For instance, general economic and financial data can often be retrieved via APIs. Depending on the maturity of an organization's analytical capabilities, making the data for lead events accessible can be challenging, especially if the data quality is low and there is no master data management in place (Wagner & Hogan, 1996).

Step 2: Harness lead events
After detecting high-potential candidate leads, it is necessary to determine whether they can be harnessed algorithmically in a data-driven way such that the lead events are technically accessible. This step is not always straightforward; if a high-potential lead cannot be retrieved, users of the method can go back to Step 1.

External and internal data sources must usually be algorithmically processed and analyzed if they are to generate useful insights. The kinds of algorithms required can vary and depend on the particular lead event as well as on the organization's analytical capabilities. The main types of algorithms and insights generated by those algorithms are (Watson, 2014):

- **Descriptive** (e.g., summary statistics, grouping, aggregation)
- **Explorative** (e.g., clustering, dimensionality reduction, visualizations)
- **Predictive** (e.g., regression, classification, time-series analysis)
- **Prescriptive** (e.g., optimization, simulation)

Steps 1 and 2 together cover the elements from question to data and from data to insights in the DDD process and reflect a full data-mining and analytics sub-process. We suggest using the cross-industry standard process for data mining (CRISP-DM; Shearer et al., 2000) for guidance in undertaking Steps 1 and 2.

Step 3: What additional insights are decision-critical? (Stakeholder involvement)
After high-potential lead events have been identified and it is determined that they can be harnessed algorithmically in a data-driven way, relevant stakeholders should be involved again to determine what additional decision-critical insights are needed to take immediate action on a generated lead. For instance, when the lead event alone is not sufficiently prescriptive, we suggest enriching the lead pipeline with further decision-critical insights to support sales representatives in their decision-making and action-taking to create value (e.g., closing a deal).

The level of uncertainty and responsibility for decisions and actions that a sales representative has depends highly on the kind of insights on which the leads are created and with which they are enriched. In the case of descriptive insights, sales professionals have a comparatively high responsibility for the eventual decision and the following action, as there is considerable uncertainty involved about why a customer shows particular characteristics, what the customer may do in the future, and what appropriate (logical) action to take.

The overall objective of Step 3 is to think of and plan for the additional insights that could support sales employees in their decision-making and action-taking. Thus, Step 3 is similar to Step 1, but while Step 1 is concerned with determining the initial lead event and is the basis for the whole lead pipeline, Step 3 is concerned with determining additional decision-critical insights to remove uncertainty from the decision-making process.

Step 4: Enrich leads with additional decision-critical insights
In Step 4, additional decision-critical insights are technically integrated into the data-driven lead pipeline. Step 4 is similar to Step 2 but is focused on additional decision-critical insights instead of the primary pipeline of lead events. Like Steps 1 and 2, Steps 3 and 4 cover the elements **From Question to Data** and **From Data to Insights** in the DDD process, so they require deploying complete data mining and analytics sub-processes. However, unlike Steps 1 and 2, Steps 3 and 4 often entail using a couple of data mining and analytics sub-processes. For instance, reducing uncertainty about an effective lead follow-up may require a combination of descriptive, explorative, predictive, and prescriptive insights.

Step 5: Automatically generate and assign leads in the CRM system
In Step 5, leads are generated in the CRM system and assigned to the right person by notifying them directly when new data-driven leads are available. Step 5 may require connecting and integrating operational sub-processes to join the high-potential lead events with additional decision-critical insights. Moreover, procedures should be put in place to automate the generation and assignment of leads as much as possible, and as long as it makes sense. Here, a trade-off between automation and customizability should be made, especially in the beta phase of a data-driven lead pipeline, as it can be advisable to keep the setting flexible and allow for quick adjustments based on stakeholder feedback.

Step 6: Lead follow-up decision
Step 6 contains the core element of the decision-making process: **From Insights to Decision**. First, sales employees decide, based on the insights provided, whether they will accept an assigned lead or not. A reason for declining a lead could be that the employee already knows about the lead event and has already acted or that the lead is incorrectly assigned, in which case, the employee should delegate the lead to the correct person or inform the project team. However, once sufficient data quality is ensured, it is expected that most generated leads will be accepted.

After a lead is accepted, the sales emplyee must decide how to act based on the insights provided. The effects of the decision can be either direct or indirect. For instance, the information could be used to contact the customer right away, which is a direct effect of the decision, or the information could be used to change the general sales strategy for the customer, which is an indirect decision effect. Overall, the greater the certainty in a decision, the more likely it is to have a direct effect. In data-driven lead generation, the level of uncertainty is influenced by the kind of insights that are provided to the decision-maker. For example, the insight that a technical manager has changed is descriptive, while additional decision-critical insights regarding the expected future transactions and churn probability of a customer are predictive. Following this, the lowest level of uncertainty is likely reached when prescriptive insights are provided.

Step 7: Change management

Step 7 addresses change management. In particular, we suggest following Kotter's (1995) eight steps to transforming an organization. The change endeavor here focuses not just on the implementation of a data-driven lead-generation pipeline but also on helping stakeholders to understand the basic principles of DDD first. Moreover, the organization's own mindset must often be changed to accept using data-driven and proactive approaches. Kotter's (1995) eight steps appear to be particularly suitable for this purpose:

1. Establish a sense of urgency.
2. Form a powerful guiding coalition.
3. Create a vision.
4. Communicate the vision.
5. Empower others to act on the vision.
6. Plan for and create short-term wins.
7. Consolidate improvements and produce still more change.
8. Institutionalize new approaches.

Step 8: Consolidate and evaluate the data-driven lead pipeline (Stakeholder involvement

In Step 8, the data-driven lead pipeline is consolidated and evaluated after the beta version has been in use for some time. Stakeholders should be involved again to determine whether the pipeline has been successful, and based on this evaluation, measures can be taken to improve the pipeline or, if it is deemed unsuccessful, to discontinue it in the beta state. However, even an unsuccessful pipeline is valuable for future pipelines, as parts of it, such as the additional decision-critical insights, can apply to many business problems and contexts in an organization.

4.2 Application of the Artifact: The Technical Manager Change Pipeline

The following sections describe a concrete application of our artifact, the data-driven lead generation artifact, using the example of the technical manager change pipeline.

In Step 1, we received the information that changes in the technical management of a ship constitute high-potential lead events. We interviewed experienced sales managers with a sound understanding of the dynamics of the marine engine after-sales business. We then contacted potential users (i.e., sales employees) to determine whether changes in a ship's technical management are appropriate lead events in their consideration. As a result of this first stakeholder involvement, it became clear that the sales employees did not have a straightforward process for retrieving information regarding changes in ships' technical management, and that there were no well-defined proactive processes for collecting and working with such information. Instead, sales representatives sometimes received information regarding changes in technical management from customers directly during ordinary sales interactions. Overall, the sales employees stated that the insights regarding recent changes in technical management would be valuable for several reasons:

1. as a conversation starter to contact the customer proactively
2. to learn more about the current customer base and the ships in the territory for which they are responsible (defined by the country in which a technical manager is registered)
3. to update a customer's metadata.

These talks led us to conclude that changes in technical managers are high-potential lead events. The next task was to evaluate how and based on what data sources insights regarding such changes could be harnessed. The plan was to investigate the possibility of using external sources to retrieve the data by simply querying it or by using a look-up algorithm to gain the desired insights.

In Step 2, we created the connection to an external data source that contains metadata of ships that are frequently updated with data from the international shipping registries. At first, it looked like data regarding changes in technical management would be comparatively easy to access by querying a column of the dataset that indicates on what date the value of the technical management field for a specific ship was changed. However, during the validation of this initial assumption with the data provider, it became apparent that the column could not be used. Therefore, we chose another approach that consisted of, firstly, creating a log of old versions of the dataset, secondly, creating a script to compare the current value of the technical management field with its latest predecessor, and finally, to trigger an event if the value changed.

In Step 3, we scheduled meetings with sales representatives and the rest of the ADR team to determine what additional decision-critical insights were required. The results of this second stakeholder involvement were to add an additional sales report and a ship and engine report to the leads in the CRM system. This was done to help sales employees to gain a quick overview of the existing and past relationships and interactions with a particular ship and customer. After involving a business manager in the design process, other decision-critical insights in the form of dates of upcoming dry-dockings were identified and added to the reports, along with key customer metrics estimated via BTYD models.

In Step 4, the planned enrichments of leads with the identified additional decision-critical insights were implemented technically. For example, to enrich the leads with key customer metrics estimated via the BTYD model, we conducted a complete data-mining process (Shearer et al., 2000). In particular, we built probabilistic models for estimating customers' future expected transactions, the probability of being alive (not churned), and estimates of future customer lifetime values (Fader & Hardie, 2009; Platzer & Reutterer, 2016). Probabilistic models of the family of BTYD models come from the field of marketing research and are particularly suitable for our setting, as they require comparatively little individual-level data (Rossi & Allenby, 2003; Abe, 2008; Van De Schoot, Broere, Perryck, Zondervan-Zwijnenburg, & Van Loey, 2015; Platzer & Reutterer, 2016).

In OEM's non-contractual market setting, technical managers with large fleets are handled by key-account managers. However, there are also many technical managers with small to medium-sized fleets that produce only small amounts of individual-level (i.e., ship-level) sales data. This can affect the predictive performance of machine-learning algorithms (Shaikhina & Khovanova, 2017). On the other hand, BTYD models (Fader & Hardie, 2009) like the Pareto/GGG (Platzer & Reutterer, 2016) apply hierarchical modeling, which allows group-level information about the selected cohort of ships to be used when individual-level data is sparse (Efron & Morris, 1977).

At the start of the BTYD modeling procedure, the required input data had to be defined and extracted from OEM's data warehouse. The comparatively simple format of the required raw-data input is another strength of BTYD models, as they usually require only a transaction log of orders as instances, along with the order date, its value, and a unique identifier of the ship for which the order was placed. The transaction log is then transferred into the programming environment R, where the data is further processed and transformed into an aggregated higher-level format where the instances are ships and the variables are, for example, the number of transactions, the date of the first transaction, the logarithms of the timing between transactions, and the sum of the transaction values. Then, we estimated the parameters and hyper-parameters of the selected Pareto/GGG model using a Markov-Chain-Monte-Carlo approach (MCMC; Platzer & Reutterer, 2016). Based on this, future transactions can be predicted in a Bayesian way by drawing from the posterior distribution. Also, future probabilities that ships are active and alive can be calculated easily. Eventually, with an additional probabilistic model for monetary value (Fader & Hardie, 2013), future CLVs can be calculated (Fig. 7).

We used around 500,000 orders as input data to predict the number of transactions one year ahead for around 24,000 ships. When we predicted the number of future expected transactions using the Pareto/GGG model that incorporates regularity parameters, the overall accuracy (predictions compared to test data) was 93% for predictions of the whole customer base. This reflects a high level of accuracy. On an individual level, the mean absolute error (MAE) was used as a performance metric. In the case of the Pareto/GGG, the MAE was 1.2.

When we applied the hierarchical Bayes version of the Pareto/NBD model, the accuracy of total predicted future transactions was 78%, with a MAE of 1.4 (Table 1).

In **Step 5**, the leads were joined with the additional decision-critical insights in an SQL database, based on which spreadsheets were created and stored so they can be associated with a lead. Another important task was to specify to which sales employees a specific lead should be assigned. We reached out to the potential users

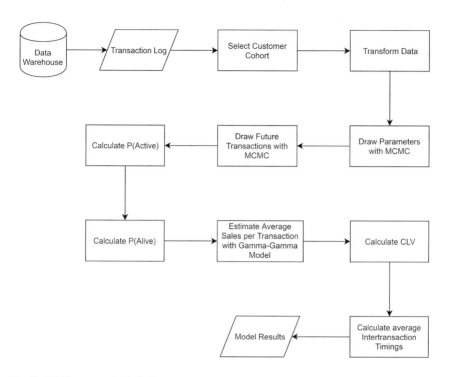

Fig. 7 BTYD process (technical manager case)

Table 1 Predictive Performance of BTYD Model

Model	Actuals/Predictions (%)	MAE
Pareto/GGG	93	1.2
Pareto/NBD (HB)	78	1.4

in OEM's regional sales companies to get the required information. However, after the beta version was implemented, users became active themselves in specifying the correct assignees.

Step 6 supplied us with feedback regarding how to improve how leads are assigned and how additional decision-critical insights can be used to improve decision-making and action-taking. This step shows that the artifact encourages the use of feedback loops throughout the lead generation process. Moreover, the degree of uncertainty with which sales employees as decision-makers were confronted can be assessed as medium to low, as they had access to descriptive insights about the lead events and additional descriptive and predictive insights that together created the basis for decision making and action-taking. For instance, sales employees had insights into recent changes in technical management and the past sales history of customers so that they could answer the "what is the lead?" question (descriptive). Based on the predictive insights regarding future transactions and churn probabilities, they could also answer the "how will the customer relation probably be?" question (predictive). This combination of insights gave the sales employees at least partial answers to the "how to approach the lead?" question (prescriptive). They could, for instance, determine that a ship with a recent change in technical management with which OEM had a good customer relationship and that had a high predicted future CLV should be contacted immediately to avoid losing a valuable business relationship. In other cases, it can be sufficient for the sales employees to use the generated insights for adjusting the general way in which they approach a customer, e.g., adapting their marketing efforts based on the generated customer insights.

In **Step 7**, change management measures were formalized loosely following Kotter's (1995) eight steps:

1. **Establish a sense of urgency**: The data-driven lead-generation artifact was presented in several business meetings, and emails targeted to all assignees of leads were sent to create awareness and inform them about the sometimes-imperfect use of the CRM systems as the preferred sales tool.
2. **Form a powerful guiding coalition**: By contacting and involving the heads of sales of the local sales companies that were involved in the project and closely involving the responsible business managers, a powerful guiding coalition was built.
3. **Create a vision**: Together with a general digitization and business transformation initiative, the project drew on the vision of proactive 360-degree sales services with a customer-centric focus.
4. **Communicate the vision**: The overall vision of the digitization and business transformation initiative was continually communicated via managers, the intranet, and other internal communication channels.
5. **Empower others to act on the vision**: The department in which the ADR team was located organized periodic meetings in which stakeholders related to analytics could share knowledge and best practices. Here, the artifact and its various iterations and sub-steps were presented several times.
6. **Plan for and create short-term wins**: From the beginning on, the plan was to create quick wins by focusing first on a few local sales companies that are well connected to the department. This was done to create initial success stories and communicate them via the intranet in order to create awareness and support in the organization.
7. **Consolidate improvements and producing still more change**: Because of its iterative nature, the versions of the technical manager change lead pipeline were consolidated and improved several times as a result of the feedback loops.
8. **Institutionalize new approaches**: By showcasing qualitative and quantitative success measures, the technical manager change lead pipeline could be institutionalized and expanded to a broader target group.

4.3 Evaluation of the Artifact

The resulting artifact and sub-artifacts were evaluated by the involved practitioners and their users throughout the entire design process. The evaluations were based on observational field notes, meeting notes, internal documents, informal interviews (especially collegial dialogue and joint problem-solving), and readily available data like usage reports on several decision-support systems and workshop outputs. We involved stakeholders and potential users continually to evaluate changes in the artifact. In particular, we were in close contact with the aftersales data analytics manager, the application manager of the CRM system, the team lead for analytics, and a selection of sales managers and sales professionals from OEM's sales companies, as potential users of the artifact. For example, we conducted at first informal interviews with potential users, then we refined the artifact based on the feedback, and eventually, we presented the refined artifact to a management audience. In short, we followed the ADR principles of reciprocal shaping, mutually influential roles, and authentic and concurrent evaluation, as Sein et al. (2011) proposed.

So far, around 650 leads have been generated in the CRM system directly from an instantiation of the data-driven lead-generation artifact. The initiative also inspired other data-driven lead campaigns that have generated another 2,000 leads. While in the beginning, just a handful of leads for one particular sales company were created, the pipeline's scope was quickly broadened to cover more than ten countries and their corresponding sales companies. This provides a clear indication that the aftersales organization sees practical value in the artifact. It is still too early to present metrics on the revenue generated through the artifact, as it is not linked directly to the quotation and ordering processes in the ERP systems. However, the feedback from the users has been positive, and the ADR team has received several suggestions for expanding the artifact to other campaigns beyond that of changes in technical management, such as to ship breakdowns and the sea trials of newly built ships. The feedback from the application manager of the CRM system has also been positive:

> It's very interesting to see what scientific theories applied to our data sources can be used for. It has been important for us to include some of the receivers/end-users of the data-driven leads in the process to make it tangible for them and to gain from their real-life expertise and not end up with a bunch of leads that only looked promising on paper. Having their stamp of approval is the first step toward a more proactive sales process and creating additional value. The data-driven leads will be an addition to their work and will save them some time when they are looking for new leads in the market, as these leads come out of the box that is our CRM system.

The artifact has also fulfilled its objective of enabling proactive sales processes, as sales representatives can take immediate action and contact customers based on the leads without having to wait for an inquiry from the customer side. As the application manager of the CRM system explained:

> We have to search for leads wherever we can, and using the data sources available is a natural next step in a more proactive sales approach. It's important that we set up an automated process around it and analyze the outcome of the data-driven leads to optimize the process over time.

One obstacle we observed is that the users of the CRM system have not yet fully adapted their work practices to the system's new capabilities. For example, users do not always document their work correctly in the system (e.g., setting a lead as qualified after being in contact with a customer).

The operational BTYD models to predict future customer behavior have been presented to managers and sales professionals on several occasions. The managers' evaluation was positive, and one business unit was interested in applying a similar approach to their particular business case. However, the feedback from sales professionals was mixed, as some saw the approach as too advanced, considering that it predicts future customer behavior while some of the current sales processes do not even use descriptive information. Nevertheless, the sub-artifacts, such as the BTYD models, have been seen as a positive outcome that, as an operational approach to analyzing the customer base, is applicable to many use cases and possible lead pipelines.

The project's main design objective was to design a DDD artifact that helps to create a new data-driven and proactive lead generation process in the CRM system. By applying an instantiation of the data-driven lead-generation artifact in the form of the technical management change pipeline, we created a new process for lead generation at OEM. Moreover, by integrating the artifact with and framing it in DDD theory, we fulfilled the objective of creating a data-driven process. The initial design principle of embeddedness was incorporated into the artifact by embedding the DDD elements into a process of stakeholder involvement and change management. The initial design principle of partial automation was incorporated by including a stage of generating leads and assigning them to sales professionals in the CRM system automatically. Moreover, we automated the process of detecting lead events as well as the lead selection, and the enrichment of leads with additional decision-critical insights. Nevertheless, transferring leads to the right assignee still needed some degree of human involvement, due to organizational constraints (e.g., admin rights). The initial design principle of proactivity is incorporated in the artifact by supporting sales professionals with prescriptive insights about how to take action.

4.4 Growth of Design Theory

Over the cycles of the ADR project, we abstracted from the original problem and the original solution instance (i.e., the technical manager change pipeline) toward a more generic data-driven lead-generation artifact. Based on our experiences while designing and implementing these solutions, we learned why the artifacts we designed are effective solutions to the problems we encountered in the field. Following the ADR methodology, we formalized these lessons into design principles. (See Thiess & Müller, 2018, for a more detailed presentation) We started out with initial design principles of being data-driven, proactivity, partial automation, and embeddedness, which were informed by the selected theory and the problem diagnoses. Throughout the building, intervention, and evaluation iterations, other nascent design principles emerged and subsumed the initial design principles. We formalized these generic and somewhat latent design principles by following the template Chandra, Seidel, and Gregor (2015) introduced, according to which the final design principles reflect material properties, enacted affordances, and constraints.

DP1: Theory-driven modeling—Given a lack of proof-of-concept, use theory-based models instead of data-driven machine learning algorithms to achieve concrete results.

Data-driven machine learning algorithms like gradient boosted trees and neural networks have proved their usefulness in work with large, high-dimensional datasets. They have shown their superior performance compared to often more theory-based applications of models like logistic regression. Therefore, we first constructed an artifact based on a data-driven machine learning algorithm. However, it became apparent that the algorithms could not find meaningful relationships among the variables in the complex dataset, which led to overfitting and low performance of the model on unseen data. As a result, we could not implement our artifact in this form, leaving us without a concrete solution to the diagnosed field problems. Moreover, we lacked a theoretical foundation to guide our modeling, as our particular data-modeling application had not been made before, nor did an explorative data analysis or the consultation of domain experts reveal associations that could have enabled us to formulate an initial theoretical model.

Therefore, we turned to the marketing literature to search for alternative approaches to predicting customers' future purchasing behavior based on customer transaction data. Hierarchical Bayes models of the BTYD type satisfied our requirements for a modeling approach, as they were developed for the problem domain of non-contractual market settings and facilitate predictions of customer purchases, allow individual-level parameter estimations from group-level data, and require little data. Moreover, BTYD models are based on sound behavioral theory and, because of the possibility of using informative priors, do not require large amounts of data to produce good predictive performance (Van De Schoot et al., 2015). In the end, choosing a theoretically grounded modeling approach enabled us to create concrete results in the form of solutions to the field problem.

DP2: Comprehensibility—Limit models' complexity to gain support from managers.

In addition to predictive accuracy, comprehensibility heavily influences user acceptance of any decision-support system (Gregor & Benbasat, 1999). We started out using machine learning to classify leads for aftersales from transactional customer data. This approach involved data-driven machine learning algorithms and a complex, highly dimensional dataset. As a result, even though the stakeholders' analytical background appeared to be strong, they had difficulty comprehending how the black-boxed algorithms processed the data to generate meaningful insights. In contrast, the BTYD models that we used later in the project seemed to be easier to comprehend even though they are mathematically complex. An explanation for this observation may be that the BTYD models require only three pieces of information about each customer as input: their recency (i.e., the time of the last transaction), frequency (i.e., the number of transactions), and the monetary value of the transaction (for calculating CLVs). This information, which can be provided in the form of an event log of purchase transactions for each customer, was in line with the experience and intuition of the involved domain experts, minimizing the gap between the predictive model and managers' mental models.

DP3: Domain Knowledge—Incorporate domain knowledge into the data-driven decision-making process to encourage acceptance by managers.

Machine learning models can detect associations between variables related to customers' purchasing behavior from historical transactional data. However, human experts have developed expertise through years of experience in marketing and selling services to customers, domain knowledge that tends to be implicit and heuristic in nature (e.g., best practices, rules of thumb). This implicit knowledge is difficult to formalize but can hold valuable information for predicting future customer behavior. In our project, we included the knowledge of domain experts via business rules that capture an experts' experience and intuition regarding the context of the field problem. For instance, we interviewed domain-specific experts at OEM to collect data regarding the types of life-cycle events that constitute a demand for spare parts and service. In addition, the BTYD models are based on Bayesian theory, which allows us to incorporate beliefs about the relationship between input and output variables (e.g., how important the recency or frequency of past transactions are in predicting future customer behavior) in the form of informative prior distributions. Eliciting and incorporating this expert knowledge into the artifact increased the user's level of participation and influence on the final design, a key success factor in ensuring acceptance of the final artifact (Hollander et al., 1973).

DP4: Actionability—Provide actionable insights instead of quantitative reports to increase use by decision-makers.

Even if a decision support system produces highly accurate decisions and wide acceptance, it is not a given that end-users will follow those decision proposals and take action. Many organizations fail to take appropriate actions based on the generated insights because of the artifacts' focus on descriptive information and lack of prescriptive theory (LaValle, Lesser, Shockley, Hopkins, & Kruschwitz, 2011). The departmental practitioners observed that analytical applications that are not based on a business process are used less often than those that are. Based on this early feedback, we decided to push the leads generated by our artifact directly into sales employees' daily newsfeed inside the CRM system instead of building extra reports or dashboards that the representatives would have to pull. The process was designed so every lead is created as a separate item and accompanied with additional information regarding what to do in the form of descriptive and predictive insights, but also via attaching clearly formulated prescriptive instructions with regard to what actions a sales employee should take, e.g., contacting the customer. Moreover, based on the meetings with the regional sales organizations, we decided to enrich the leads with additional ship and customer transaction information, so the sales employees have all the information they need for their regular lead follow-ups at their fingertips. This approach "makes it harder for decision makers to avoid using analytics—which is usually a good thing" (Davenport, 2013).

5 Key Lessons

Our experience in applying ADR in a real organizational setting gave us the chance to be directly involved in the organization's operational processes. It provided us with an insider perspective that enabled us to collect and process large amounts of empirical data in the form of, for example, field notes, informal interviews, internal documents, and readily available data. Because of ADR's emphasis on authentic rather than controlled settings, we were able to inform our artifact design with empirical findings, creating a dynamic design process in which we could shape the artifact at high speed based on quickly executed cycles of building new features, demonstrating the features to practitioners, and evaluating their responses. However, we found it particularly challenging to report on our experiences during our design journey using the traditional structure for academic publications. For instance, if we wanted to report on every new design iteration, we would have had to describe more than a hundred micro-iterations. Therefore, we decided to report on only major changes to the artifact and to group the micro-iterations that went into such major changes under one umbrella iteration.

Moreover, we found that it is helpful to distinguish initial theory-informed design principles from design principles that emerged throughout the design iterations because they represent two approaches to theory generation and so two research contributions. Theory-informed design principles that are tested via an artifact in a field setting represent a deductive approach and, thus, a deductive research contribution, while design principles that emerge out of the design process without being informed by theory represent an inductive approach, and, thus, an inductive research contribution. As a third research contribution and an attempt to generalize our context-specific findings, we found it helpful to relate and abstract both kinds of design principles back to theory when formalizing them in the last ADR stage, which represents an abductive theorizing approach.

In our next ADR application, we hope to use the notion of affordances more stringently as an analytical tool, as doing so will help to articulate the relationships among material properties, constraints, and intended effects in terms of user behavior (affordances; Seidel, Chandra Kruse, Székely, Gau, & Stieger, 2018). We hope to use the ethnographic method of shadowing that is popular in interaction design to determine how material properties enact affordances and how those affordances may differ from those that are intended.

References

Abe, M. (2008). 'Counting your customers' one by one: A hierarchical bayes extension to the Pareto/NBD model. *Marketing Science, 28*(3), 541–553.

Beverungen, D., Müller, O., Matzner, M., Mendling, J., & Vom Brocke, J. (n.d.). Conceptualizing smart service systems.

Brynjolfsson, E., Hitt, L. M., & Kim, H. H. (2011). Strength in numbers: How does data-driven decisionmaking affect firm performance? *SSRN Electronic Journal.*

Chandra, L., Seidel, S., & Gregor, S. (2015). Prescriptive knowledge in IS research: Conceptualizing design principles in terms of materiality, action, and boundary conditions. In: *2015 48th Hawaii International Conference on System Sciences* (pp. 4039–4048). IEEE.

Davenport, T. H. (2013, December). 'Analytics 3.0'.

Dearden, A. (2001). IDA-S: A conceptual framework for partial automation. In *People and computers XV—interaction without frontiers* (pp. 213–228). London: Springer.

Efron, B., & Morris, C. (1977). Stein's paradox in statistics. *Scientific American, 236*(5), 119–127.

Fader, P. S., & Hardie, B. G. S. (2009). Probability models for customer-base analysis. *Journal of Interactive Marketing, 23*(1), 61–69.

Fader, P. S., & Hardie, B. G. (2013). *The Gamma-Gamma model of monetary value.*

Gregor, S., & Benbasat, I. (1999). Explanations from intelligent systems: Theoretical foundations and implications for practice. *MIS Quarterly.*

Hevner, A. (2007). A three cycle view of design science research. *Scandinavian Journal of Information Systems, 19*(2).

Hollander, E. P., Vroom, V. H., & Yetton, P. W. (1973). Leadership and decision-making. *Administrative Science Quarterly.*

International Maritime Organization. (2015). *Survey Guidelines under the Harmonized System Of Survey And Certification (HSSC).*

Kayande, U., De Bruyn, A., Lilien, G. L., Rangaswamy, A., & van Bruggen, G. H. (2009). How incorporating feedback mechanisms in a DSS affects DSS evaluations. *Information Systems Research.*

Kotter, J. P. (1995). Leading change: Why transformation efforts fail.

LaValle, S., Lesser, E., Shockley, R., Hopkins, M. S., & Kruschwitz, N. (2011). Big data, analytics and the path from insights to value. *MIT Sloan Management Review, 52*(2), 21.

Leek, J. T., & Peng, R. D. (2015). What is the question? *Science, 347*(6228), 1314–1315.

Müller, O., Fay, M., & vom Brocke, J. (2018). The effect of big data and analytics on firm performance: An econometric analysis considering industry characteristics. *Journal of Management Information Systems, 35*(2), 488–509.

Orlikowski, W. J., & Iacono, C. S. (2001). Research commentary: Desperately seeking the 'IT' in IT research—A call to theorizing the IT artifact. *Information Systems Research, 12*(2), 121–134.

Platzer, M., & Reutterer, T. (2016). Ticking away the moments: Timing regularity helps to better predict customer activity. *Marketing Science, 35*(5), 779–799.

Purao, S., Rossi, M., & Sein, M. K. (2010). *On integrating action research and design research* (pp. 179–194).

Ransbotham, S., Kiron, D., & Prentice, P. K. (2015). The talent dividend. *MIT Sloan Management Review, 56*(4), 1.

Rossi, P. E., & Allenby, G. M. (2003). Bayesian statistics and marketing. *Marketing Science, (3),* 304.

SAS. (2012). *The evolution of decision making: How leading organizations are developing a data-driven culture—Sponsor content from SAS*. Retrieved from https://hbr.org/sponsored/2016/04/the-evolution-of-decision-making-how-leading-organizations-are-developing-a-data-driven-culture.

Seidel, S., Chandra Kruse, L., Székely, N., Gau, M., & Stieger, D. (2018). Design principles for sensemaking support systems in environmental sustainability transformations. *European Journal of Information Systems.*

Sein, H., Purao, R., & Lindgren, R. (2011). Action design research. *MIS Quarterly.*

Shaikhina, T., & Khovanova, N. A. (2017). Handling limited datasets with neural networks in medical applications: A small-data approach. *Artificial Intelligence in Medicine, 75,* 51–63.

Sharma, R., Mithas, S., & Kankanhalli, A. (2014). Transforming decision-making processes: A research agenda for understanding the impact of business analytics on organisations. *European Journal of Information Systems.*

Shearer, C., Watson, H. J, Grecich, D. G., Moss, L., Adelman, S., Hammer, K., & Herdlein, S. a. (2000). The CRISP-DM model: The new blueprint for data mining. *Journal of Data Warehousing.*

Susman, G. I., & Evered, R. D. (1978). An assessment of the scientific merits of action research. *Administrative Science Quarterly, 23*(4), 582.

Thiess, T., & Müller, O. (2018). Towards design principles for data-driven decision making-an action design research project in the maritime industry. In *Proceedings of the 26th European Conference on Information Systems (ECIS).* Portsmouth: European Conference on Information Systems (ECIS).

Van De Schoot, R., Broere, J. J., Perryck, K. H., Zondervan-Zwijnenburg, M., & Van Loey, N. E. (2015). Analyzing small data sets using Bayesian estimation: The case of posttraumatic stress symptoms following mechanical ventilation in burn survivors. *European Journal of Psychotraumatology.*

vom Brocke, J., Debortoli, S., Müller, O., & Reuter, N. (2014). How in-memory technology can create business value: Insights from the hilti case. *Communications of the Association for Information Systems.*

Wagner, M. M., & Hogan, W. R. (1996). The accuracy of medication data in an outpatient electronic medical record. *Journal of the American Medical Informatics Association, 3*(3), 234–244.

Watson, H. J. (2014). Tutorial: Big data analytics: Concepts, technologies, and applications. *CAIS, 34,* 65.

Wu, L., & Hitt, L. M. (2016). How do data skills affect firm productivity: Evidence from process-driven versus innovation-driven practices.

Wu, L., Hitt, L. M., & Lou, B. (2017, February 28). Data analytics skills, innovation and firm productivity.

e-Government Capacity Building in Bangladesh: An Action Design Research Program

Shirley Gregor, Ahmed Imran, and Tim Turner

Abstract e-Government systems have the potential to improve societal conditions in developing countries, and yet design knowledge to inform interventions to encourage uptake and use of these systems is sparse. An action design research program addressed the problem of limited adoption of e-government in Bangladesh. Inadequate knowledge of the nature of e-government systems was identified as an underlying cause of many other problems. The program aimed to reduce knowledge deficiencies among key decision makers through activities that included the delivery of a custom-made training program supported by a handbook targeted at senior government officers. The project had modest resources and yet yielded significant outcomes. Critical reflection established a number of design principles for a 'sweet spot change strategy' for interventions of this type, with the most important principle being to first identify a 'sweet spot', a point of maximum leverage, and then to act on it. Issues in achieving academic outcomes from action design research are noted.

1 Introduction

Appropriate use of information systems (IS) by governments and citizens of least developed countries (LDCs) can have significant benefits in improving the economic and societal conditions for the large proportion of the world's population who live in

S. Gregor (✉)
College of Business and Economics, Australian National University, Canberra, ACT, Australia
e-mail: shirley.gregor@anu.edu.au

A. Imran
School of Engineering and Information Technology, School of Information Technology and Systems, Faculty of Science and Technology, University of Canberra, Canberra, ACT, Australia
e-mail: ahmed.imran@canberra.edu.au

T. Turner
Apis Group, Canberra, ACT, Australia
e-mail: tim.turner@apisgroup.com.au

© Springer Nature Switzerland AG 2020
J. vom Brocke et al. (eds.), *Design Science Research. Cases*, Progress in IS,
https://doi.org/10.1007/978-3-030-46781-4_13

these countries.[1] The field of research that is engaged with these problems is known as information and communication technology for development (ICT4D). However, despite the efforts of bodies such as the United Nations, the World Bank, and the European Union, many interventions designed to yield desirable improvements have had little or no lasting effect, and the knowledge building of solutions appears far from cumulative. Heeks and Bailur (2007) characterized the problem as "random rocks being thrown into a pool rather than building cairns of knowledge" (p. 256). The problem is serious as the development of systemized knowledge (design theory) can mean that lessons learned across projects inform subsequent interventions and reduce the chance of failure.

e-Government is a particularly important area for LDCs. Successful e-government can lead to increased compliance with international codes, norms, and standards, which means higher levels of accountability, reduced corruption, and more-effective systems in important areas such as health and security (Banerjee & Chau, 2004; Cho & Choi, 2004; Kraemer & King, 2006; Von Haldenwang, 2004). Prior studies indicate that the use of information communication technologies (ICT) in government has flow-on effects to other sectors, which improves productivity and reduces poverty (Pilat & Lee, 2001; Walsham & Sahay, 2006; World Bank, 2002). According to Heeks (2003), however, 35% of e-government initiatives in developing countries were failures (e-government was not implemented or was implemented but immediately abandoned) and 50% were partial failures (major goals were not attained or there were undesirable outcomes). As such, for both research and practice, we needed to more thoroughly understand how to achieve specific aims with e-government interventions in LDCs.

Some researchers saw problems in theorizing in the context of ICT4D because they perceive an explosion of work on ICTs that is descriptive rather than analytical and that does not provide ground for solid theorizing (Heeks, 2006). These perceptions have arisen despite the wide range of theories that ICT4D studies include, such as actor network theory, structuration theory, institutional theory, and innovation theory (see Avgerou, 2008, 2009; Silva & Westrup, 2009; Stanforth, 2006; Walsham & Sahay, 2006). Reviews in the e-government field have characterized much work as "case stories"—event descriptions with no analyzable data or theory application (Grönlund, 2004; Norris & Lloyd, 2006). The situation may be changing, however, as more recent attempts to address the phenomena employ different approaches. For instance, research now documents historical inventories or longitudinal analysis (Heeks & Stanforth, 2007) and the application of different theories, such as general systems theory (GST) (Turpin, Phahlamohlaka, & Marais, 2009; Wahid, 2011). Still, there has been comparatively little work that addresses the need to give interventions in LDCs a sound theoretical foundation in terms of design principles and design theory—systemized knowledge that provides a basis for design and action (Gregor, 2006; Gregor & Jones, 2007).

---

[1]This chapter incorporates material from previously published work, including Gregor, Imran and Turner (2014) and Imran and Gregor (2010).

In this chapter we report the practical interventions that were designed and implemented in an applied research program over a five year period in Bangladesh, including the PhD study of one of the authors (Imran, 2010) as well as the systemized knowledge that was developed from the project. In this work the primary artifact that was developed can be characterized as a change strategy, the *Sweet Spot Change (SSC) Strategy* for developing countries, with overarching design principles developed from reflection during and after the projects. There were, however, other artifacts such as course syllabi and strategy documents developed in the course of the project as part of the overall change strategy.

2 The Context

The context of the problem is described as it was before 2008 and the program began (see Imran & Gregor, 2010). Bangladesh, one of the 49 LDCs, is a small south Asian country and was an example of a typical LDC lagging in ICT adoption in the public sector. Bangladesh was densely populated with 162.2 million inhabitants. The country has a parliamentary form of government, with the President as the Head of State and the Prime Minister as the Head of the Government. The Prime Minister was assisted by a council of ministers, with the secretaries belonging to the civil service. Bangladesh is also a country with a "high power distance", where the typical hierarchical administrative culture inherited from the British colonial system has evolved into distinctive hierarchical attitudes with respect to the interactions with the common citizens, superior–subordinate relationships and the method of delivery of government services (Jamil, 2007; Siddiqui, 1996). Little change occurred in the culture and the regulation of the public service following British rule and then independence in 1971; bureaucrats still felt comfortable working in high-power distance relationships rather than as equals (Jamil, 2007). The concepts of setting priorities and achieving cost-benefits was considered a foreign tradition; following established norms was more important than achieving results. Similarly, the principle that the consumers or subscribers have a right to good service was frequently ignored in the service sector of Bangladesh (Jamil, 2007). The issue of good governance was receiving increasing attention from the public as well as from developmental partners. According to a survey carried out in 1996 by the World Bank, the Government was seen to be "preoccupied with process; too pervasive; highly centralized; overly bureaucratic" (World Bank, 1996, p ii). In such an environment, creativity and innovation are not usually appreciated, and new ideas and new ways of doing things were considered to be foreign values that foster competition and conflict, which may threaten the stability of the system. A government officer, therefore, was not expected to engage in finding new ways of solving societal problems; neither does he encourage subordinates to nurture innovative ideas (Jamil, 2007; Sein et al., 2008). Overall, the administration of Bangladesh was influenced by political instability and political influence and was seen as lacking in understanding, planning and initiative;

all of which are further aggravated by a poor infrastructure and a lack of training and skill (Jamil, 2007, p. 14).

Unfortunately, ICT in Bangladesh was still seen primarily in terms of a hardware and software industry and much of its wider implication for the national economy in terms of information processing was not understood (Imran, 2009). The lack of vision in this area was felt at all levels. Some wanted ICT to be implemented but did not know how to go about it, missing the "big picture" surrounding ICT innovation. As a result, many computerisation initiatives with a strong techno-centric focus had not changed the situation or improved efficiency and effectiveness significantly. The UN Global e-government Readiness Report (UN, 2004, 2005, 2008), which gives data on 192 member states, shows a bleak picture of progress within the region. In this report, each member state is given an e-government readiness index based on a weighted average composite figure calculated from an assessment of websites, telecommunications infrastructure and human resource endowments. In 2004 and 2005, Bangladesh was shown as falling significantly behind other LDCs, even compared with the neighbouring South Asian Association of Regional Cooperation (SAARC) member countries, with an index much below the SAARC average. However, in 2008, Bangladesh had improved its position from 162 to 142 on the e-government readiness index through the increased presence of Government department websites. This e-government index is not a complete measure, but provides an indication of the relative position compared with the region and the world. There were some encouraging signs. The interim Government (2007–2008) successfully completed a massive national voter and ID project, which successfully registered and issued ID cards for about 80 million people, one of the largest databases in the world. Although this project was aimed primarily at ensuring a correct voter list for the last election, it opened up a number of opportunities for multipurpose use.

3   The Journey

The overall project is considered in terms of the action design research (ADR) framework of Sein et al. (2011). Elements of both action research and design science research (DSR) were envisaged from the outset of the project. We chose action research for our project because we were faced with an immediate problematic situation in which we proposed to intervene to bring about change. We also had to work with AusAID and partner organizations in Bangladesh with whom we had to establish an ethical and feasible collaborative relationship. Furthermore, we incorporated elements of DSR because we aimed to contribute to design theory through reflection during and following our work by elucidating some general design principles (Gregor & Jones, 2007; Peffers, Tuunanen, Rothenberge, & Chatterjee, 2008).

Table 1 shows our activities in each stage of the program. Note that these activities did not follow in a strictly linear fashion as recognized in the iterative ADR process of Sein et al. (2011). Reflection and learning occurred throughout the project as would be expected in action research: some elements of the problem became clearer, and we

Table 1 The action design research process

Stage 1: Problem formulation
Research was driven by the problem of inadequate use of ICT in the public sector of Bangladesh—a problem linked to public sector inefficiency and lack of transparency, with negative impact on socio-economic growth
We elucidated the dimensions of the problem in a theoretical process model of inhibitors to e-government in LDCs, which was based on a three year study in Bangladesh (Imran, 2010; Imran & Gregor, 2010). This work was informed initially by theories of innovation and change
Stage 2: Building, intervention and evaluation
An initial project was funded by AusAID in Bangladesh in 2008 and a taskforce was formed with representatives from stakeholder organizations
A strategy document (Imran, Gregor, & Turner, 2008), training program, handbook (Gregor, Imran, & Turner, 2008) and awareness-raising activities were developed and implemented. Evaluation specifically involved counterparts and LDC recipients and included pilot testing and qualitative and quantitative data gathering. The counterpart organizations were involved with successive versions of the deliverables
The initial design of materials for the training course was based on existing technology (best practice guides from a government agency) and strategies used in developed countries (see MIT, 2010). The learning approach was one of constructivism (Marton & Saljo, 1997). The strategic pathway document followed sources including (Credé & Mansell, 1998; Labelle, 2005)
Stage 3: Guided emergence
The complex nature of the deliverables and the web of surrounding activities needed for their realization emerged
A formal deed of agreement for the second funded project was signed between the research group, AusAID, and counterpart organizations in Bangladesh. The activities proposed in the agreement were based on the initial theoretical understanding gained in Stages 1 and 2
The second funded project involved institutionalizing knowledge of e-government management in a regular course at the Bangladesh Public Administration Training Center (BPATC). The project deliverables were refined as the need to tailor ideas for the LDC context and to gain maximum impact became more evident. The appreciation of how the intervention was effectively achieving outcomes in the SSC strategy emerged
Stage 4: Formalization of learning
The problem and intervention were generalized as belonging to the change strategy class of problems—the abstraction activity in theorizing (Lee, Pries-Heje, & Baskerville, 2011). Principles were identified through reflective judgment that had a high probability of necessity for positive outcomes (Pearl, 2000)
A set of design principles for a sweet spot intervention was articulated and reflected upon

sought evaluation and feedback at several points during the design of the deliverable products (strategy document, training program, handbook and awareness activities) that were used in the intervention.

4   Interventions and Outcomes

In this action design research process a number of tangible artifacts were developed in an iterative process and evaluated in summative testing. The final artifact is the sweet spot change strategy, which was described in design principles. This section describes ongoing project deliverables and outcomes.

4.1   Problem Modelling

In the first stage of the research program, exploratory research resulted in a process model of inhibitors to the adoption of e-government in a LDC (Imran & Gregor, 2010). This initial research proved to be a critical element of the project and underpinned the primary design principle. The exploration started with a broad, open question: "Why isn't e-government being adopted in Bangladesh?" A series of focus groups and interviews with relevant Bangladeshi stakeholders offered a substantial body of findings from which to identify an answer. These findings were analyzed using classical grounded theory content analysis techniques by our research team member with personal experience in the Bangladesh public service. An initial view of the key inhibitors was developed by the researcher and tested through a survey and further focus groups; again involving key Bangladeshi stakeholders.

The research revealed a critical stumbling block for successful adoption of e-government in the Bangladesh public sector—namely, that decision makers lacked fundamental knowledge and understanding of ICT, and also demonstrated a lack of awareness of the strategic use and implications of ICT systems for government business processes. This finding was significant as this lack of knowledge was found to inhibit adoption of solutions to a range of other typically identified barriers such as poor infrastructure, low socio-economic conditions, and a lack of leadership with respect to ICT. We identified the lack of knowledge and the attitudes of public sector decision makers as key barriers to address to facilitate further success in e-government initiatives. The extent to which the inhibitors influenced each other (e.g. the lack of knowledge about ICT influencing the lack of adoption of solutions to technology issues) was articulated in a causal map of the inhibitors identified by the respondents (see Imran & Gregor, 2010; Gregor, Imran, & Turner, 2014).

4.2   First Funded Project—Capacity Building

The first phase of the project was conducted in 2008 to develop "know-how" among key decision makers and government officials in Bangladesh concerning the effective use of ICT in public sector organizations. The counterpart public service agency of the project was the Ministry of Science and Information and Communication Technology

(MOSICT) of Bangladesh. The Bangladesh Institute of Peace and Security Studies (BIPSS) provided support as a third-party organization.

Our research showed that many of the government officials at the level of Joint Secretary and Deputy Secretaries who were nominated as ICT focal points for their ministry were lacking in knowledge on e-Government processes and the associated project management techniques. The project addressed this issue in a very pragmatic way with consideration of the local context and developed a two-day intensive training program aimed at effectively changing the attitude of officials toward ICT. This project led to: (i) a comprehensive strategic direction and recommendation prepared in the form of a book, "e-Government for Bangladesh: A Strategic Pathway to Success" (Imran, Turner, & Gregor, 2008); (ii) a custom-built intensive training workshop for senior government officials (see Fig. 1), (iii) delivery of training workshops to 107 senior and mid-level government officers (ICT focal points in the various ministries, Joint Secretaries and Deputy Commissioners) at the Bangladesh Computer Council (BCC), and (iv) the production and distribution of a concise ICT Management Handbook to support participants' learning with a good understanding of major IT management issues and how to deal with them effectively and professionally (Gregor, Imran, & Turner, 2008). The handbook served as a ready reckoner for day-to-day management of ICT.

The workshop teaching package was self-contained, was re-used over multiple offerings, and was regularly delivered by people other than the original developers. It comprised four modules that consisted of 4 h of delivery for each, including a 30 min break; i.e. 3.5 h lesson time. The whole training package, including the associated workbook, was handed to the Bangladesh government for wider dissemination among government officers through a Train-the-Trainer program. The project included an awareness program in the form of seminars, posters, and other outreach materials.

Fig. 1 Workshop with senior government officials, Dhaka, 2008

Fig. 2 Training course at Bangladesh public administration training centre, Dhaka, 2011

4.3 Second Funded Project—Institutionalization

Building on the success of the first project, the second project in 2010–2012 was designed to further institutionalize knowledge on e-government management through a well-designed comprehensive training course tailored to the local context. This objective was achieved through the development and implementation of a training course included in the regular curriculum of the BPATC. The course curriculum was developed as the equivalent of full semester with lectures, tutorials, and workshops, and was run through month long intensive course at the BPATC. Through the delivery of three courses over two years, more than 100 officers and educators were trained, and the course became a part of the annual curriculum of BPATC (Fig. 2).

4.4 Evaluation of Intervention

We applied a formative evaluation approach to key elements of the project while it was underway. At the conclusion of the second funded project, we conducted a more conventional evaluation including pre- and post-training surveys. The formative evaluation of the intervention took a variety of forms, including workshops in which we presented plans for the project for discussion and sought feedback from stakeholders, observation, feedback forms at the training sessions, scrutiny of reports of the program and related material in the media, and informal feedback by email and in interviews. Follow-up evaluation occurred 18 months after the project concluded. We kept a project logbook to document observations, evaluation, and design decisions as they occurred. Gregor et al. (2014) provides evidence of the program's worth from sources that include evaluation activities in training workshops, media reports, feedback from the funding agency and in follow-up evaluation.

Further compelling evidence for the worth of the overall strategy comes from the ongoing change activities that the project has leveraged. The handbook enjoyed some popularity. We distributed all 300 copies from the initial release and there was continuing demand. Many senior officers who were unable to attend the training program requested copies of the books and some bought extra copies for their department. On the basis of this demand, MOSICT reprinted another 500 copies of the handbook at its own cost. The textbook developed in the second phase to support the training course on e-government management was the first of its kind for developing countries and has now been commercially published (Imran, Turner, & Gregor, 2017). Three hundred initial copies of the book were donated to BPATC for subsequent courses.

More generally, recognition of the importance of ICT in the government sector of Bangladesh is noticeable. The subsequent developments and initiatives of Bangladesh Government in this area—for example: increased interest in e-government at political and decision-making levels, and establishment of e-government portals for all the districts—demonstrate government's positive change. It is difficult to establish any strong causal links between a specific project such as ours and a high-level change in a complex socio-technical environment. We do, however, believe that our project has made important contribution to these ICT initiatives.

4.5 Growth of Design Theory

We identified high-level design principles with the assistance of Sein et al. (2011, p. 45) and Lee, Pries-Heje and Baskerville (2011) recommendations to enhance generalization by focusing on the problem that is addressed as an instance of a class of problems. Table 2 shows the design principles elucidated, with more detail provided in Gregor et al. (2014).

5 Key Learning

The key lessons from the project regarding the problem context are represented in the design principles for the Sweet Spot Change Strategy for Least Developed Countries (Table 2). It is to be hoped that these principles can be of use in the future to others who are engaged as change agents in a similar complex situation.

Here we reflect on the action design research process itself as we experienced it. First, we can say that this research program was tremendously rewarding personally.

Table 2 Sweet spot change strategy for developing countries design principles

Number	Principles	Relevant artefact
Principle 1	Identify and Act on the Sweet Spot(s)	A theoretical process model was produced that showed casual linkages amongst key inhibitors to adoption of e-government in an LDC (see Imran, 2010; Imran & Gregor, 2010)
	Undertake a thorough analysis to identify the primary underlying inhibitor(s) for a desired outcome and target the initial intervention activity to address and overcome the primary inhibitor(s)	
Principle 2	Engage Influential Stakeholders	The change process included at an early stage a series of meetings and establishment of linkages with high level stakeholders including relevant ministers, secretaries and organizational heads both in Bangladesh and Australia
	An intervention in an LDC should seek to multiply its effect by engaging highly-influential participants	
Principle 3	Local Knowledge is Mandatory	The change process was undertaken by a team that included as a chief investigator a native Bangladeshi with lengthy experience with ICT in government in Bangladesh
	Intervention projects must include team members from the LDC.	
Principle 4	Tailor the Intervention to Suit the LDC with Existing Knowledge as a Base	All artifacts developed for training and strategy support followed user-centered design principles so as be appropriate for the context. These artifacts included:
	Any intervention should be tailored to address the specific requirements for the country, which are identified after careful investigation. Best practice, knowledge, and theory from other contexts can be used as an initial base for artifacts and activities comprising an intervention.	• the Five Year Strategic Pathway publication (Imran et al., 2008) • the ICT Management Handbook for government officials (Gregor et al., 2008) • the short burst (12 h) training workshop • awareness poster and promotional material • the eGov Management course introduced at BPATC • the eGov Management Text Book (Imran et al., 2017)

We felt that we were being helpful with a program that had the potential for great societal benefit. It was extremely rewarding to work as part of a team in a foreign country (for some of us) where we were made to feel welcome and where the other stakeholders and participants in training workshops were appreciative of what we were doing.

Through this project's preliminary assessment, it was determined that no similar long-term plan had been undertaken to address the central goals of this project. Other initiatives that existed were smaller and limited in scope. The first phase was the initial step towards adopting sustainable and workable eGovernment in Bangladesh and played a significant role as an ice breaker to start that process. Initial workshops provided rich insights into training needs and in formulating the right strategy for Bangladesh. Interest in the training was demonstrated by the day-long presence and participation of senior officers throughout the workshop. Before commencing the first workshop in the first phase, many senior officers, who held important and busy portfolios within the government, gave an indication that they might not be able to remain for more than 1–2 h. However, none of them left the workshop; some cancelled their meetings by phone. Some commented that they had attended other foreign-led training workshops before which they could not relate to their local context; however, they found the workshop was exceptional in addressing the problems they encountered day-to-day in their own work environment. Some senior officers told us later that they always carried the Handbook and read it whenever they had time. Many others requested copies of the books and some intended to buy extra copies for their whole department. Even after the change of government of Bangladesh following an election with a new minister and a new secretary in place, the Ministry of Science, Information and Communication Technology (MOSICT) still went ahead with printing extra copies of the Handbook, using their own budget. The strategy document was presented to the government at a formal ceremony attended by dignitaries and officials including the Australian High Commissioner to Bangladesh.

One of our universities recognized our achievements with a Vice-Chancellor's award for outreach. Living in the BPATC staff quarters was an interesting experience. Bangladesh was undergoing some political instability at that time. BPATC is an academic institution and is away from the central political structure. As such, our project was sheltered from much of the political uncertainties. Being a residential training institution, it was pleasing to see student officers were engaged in project work in groups after the class hour even at night in libraries and dormitories with much enthusiasm. We often encountered them for clarification and discussion beyond the classrooms during games period or in the dining hall. Evidence also shows that following the course some participants played a championship role in initiating e-government projects and some have made policy contributions in their organizations.

In 2018, the e-government readiness ranking for Bangladesh had improved in position to 115 compared from 142 in 2008 and it is shown as having the highest ranking of all the 47 LDCs (UN, 2018, p. 143).

Looking back, we can see challenges that, on reflection, also meant lessons learned in addition to the design principles. These challenges included:

1. *Ownership and maintaining interest.* A risk minimization strategy was to keep the counterpart stakeholders involved in the project at all steps so that a feeling of ownership was developed. It was important to maintain the interest of the stakeholders toward the program through regular commitments, communications and timely responses and delivery of programs.
2. *Maintenance of the integrity of the program.* There was a tendency to mix the training course with existing course material by external instructors, so it was more familiar to them. However, the project team was alert so as not to allow the integrity of the program to be threatened. We emphasized the importance of keeping the program intact not only to maintain the chronological understanding

of the study material but also so as potentially to attain Australian or standard university recognition in the future.

3. *Immediate benefit realisation.* It is often difficult to demonstrate any quick return from an institutional intervention that may take a considerable time to realise maximum benefits. Some students who attended the course may not have had the opportunity to utilise their knowledge immediately due to their postings, transfer and nature of employment. We expected that when a critical mass of officers were trained over the next 5–10 years, and when some of participants were promoted to higher ranks in the decision making roles, then they would be able to make greater impact.

4. *Transfer of officials.* Transfer of officials and instructors who were already trained to train others could not be avoided during the duration of the activity. These transfers meant wastage, which was covered with contingency plans; for example, substituting instructors or borrowing from external resources/universities in Bangladesh.

5. *Political instability.* This is an inherent problem in many LDCs, beyond the control and scope of a project team. Political instability and unrest often hinders the smooth running of an activity, which also influences and creates uncertainty for the future. However, as BPATC is located away from Dhaka city, some political agitation could be avoided. Some of our Australian instructors, however, were at times confined to a city hotel due to the Hartal (general strike) called by the opposition party.

6. *Length of the training course.* Some students complained that the length of the course was too short compared with the amount of content they had to absorb. In part this situation arose because of too many holidays and extracurricular activities in between some courses. A week's extension of the course was suggested to the authorities for the future.

7. *Demanding time schedule.* Managing the time schedule and commitment of all stakeholders to match the BPATC program calendar was also challenging. Significant time had to be spent on negotiation and correspondence between BPATC and ANU on training, coordination and financial matters.

8. *Book publishing.* The text book publishing required substantial effort and time in acquiring permissions for using third party references, photos, case studies and so on. Preparation of teaching notes, exercises, questions, and answers also demanded significant effort and time to attain international standards, which were not anticipated during initial planning. The research team had to devote additional time and energy beyond what was anticipated.

As an additional comment, this research program was one where the societal benefit was easier to see than rewards in an academic sense. The program as a whole was time-intensive and spread over 10 years, when the publication of the textbook in 2017 is included. We did have a strong motivational force in the commitment of our team member Ahmed Imran who is a native Bangladeshi and is passionate about reaping benefits from information technology in LDCs. However, realizing research outputs from a program that was in part an application of the professional skills that our team possessed was not easy. It was a struggle to have research articles published and to have a change strategy recognized as an artifact in the information systems community. Possibly publication problems are relatively common with action research programs.

What was important for the publications that have appeared was that we were able to reflect and abstract from our experiences. For the Sweet Spot change strategy paper (Gregor et al., 2014), it was important that we classified our field problem as an instance of change strategy problems (and named the artifact the SSC strategy so it was clear what type of artifact it was). By doing this, we were able to separate the important principles that related to the change strategy from the potential principles that related to more specific, low-level activities that occurred in this particular instantiation (see Lee et al., 2011). For example, at one point, we had principles relating to the design of the learning materials. The specific learning program we implemented appeared to be effective, but there are certainly other means through which knowledge enhancement (if that is a sweet spot) can be produced. The specific design of the learning program in our project was not an essential part of the higher-level SSC strategy. Similarly, we used focus group discussions with the nominal group technique and interviews to identify the sweet spot in the first stage, but it is possible that some other method could also be used to identify a sweet spot.

Theory evolution went hand-in-hand with the ADR process (see also Sein et al., 2011). Our ideas concerning the change strategy were more atheoretical at the beginning, although we conceptualized the problem in terms of "breaking the log jam" or "ice breaking" for e-government diffusion as informed by Rogers (2003). It was not until we were well into the second project that we realized that what we were doing could be more appropriately conceptualized in terms of complex systems theory and points of leverage in self-reinforcing cycles. Our experience matches the idea of design research being a process of discovery and of theory-building through abduction, deduction, and induction (Fischer and Gregor 2011; Lee et al., 2011; Simon, 1996).

As there appear to be relatively few action design research programs that produce design principles for a process-method artifact such as a strategy, we hope that our example may provide some guidance to others.

Recently we have been able to use the experiences and data from the project to produce a more conventional behavioral-type publication that explores with quantitative analysis one of the phenomena that was encountered, a "mind-set" amongst government official that hinders ICT adoption (Imran and Gregor, 2019). Thus, our project provides an interesting example of an action design research project leading to both prescriptive and descriptive theorizing.

References

Avgerou, C. (2008). Information systems in developing countries: A critical research review. *Journal of Information Technology, 23*(3), 133–146.

Avgerou, C. (2009, May 6–28). Discourses on innovation and development in information systems in developing countries' research. *Paper presented at the 10th International Conference of the IFIP 9.4 working group on Social Implications of Computers in Developing Countries Dubai, UAE.*

Banerjee, P., & Chau, P. (2004). An evaluative framework for analysing e-government convergence capability in developing countries. *Electronic Government, 1*(1), 29–48.

Cho, Y. H., & Choi, B. (2004). E-government to combat corruption: The case of Seoul metropolitan government. *International Journal of Public Administration, 27*(10), 719–735.

Credé, A., & Mansell, R. (1998). *Knowledge societies in a nut shell IDRC and the UN commission on science and technology for development.* Oxford, UK: Oxford University Press.

Fischer, C., & Gregor, S. (2011). Forms of reasoning in the design science research process. In H. Jain, A. Sinh & P. Vitharana (Eds.), Service-oriented perspectives in design science research (6th DESRIST), *Lecture Notes in Computer Science* (pp. 17–31), Springer.

Gregor, S. (2006). The nature of theory in information systems. *MIS Quarterly, 30*(3), 611–642.

Gregor, S., & Jones, D. (2007). The anatomy of a design theory. *Journal of the Association of Information Systems, 8*(5), 312–335.

Gregor, S., Imran, A., & Turner, T. (2008). *ICT management handbook: A guide for government officers in Bangladesh.* Canberra, Australia: National Centre for Information Systems Research.

Gregor, S., Imran, A., & Turner, T. (2014). A 'Sweet Spot" intervention in a least developed country: Leveraging eGovernment outcomes in Bangladesh. *European Journal of Information Systems, 23*(6), 655–671.

Grönlund, Å. (2004). State of the art in e-gov research—a survey. *Electronic Government Lecture Notes in Computer Science, 3183,* 178–185.

Heeks, R. (2003). *Most e-Government-for-development projects fail: how can risks be reduced?* IDPM i-Government working paper no.14. University of Manchester. UK. Retrieved from http://unpan1.un.org/intradoc/groups/public/documents/NISPAcee/UNPAN015488.pdf.

Heeks, R. (2006). Theorizing ICT4D research. *Information Technologies & International Development, 3*(3), 1–4.

Heeks, R., & Bailur, S. (2007). Analyzing e-Government research: Perspectives, philosophies, theories, methods, and practice. *Government Information Quarterly, 24*(2), 243–265.

Heeks, R., & Stanforth, C. (2007). Understanding e-government project trajectories from an actor network perspective. *European Journal of Information Systems, 16,* 165–177.

Imran, A., Turner, T., & Gregor, S. (2008). *eGovernment for Bangladesh: A strategic pathway for success.* Canberra, Australia: National Centre for Information Systems Research.

Imran, A. (2009). Knowledge and attitude, the two major barriers to ICT adoption in LDC are the opposite sides of a coin; an empirical evidence from Bangladesh. In *Proceedings of the 42nd Hawaii International Conference on System Sciences.* Washington DC: IEEE Computer Society.

Imran, A. (2010). *Information communication technology adoption in governments of the least developed countries: A case study of Bangladesh.* Unpublished Ph.D. thesis. The Australian National University.

Imran, A., & Gregor, S. (2010). Uncovering the hidden issues in e-Government adoption in a least developed country: The case of Bangladesh. *Journal of Global Information Management, 18*(2), 30–56.

Imran, A., & Gregor, S. (2019). Conceptualizing an IT mindset and its relationship to IT knowledge and intention to explore IT in the workplace. *Information Technology & People, 32*(6), 1536-1563.

Imran, A., Turner, T., & Gregor, S. (2017). *e-Government management for developing countries.* Reading, UK: Academic Conferences and Publishing International Limited.

Jamil, I. (2007). *Administrative culture in Bangladesh.* Dhaka: A H Development Publishing House.

Kraemer, K., & King, J. (2006). Information technology and administrative reform: Will e-government be different. *International Journal of Electronic Government Research, 2*(1), 1–20.

Labelle, R. (2005). ICT policy formulation and e-strategy development: A comprehensive guidebook. Bangkok Asia-Pacific Development Information Programme.

Lee, J., Pries-Heje, J., & Baskerville, R. (2011). Theorizing in design science research. In H. Jain, A. Sinh, & P. Vitharana (Eds.), Service-oriented perspectives in design science research (6th DESRIST), *Lecture Notes in Computer Science* (pp. 1–16), Springer.

Marton, F., & Saljo, R. (1997). Approaches to learning. In F. Marton, D, Hounsell, & N. Entwistle (Eds.), *The experience of learning: Implications for teaching and studying in higher education* (2nd ed.), Scottish Academic Press.

MIT. (2010). transforming your business through IT (formerly IT for the non-IT executive). *Executive Education* Retrieved April 12, 2010, from http://mitsloan.mit.edu/execed/coursedetails.php?id=766.

Norris, D. F., & Lloyd, B. A. (2006). The scholarly literature on e-government: Characterizing a nascent field. *International Journal of Electronic Government Research, 2*(4), 40–56.

Pearl, J. (2000). *Causality.* Cambridge, UK: Cambridge University Press.

Peffers, K., Tuunanen, T., Rothenberge, M., & Chatterjee, S. (2008). A design science research methodology for information systems research. *Journal of MIS, 24*(3), 45–77.

Pilat, D., & Lee, F. C. (2001). *Productivity growth in ICT-producing and ICT-using industries: A source of growth differentials in the oecd?.* Paris: OECD.

Rogers, E. M. (2003). *Diffusion of innovations* (5th ed.). New York: Free Press.

Sein, M., Ahmad, I., & Harindranath, G. (2008). Sustaining ICT for development: The case of grameenphone CIC. Retrieved from https://www.academia.edu/5075631/Sustaining_ICT_for_Development_Projects_The_Case_of_Grameenphone_CIC.

Sein, M. K., Henfridsson, O., Purao, S., Rossi, M., & Lindgren, R. (2011). Action design research. *MIS Quarterly, 35*(1), 37–56.

Siddiqui, K. (1996). *Towards good governance in Bangladesh: Fifty unpleasant essays.* Dhaka: University Press Limited.

Simon, H. (1996). *The sciences of the artificial* (3rd ed.). Boston: MIT Press.

Silva, L., & Westrup, C. (2009). Development and the promise of technological change. *Information Technology for Development, 15*(2), 59–65.

Stanforth, C. (2006). Using actor-network theory to analyze e-government implementation in developing countries. *Information Technologies & International Development, 3*(3), 35–60.

Turpin, M., Phahlamohlaka, J., & Marais, M. (2009). The multiple perspectives approach as a framework to analyze social systems in a developing country context. *Paper presented at the 10th International Conference on Social Implications of Computers in Developing Countries, Dubai, United Arab Emirates.*

UN. (2004). *Global e-Government readiness report 2004—towards access for opportunity.* Department of Economic and Social Affairs, Division for Public Administration and Development Management, United Nations. Retrieved from http://www.unpan.org/e-Government4.asp.

UN. (2005). *Global eGovernment Readiness Report 2005- From eGovernment to e-Inclusion.* Department of Economic and Social Affairs, Division for Public Administration and Development Management, United Nations.

UN. (2008). *The United Nations e-Government Survey 2008: From e-Government to Connected Governance.* Department of Economic and Social Affairs Division for Public Administration and Development Management, United Nations.

UN. (2018). *United Nations e-Government Survey 2018.* Department of Economic and Social Affairs, New York: United Nations.

Von Haldenwang, C. (2004). Electronic government (e-government) and development. *The European Journal of Development Research, 16*(2), 417–432.

Wahid, F. (2011). Explaining history of e-Government implementation in developing countries: An analytical framework. *Paper presented at the EGOV IFIP International Federation for Information Processing.*

Walsham, G., & Sahay, S. (2006). Research on information systems in developing countries: current landscape and future prospects. *Information Technology for Development, 12*(1), 7–24.

World Bank. (1996). *Bangladesh, Government that works: Reforming the public sector. South Asia Region.*

World Bank. (2002). *The e-Government handbook for developing countries.* Center for Democracy and Technology. Retrieved from http://www.eldis.org/static/DOC11473.htm.

Printed in the United States
by Baker & Taylor Publisher Services